MICROCOMPUTER EXPERIMENTATION WITH THE MOTOROLA MEK6800D2

LANCE A. LEVENTHAL

Emulative Systems Company
San Diego, California

PRENTICE-HALL, INC., *Englewood Cliffs, New Jersey 07632*

Library of Congress Cataloging in Publication Data

LEVENTHAL, LANCE A   date
    Microcomputer experimentation with the Motorola
MEK6800D2.

    Bibliography: p.
    1. Microcomputers—Laboratory manuals.
2. Microprocessors—Laboratory manuals.   I. Title.
QA76.5.L488   001.64'04'028   80-21444
ISBN   0-13-580761-1

Editorial/production supervision by Daniela Lodes
Interior design by Virginia Huebner
Cover Design by Edsal Enterprises
Manufacturing buyer: Anthony Caruso

This book is dedicated,
with my warmest personal regards, to
Karl Karlstrom,
in appreciation of his support and encouragement.

Printed in the United States of America

10   9   8   7   6   5   4   3   2   1

PRENTICE-HALL INTERNATIONAL, INC., *London*
PRENTICE-HALL OF AUSTRALIA PTY. LIMITED, *Sydney*
PRENTICE-HALL OF CANADA, LTD., *Toronto*
PRENTICE-HALL OF INDIA PRIVATE LIMITED, *New Delhi*
PRENTICE-HALL OF JAPAN, INC., *Tokyo*
PRENTICE-HALL OF SOUTHEAST ASIA PTE. LTD., *Singapore*
WHITEHALL BOOKS LIMITED, WELLINGTON, *New Zealand*

Contents

LABORATORY 6—PROCESSING DATA ARRAYS

LABORATORY 7—FORMING DATA ARRAYS

LABORATORY 8—DESIGNING AND DEBUGGING PROGRAMS

LABORATORY 9—ARITHMETIC

LABORATORY A—SUBROUTINES AND THE STACK

LABORATORY B—INPUT/OUTPUT USING HANDSHAKES

LABORATORY C—INTERRUPTS

LABORATORY D—TIMING METHODS

LABORATORY E—SERIAL INPUT/OUTPUT

LABORATORY F—MICROCOMPUTER TIMING AND CONTROL

Preface

The aim of this manual is to provide experimental training in the use of microcomputers for students of engineering, engineering technology, computer science, the physical sciences, the health sciences, and related fields. The emphasis throughout is on the design of controllers for industrial and laboratory applications. The experiments, examples, and problems were adapted from applications in instrumentation, test equipment, communications, computers and peripherals, industrial control, process control, business equipment, aerospace and military systems, and consumer products. The manual describes functions and procedures that are essential in all of these applications—interaction with switches and lights (front panel interface), keyboard and display interface, data collection and processing, code conversion, arithmetic, interface with simple handshaking peripherals (such as printers and terminals), timing, and serial communications.

First, the manual describes the operation of the microcomputer and then introduces assembly language programming, shows how to perform simple controller functions, discusses hardware/software tradeoffs, describes the design and development of programs, demonstrates alternative approaches to input/output and timing, presents the advantages and uses of programmable LSI devices, and describes communications methods. Included are numerous examples drawn from actual applications, but simplified so as not to require extensive background, special equipment (beyond the microcomputer itself), or long setup times. The manual is self-contained, so that it can be used in a variety of disciplines at differing levels.

The manual is based on the Motorola MEK6800D2 microcomputer because of its low cost, wide availability, completeness, and ease of use. The MEK6800D2 does not require expensive peripherals (such as a terminal), has adequate documentation, is easy to assemble, includes a prototyping area and expansion facilities, and provides all the components of typical microcomputer systems. The MEK6800D2 has a ROM-based monitor that handles simple functions and has enough memory and input/output lines for a variety of useful and relevant examples.

This manual emphasizes the control of systems with software. This control is illustrated with the simplest possible examples using switches, single displays, and the on-board peripherals. More advanced programming and interfacing will be covered in a later text. The intent here has been to provide realistic exercises that require little additional hardware and can be performed in short time periods. Numerous programs are included as starting points for students and as references for examination and comparison.

The standard format throughout this manual conforms with other textbooks, manuals, and reference materials. I have used the notation from the 6800 assembler provided by Motorola. I have tried to make all programs clear, simple, well-structured, and well-documented. Programming tricks have been avoided even when they would make programs somewhat shorter and faster. Good programming practices are essential for users of microcomputers and I have tried to provide sound, fully-tested examples for students to follow.

This manual does not describe the Motorola 6800 microprocessor in detail. Nor does it provide a complete discussion of 6800 assembly language programming. I have therefore provided extensive references to appropriate text books, 6800 manuals, and programming books. Because the manual is self-contained, it can be used independently of the reference materials.

Each experiment in the manual is itself self-contained. Each includes a list of goals, definitions of new terms, references (with page numbers), a description of new instructions that are being introduced, a list of required equipment, and a key point summary. Each contains numerous problems that are closely linked to the discussion. The problems are intended as further learning experiences, not as rote tasks or repetition of simple points. I have tested all the problems and have provided sample data, hints, and discussions.

Many people contributed to the writing of this manual. In particular, Mr. Irvin Stafford of Burroughs Corporation constructed most of the hardware, checked the examples and problems, and suggested many improvements and corrections. Others who helped include Mr. Colin

Walsh of Tandberg Data, Mr. Michael Lehman of MT Microsystems, and Mr. Winthrop Saville of Sorrento Valley Associates. I would also like to thank Victor Wintriss, Chuck Bennett, Charles Matthews, Charles McMahan, and Edward Simms for their encouragement. The staff of Motorola Semiconductor Products' Technical Information Center provided both encouragement and materials; I would especially like to thank Mr. Lothar Stern and Mr. Marshall Rothen. The reviewers of the original manuscript, all of them anonymous except for Mr. Sol Libes of Union County Technical Institute (New Jersey), provided many useful suggestions. My editors, Mr. Paul Becker and Mr. Bernard Goodwin, encouraged this project as did Mr. Walter Welch, the local representative of Prentice-Hall. My wife, Donna, and my daughter, Amanda Catherine, were patient and understanding, particularly as this project neared completion. Of course, I am responsible for all remaining errors and I hope that the users of this manual will take the time to inform me of any that they find.

LANCE A. LEVENTHAL

San Diego, California

☐ *Laboratory* **0**

Introduction to the
MEK6800D2 Microcomputer

PURPOSE

To learn how to operate the MEK6800D2 microcomputer.

PARTS REQUIRED

An assembled MEK6800D2 microcomputer with a 5-V power supply.

REFERENCE MATERIALS

MEK6800D2 Evaluation Kit II Manual, Motorola Semiconductor Products Inc., Austin, TX, 1977, pp. 1-1 through 1-9 (general description and monitor commands).

WHAT YOU SHOULD LEARN

1) How to reset the computer.
2) How to examine the contents of a memory location.
3) How to change the contents of a memory location.
4) How to enter and execute a simple program.

Central processing unit (CPU)–the control section of the computer; the part that controls its operations, fetches and executes instructions, and performs arithmetic and logical functions.

Hexadecimal (or hex)–number system with base 16. The digits are the decimal numbers 0 through 9, followed by the letters A through F.

Microcomputer–a computer that has a microprocessor as its central processing unit.

Microprocessor–a complete central processing unit for a computer constructed on one or a few chips of silicon.

Monitor–a program that allows the computer user to enter programs and data, run programs, examine the contents of the computer's memory and registers, and utilize the computer's peripherals.

Nonvolatile memory–a memory that retains its contents when power is removed.

Random-access memory (RAM)–a memory that can be both read and altered (written) in normal operation.

Read-only memory (ROM)–a memory that can be read but not altered in normal operation.

Register–a storage location inside the CPU.

Reset–a control signal that forces the computer into a known initial (or startup) state.

Volatile memory–a memory that loses its contents when power is removed.

6800 INSTRUCTIONS

SWI (3F hex)–Software interrupt; on the MEK6800D2 microcomputer, this instruction returns control to the monitor (JBUG) program.

OVERVIEW

The Motorola MEK6800D2 (or Microcomputer Evaluation Kit 6800, Version 2) is an inexpensive microcomputer based on the widely used Motorola 6800 microprocessor. Section 1-2 of the *MEK6800D2 Evaluation Kit II Manual* contains assembly instructions for the kit. The kit (see Figure 0-1) consists of two separate circuit boards: the Microcomputer

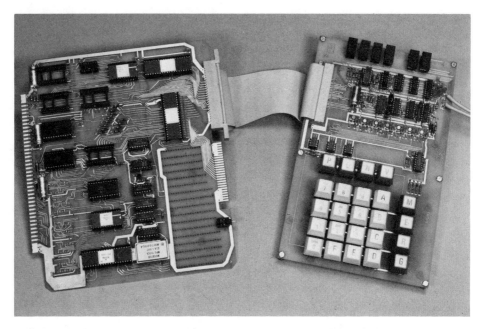

FIGURE 0-1. The assembled MEK6800D2 microcomputer. (Photo courtesy Motorola Semiconductor Products Inc.)

Module and the Keyboard/Display Module. These modules contain the following items:

- A 6800 microprocessor, which serves as the central processing unit or "brain."

- Read-only memory or ROM (a 6830 device that contains a monitor program called JBUG). Each 6830 ROM contains 1K 8-bit words (1K = 2^{10} = 1024).

- Read/write memory or RAM (three 6810 devices into which the user can enter data and programs). Each 6810 RAM contains 128 8-bit words.

- Keyboard/display interface (a 6821 Peripheral Interface Adapter or parallel interface).

- User I/O interface (a 6821 Peripheral Interface Adapter that is available for user-defined input or output).

- 24-key keyboard. The 16 white keys are used to enter data as hexadecimal digits. The 8 blue keys are used to enter commands.

- Six-digit seven-segment LED display.
- An audio cassette interface that includes a 6850 Asynchronous Communications Interface Adapter (a UART or serial interface) and clock generation circuitry.
- Expansion area.
- Prototyping area (upper left-hand corner of the Keyboard/ Display Module).

Complete descriptions of the various devices are in the *M6800 Microcomputer System Design Data Book* (Motorola Semiconductor Products Inc., Phoenix, AZ, 1976) and in the *M6800 Microprocessor Applications Manual* (Motorola Semiconductor Products Inc., Phoenix, AZ, 1975; also available from McGraw-Hill, New York, 1976). Appendix 3 contains parts of those descriptions.

RESETTING THE COMPUTER

To start using the Motorola MEK6800D2 microcomputer, you must reset it. The RESET switch is in the lower right-hand corner of the Microcomputer Module; press and release it. If the computer is working correctly, the displays should be all blank except for a dash (−) in the leftmost digit.

− (in leftmost digit)

The microcomputer is now executing the JBUG monitor program stored in the 6830 read-only memory. This program allows you to control the microcomputer from the keyboard. You can place programs and data in read/write memory, execute programs, examine and change the contents of memory and registers, and perform other functions which we will describe later.

EXAMINING MEMORY

The basic MEK6800D2 microcomputer contains 384 bytes of read/write memory which occupy addresses 0000 through 00FF hexadecimal and A000 through A07F hexadecimal. Since the monitor uses the addresses from A000 through A031, we will not use those locations.

Note that each memory location has a 16-bit address (four hexadecimal digits) and contains 8 bits of data (two hexadecimal digits). Table 0-1 is a list of the hexadecimal digits and their binary and decimal equivalents. Use this table if you need help converting numbers to and from the hexadecimal representation.

Table 0-1

HEXADECIMAL-TO-DECIMAL CONVERSION TABLE

HEXADECIMAL DIGIT	DECIMAL VALUE	BINARY VALUE
0	0	0000
1	1	0001
2	2	0010
3	3	0011
4	4	0100
5	5	0101
6	6	0110
7	7	0111
8	8	1000
9	9	1001
A	10	1010
B or b	11	1011
C	12	1100
D or d	13	1101
E	14	1110
F	15	1111

To examine the contents of memory, you must enter a four-digit address and then press the M or Memory Examine and Change key. Remember that the digits are hexadecimal (see Table 0-1) and note that the digits B and D are shown as lowercase letters (b and d, respectively) because of the limitations of the inexpensive calculator-like displays. If nothing happens or you get an unexpected display, press the RESET switch again or press the blue E key (the key immediately under M in the rightmost column of the keyboard). The blue E key is an Escape or Abort key that returns control to the monitor. Do not confuse the blue E key with the white E key, which is used to enter the hexadecimal digit E; we will try to maintain the color distinction, but you should interpret references to "the E key" (both in this manual and in the *MEK6800D2 Evaluation Kit II Manual)* as references to the blue E key. Obviously, a slight improvement in the key markings would eliminate this confusion.

For example, enter the four-digit address 0, 0, 0, 0. Note that the digits appear on the displays from left to right; this is easier to see if you try an address in which all the digits are different, such as A, 0, 5, 7. The two rightmost displays remain blank. Remember that all the displays are in hexadecimal and that addresses (shown on the leftmost displays) are four digits long, whereas data entries (shown on the rightmost displays) are two digits long.

Now press the M key at the top of the rightmost column of the keyboard. The two rightmost displays show the contents of memory location 0000 (hex). The value is arbitrary, because the 6810 RAM loses its contents when power is removed and could start in any state whatsoever. Such a memory is said to be *volatile*. To demonstrate this volatility, simply unplug the MEK6800D2's power supply and repeat the examination procedure. Try this several times if you are not easily convinced.

The following procedure thus allows you to examine the contents of a memory location:

1) (if necessary) Reset the computer with the RESET switch.
2) Enter the address as four hexadecimal digits starting with the most significant digit.
3) Press the M key.

Before you press the M key, be sure that you have entered the address correctly. If not, press the blue E key or RESET and enter the correct address. Note that you cannot change the address by simply entering more digits; the additional digits appear only on the two rightmost displays (in pairs) and affect the contents of the memory location but not its address. If you make a mistake or get confused, press the blue E key or RESET until you get back to the starting condition, in which a dash character (the JBUG prompt symbol) appears on the leftmost display.

PROBLEM 0-1

Examine the contents of memory location 0038 (hex).

PROBLEM 0-2

Examine the contents of memory location E2BD (hex). Its value should be E7. Disconnect the power supply and examine this location again. The result will be the same, since this memory location is in the *nonvolatile* read-only memory.

Note the following special features of the MEK6800D2 displays:

1) The digits B and D are shown as lowercase letters (b and d, respectively) because of the limitations of the displays.
2) The digit 6 appears with a bar at the top so that you can differentiate it from "b."

Be careful; these special features can lead to errors until you get used to them.

Once you have examined a memory location, you can examine the next location by pressing the G key (bottom of the rightmost column). Try examining memory locations 0000 (hex) through 0010 (hex). Note that you can go forward but not backward. Note also the sequence of the hexadecimal digits (remember Table 0-1). If you wish to stop examining memory, press the blue E key.

CHANGING MEMORY

Once you have examined a memory location, you can change its contents by simply entering two digits. For example, to change the contents of memory location 0000 to 3F, first examine that location and then press

```
3         (rightmost displays are unchanged)
F         (rightmost displays now read 3F)
blue E or G
```

To verify that the data is there, repeat the examination. Wouldn't it be nice to have a key that decremented the memory address? (Suggest one to your Motorola representative.) Be careful of the fact that the first digit entry does not affect the displays at all; both rightmost displays change after you press the key for the less significant digit.

So the following procedure allows you to change the contents of a memory location (after examining it):

4) Enter the data as two hexadecimal digits, starting with the more significant digit.

5) Press the blue E key. The G key has the same effect, except that it proceeds to the next memory location rather than terminating.

Be sure that you have entered the data correctly before you press the blue E or G key. If not, simply enter the correct data. Note that the JBUG monitor changes the contents of memory as soon as you enter two digits. Check this by entering 3F into memory location 0000; examining it again; pressing 8, 6, RESET (on the Microcomputer Module); and examining memory location 0000 once more. It should contain 86 even though we pressed RESET rather than blue E or G after changing it. What happens if you enter only one digit before pressing RESET?

PROBLEM 0-3

Enter the following data into memory locations 0000 through 0002:

MEMORY ADDRESS (HEX)	MEMORY CONTENTS (HEX)
0000	86
0001	6A
0002	3F

Verify the values after you enter them. You should press the blue E key after entering the contents of memory location 0002. If you press G instead, the JBUG monitor will proceed to memory address 0003 and you must then press the blue E key to conclude the entry.

PROBLEM 0-4

Try changing the contents of memory location E2BD to 86 (hex). Do the right-most displays change? What happens when you examine the location again? Remember that this address is in the read-only memory, not in the read/write memory.

EXECUTING A PROGRAM

To execute a program, enter the four-digit address at which you want the computer to start and then press the G key. A simple program consists of the single instruction SWI (SOFTWARE INTERRUPT or TRAP), which just forces the computer to return to the monitor program.

Enter and run this program as follows:

1)   Press the RESET switch.
2)   Press 0, 0, 0, 0. This is the memory address in which we will place the SWI instruction.
3)   Press M.

You can now see the contents of memory location 0000.

4)   Press 3, F.

This is the hexadecimal version of SWI. Look it up on your programming card or in Appendix 1 of this manual.

5)   Press the blue E key.

3F (SWI) has now been entered into memory location 0000 and the computer is ready for another command. If you press G instead of E, the computer will enter the data into memory and display the contents of memory location 0001. Remember to press RESET if you get confused or lost.

6)   Press 0, 0, 0, 0. This is the address at which the computer will start executing the program.

7)   Press G. What happens?

The computer simply displays the last address it has executed (0000) and the contents of that address (3F). We have no way of knowing whether anything actually happened, except that the computer did not wander off aimlessly.

PROBLEM 0-5

Try entering and executing the same program in memory location 002A.

PROBLEM 0-6

Try entering and executing the same program in memory location E05C. What happens and why?

KEY POINT SUMMARY

1)   The MEK6800D2 microcomputer has a monitor program (called JBUG) stored in read-only memory (ROM) in addresses E000 through E3FF. This memory is nonvolatile and the user cannot change it.

2)   You can transfer control to the JBUG monitor by pressing the RESET switch or the blue E (Escape or Abort) key. The monitor program is ready to accept entries from the keyboard when a dash character (the JBUG prompt symbol) appears alone in the leftmost display.

3)   The MEK6800D2 microcomputer has read/write memory (RAM) in addresses 0000 through 00FF. This memory is volatile (its contents change when power is lost) and the user can change it.

4)   Each memory location is characterized by a 16-bit address (four hexadecimal digits); its contents are an 8-bit number (two hexadecimal digits).

5)   You can examine an MEK6800D2 memory location by entering its address and pressing the M key. You can then change the

contents by entering two hexadecimal digits as the new data, proceed to the next higher address by pressing the G key, or return to the JBUG monitor by pressing the blue E key. This procedure allows you to see the contents of memory and to enter programs and data into memory.

6)   You can have the MEK6800D2 microcomputer execute a program by entering its starting address and pressing the G key. All programs should end with an SWI instruction (3F hex) so that control returns to the JBUG monitor when the program is finished.

Laboratory 1

Writing and Running Simple Programs

PURPOSE

To learn how to write, enter, and run simple programs on the MEK6800D2 microcomputer.

PARTS REQUIRED

An assembled MEK6800D2 microcomputer with a 5-V power supply.

REFERENCE MATERIALS

L. A. Leventhal, *Introduction to Microprocessors: Software, Hardware, Programming,* Prentice-Hall, Englewood Cliffs, NJ, 1978, pp. 66-68, 104-121, 152-153, 166-179.

L. A. Leventhal, *6800 Assembly Language Programming,* Osborne/McGraw-Hill, Berkeley, CA, 1978, Chapter 4.

W. J. Weller, *Practical Microcomputer Programming: The M6800,* Northern Technology Books, Evanston, IL, 1977, Chapters 2-5.

MEK 6800D2 Evaluation Kit II Manual, Motorola Semiconductor Products Inc., Austin, TX, 1977, pp. 1-6 through 1-9 (operating procedures).

WHAT YOU SHOULD LEARN

1) How to enter simple programs into memory.
2) How to determine the length of instructions.
3) How to place addresses in instructions.
4) How to store data in memory.
5) How to examine the results of programs.
6) How to use the index register and indexed addressing.
7) How to examine registers and change their contents.

TERMS

Accumulator—a register that is the source of one operand and the destination of the result for most arithmetic and logical operations.

Addressing methods (modes)—the methods for specifying the addresses to be used in executing an instruction. Common addressing methods include direct, immediate, indexed, and relative.

Assembler—a computer program that converts assembly language programs into a form (machine language) that the computer can execute directly. The assembler translates mnemonic operation codes and names into their numerical equivalents and assigns locations in memory to data and instructions.

Assembly language—a programming language in which the programmer can use mnemonic operation codes, labels, and names to refer to their numerical equivalents.

Byte—the smallest grouping of bits that the computer can process at one time, usually consists of 8 bits.

Comment—a section of a program that has no function other than to explain the meaning of part of the program. Comments are neither translated nor executed; they are simply copied into the program listing.

Condition code register—a register that defines the current state of the computer, often contains various bits indicating internal conditions.

Direct addressing—an addressing method in which the address required by an instruction is part of the instruction, typically following the operation code in memory. In 6800 terminology, direct addressing refers to the case in which the 8 most significant bits of the address are all zeros and need not be specifically included in the instruction.

Effective address—the actual address used by an instruction to fetch or store data.

Extended addressing—in 6800 terminology, a form of direct addressing in which the 8 most significant bits of the address are not all zeros and those bits must therefore be included specifically in the instruction.

Immediate addressing—an addressing method in which the data required by an instruction is part of the instruction, usually immediately following the operation code in memory.

Indexed addressing—an addressing method in which the address included in the instruction is modified by the contents of an index register in order to calculate the actual address of the data.

Indexed offset—the offset from the current value of the index register.

Index register—a register that can be used to modify memory addresses.

Inverter—a logic device that complements the input.

Low-level language—a language in which each instruction or statement is translated into a single machine language instruction.

Machine language—the programming language that the computer can directly execute with no translation other than numeric conversions.

Mnemonic—symbolic name for an instruction, register, or memory location that suggests its actual purpose or function.

One's complement—a bit-by-bit logical complement of a binary number.

Operation code (op code)—the part of an instruction that specifies the operation to be performed.

Program counter—a register that contains the address of the next instruction to be fetched from memory.

Stack pointer—a register that contains the address of the top of a stack.

Two's complement—a binary number that, when added to the original number in a binary adder, produces a zero result. The two's complement is the one's complement plus 1.

Word—the basic grouping of bits that the computer can process at one time. The 6800 microprocessor has an 8-bit word. Eight bits are sometimes referred to as a *byte.*

ADD—add; add the contents of the specified memory location to the contents of an accumulator. The result is placed in the accumulator.

COM—one's complement; perform a bit-by-bit logical complement of the contents of an accumulator or memory location.

DEX—decrement index register; subtract 1 from the 16-bit contents of the index register.

INX—increment index register; add 1 to the 16-bit contents of the index register.

LDA—load accumulator; load an accumulator from the specified memory address.

LDX—load index register; load the index register from the specified memory address and the next higher address. Note that two memory locations are required to load the 16-bit index register, with the most significant bits coming from the lower address.

NEG—two's complement (negate); add 1 to the bit-by-bit logical complement of the contents of an accumulator or memory location. The result is a number that, when added to the original data, produces a sum of zero (plus a carry).

STA—store accumulator; store the contents of an accumulator in the specified memory address.

STX—store index register; store the contents of the index register in the specified memory address and the next higher address. Note that two memory locations are required to store the 16-bit index register, with the most significant bits going into the lower address.

ONE'S-COMPLEMENT PROGRAM

The first actual program that we will write is an inverter or one's-complement program. This program will simply take the contents of memory location 0040 (hex), complement (or invert) each bit, and place the result in memory location 0041. The computer here does exactly what eight inverter gates would do; we could accomplish the same function in TTL logic with two 7404 inverter packages. The program is

```
LDAA      $40               GET DATA
COMA                        COMPLEMENT DATA
STAA      $41               STORE RESULT
SWI                         RETURN TO MONITOR
```

We are using the Motorola assembler format (see Figure 1-1), in which a $ before a number means "hexadecimal" and the accumulator designation (A or B) can be added to the operation code without a space. The comments at the end of the line (separated from the data or addresses by one or more spaces) are intended solely for documentation and do not affect the program that the computer executes. Figure 1-2 is a programming model of the 6800 microprocessor, showing the various registers that the programmer can use.

Before a number:

$ - hexadecimal
% - binary
@ - octal

The default case (i.e., unmarked) is decimal.

Other symbols:

\# - immediate addressing
,X - indexed addressing (but note that the assembler accepts X alone as equivalent to 0, X)
' - before an ASCII character
* - indicates an entire line of comments.

A space is required after a label and before a comment.

FIGURE 1-1. Motorola 6800 assembler format.

Let us now look at each instruction:

1)   LDAA $40 loads accumulator A with the contents of memory location 0040 (hexadecimal). The $ means hexadecimal and the leading zeros can be omitted as in common practice. Remember that the address is four digits (16 bits) long but the data stored at that address is two digits (8 bits) long.

2)   COMA complements the contents of accumulator A; that is, it replaces each 0 bit with a 1 and each 1 bit with a 0, just like a set of inverter gates.

3)   STAA $41 stores the contents of accumulator A in memory location 0041 (hex). Here again, the address is four digits long, whereas the data is two digits long.

4)   SWI (SOFTWARE INTERRUPT) returns control to the monitor. You should put this instruction at the end of every program. The computer will then return control to the monitor rather than wandering off aimlessly after it has finished your program.

To enter the program into the computer's memory, you must look up the hexadecimal operation codes on the instruction card (or Instruc-

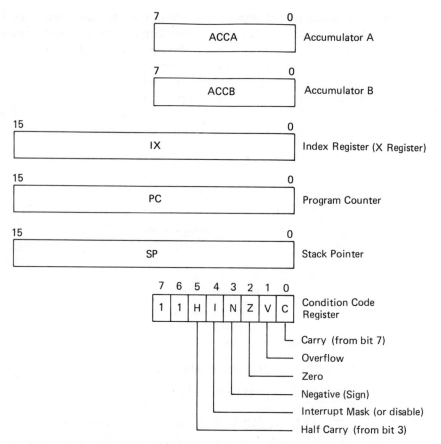

FIGURE 1-2. Programming model of the 6800 microprocessor.

tion Set Summary). Appendix 1 of this book also contains a summary of the 6800 instruction set, but you will probably find the self-contained card more convenient to use. Note that each instruction has several different operation (or op) codes, depending on the addressing method (mode) involved. Each operation code is followed by two numbers: one (under ~) indicates the number of clock cycles required to execute the instruction and the other (under #) indicates the number of words of memory the instruction occupies. We will explain the various addressing modes as we use them.

Note that we are writing the program originally in a form in which we can refer to the instructions by name. This form is called *assembly language*. However, the MEK6800D2 microcomputer does not allow us to enter names; it only accepts hexadecimal numbers. The form in which the actual numbers appear is called *machine language*. Converting assembly language to machine language is a simple (but highly repetitive) matter of looking up operation codes on a card or in a table; we can do the conversion by hand or we can let the computer do this rote task by using a program called an *assembler*. Assembly language is much easier for the programmer to write than is machine language, since assembly language is based on meaningful names or *mnemonics* rather than arbitrary numbers.

Program 1-1 is the hexadecimal (machine language) version of the one's-complement program.

PROGRAM 1-1

MEMORY ADDRESS (HEX)	MEMORY CONTENTS (HEX)	INSTRUCTION (MNEMONIC)	
0000	96	LDAA	$40
0001	40		
0002	43	COMA	
0003	97	STAA	$41
0004	41		
0005	3F	SWI	

Note the following:

1) With both LDAA and STAA, we have used the direct addressing mode in which the word of memory following the operation code contains the address to be used in the instruction. This address is actually 16 bits long, but if the 8 most significant bits are all zeros, we can omit them. This is like the common practice of referring to amounts under a dollar as "60 cents" rather than "zero dollars and 60 cents." If the 8 most significant bits of the address are not all zeros, we cannot omit them and must use the extended addressing mode.

2) In the direct addressing mode, the second word of the instruction contains an address. Note that LDAA $40 means "load Accumulator A with the contents of memory address 0040." That address could contain any 8-bit number; it need not contain 40.

3) COMA does not require an address or any additional words of memory, since the computer knows what to do from the operation code alone.

4) The instructions vary in length—LDAA $40 and STAA $41 require two words of memory, whereas COMA and SWI require only one.

Let us now try this program with the data C9 (binary 11001001) in memory location 0040. The answer should be 36 (binary 00110110) in memory location 0041. Why? Remember that you can use Table 0-1 to convert hexadecimal to binary, and vice versa. For example, C9 hexadecimal is 11001001 binary since C is 1100 binary and 9 is 1001 binary. Going the other way, 00110110 binary is 36 hexadecimal since 0011 binary is 3 in hexadecimal and 0110 binary is 6 in hexadecimal. Note that you must split the 8-bit binary word down the middle.

ENTERING AND RUNNING THE ONE'S-COMPLEMENT PROGRAM

Enter and run the program as follows:

ENTER PROGRAM

1) Press RESET if necessary.
2) Examine memory location 0000 with the key sequence

> 0
> 0
> 0
> 0
> M

3) Enter the hexadecimal program with the key sequence

> 9
> 6
> G
> 4
> 0
> G
> 4
> 3
> G
> 9
> 7
> G
> 4
> 1
> G
> 3
> F
> blue E

You can verify that the program has been entered correctly by first examining memory location 0000 and then using the G key to examine subsequent locations.

ENTER DATA

1) Examine memory location 0040 (hex) with the key sequence

0
0
4
0
M

2) Enter the data with the key sequence

C
9
blue E

RUN PROGRAM

You can now execute the program with the key sequence

0
0
0
0
G

Remember that the program starts in memory location 0000. The final G transfers control from the monitor to the program that you just entered. Control will return to the monitor when the computer executes the SWI instruction.

EXAMINE RESULTS

Finally, you can examine the result (after running the program) with the key sequence

blue E
0
0
4
1
M

Remember that the program stores the result in memory location 0041. The computer does not tell you the answer by itself (regardless of what some fiction writers think). All the computer does is execute the program (which takes about 30 μs) and return control to the monitor (since you put an SWI instruction at the end). When the computer executes SWI, it displays the address it has just executed (0005 in this case) and the contents of that address (3F in this case). You must press the blue E key to get the JBUG prompt.

Watch out for the following common errors (we know them from experience):

1) Accidentally executing the data instead of the program. That is, pressing 0, 0, 4, 0, G instead of 0, 0, 4, 0, M or 0, 0, 0, 0, G. This is an easy error to make and causes the computer to execute the data entries as if they were instructions. One way to limit the damage is to enter 1 or 2 SWI (3F) instructions at the end of the data. The computer will usually encounter one of these and return control to the monitor.

2) Forgetting to run the program. That is, entering the program and the data and waiting for something to happen. This is comparable to entering data into your calculator and waiting for it to produce a result. Neither a computer nor a calculator will produce an answer until it has been directed to execute a program.

3) Starting the program at the wrong address. This causes the computer to execute whatever instructions it finds at the specified address. This is a particularly annoying problem if you have several programs in memory or if you vary your starting addresses. One partial solution is to place SWI instructions at the addresses that you might enter accidentally.

Quite often, you will make an error that causes the computer to get lost and never return to the monitor. If this happens, press RESET or the blue E key to restore the JBUG prompt. One or two extra SWI instructions at the end of the program will reduce the frequency with which this happens (the computer occasionally gets past the first SWI), but no amount of caution will ever completely eliminate this frustrating experience.

PROBLEM 1-1

Run Program 1-1 again with the following data:

a) 36. The answer should be C9.

b) 00. The answer should be FF.

PROBLEM 1-2

Make Program 1-1 use accumulator B instead of accumulator A. Remember to change all three operation codes, (i.e., replace LDAA with LDAB, COMA with COMB, and STAA with STAB). The two 6800 accumulators are nearly equivalent, with some small differences that we will note later.

PROBLEM 1-3

Make Program 1-1 do the following:

a)   Store the result in memory location 0042.

b)   Load the data from memory location 0041 and store the result in memory location 0040.

PROBLEM 1-4

Write and run a program that calculates the two's complement of the contents of memory location 0040 and stores the result in memory location 0041. The two's complement is the one's complement plus 1; note that adding a number to its two's complement gives a result of zero (what is the result of adding a number and its one's complement?).

Sample Problems (The parentheses around a memory address indicate "contents of"):

1)   (0040) = C9
     Result: (0041) = 37
2)   (0040) = 00
     Result: (0041) = 00

(**Hint:** Use the NEG instruction instead of COM.)

USING THE INDEX REGISTER

A unique feature of the Motorola 6800 microprocessor is its indexed addressing mode. The index register is a 16-bit register which can hold a complete memory address. In the indexed addressing mode, the instructions contain 8-bit offsets that are added to the contents of the index register to determine the actual address of the data. This actual address is called an *effective address.* Note that the addition of an 8-bit offset and the 16-bit contents of the index register produces a 16-bit address which is then used to transfer data to or from memory. We can revise the one's-complement program to use the index register as follows:

```
LDX        #$40          GET STARTING ADDRESS OF DATA
LDAA       0,X           GET DATA
COMA                     COMPLEMENT DATA
STAA       1,X           STORE RESULT
SWI
```

Note that # means "immediate" and NUM,X means the indexed address-ing mode with an offset of NUM. Most 6800 assemblers allow you to omit a zero offset (i.e., LDAA 0,X may be abbreviated as LDAA X).

Let us look next at each instruction in this program (Program 1-2 is the hexadecimal version).

PROGRAM 1-2

MEMORY ADDRESS (HEX)	MEMORY CONTENTS (HEX)	INSTRUCTION (MNEMONIC)	
0010	CE	LDX	#$40
0011	00		
0012	40		
0013	A6	LDAA	0,X
0014	00		
0015	43	COMA	
0016	A7	STAA	1,X
0017	01		
0018	3F	SWI	

1) LDX #$40 loads the index register with the contents of the two memory locations *immediately* following the operation code. This is the immediate addressing mode in which the data (and not the address of the data) follows the operation code. Note that 0040 occupies two memory locations, with 00 (the 8 most significant bits) in the first one and 40 (the 8 least significant bits) in the second one.

2) LDAA 0,X loads accumulator A with the contents of the memory address calculated by adding 0 (the offset) to the contents of the index register. The result here is to load accumulator A with the contents of memory location 0040 (hex). Note that the offset (00) follows the operation code (A6) for "LDAA indexed" in the machine language version.

3) COMA is the same as before.

4) STAA 1,X stores accumulator A in the memory address calculated by adding 1 (the offset) to the contents of the index register.

The result here is to store the contents of accumulator A in memory location 0041. Note that the index register is only loaded once and the other addresses are specified relative to its contents.

In the immediate addressing mode (LDX #$40), the instruction contains the data that it needs. Note that LDX #$40 loads the index register with the number 0040, not the contents of memory address 0040. Explain how immediate and direct addressing differ. Can STA or STX be used in the immediate mode? Why not?

Be careful of the fact that the index register is 16 bits long, whereas the accumulators (and the memory locations) are only 8 bits long. Two memory locations are needed to load the index register or to store its contents.

The instructions LDAA 0,X and STAA 1,X use *indexed addressing* in which the instructions specify (with an 8-bit offset) the address relative to the contents of the index register. Note that we can change the contents of the index register with such instructions as LDX (LOAD INDEX REGISTER), INX (INCREMENT INDEX REGISTER BY 1), and DEX (DECREMENT INDEX REGISTER BY 1). These are all 16-bit operations.

In this approach it is very important to keep all the data close together since the offset is only 8 bits long. Does it matter in the earlier program whether the addresses are close together? (What if one or the other is larger than 00FF?) We have started the hexadecimal version of this program (Program 1-2) in address 0010 to avoid interfering with Program 1-1. Program 1-2 occupies three more memory locations than Program 1-1 because of the LDX #$40 instruction. Note that LDAA 0,X and STAA 1,X both occupy two words of memory. Here the instructions vary from one to three words in length; this variation is a nuisance when you are assembling programs by hand, but the assembler takes care of it automatically.

Enter Program 1-2 into memory and execute it. Try the same sample problems as before:

1) Data: (0040) = 36
    Result: (0041) = C9

2) Data: (0040) = C9
    Result: (0041) = 36

3) Data (0040) = 00
    Result: (0041) = FF

Remember to start program execution in memory location 0010, not 0000.

PROBLEM 1-5

Revise Program 1-2 to do the following:

a) Store the result in memory location 0042.

b) Load the data from memory location 0041 and store the result in memory location 0040.

c) Load the data from memory location 0031 and store the result in memory location 0030.

d) Use accumulator B instead of accumulator A.

PROBLEM 1-6

Make Program 1-2 calculate the one's complements of two successive memory locations and store them in the next two memory locations (i.e., it should store the one's complement of location 0040 in 0042 and the one's complement of 0041 in 0043).

Sample Problem:

$$(0040) = C9$$

$$(0041) = 00$$

Result:

$$(0042) = 36$$

$$(0043) = FF$$

EXAMINING REGISTERS

One way to compare the two versions of the one's-complement program is to compare the final contents of the registers. Once you are in the mode in which the JBUG prompt is being displayed, you can examine the registers by pressing the R key (second key from the bottom in the rightmost column). Remember that you can restore the JBUG prompt by pressing RESET or the blue E key. When you press R, the program counter will appear in the address displays and the contents of that address in the data displays. You may then examine the remaining registers one at a time by pressing the G key repeatedly; the order in which the registers appear is listed below (see also Table 1-1). Unfortunately, JBUG does not identify the register that is being displayed.

Program Counter (16 bits) and contents
of address in Program Counter (8 bits)

Index Register (16 bits)

Accumulator A (8 bits)

Accumulator B (8 bits)

Condition Code Register (8 bits)

Stack Pointer (16 bits)

We will discuss the condition code register (see Laboratory 2) and the stack pointer (see Laboratory A) later.

The program counter, index register, and stack pointer are all four digits (16 bits) long, since they contain memory addresses rather than data. The program counter contains the address of the next instruction that the CPU will fetch from memory. Each time the CPU uses the program counter, it adds one to its contents. Thus the computer will execute instructions sequentially unless it is specifically told to do otherwise.

> **Warning**: If you want to examine the current contents of the registers, do not press RESET. This switch reinitializes the CPU and may change the registers. If necessary, exit from the current command by pressing the blue E key.

Table 1-1

ORDER FOR REGISTER DISPLAY

When the R key is pressed, registers appear in the following order:

Program Counter and contents of address in Program Counter

Index Register

Accumulator A

Accumulator B

Condition Code Register

Stack Pointer

The sequence is circular, so pressing G after examining the stack pointer causes the program counter to appear again. Since the stack is used to hold the register values, the actual value of the stack pointer is seven larger than the displayed value.

CHANGING REGISTERS

Unfortunately, you cannot change the contents of the registers as part of the examination procedure. You can, however, change the registers by changing the memory locations that the monitor program uses for temporary storage of their contents. The area that the monitor uses for this purpose can be determined by examining memory locations A008 and A009, which contain the monitor Stack Pointer. If the address in those two locations is S, the registers may be examined and changed by examining

S + 1—Condition Code Register

S + 2—Accumulator B

S + 3—Accumulator A

S + 4—High-order (most significant) byte of Index Register

S + 5—Low-order (least significant) byte of Index Register

S + 6—High-order (most significant) byte of Program Counter

S + 7—Low-order (least significant) byte of Program Counter

For example, let us assume that we want to place 4C in accumulator B. We must first examine memory locations A008 and A009 using the M and G keys. Let us assume that they contain

(A008) = A0 (MSBs of Stack Pointer)

(A009) = 78 (LSBs of Stack Pointer)

To change accumulator B, we must change memory location S+2 or A07A to 4C. Make this change and verify it by using the R key to examine the registers. Note that you have to remember the order of the registers and the memory locations (see Tables 1-1 and 1-2), since the monitor does not identify the registers when they are displayed and provides no way to change them directly.

Table 1-2

ADDRESSES FOR REGISTER CHANGES

A008—MSBs of Stack Pointer (S_H)
A009—LSBs of Stack Pointer (S_L)

$S_H S_L$+1—Condition Code Register
$S_H S_L$+2—Accumulator B
$S_H S_L$+3—Accumulator A
$S_H S_L$+4—High-order (most significant) byte of Index Register
$S_H S_L$+5—Low-order (least significant) byte of Index Register
$S_H S_L$+6—High-order (most significant) byte of Program Counter
$S_H S_L$+7—Low-order (least significant) byte of Program Counter

Example:

If (A008) = A0
  (A009) = 78

the registers can be accessed in the following memory locations.

MEMORY ADDRESS (HEX)	CONTENTS (REGISTER)
A079	Condition Code Register
A07A	Accumulator B
A07B	Accumulator A
A07C	High-order (most significant) byte of Index Register
A07D	Low-order (least significant) byte of Index Register
A07E	High-order (most significant) byte of Program Counter
A07F	Low-order (least significant) byte of Program Counter

COMPARING PROGRAMS

Try the following experiment. Clear accumulator A and the index register and run the first version of the one's-complement program. What are the final contents of accumulator A, the index register, and the program counter? Clear accumulator A and the index register again and run the second version of the one's-complement program. What are the final contents of accumulator A, the index register, and the program counter? What is the advantage of each version? Note that executing SWI causes the microcomputer to display the current program counter and the contents of that address, just as if you had pressed the R key. You can then use G to examine the other registers (remember Table 1-1) and the blue E key to exit.

> **Important Note:** Although we will not use the stack pointer untill much later (Laboratory A), you must be careful that it always contains an actual RAM address. One way to do this is to place A078 in memory locations A008 and A009. This patch (sort of like a well-placed kick) can sometimes solve a very mysterious operating problem.

ADDING TWO NUMBERS

Either version of the one's-complement program can easily be changed to an addition program. The problem now is to add the contents of memory locations 0040 and 0041 and place the result in memory location 0042. The second approach results in the following program:

```
LDX      #$40      GET STARTING ADDRESS OF DATA AREA
LDAA     0,X       GET FIRST OPERAND
ADDA     1,X       ADD SECOND OPERAND
STAA     2,X       STORE RESULT
SWI
```

Program 1-3 is the hexadecimal version.

PROGRAM 1-3

MEMORY ADDRESS (HEX)	MEMORY CONTENTS (HEX)	INSTRUCTION (MNEMONIC)	
0010	CE	LDX	#$40
0011	00		
0012	40		
0013	A6	LDAA	0,X
0014	00		
0015	AB	ADDA	1,X
0016	01		
0017	A7	STAA	2,X
0018	02		
0019	3F	SWI	

Enter Program 1-3 and execute it for the following sample cases:

1) Data: (0040) = 23
   (0041) = 34
   Result: (0042) = 57

2) Data: (0040) = 58
   (0041) = 42
   Result: (0042) = 9A

Remember that all numbers are hexadecimal.

3) Data: (0040) = B9
   (0041) = 7E
   Result: (0042) = 37

28

What happened to the carry?

PROBLEM 1-7

Make Program 1-3 logically AND the two data entries and store the result. How would you implement a logical OR? Logical EXCLUSIVE OR? Use Table 3-3 if you cannot remember how the logical functions work.

Sample Problem:

Data: (0040) = 23
　　　(0041) = 34
Result: (0042) = 20 for logical AND
　　　　　　　= 37 for logical OR
　　　　　　　= 17 for logical EXCLUSIVE OR

PROBLEM 1-8

Modify Program 1-1 so that it performs an addition. Do not use the index register. Which version is better, and why?

PROBLEM 1-9

Modify Program 1-3 and the answer to Problem 1-8 so that they add the contents of memory locations 0050 and 0051 and place the result in memory location 0052. Which one is easier to change, and why? Which would be easier to change if the required memory addresses were A050, A051, and A052?

KEY POINT SUMMARY

1) Most simple 6800 programs use an accumulator (either A or B) as the center of operations. The programs begin by loading the accumulator from memory and end by storing the result in memory.

2) The easiest addressing mode to use for loading and storing data is the one in which the instruction contains the address the CPU needs to perform the operation. This address follows the operation code in memory. If the address's 8 most significant bits are all zero, they can be omitted and the direct addressing mode can be used. If they are not all zero, the extended mode must be used, in which the address occupies two words of memory with the 8 most significant bits in the first word.

3) To run a program on the MEK6800D2 microcomputer, you must enter the program and data into memory, execute the program, and examine the results.

4) In the indexed addressing mode, the actual (effective) address is calculated by adding the offset to the contents of the index register. The offset follows the operation code in memory and is 8 bits long. The

index register is 16 bits long. Indexed addressing is often convenient since addresses can be specified relative to the value in the index register and that value can be changed by means of the instructions LDX, INX, or DEX.

5) In immediate addressing, the actual data (not its address) follows the operation code in memory. This mode is used to provide constant values for use in instructions. Instructions such as LDX require 16 bits of data (two memory locations with the most significant bits first).

6) You can examine the microprocessor's registers by pressing the R key to start the register display and the G key to cycle through the display. You must remember the arbitrary order in which registers are displayed since the monitor does not identify them. You can change the contents of the registers by changing the memory locations that the monitor uses for temporary storage.

Simple Input for the
MEK6800D2 Microcomputer

PURPOSE

To learn how to use the input ports on the MEK6800D2 microcomputer.

PARTS REQUIRED

Eight switches or pushbuttons attached to the user Peripheral Interface Adapter as shown in Figure 2-1. The pin assignments needed for I/O port connector J1 are listed in Table 2-1 (and in Figure A3-b of the *MEK6800D2 Evaluation Kit manual*).

REFERENCE MATERIALS

L. A. Leventhal, *Introduction to Microprocessors: Software, Hardware, Programming,* Prentice-Hall, Englewood Cliffs, NJ, 1978, pp. 104-121, 363-365, 369, 408-409.

L. A. Leventhal, *6800 Assembly Language Programming,* Osborne/McGraw-Hill, Berkeley, CA, 1978, pp. 11-12 through 11-26.

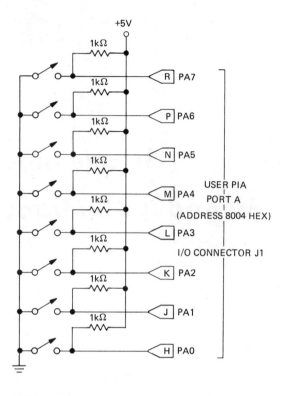

FIGURE 2-1. Attachment of switches to user PIA port A.

W. J. Weller, *Practical Microcomputer Programming: The M6800,* Northern Technology Books, Evanston, IL, pp. 38-55, 211-216.

MEK6800D2 Evaluation Kit II Manual, Motorola Semiconductor Products Inc., Austin, TX, p. 1-11, p. 2-3.

M6800 Programming Reference Manual, Motorola Semiconductor Products Inc., Phoenix, AZ, 1976, pp. 2-4 through 2-6, Chapter 4.

WHAT YOU SHOULD LEARN

1) How to use the user Peripheral Interface Adapter (PIA) for input.
2) How to use the LDA and STA instructions for input and output.
3) How to determine whether a switch is open or closed.
4) How to examine single bits in a word.
5) How to use conditional jump (branch) instructions.
6) How to calculate relative offsets for branch instructions.

7) Which bit positions can be accessed most easily.

8) How to use shift instructions.

9) What flags are available on the 6800 CPU.

10) How to examine the flags.

11) How 6800 instructions affect the flags.

12) How to handle a series of switch closures.

13) How to recognize a starting character in communications.

Table 2-1

**I/O CONNECTOR J1 PIN
ASSIGNMENTS FOR USER PIA PORT A**

ASSIGNMENT	PIN
Bit 0 (PA0)	H
Bit 1 (PA1)	J
Bit 2 (PA2)	K
Bit 3 (PA3)	L
Bit 4 (PA4)	M
Bit 5 (PA5)	N
Bit 6 (PA6)	P
Bit 7 (PA7)	R

TERMS

Arithmetic-logic unit (or **ALU**)—a device that can perform any of a variety of arithmetic or logical functions; function inputs select which function is performed during a particular cycle.

Arithmetic shift—a shitt operation that preserves the value of the sign bit (most significant bit). Be careful—the 6800's ARITHMETIC SHIFT LEFT instruction is actually a logical shift.

Branch instruction—*see* Jump instruction.

Carry flag—a flag that is 1 if the last operation generated a carry from the most significant bit and 0 if it did not.

Flag (or **condition code** or **status bit**)—a single bit that indicates a condition within the computer, often used to choose between alternative instruction sequences.

Flip-flop—a digital electronic device with two stable states that can be made to switch from one state to the other in a reproducible manner.

Floating—not tied to any logic level. TTL and MOS devices usually interpret a floating input as a logic 1.

Isolated input/output—an addressing method for I/O ports that uses a decoding system distinct from that used by the memory section. I/O ports do not occupy memory addresses.

Jump instruction (or **branch instruction**)—an instruction that places a new value in the program counter, thus departing from the normal one-step incrementing. Jump instructions may be conditional; that is, the new value may only be placed in the program counter if certain conditions are met.

Label—a name attached to an instruction or statement in a program that identifies the location in memory of the machine language code or assignment produced from that instruction or statement.

Logical shift—a shift operation that places zeros in the empty bits.

Mask—a bit pattern that isolates 1 or more bits from a group of bits.

Memory-mapped input/output—an addressing method for I/O ports that uses the same decoding system used by the memory section. The I/O ports thus occupy memory addresses.

Parallel interface—an interface between a CPU and input or output devices that handle data in parallel (more than one bit at a time).

Peripheral Interface Adapter—the 6800 family version of a parallel interface. The 6820 and 6821 devices are virtually interchangeable.

Port—the basic addressable unit of the computer input/output section.

Relative addressing—an addressing method in which the address specified in the instruction is the offset from a base address. Relative addressing allows programs to be easily relocated in memory.

Relocatable—can be placed anywhere in memory without changes: that is, a program that can occupy any set of consecutive memory addresses.

Serial—one bit at a time.

Shift instruction—an instruction that moves all the bits of the data by a certain number of bit positions, just as in a shift register.

Sign flag—a flag that contains the most significant bit of the result of the previous operation.

SPST switch—single-pole, single-throw switch with one common line and one output line.

Status register (or **status word** or **condition code register**)—a register that contains bits describing the current state of the computer. This register usually holds all the flags.

Synchronization (or **sync**) **character**—a character that is used only to synchronize the transmitter and the receiver. The character does not contain any actual information.

Zero flag—a flag that is 1 if the last operation produced a result of zero and 0 if it did not.

6800 INSTRUCTIONS

AND—logical AND; logically AND the contents of an accumulator with the contents of the specified memory location.

ASL—arithmetic shift left; shift each bit of an accumulator or memory location left one position and clear the least significant bit (see Figure 2-2).

BCC—branch if carry clear; jump over the specified number of memory locations if the CARRY flag is 0; otherwise, proceed to the next instruction in sequence.

BCS—branch if carry set; jump over the specified number of memory locations if the CARRY flag is 1; otherwise, proceed to the next instruction in sequence.

BEQ—branch if equal to zero; jump over the specified number of memory locations if the ZERO flag is 1; otherwise, proceed to the next instruction in sequence.

BIT—bit test (logical AND with no result saved); logically AND the contents of an accumulator with the contents of the specified memory location but leave the final contents of the accumulator unchanged. This instruction affects only the flags.

BMI—branch if minus; jump over the specified number of memory locations if the NEGATIVE (SIGN) flag is 1; otherwise, proceed to the next instruction in sequence.

BNE—branch if not equal to zero; jump over the specified number of memory location if the ZERO flag is 0; otherwise, proceed to the next instruction in sequence.

BPL—branch if plus; jump over the specified number of memory locations if the NEGATIVE (SIGN) flag is 0; otherwise, proceed to the next instruction in sequence.

CLR—clear; place zero in the specified accumulator or memory location.

CMP—compare; subtract the contents of the specified memory location from the contents of an accumulator but leave the contents of the accumulator unchanged. This instruction affects only the flags.

LSR—logical shift right; shift each bit of an accumulator or memory location right one position and clear the most significant bit (see Figure 2-2).

SUB—subtract; subtract the contents of the specified memory location from the contents of an accumulator.

TST—test zero or minus; subtract zero from the contents of the specified accumulator or memory location and change the flags accordingly. This instruction affects only the flags.

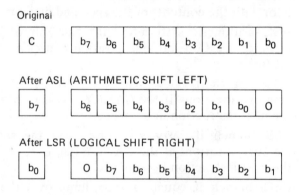

FIGURE 2-2. 6800 shift instructions ASL and LSR.

6800 INPUT/OUTPUT OPERATIONS

The 6800 microprocessor has no specific input/output (I/O) instructions. Instead, it treats I/O ports as if they were memory locations. (This approach is referred to as *memory-mapped input/output,* as opposed to *isolated input/output,* in which I/O ports and memory locations are addressed separately.) Note that the processor really cannot tell memory from I/O; all the processor does is produce addresses and control signals and transfer data.

In memory-mapped input/output, any instruction that transfers data to or from memory can serve as an I/O instruction. The 6800 instructions that are most commonly used to perform I/O are:

- LDA (LOAD ACCUMULATOR) transfers 8 bits of data from the specified memory address (actually an input port) to an accumulator.

- STA (STORE ACCUMULATOR) transfers 8 bits of data from an accumulator to the specified memory address (actually an output port).
- CLR (CLEAR) places zeros on a set of output pins.
- BIT (BIT TEST) sets the flags as if the values of a set of input pins had been logically ANDed with the contents of an accumulator. The contents of the accumulator are unchanged.
- CMP (COMPARE ACCUMULATOR) sets the flags as if the values of a set of input pins had been subtracted from the contents of an accumulator. The contents of the accumulator are unchanged.

One difficulty with memory-mapped input/output is that input/output operations are not clearly distinguished from simple transfers of data to or from memory. Complex I/O operations can be concealed in instructions with no obvious functions. Memory-mapped input/output always requires very careful and thorough documentation.

SIMPLE INPUT

The MEK6800D2 microcomputer has a parallel interface (a 6821 Peripheral Interface Adapter) that is not used by the monitor and can be employed for user input/output. It occupies memory addresses 8004 through 8007. Note that we must use the extended addressing mode when referring to these addresses. The input port that we will use occupies memory address 8004 (hex).

The Peripheral Interface Adapter or PIA is a complex I/O system on a chip. We will describe it later in Laboratories B and C. For now, let us note that the following initialization program allows us to use address 8004 as an input port:

```
CLR     $8005           MAKE LINES INTO INPUTS
CLR     $8004
LDAA    #%00000100      ENABLE DATA TRANSFERS THROUGH PORT
STAA    $8005
```

You must include this initialization in every program that reads the switches attached to the user PIA. These instructions only have to be executed once; the switches can be read many times afterward. Program 2-1 is the hexadecimal version of the initialization.

Note that CLR $8005, CLR $8004, and STAA $8005 all use the extended addressing mode, since the 8 most significant bits of the addresses are not all zeros. In each case, the address occupies the two words of memory immediately following the operation code. The 8 most significant bits always come first; this is the standard Motorola method for storing addresses or 16-bit data but is the opposite of that used by many other manufacturers.

PROGRAM 2-1

MEMORY ADDRESS (HEX)	MEMORY CONTENTS (HEX)	INSTRUCTION (MNEMONIC)	
0000	7F	CLR	$8005
0001	80		
0002	05		
0003	7F	CLR	$8004
0004	80		
0005	04		
0006	86	LDAA	#%00000100
0007	04		
0008	B7	STAA	$8005
0009	80		
000A	05		

To begin the experiment, leave all the switches open. The following program initializes the input port and loads accumulator A with the data from the switches. Program 2-2 contains the required additions to Program 2-1 in hexadecimal.

CLR	$8005	MAKE LINES INTO INPUTS
CLR	$8004	
LDAA	#%00000100	ENABLE DATA TRANSFERS
STAA	$8005	
LDAA	$8004	READ DATA FROM SWITCHES
SWI		

PROGRAM 2-2

MEMORY ADDRESS (HEX)	MEMORY CONTENTS (HEX)	INSTRUCTION (MNEMONIC)	
000B	B6	LDAA	$8004
000C	80		
000D	04		
000E	3F	SWI	

Reset the computer and execute Programs 2-1 and 2-2. What are the final contents of accumulator A? What happens if you replace LDAA $8004 with LDAA $8005? LDAA $8004 and LDAA $8005 look similar but have different physical meanings, since memory location 8005 is not connected to the outside world.

Now close the switch attached to bit position 5 of address 8004 (pin PA5). Execute Programs 2-1 and 2-2 (accessing address 8004) again. What are the final contents of accumulator A?

Note that the standard procedure in the computer industry is to number bit positions starting with zero at the right. Thus, in an 8-bit word, the bits are numbered 0 through 7 from right to left, with bit 0 being least significant and bit 7 most significant. Figures 2-2 and 2-3 contain examples of the standard numbering.

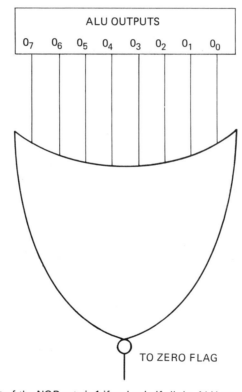

The output of the NOR gate is 1 if and only if all the ALU outputs are zero.

FIGURE 2-3. Implementation of a ZERO flag.

PROBLEM 2-1

The computer interprets an unconnected or floating input as a logic _____ , an open switch as a logic _____ , and a closed switch as a logic _____ .

PROBLEM 2-2

Determine the data input if

a) A switch attached to bit position 2 of address 8004 is closed.

b) Switches attached to bit positions 2 and 5 are closed.

c) Switches attached to bit positions 0, 6, and 7 are closed.

Assume that all other switches are open.

PROBLEM 2-3

Revise the initialization routine (Program 2-1) to use the index register. Which version uses less memory? Which version is executed faster?

FLAGS AND CONDITIONAL BRANCHES

To determine if a switch is open or closed, we must use

1) The flags (also called *condition codes* or *status bits*).
2) The conditional branch instructions.

The flags are set according to the results of previous instructions. The conditional branch (or jump) instructions allow the computer to choose among alternative instruction sequences based on the values of the flags. The most important 6800 flags are:

C (CARRY)—1 if the last arithmetic or shift instruction produced a carry or a borrow, 0 if it did not.

N (NEGATIVE or SIGN)—1 if the result of the last instruction had a 1 in its most significant bit, 0 if it did not.

Z (ZERO)—1 if the result of the last instruction was zero, 0 if it was not zero.

These flags are simply flip-flops inside the 6800 processor. Figure 2-3 shows, for example, how the ZERO flag could be implemented on the 6800 chip with an eight-input logical NOR gate. The NEGATIVE (SIGN) and CARRY flags can be derived directly from the outputs of an accumulator or an arithmetic-logic unit (ALU).

The 6800 conditional branch (jump) instructions place a new value in the program counter if the specified flag or combination of flags has the specified value. If the condition does not hold, the computer simply proceeds to the next instruction in sequence. These instructions make the computer "smart," that is, capable of making decisions based on current information. The computer thus becomes an intelligent controller. Table 2-2 lists the major 6800 conditional branch instructions.

Table 2-2

**MAJOR 6800 CONDITIONAL
BRANCH INSTRUCTIONS***

INSTRUCTION	FLAG USED	VALUE ON WHICH BRANCH OCCURS
BCC	CARRY	0
BCS	CARRY	1
BNE	ZERO	0
BEQ	ZERO	1
BPL	NEGATIVE (SIGN)	0
BMI	NEGATIVE (SIGN)	1

*If the specified flag does not have the specified value, no branch occurs.

WAITING FOR A SWITCH CLOSURE

Let us concentrate for now on the switch attached to bit 5 of address 8004 (pin PA5). The following program will wait until you close the switch and will then return control to the monitor. Remember that an open switch is a logic 1 and a closed switch is a logic 0 (see Figure 2-1).

```
        CLR     $8005           MAKE LINES INTO INPUTS
        CLR     $8004
        LDAA    #%00000100      ENABLE DATA TRANSFERS
        STAA    $8005
WAITC   LDAA    $8004           GET INPUT DATA
        ANDA    #%00100000      IS SWITCH 5 CLOSED?
        BNE     WAITC           NO, WAIT
        SWI
```

Let us now look at each of the instructions in the main program (after the standard initialization):

1)   LDAA $8004 loads accumulator A with the contents of the port attached to the eight switches. Note that the CPU must fetch 8 bits even though we are only interested in one of them.

WAITC is a name that we have given to the memory address in which the instruction LDAA $8004 starts. Such a name is called a *label*; its sole purpose is to make the program easier to read and understand. People find names easier to remember than hexadecimal numbers; however, the computer only accepts numbers, so the programmer (or the assembler program) must replace all labels with the actual addresses to which they refer. For example, if the last program starts in memory location 0000, the label WAITC refers to address 000B and the instruction BNE WAITC must actually cause a branch to that address. Labels are convenient because they are easy to find and change in a program listing. The name WAITC is arbitrary; we selected it because it suggests the idea of *wait*ing for a *c*losure.

2) ANDA #%00100000 logically ANDs the contents of accumulator A with the binary number 00100000. The % means "binary" and the # before the number means "immediate" (i.e., the data is in the next word of program memory). The result of the logical AND is 0 if the switch is closed (an 8-bit zero, remember) and 00100000 if the switch is open (verify this!) This process is called *masking*.

The ANDA instruction has the same effect as eight two-input AND gates. A TTL implementation would require two 7408 (quad two-input AND) packages.

3) BNE WAITC causes the processor to execute the instruction in memory location WAITC next if the ZERO flag is zero. Otherwise, the processor proceeds to the next instruction in sequence (SWI in this case). The ZERO flag is a flip-flop inside the 6800 CPU which is set to 1 if an operation produces a zero result. Watch out—the ZERO flag is *1* if the result was zero.

Program 2-3 is the hexadecimal version. Note the following features:

PROGRAM 2-3

MEMORY ADDRESS (HEX)	MEMORY CONTENTS (HEX)	INSTRUCTION (MNEMONIC)	
0000	7F	CLR	$8005
0001	80		
0002	05		
0003	7F	CLR	$8004
0004	80		
0005	04		

MEMORY ADDRESS (HEX)	MEMORY CONTENTS (HEX)		INSTRUCTION (MNEMONIC)	
0006	86		LDAA	#%00000100
0007	04			
0008	B7		STAA	$8005
0009	80			
000A	05			
000B	B6	WAITC	LDAA	$8004
000C	80			
000D	04			
000E	84		ANDA	#%00100000
000F	20			
0010	26		BNE	WAITC
0011	F9			
0012	3F		SWI	

1)　LDAA $8004 requires a full 16-bit memory address in the two words of memory following the operation code. The extended addressing mode is used.

2)　The ANDA #%00100000 instruction requires 8 bits of data in the next word of memory. Remember that you must convert the binary pattern 00100000 to hexadecimal—0010 is 2 in hexadecimal and 0000 is 0 (use Table 0-1).

3)　The BNE instruction requires an 8-bit relative offset in the next word of memory. This offset determines how many locations the computer should jump over (going backward or forward) from the end of the instruction (address 0012 in this case). A positive offset (most significant bit = 0) is added to the final address (e.g., an offset of 02 would be added to 0012 to make the destination 0014); the maximum positive offset is 7F or +127 decimal. A negative offset (most significant bit = 1) tells the computer how many locations backward to go (one back is FF, two back is FE, etc.). You can calculate the offset by subtracting the final address from the destination address; in our case, the subtraction is

$$
\begin{array}{ll}
000B & \text{(destination address)} \\
\underline{-0012} & \text{(final address at the end of the BNE instruction)} \\
FFF9 &
\end{array}
$$

Only the F9 is significant; the largest negative offset is 80 hex or −128 decimal.

The usual way to perform hexadecimal subtraction is to calculate the two's complement of the number to be subtracted and add it to the

43

other number. Table 2-3 contains the two's complements of all two-digit hexadecimal numbers and Table 2-4 is a hexadecimal addition table. Using these tables, we can calculate the offset as follows:

Table 2-3

TWO'S COMPLEMENTS OF TWO-DIGIT HEXADECIMAL NUMBERS

LSD	MSD															
	0	1	2	3	4	5	6	7	8	9	A	B	C	D	E	F
0	00	F0	E0	D0	C0	B0	A0	90	80	70	60	50	40	30	20	10
1	FF	EF	DF	CF	BF	AF	9F	8F	7F	6F	5F	4F	3F	2F	1F	0F
2	FE	EE	DE	CE	BE	AE	9E	8E	7E	6E	5E	4E	3E	2E	1E	0E
3	FD	ED	DD	CD	BD	AD	9D	8D	7D	6D	5D	4D	2D	2D	1D	0D
4	FC	EC	DC	CC	BC	AC	9C	8C	7C	6C	5C	4C	3C	2C	1C	0C
5	FB	EB	DB	CB	BB	AB	9B	8B	7B	6B	5B	4B	3B	2B	1B	0B
6	FA	EA	DA	CA	BA	AA	9A	8A	7A	6A	5A	4A	3A	2A	1A	0A
7	F9	E9	D9	C9	B9	A9	99	89	79	69	59	49	39	29	19	09
8	F8	E8	D8	C8	B8	A8	98	88	78	68	58	48	38	28	18	08
9	F7	E7	D7	C7	B7	A7	97	87	77	67	57	47	37	27	17	07
A	F6	E6	D6	C6	B6	A6	96	86	76	66	56	46	36	26	16	06
B	F5	E5	D5	C5	B5	A5	95	85	75	65	55	45	35	25	15	05
C	F4	E4	D4	C4	B4	A4	94	84	74	64	54	44	34	24	14	04
D	F3	E3	D3	C3	B3	A3	93	83	73	63	53	43	33	23	13	03
E	F2	E2	D2	C2	B2	A2	92	82	72	62	52	42	32	22	12	02
F	F1	E1	D1	C1	B1	A1	91	81	71	61	51	41	31	21	11	01

Table 2-4

HEXADECIMAL ADDITION TABLE

+	0	1	2	3	4	5	6	7	8	9	A	B	C	D	E	F
0	0	1	2	3	4	5	6	7	8	9	A	B	C	D	E	F
1	1	2	3	4	5	6	7	8	9	A	B	C	D	E	F	10
2	2	3	4	5	6	7	8	9	A	B	C	D	E	F	10	11
3	3	4	5	6	7	8	9	A	B	C	D	E	F	10	11	12
4	4	5	6	7	8	9	A	B	C	D	E	F	10	11	12	13
5	5	6	7	8	9	A	B	C	D	E	F	10	11	12	13	14
6	6	7	8	9	A	B	C	D	E	F	10	11	12	13	14	15
7	7	8	9	A	B	C	D	E	F	10	11	12	13	14	15	16
8	8	9	A	B	C	D	E	F	10	11	12	13	14	15	16	17
9	9	A	B	C	D	E	F	10	11	12	13	14	15	16	17	18
A	A	B	C	D	E	F	10	11	12	13	14	15	16	17	18	19
B	B	C	D	E	F	10	11	12	13	14	15	16	17	18	19	1A
C	C	D	E	F	10	11	12	13	14	15	16	17	18	19	1A	1B
D	D	E	F	10	11	12	13	14	15	16	17	18	19	1A	1B	1C
E	E	F	10	11	12	13	14	15	16	17	18	19	1A	1B	1C	1D
F	F	10	11	12	13	14	15	16	17	18	19	1A	1B	1C	1D	1E

0B   (destination address)

− 12   (address immediately following the end of the BNE instruction)

The two's complement of 12 if EE from Table 2-3. So the subtraction is equivalent to

$$
\begin{array}{r}
0B \\
+\,EE \\
\hline
F9
\end{array}
$$

where we used Table 2-4 to perform the hexadecimal addition.

Clearly this method is, at best, only slightly less cumbersome than counting on one's fingers (counting is substantially easier if you happen to have 16 fingers or are a whiz at counting backward in hexadecimal). There are several ways out of this predicament:

1) Use an assembler, which will automatically perform this rote task for you.

2) Buy a calculator that does hexadecimal arithmetic. The Texas Instruments Programmer is a popular model.

3) Use the feature in the JBUG monitor which we will describe later in this laboratory.

Henceforth, we will occasionally show how we obtained some of the hexadecimal offsets, but we will not emphasize hexadecimal arithmetic. In practical applications, one should always find a way to avoid this annoying rote task. If you must perform it by hand, always check your arithmetic (assuming that you are no better at it than we are).

Enter and run Program 2-3. What happens if you leave the switch attached to bit position 5 open? What happens if you close a switch attached to some other bit position?

PROBLEM 2-4

Make Program 2-3 wait for the closure of a switch attached to bit position 4 of memory location 8004. Next try bit position 2 and then bit position 6. How easily could you change from one bit position to another if the system were implemented entirely in TTL logic?

PROBLEM 2-5

Change Program 2-3 so that it starts in memory location 0010. A program that can be placed anywhere in memory without any changes is called *relocatable*. Is Program 2-3 relocatable? Explain why the use of relative addressing in branch instructions is the key to this program's relocatability. Would the program be relocatable if the BNE instruction actually specified the complete destination address? Suggest some reasons why relocatable programs are desirable.

PROBLEM 2-6

What happens if you replace ANDA #%00100000 with BITA #%00100000? All that you must do is replace the 84 in memory location 000E with 85. Assume that switch 5 is closed and all the other switches are open. What values are in accumulator A before and after ANDA #%00100000 is executed? How about before and after BITA #%00100000 is executed? Why is the BIT instruction advantageous?

SPECIAL BIT POSITIONS

The processor handles all 8 bits at once in most instructions, so there is little to differentiate one bit position from another. However, some instructions and internal processor facilities make certain bit positions more accessible than others. For example:

1) The instruction ASL (see Figure 2-2) shifts each bit left one position. The old value of bit 6 is placed in the NEGATIVE or SIGN flag; it can then be used as a branch condition by the instructions BMI and BPL.

2) The instruction LSR (see Figure 2-2) similarly places the value of bit 0 in the CARRY. It can then be used as a branch condition by the instructions BCC and BCS.

3) The instruction LDA sets the NEGATIVE or SIGN flag according to the value of bit 7; it can then be used as a branch condition by the instructions BMI and BPL.

So the following program will respond to a switch closure in bit position 7:

```
WAITC    LDAA    $8004    GET INPUT DATA
         BMI     WAITC    WAIT UNTIL SWITCH 7 IS CLOSED
```

The hexadecimal version (after the usual initialization) is Program 2-4. Note that Program 2-4 is considerably shorter than Program 2-3. Enter and run the program; try the following variations.

PROBLEM 2-7

Write two programs that wait for a switch closure in bit position 0, one using a logical AND instruction and one using the LSR instruction. Which program is shorter? Which is faster?

PROBLEM 2-8

Write two programs that wait for a switch closure in bit position 6, one using a logical AND instruction and one using the ASL instruction. Which program is shorter? Which is faster?

PROBLEM 2-9

What happens if you replace LDAA $8004 in Program 2-4 with TST $8004 (i.e., replace the B6 in memory address 000B with 7D)? Determine the values of accumulator A before and after the execution of LDAA $8004. How do they differ from the values before and after the execution of TST $8004? Why is the TST instruction advantageous?

PROGRAM 2-4

MEMORY ADDRESS (HEX)	MEMORY CONTENTS (HEX)	INSTRUCTION (MNEMONIC)		
000B	B6	WAITC	LDAA	$8004
000C	80			
000D	04			
000E	2B		BMI	WAITC
000F	FB			
0010	3F		SWI	

The relative offset in Program 2-4 is given by

$$\begin{array}{r} 0B \\ -\ \underline{10} \end{array} = \begin{array}{r} 0B \\ +\ \underline{F0} \\ \hline FB \end{array}$$

where we obtained the two's complement of 10 from Table 2-3.

If you have only one or two switches (or other serial inputs) to attach to a port, which bit positions would you use and why? Which bit positions would you use for the switches that are used most frequently or that have the highest priority?

EXAMINING FLAGS

Note that you can always determine the current states of the 6800's flags or condition codes by examining the condition code (CC) or P register. This register may also be referred to as a *status register.* Be careful—some manuals occasionally refer to the program counter as the P register; we refer to the program counter as PC to avoid confusion.

Figure 2-4 shows the organization of the Condition Code register. We will describe the seldom used HALF-CARRY (H), INTERRUPT (I), and OVERFLOW (V) flags later. Here the hexadecimal notation is a nuisance, because only the binary values are meaningful. You can use Table 0-1 to convert hexadecimal to binary.

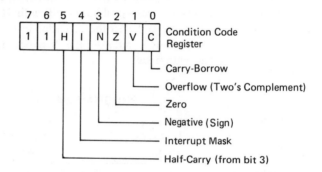

FIGURE 2-4. Organization of the 6800 Condition Code register (referred to as the CC, CCR, or P register). Bits 6 and 7 are not used and always appear as logic 1's.

The designers of the microprocessor decide how its instructions will affect its flags. The only way you can predict what will happen is by consulting the Instruction Set Summary Card or Appendix A of the *M6800 Programming Reference Manual.* Fortunately, the designers of the 6800 generally chose the effects of instructions on flags to be those you would reasonably expect. You can actually see how an instruction affects the flags by initializing the condition code register, specifying the operands, letting the computer execute the instruction, and then examining the final value of the condition code register. The results will depend on the instruction and on the operands. Remember not to press RESET because that changes the flags.

For example, if we start with (A) = 80 hex and (CC) = 10 hex (leaving I equal to 1 to disable interrupts), executing the instruction ADD #$80 results in (CC) = 15 (hex). This translates to (considering major flags only)

$$\begin{aligned} \text{NEGATIVE (SIGN)} &= 0 \\ \text{ZERO} &= 1 \\ \text{CARRY} &= 1 \end{aligned}$$

These results reflect the fact that adding 80 hex to 80 hex produces a sum of 00 (remember Table 2-4) plus a CARRY of 1. Since the sum is zero, the ZERO flag is set to 1 and the NEGATIVE flag to 0 (the most significant bit of 00 is zero). Remember that you must use the procedure described in Laboratory 1 to initialize the condition code register and accumulator A (see Table 1-2).

PROBLEM 2-10

Determine the final values of NEGATIVE, ZERO, and CARRY after the processor executes ADDA #$80 for the following initial conditions:

a) (A) = 80
    (CC) = FF

b) (A) = 7F
    (CC) = 10

c) (A) = 7F
    (CC) = FF

Hint: Use the program

```
ADDA      #$80
SWI
```

Do the final values of the flags depend on their initial values? What happens to information that is stored in the flags if the instruction ADDA #$80 is executed?

PROBLEM 2-11

Determine the final values of NEGATIVE, ZERO, and CARRY after the processor executes ANDA #$80 for the following initial conditions:

a) (A) = 80
    (CC) = 10

b) (A) = 80
    (CC) = FF

c) (A) = 00
    (CC) = 10

d) (A) = 00
    (CC) = FF

Which flags does AND affect and how? What happens to information that is stored in the flags if the instruction ANDA #$80 is executed?

WAITING FOR TWO CLOSURES

You can easily combine programs to wait for more than one closure. The following program will wait for switches attached to bits 2 and 5 to be closed in that order.

```
WAIT1    LDAA    $8004          GET INPUT DATA
         ANDA    #%00000100     IS SWITCH 2 CLOSED?
         BNE     WAIT1          NO, WAIT
WAIT2    LDAA    $8004          GET INPUT DATA
         ANDA    #%00100000     IS SWITCH 5 CLOSED?
         BNE     WAIT2          NO, WAIT
         SWI
```

Enter and run this program; the hexadecimal version is Program 2-5 and should follow the usual initialization. What happens if you close the switch attached to bit 2 and then the switch attached to bit position 5? What happens if you close switches attached to other bit positions?

PROBLEM 2-12

Make Program 2-5 respond only to the closure of the switch attached to bit position 3 followed by the closure of the switch attached to bit position 1. What happens if you leave one of the switches closed?

PROGRAM 2-5

MEMORY ADDRESS (HEX)	MEMORY CONTENTS (HEX)	INSTRUCTION (MNEMONIC)		
000B	B6	WAIT1	LDAA	$8004
000C	80			
000D	04			
000E	84		ANDA	#%00000100
000F	04			
0010	26		BNE	WAIT1
0011	F9			
0012	B6	WAIT2	LDAA	$8004
0013	80			
0014	04			
0015	84		ANDA	#%00100000
0016	20			
0017	26		BNE	WAIT2
0018	F9			
0019	3F		SWI	

Enter a combination of switch closures and let someone else try to break the combination. What happens if the other person simply closes all the switches? You can eliminate this deficiency by using the instruction SUBA or CMPA instead of ANDA. Why does this change the situation? Remember that SUB or CMP will only produce a zero result if the two operands are equal, so you will have to either change the masks or set the unused switches appropriately. For example, if we use the instruction sequence

```
        LDAA          $8004                GET INPUT DATA
        CMPA          #%00100000
```

the ZERO flag will only be set to 1 if all eight switches are in the positions specified by the operand of the CMPA instruction (0 = open, 1 = closed). That is, the ZERO flag will only be set to 1 if all the following conditions hold:

Switch 7 is closed.

Switch 6 is closed.

Switch 5 is open.

Switch 4 is closed.

Switch 3 is closed.

Switch 2 is closed.

Switch 1 is closed.

Switch 0 is closed.

Note how different this is from the condition needed to set the ZERO flag if ANDA is used. Remember that AND is a bit-by-bit operation whereas CMP (and SUB) are byte-wide operations.

PROBLEM 2-13

Explain the difference between SUBA and CMPA. What are the final values of NEGATIVE, ZERO, CARRY, and accumulator A after the processor executes SUBA #$80 and after the processor executes CMPA #$80 for the following initial conditions?

a) (A) = 80
    (CC) = 10
b) (A) = 80
    (CC) = FF

c)　(A)　= 7F
　　(CC) = 10

d)　(A)　= 7F
　　(CC) = FF

Why is the CMP instruction advantageous?

PROBLEM 2-14

Write a program that waits for the switch attached to bit position 0 to be closed and then for the switch attached to bit position 7 to be closed. Write one version that ignores the states of other switches and one that only works if all the other switches are open. What happens in the second version if you leave one of the switches closed?

PROBLEM 2-15

Write a program that waits for switches attached to bit positions 2 and 5 to be closed at the same time and then for switches attached to bit positions 0 and 7 to be closed at the same time.

PROBLEM 2-16

Write a program that waits for either a switch attached to bit position 2 to be closed followed by a switch attached to bit position 5 or a switch attached to bit position 5 followed by a switch attached to bit position 2.

SEARCHING FOR A STARTING CHARACTER

In communications applications, the input data will be the last character received from the channel. Of course, if the transmitter is inactive, that character will just be random noise. Assume that the transmitter starts every message with the hexadecimal pattern 7F (a so-called synchronization or sync character since it is not part of the actual data).

PROBLEM 2-17

Write and run a program that waits for the value 7F to appear in memory location 8004. An easy way to produce 7F is to first open all the switches (producing FF) and then close the switch attached to bit position 7.

If the input data is random noise, how often will the computer think that it has found a message? That is, what is the probability that the random input will be 7F? How often would the computer find a message erroneously if the required starting pattern were two 7F characters? How about three 7F characters?

Clearly, a longer synchronizing pattern leads to fewer false messages. On the other hand, noise in the communications channel could cause a 7F character to be received as something else and a valid message would then be missed.

PROBLEM 2-18

Write and run a program that will accept the input as 7F even if bit 2 is received incorrectly. How often would this program find a message erroneously (i.e., what is its probability of finding an acceptable random input)?

USING THE MONITOR TO CALCULATE RELATIVE OFFSETS

The JBUG monitor in the MEK6800D2 microcomputer contains a program that will calculate a relative offset for you. You can use this program as follows:

1)   Enter the destination address into accumulators B and A with the 8 most significant bits in B.

2)   Enter the address in which the operation code of the branch instruction is located into the index register.

3)   Execute the program starting at memory location E000 hex.

4)   The result will be in accumulator A. Accumulator B will contain FF if the offset is valid and negative, 00 if the offset is valid and positive, and some other value if the offset is invalid (i.e., the specified branch is too far for an 8-bit offset).

Use the monitor program to verify the relative offsets in Programs 2-3, 2-4, and 2-5.

KEY POINT SUMMARY

1)   The 6800 microprocessor has no specific input/output instructions. Instead, input and output ports are addressed as memory locations (memory-mapped I/O), and any instruction that transfers data to or from memory can be used as an I/O instruction.

2)   The MEK6800D2 microcomputer has a user PIA which occupies addresses 8004 through 8007 hexadecimal. A simple sequence of steps makes address 8004 into an input port.

3)   The 6800 microprocessor has three major flags, which are set according to the results of certain instructions. These are the CARRY, ZERO, and NEGATIVE (or SIGN) flags. Almost all instructions affect the ZERO and NEGATIVE flags, whereas only arithmetic and shift instructions affect the CARRY flag.

4)   A conditional branch (jump) instruction forces a jump if the specified condition is true. If the condition is false, the microprocessor continues executing instructions in their normal sequence. Conditional branch instructions are the keys to computer decisionmaking.

5)   The processor can determine the value of a specific bit in a register or memory location by logically ANDing the contents with a mask. The mask has a 1 in the specified bit position and 0's elsewhere. The result is zero if and only if the specified bit position contains zero. Bit positions at either end of the word can be handled by using the SIGN or CARRY flag and the load or shift instructions.

6)   The processor can determine whether a register or memory location contains a specified value by subtracting the value from the contents. The result is zero if and only if the operands are equal (i.e., if the register or memory location contains the specified value).

7)   The processor performs logical operations (AND, OR, EX-CLUSIVE OR, NOT) bit by bit, 8 bits at a time. However, arithmetic operations (ADD, SUBTRACT) involve carries or borrows, so the bit positions are not independent.

☐ Laboratory **3**

Simple Output for the
MEK6800D2 Microcomputer

PURPOSE

To learn how to use the output ports on the MEK6800D2 microcomputer.

PARTS REQUIRED

Eight single LEDs (light-emitting diodes) attached to the user Peripheral Interface Adapter as shown in Figure 3-1. The pin assignments needed for I/O port connector J1 are in Table 3-1 (and in Figure A3-b of the *MEK6800D2 Evaluation Kit Manual*).

REFERENCE MATERIALS

L. A. Leventhal, *Introduction to Microprocessors: Software, Hardware, Programming,* Prentice-Hall, Englewood Cliffs, NJ, 1978, pp. 343-345, 363-369, 376-377, 413-414.

L. A. Leventhal, *6800 Assembly Language Programming,* Osborne/McGraw-Hill, Berkeley, CA, 1978, pp. 11-8 through 11-21, 11-37 through 11-39.

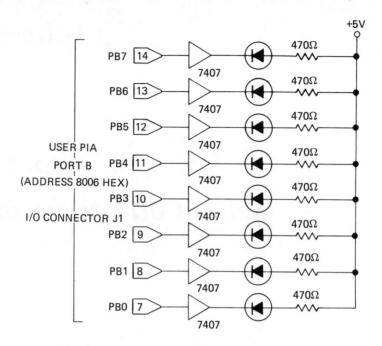

FIGURE 3-1. Attachment of LEDs to user PIA port B.

W. J. Weller, *Practical Microcomputer Programming: The M6800,* Northern Technology Books, Evanston, IL, 1977, pp. 211-216.

MEK6800D2 Evaluation Kit II Manual, Motorola Semiconductor Products Inc., Austin, TX, p. 2-3.

WHAT YOU SHOULD LEARN

1) How to employ the user Peripheral Interface Adapter (PIA) for output.

2) How to make PIA I/O lines into inputs or outputs.

3) How to turn LEDs on and off.

4) How to write a delay routine.

5) How to produce short and long delays.

6) How to turn individual LEDs on and off by using the logical functions.

7) How to establish a duty cycle for LEDs.

8) How to control the appearance of displays with software.

Table 3-1

**I/O CONNECTOR J1 PIN
ASSIGNMENTS FOR USER PIA PORT B**

ASSIGNMENT	PIN
Bit 0 (PB0)	7
Bit 1 (PB1)	8
Bit 2 (PB2)	9
Bit 3 (PB3)	10
Bit 4 (PB4)	11
Bit 5 (PB5)	12
Bit 6 (PB6)	13
Bit 7 (PB7)	14

TERMS

Active-high—the active state is a high logic level.

Active-low—the active state is a low logic level.

Anode—positive terminal.

Cathode—negative terminal.

Control register—a register whose contents determine the state of a transfer or the operating mode of a device.

Data direction register—a register that determines whether I/O lines are inputs or outputs.

Duty cycle—the period of time during which a device is active as part of a total period of continuous operation.

Light-emitting diode (LED)—a semiconductor device that emits light when biased in the forward direction.

Multiplex—to use one functional unit for several different purposes on a shared basis.

Negative logic—circuitry in which a logic zero is the active or "on" state.

Nesting—constructing programs, subroutines, or interrupt service routines so that one level is contained within another, and so on. The nesting level is the number of transfers of control required to reach a particular routine without returning.

Software delay—a program that has no function other than to waste time.

Turn-on time—the time required for a device to enter the "on" state after the signal to do so has been received.

BRA—branch always (or unconditionally); jump over the specified number of memory locations.

DEC—decrement (by 1); subtract one from the contents of the specified accumulator or memory location.

EOR—logical EXCLUSIVE OR; logically EXCLUSIVE OR the contents of an accumulator with the contents of the specified memory location.

INC—increment (by 1); add one to the contents of the specified accumulator or memory location.

ORA—logical (INCLUSIVE) OR; logically OR the contents of an accumulator with the contents of the specified memory location.

ATTACHING THE LEDS

Attach eight single LEDs to the user PIA as described in Table 3-1 and Figure 3-1. An LED will light when its cathode is sufficiently negative with respect to its anode. The computer can therefore light the LED either by grounding the cathode (if the anode is tied to +5 V) or by applying +5 V to the anode (if the cathode is grounded). The PIA output ports (like most TTL and MOS devices) can drive the cathodes of LEDs better than the anodes, so we will use the configuration of Figure 3-1. Note that a logic 0 from the computer lights the LED; that is, the LED is *active-low* or uses *negative logic.*

PIA INPUT/OUTPUT PORTS

In Laboratory 2, we used part of the PIA as an input port. In fact, a PIA contains two 8-bit I/O ports (A and B), along with other registers that determine how the PIA operates. Each bit of the two I/O ports can be either an input or an output. The choice is made as follows:

1)   A 0 in a bit of the port's data direction register makes the corresponding bit position of the I/O port an input.

2)   A 1 in a bit of the port's data direction register makes the corresponding bit position of the I/O port an output.

The data direction registers themselves occupy memory addresses (see Table 3-2. In fact, the data direction register for each I/O port occupies

Table 3-2

THE USER PIA I/O ADDRESSES

ADDRESS (HEX)	FUNCTION
8004	I/O port A or data direction register for port A*
8005	Control register for port A
8006	I/O port B or data direction register for port B*
8007	Control register for port B

*Bit 2 of PIA control register A (B) is 1 to activate the I/O port and 0 to activate the data direction register.

the same memory address as the port itself. How, then, can we distinguish them? Note that each port also has a control register; Table 3-2 contains the memory addresses occupied by the two control registers for the user PIA. Bit 2 of the control register for a port determines whether the other address refers to the I/O port (also called a data or peripheral register) or to the data direction register. If that bit is 0, the data direction register is activated while if that bit is 1, the I/O port is activated. This is why we had to first clear memory location 8005 (the control register for user PIA port A) and later set bit 2 of that location in Program 2-1. Note that only the I/O ports are connected to the outside world; the data direction registers and control registers are inside the PIA chip.

Note the following examples:

1) Storing 00 in the data direction register for port A makes all the bits of port A inputs. The required instructions are

```
CLR    $8005          ACCESS DATA DIRECTION REGISTER
CLR    $8004          MAKE PORT A INPUTS
LDAA   #%00000100     ACCESS I/O PORT
STAA   $8005
```

Note that we can clear a memory location directly without using an accumulator.

2) Storing FF in the data direction register for port B makes all the bits of port B outputs. The required instructions are

```
CLR    $8007          ACCESS DATA DIRECTION REGISTER
LDAA   #$FF           MAKE PORT B OUTPUTS
```

```
STAA   $8006
LDAA   #$00000100      ACCESS I/O PORT
STAA   $8007
```

Note that it takes two instructions to place FF (hex) in the data direction register.

3)   Storing 0F in the data direction register for port A makes bits 4 through 7 of port A inputs and bits 0 through 3 outputs. The required instructions are

```
CLR    $8005           ACCESS DATA DIRECTION REGISTER
LDAA   #$0F            MAKE BITS 4-7 OF PORT A OUTPUTS, 0-3 INPUTS
STAA   $8004
LDAA   #%00000100   ACCESS I/O PORT
STAA   $8005
```

4)   Storing AA (hex)—10101010 binary—in the data direction register for port B makes bits 1, 3, 5, and 7 outputs and 0, 2, 4, and 6 inputs. The required instructions are

```
CLR    $8007           ACCESS DATA DIRECTION REGISTER
LDAA   #$AA            MAKE BITS 1,3,5,7 OF PORT B OUTPUTS,
                              BITS 0,2,4,6, INPUTS
STAA   $8006
LDAA   #%00000100   ACCESS I/O PORT
STAA   $8005
```

Of course, determining the effects of values is much simpler if we see them in binary rather than in hexadecimal. Here again, hexadecimal is a nuisance, since we are concerned with the values of individual bits.

The Peripheral Interface Adapter has the following important features:

1)   RESET clears the control registers, thus accessing the data direction registers. You can check this by resetting the MEK6800D2 computer and examining memory locations 8005 and 8007. The initialization routine must select the proper arrangement of input and output bits before the program transfers any data.

2)   The ports can consist of any combination of input and output bits. This adds to the flexibility and usefulness of the MEK6800D2, since users can select the numbers and arrangements of input and output lines rather than having to modify designs to accommodate a fixed arrangement. This is the advantage of programmability; it allows a single board to be modified by software to handle varied applications.

3)   In a particular application, the initialization routine (starting from RESET) must establish the required arrangement; the main program will usually transfer data to or from the I/O ports as if the arrangement were fixed.

PROBLEM 3-1

Write a program that makes port A of the user PIA an input port and port B an output port. How would you check this program to see if it had executed correctly? What happens when you clear port B (by executing CLR $8006) after running this program?

PROBLEM 3-2

Revise the initialization routine from Problem 3-1 so that it makes bit 0 of port B an output and all other bits of port B inputs. What happens when you clear port B after running this program?

PROBLEM 3-3

Revise the initialization routine from Problem 3-1 so that it uses the index register. Which version is shorter (the one using extended addressing or the one using indexed addressing)? Which version executes faster?

TURNING ON AN LED

The following program will light the LED attached to bit 3 of port B of the user PIA (address 8006):

```
CLR    $8007           ACCESS DATA DIRECTION REGISTER
LDAA   #$FF            MAKE PORT B OUTPUTS
STAA   $8006
LDAA   #%00000100      ACCESS I/O PORT
STAA   $8007
LDAA   #%11110111      LIGHT LED 3
STAA   $8006
SWI
```

Remember that the LEDs are attached to the I/O port by their cathodes, so a 0 turns an LED on and a 1 turns it off. We must access the data direction register before selecting the inputs and outputs, and we must access the I/O port before transferring data. Program 3-1 is the hexadecimal version; enter and run this program. What happens if you press RESET after running Program 3-1?

PROGRAM 3-1

MEMORY ADDRESS (HEX)	MEMORY CONTENTS (HEX)	INSTRUCTION (MNEMONIC)	
0000	7F	CLR	$8007
0001	80		
0002	07		
0003	86	LDAA	#$FF
0004	FF		
0005	B7	STAA	$8006
0006	80		
0007	06		
0008	86	LDAA	#%00000100
0009	04		
000A	B7	STAA	$8007
000B	80		
000C	07		
000D	86	LDAA	#%11110111
000E	F7		
000F	B7	STAA	$8006
0010	80		
0011	06		
0012	3F	SWI	

Try the following variations:

PROBLEM 3-4

Write a program that lights the LED attached to bit 4 of port B and turns off all the other LEDs. How would you make the program light only the LEDs attached to bits 2 and 5 of port B?

PROBLEM 3-5

Write a program that makes the LEDs show the contents of memory location 0040. An LED should be lit if the corresponding bit in location 0040 is 1.

PROVIDING A DELAY

Of course, in real applications we seldom want to turn an output on and leave it on. More frequently, we want to leave an output on for a specified amount of time. The microprocessor can simply waste time counting as follows:

1) Load a register with a specified value.

2)   Decrement the contents of the register until they become zero.

The program that performs these steps using accumulator B is

```
              LDAB      #COUNT
      DLY     DECB
              BNE       DLY
```

This program works like telling someone to count to 10 before opening his or her eyes.

The time wasted can be calculated from the following information:

INSTRUCTION	NUMBER OF TIMES EXECUTED	CLOCK CYCLES PER EXECUTION
LDAB # (IMMEDIATE)	1	2
DECB	COUNT	2
BNE	COUNT	4

The execution times are given in Appendix 1 and in Figure 4-1 of the *M6800 Programming Reference Manual.* The total amount of time wasted is

$$(6 \times COUNT + 2) \times t_C$$

where t_C is the clock period of the microcomputer. Since the MEK6800D2 uses a 614.4-kHz clock (see p. 2-3 of the *MEK6800D2 Evaluation Kit II Manual*), $t_C = 1.63$ μs.

For example, if COUNT = 10 the time wasted is

$$(6 \times 10 + 2) \times 1.63 = 101 \ \mu s$$

The maximum delay is

$$(6 \times 256 + 2) \times 1.63 = 2507 \ \mu s \quad \text{or} \quad 2.5 \ ms$$

What value of COUNT produces this delay?

Add a delay to the output program as follows:

```
      CLR     $8007           ACCESS DATA DIRECTION REGISTER
      LDAA    #$FF            MAKE PORT B OUTPUTS
      STAA    $8006
      LDAA    #%00000100      ACCESS I/O PORT
      STAA    $8007
      LDAA    #%11110111      LIGHT LED 3
```

```
            STAA    $8006
            LDAB    #COUNT          DELAY
    DLY     DECB
            BNE     DLY
            LDAA    #%11111111      TURN OFF LED 3
            STAA    $8006
            SWI
```

Program 3-2 is the hexadecimal version assuming the same PIA initialization routine (memory locations 0000 through 000C) as in Program 3-1; enter and run the program, setting COUNT to 00 initially.

PROGRAM 3-2

MEMORY ADDRESS (HEX)	MEMORY CONTENTS (HEX)		INSTRUCTION (MNEMONIC)	
000D	86		LDAA	#%11110111
000E	F7			
000F	B7		STAA	$8006
0010	80			
0011	06			
0012	C6		LDAB	#COUNT
0013	COUNT			
0014	5A	DLY	DECB	
0015	26		BNE	DLY
0016	FD			
0017	86		LDAA	#%11111111
0018	FF			
0019	B7		STAA	$8006
001A	80			
001B	06			
001C	3F		SWI	

PROBLEM 3-6

The smallest value of COUNT for which the light is visible is _____.

A LONGER DELAY

You can lengthen the delay by placing one time-wasting routine inside another (called *nesting* the routines): that is,

```
            LDAA    #CT1            SET MULTIPLYING FACTOR
    DLY1    LDAB    #CT2            SET DELAY FACTOR
```

```
DLY2    DECB
        BNE     DLY2
        DECA
        BNE     DLY1
```

How long does this program take to execute? Program 3-3 contains the additions required to lengthen the delay in Program 3-2.

PROGRAM 3-3

MEMORY ADDRESS (HEX)	MEMORY CONTENTS (HEX)		INSTRUCTION (MNEMONIC)	
0012	86		LDAA	#CT1
0013	CT1			
0014	C6	DLY1	LDAB	#CT2
0015	CT2			
0016	5A	DLY2	DECB	
0017	26		BNE	DLY2
0018	FD			
0019	4A		DECA	
001A	26		BNE	DLY1
001B	F8			
001C	86		LDAA	#%11111111
001D	FF			
001E	B7		STAA	$8006
001F	80			
0020	06			
0021	3F		SWI	

PROBLEM 3-7

If you set CT1 to 100 (64 hex), what value of CT2 produces a 10-ms delay? What value of CT2 produces a 100-ms delay?

PROBLEM 3-8

Revise the nested delay program so it counts up instead of down. What value of CT2 produces a 10-ms delay if you set CT1 to −100 (9C hex)?

PROBLEM 3-9

Another way to lengthen the delay is to use the 16-bit index register as a counter. Write a routine to do this; calculate how much time is wasted as a function of the initial value in the index register.

CONTROLLING INDIVIDUAL BITS

Often, we want to turn individual displays on or off without affecting other displays that may have unrelated meanings. This can be done as follows:

     1)   Logically ANDing a number with a mask clears those bit positions which are 0's in the mask but does not affect those bit positions which are 1's (see Table 3-3).

     2)   Logically ORing a number with a mask sets those bit positions which are 1's in the mask but does not affect those bit positions which are 0's (see Table 3-3).

     3)   Logically EXCLUSIVE ORing a number with a mask complements those bit positions which are 1's in the mask but does not affect those bit positions which are 0's (see Table 3-3).

So in the program with the short delay (Program 3-2), we could turn off LED 3 alone by using the instruction ORAA #%00001000; that is,

0017	8A	ORAA	#%00001000
0018	08		

Make this change and run the revised program. If you use the nested delay, remember that it changes the value in accumulator A. You will have to add the following sequence to Program 3-3:

LDAA	$8006	RECOVER DATA
ORAA	#%00001000	TURN OFF LED 3
STAA	$8006	
SWI		

or in hexadecimal

001C	B6	LDAA	$8006
001D	80		
001E	06		
001F	8A	ORAA	#%00001000
0020	08		
0021	B7	STAA	$8006
0022	80		
0023	06		
0024	3F	SWI	

Table 3-3

EFFECTS OF LOGICAL INSTRUCTIONS

Logical AND

ORIGINAL VALUE	MASK VALUE	FINAL VALUE
0	0	0
1	0	0
0	1	0
1	1	1

The final value is 0 if the mask value is 0 and the same as the original value if the mask value is 1.

Logical OR

ORIGINAL VALUE	MASK VALUE	FINAL VALUE
0	0	0
1	0	1
0	1	1
1	1	1

The final value is 1 if the mask value is 1 and the same as the original value if the mask value is 0.

Logical EXCLUSIVE OR

ORIGINAL VALUE	MASK VALUE	FINAL VALUE
0	0	0
1	0	1
0	1	1
1	1	0

The final value is the complement of the original value if the mask value is 1 and the same as the original value if the mask value is 0.

PROBLEM 3-10

Write a program that turns LED 4 off, delays for a while, and then turns LED 4 on without affecting any other displays.

PROBLEM 3-11

Write a program that gets the values for the LEDs from memory location 0040, delays for a while, and then complements LEDs 1 and 5 without affecting any other displays.

PROBLEM 3-12

Write a program that gets the values for the LEDs from memory location 0040, turns LEDs 2 and 6 on, delays for a while, turns LED 6 off, delays again, and finally turns LED 2 off and LED 6 on without affecting any other displays.

Remember that you can change a particular bit of accumulator A (bit position 5, for example) as follows:

1) Make it 1 with ORAA #%00100000.
2) Make it 0 with ANDA #%11011111.
3) Complement it with EORA #%00100000.

ESTABLISHING A DUTY CYCLE

We can establish a duty cycle for an LED simply by turning it on and then off for specified periods of time. The following program will do the job:

```
            CLR     $8007           ACCESS DATA DIRECTION REGISTER
            LDAA    #$FF            MAKE PORT B OUTPUTS
            STAA    $8006
            LDAA    #%00000100      ACCESS I/O PORT
            STAA    $8007
CYCLE       LDAA    #%11110111      TURN ON LED 3
            STAA    $8006
            LDAA    #CT1            DELAY WHILE ON
DLY1        LDAB    #CT2
DLY2        DECB
            BNE     DLY2
            DECA
            BNE     DLY1
            LDAA    #%11111111      TURN OFF LED 3
            STAA    $8006
            LDAA    #CT3            DELAY WHILE OFF
DLY3        LDAB    #CT4
DLY4        DECB
            BNE     DLY4
            DECA
            BNE     DLY3
            BRA     CYCLE
```

Program 3-4 is the hexadecimal version (assuming the PIA initialization from Program 3-1). Enter and run Program 3-4; try various values for the delay constants.

PROGRAM 3-4

MEMORY ADDRESS (HEX)	MEMORY CONTENTS (HEX)	INSTRUCTION (MNEMONIC)		
000D	86	CYCLE	LDAA	#%11110111
000E	F7			
000F	B7		STAA	$8006
0010	80			
0011	06			
0012	86		LDAA	#CT1
0013	CT1			
0014	C6	DLY1	LDAB	#CT2
0015	CT2			
0016	5A	DLY2	DECB	
0017	26		BNE	DLY2
0018	FD			
0019	4A		DECA	
001A	26		BNE	DLY1
001B	F8			
001C	86		LDAA	#%11111111
001D	FF			
001E	B7		STAA	$8006
001F	80			
0020	06			
0021	86		LDAA	#CT3
0022	CT3			
0023	C6	DLY3	LDAB	#CT4
0024	CT4			
0025	5A	DLY4	DECB	
0026	26		BNE	DLY4
0027	FD			
0028	4A		DECA	
0029	26		BNE	DLY3
002A	F8			
002B	20		BRA	CYCLE
002C	E0			

PROBLEM 3-13

Set CT2 = CT4 = 0. Start with CT1 = CT3 = 0 and run Program 3-4. Then try the following sequence of hexadecimal values for CT1 and CT3: 80, 40, 20, 10, 08, 04, 02, 01. What is the smallest value for which the LED flickers? How many times per second is the LED being turned on and off at this value?

PROBLEM 3-14

Set CT2 = CT4 = 0. Start with CT1 = CT3 = 10 (hex) and run Program 3-4. Try the following pairs of hexadecimal values for CT1 and CT3: (1) CT1 = 1C, CT3 = 04; (2) CT1 = 18, CT3 = 08; (3) CT1 = 08, CT3 = 18; (4) CT1 = 04, CT3 = 1C. Describe the effects of the varied values on the brightness and continuity of the LEDs. Compare the effects to those seen in Problem 3-10.

PROBLEM 3-15

Set CT2 = CT4 = 0 and CT1 = CT3 = 20 (hex). Write a program that flashes the LED on and off for 5 s before turning it off permanently. Use memory location 0040 as an overall counter and load it initially from the keyboard (before executing the program).

Note the following characteristics of LEDs:

1)   LEDs have a very short turn-on time, typically only a few microseconds. It is therefore easy to handle many LEDs from one port (i.e., to multiplex them).

2)   LEDs dissipate less power and last longer if they are pulsed rather than left on continuously.

3)   Display time constants can easily be varied in software to achieve a suitable balance among power dissipation, visibility, and life span. How would you implement such changes in hardware? In many applications the operator may wish to control the displays in order to adapt them to local lighting conditions or to avoid distraction.

4)   A microprocessor can easily handle LED displays while performing other tasks, since the LEDs need only be controlled at a very slow rate to satisfy human observers.

KEY POINT SUMMARY

1)   The ports in the Peripheral Interface Adapter (PIA) can be either inputs or outputs. Each bit is individually selected as an input or output by storing the appropriate value (0 for input, 1 for output) in the corresponding bit position of the data direction register. The data direction registers occupy the same memory addresses as the actual I/O ports; a data direction register can be addressed by placing a '0' in bit 2 of the port's control register.

2)   By storing the proper values in the data direction registers, the user can easily vary the numbers and arrangements of inputs and outputs to handle different applications. The arrangement for a particular application is specified in the initialization routine and left unchanged in most programs.

3)   You can implement a delay program by having the processor count for a specified amount of time. The length of the delay depends on the number of instructions in the program and their execution times. Delay programs can be nested as long as there are registers or memory locations available to hold counters.

4)   A particular bit can be cleared, set, or complemented by means of logical operations with appropriate masks.

5)   You can establish a duty cycle by providing appropriate delays after turning the peripheral device on or off.

6)   You can easily modify control functions that are implemented in software, since the only changes required are a few constants or instructions in the program.

☐ *Laboratory* **4**

Processing Data Inputs

To learn how to process data inputs using the MEK6800D2 microcomputer.

PARTS REQUIRED

- Eight single switches or pushbuttons attached to port A of the user Peripheral Interface Adapter as shown in Figure 2-1. Table 2-1 lists the pins used on I/O connector J1. An unencoded rotary or thumbwheel switch may be used instead of the single switches. It should have at least eight positions, which can be connected as shown in Figure 4-1.

- Eight switches attached through an encoder to port A of the user PIA as shown in Figure 4-2. This add-on can employ the same switches as the add-on shown in Figure 2-1.

- A 74148 priority encoder (see Table 4-2 and Figure 4-6 for descriptions of this device).

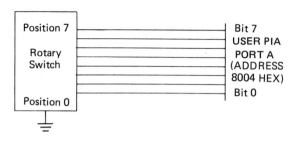

FIGURE 4-1. Connections for an unencoded rotary switch.

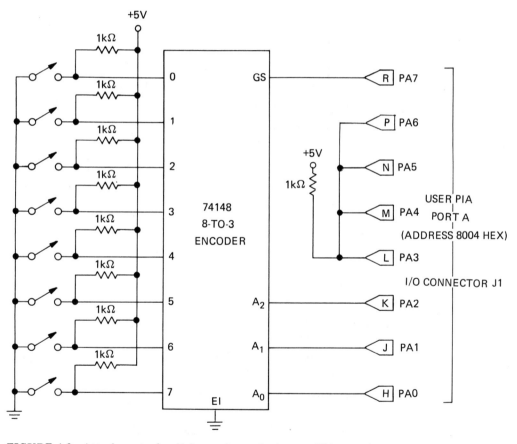

FIGURE 4-2. Attachment of switches and encoder to user PIA port A.

73

REFERENCE MATERIALS

L. A. Leventhal, *Introduction to Microprocessors: Software, Hardware, Programming*, Prentice-Hall, Englewood Cliffs, NJ, 1978, pp. 369-376, 408-412.

L. A. Leventhal, *6800 Assembly Language Programming*, Osborne/McGraw-Hill, Berkeley, CA, 1978, pp. 11-21 through 11-36.

W. J. Weller, *Practical Microcomputer Programming: The M6800*, Northern Technology Books, Evanston, IL, 1977, Chapter 14.

The TTL Data Book for Design Engineers, Texas Instruments Inc., Dallas, TX, 1976, pp. 6-64 through 6-67 (74121 one-shot), 7-151 through 7-156 (74148 encoder).

WHAT YOU SHOULD LEARN

1) How to wait for a switch to close.
2) How to wait for a switch to close and reopen.
3) How to debounce a switch.
4) How to count switch closures.
5) How to determine the bit position of a switch closure.
6) How to use a TTL encoder.
7) How to make simple tradeoffs between hardware and software.

TERMS

Bounce—move back and forth between states before reaching a final state.

Cross-coupled—when two devices each have their output fed back into the other's input.

Debounce—convert the output from a contact with bounce into a single, clean transition between states.

Debounce time—the amount of time required to debounce a change of state.

Enable—allow an activity to proceed or a device to produce data outputs.

Encoder—a device that produces coded outputs from unencoded inputs. A *priority encoder* only accepts the input with the highest priority if two or more are simultaneously active.

Group select (GS)—a single that indicates if there is any activity within a particular level or group of signals, used to combine devices in a prioritized manner.

Normal closed (NC)—a switch output that is connected to the common line if the switch is in its marked closed position.

Normal open (NO)—a switch output that is connected to the common line if the switch is in its marked open position.

One-shot (or **monostable multivibrator**)—a device that produces a single pulse of known length in response to a pulse input.

SPDT switch—single-pole, double-throw switch with one common line and two output lines.

6800 INSTRUCTIONS

BEQ—branch if equal to zero; jump over the specified number of memory locations if the ZERO flag is 1; otherwise, proceed to the next instruction in sequence. Note that the ZERO flag is 1 if the last result *was zero.*

CBA—compare accumulators; subtract the contents of accumulator B from accumulator A but leave the accumulators unchanged. This instruction affects only the flags.

CMP—compare; subtract the contents of the specified memory location from the contents of an accumulator but leave the contents of the accumulator unchanged. This instruction affects only the flags.

DEX—decrement index register; subtract 1 from the 16-bit contents of the index register.

JMP—jump unconditionally; jump to the specified memory address. JMP can only be used with indexed or extended addressing. You may find JMP more convenient than BRA in the examples because JMP does not require the calculation of a relative offset.

TAB—transfer accumulator A to accumulator B; transfer the contents of accumulator A to accumulator B. Accumulator A is not changed.

TBA—transfer accumulator B to accumulator A; transfer the contents of accumulator B to accumulator A. Accumulator B is not changed.

PROCESSING DATA INPUTS

Normally, we would like the microprocessor to do more than just determine the value of a particular binary input. Rather, we want the processor to handle a series of inputs and convert the input data into useful forms. The processor should also be able to perform such simple tasks as smoothing the input data and accounting for the time constants of input peripherals. An important consideration is that either software or hardware can perform these tasks. Extra hardware can transform the inputs so that the processor can easily handle them. Designers must make trade-offs based on per-unit cost, development time and cost, reliability, compatibility with other applications, power dissipation, board space, and number of available input pins.

WAITING FOR ANY SWITCH CLOSURE

Table 4-1 contains the binary inputs resulting from the closure of one of a set of single switches. If no switches are closed, the input data is all 1's (i.e., FF hexadecimal). So the following program will wait until you close any of the switches:

```
        CLR    $8005         ACCESS DATA DIRECTION REGISTER
        CLR    $8004         MAKE PORT A INPUTS
        LDAA   #%00000100    ACCESS DATA REGISTER
        STAA   $8005
WAITC   LDAA   $8004         GET INPUT DATA
        CMPA   #$FF          ARE ANY SWITCHES CLOSED?
        BEQ    WAITC         NO, WAIT
        SWI
```

The hexadecimal version of the program is given in Program 4-1. Note that the instruction CMPA #$FF subtracts FF from the contents of accumulator A and sets the flags appropriately but does not save the result anywhere. Thus the data from memory address 8004 is still in accumulator A at the end of the program. (Verify this!)

Enter and run Program 4-1. Check to see that it responds to the closure of any switch. What happens if you close several switches at once? What happens if you close switches before executing the program? Note the final contents of accumulator A in each case.

We can easily add a section to Program 4-1 that waits until the switch is opened again. The addition is

```
WAITO   LDAA   $8004         GET INPUT DATA
        CMPA   #$FF          ARE ANY SWITCHES CLOSED?
        BNE    WAITO         YES, WAIT
```

The condition for the branch instruction is the inverse of the one used in Program 4-1, since the aim here is to wait until the switch closure ends.

Table 4-1

BIT POSITION OF CLOSED SWITCH	INPUT	
	BINARY	HEX
0	11111110	FE
1	11111101	FD
2	11111011	FB
3	11110111	F7
4	11101111	EF
5	11011111	DF
6	10111111	BF
7	01111111	7F
None	11111111	FF

PROGRAM 4-1

MEMORY ADDRESS (HEX)	MEMORY CONTENTS (HEX)	INSTRUCTION (MNEMONIC)	
0000	7F	CLR	$8005
0001	80		
0002	05		
0003	7F	CLR	$8004
0004	80		
0005	04		
0006	86	LDAA	#%00000100
0007	04		
0008	B7	STAA	$8005
0009	80		
000A	05		
000B	B6	WAITC LDAA	$8004
000C	80		
000D	04		
000E	81	CMPA	#$FF
000F	FF		
0010	27	BEQ	WAITC
0011	F9		
0012	3F	SWI	

The complete program now is

```
CLR    $8005          ACCESS DATA DIRECTION REGISTER
CLR    $8004          MAKE PORT A INPUTS
LDAA   #%00000100     ACCESS DATA REGISTER
```

```
              STAA   $8005
      WAITC   LDAA   $8004        GET INPUT DATA
              CMPA   #$FF         ARE ANY SWITCHES CLOSED?
              BEQ    WAITC        NO, WAIT
      WAITO   LDAA   $8004        GET INPUT DATA
              CMPA   #$FF         ARE ANY SWITCHES CLOSED?
              BNE    WAITO        YES, WAIT
              SWI
```

The hexadecimal additions to Program 4-1 are given in Program 4-2. Enter and run this program; try the variations in Problems 4-1, 4-2, and 4-3.

PROGRAM 4-2

MEMORY ADDRESS (HEX)	MEMORY CONTENTS (HEX)	INSTRUCTION (MNEMONIC)		
0012	B6	WAITO	LDAA	$8004
0013	80			
0014	04			
0015	81		CMPA	#$FF
0016	FF			
0017	26		BNE	WAITO
0018	F9			
0019	3F		SWI	

PROBLEM 4-1

Make the combined program wait for a switch attached to bit position 5 to be closed and opened while all other switches are open.

PROBLEM 4-2

Write a version of the combined program that waits for a switch attached to bit position 5 to be closed and opened, regardless of the states of the other switches.

PROBLEM 4-3

Write a version of the combined program that waits for a switch attached to bit position 5 to be closed, opened, and then closed again, regardless of the states of the other switches.

DEBOUNCING A SWITCH

If you run Programs 4-1 and 4-2 several times, you will probably find that the computer often exits before you open the switch. This is because a mechanical switch (or a key on a keyboard) does not change state cleanly. Instead, the switch bounces back and forth for a while before it settles into its final position. The computer may mistake the bounce for the opening of the switch, since both result in a logic 1 in the input bit.

The solution to this problem is to debounce the switch. This can be done in hardware with a one-shot (see Figure 4-3) or with cross-coupled NAND gates (see Figure 4-4). But we can also debounce the switch in software at the cost of a few bytes of memory. All we need is a short delay program that waits until the switch stops bouncing. Since the bounce usually lasts less than 1 ms, the following program will do the job:

B 74121 Q
INPUT
PORT

FIGURE 4-3. Debouncing a switch with a one-shot.

74121 Function Table

INPUTS			OUTPUTS	
A1	A2	B	Q	$\overline{Q}$
L	X	H	L	H
X	L	H	L	H
X	X	L	L	H
H	H	X	L	H
H	↓	H	⊓	⊔
↓	H	H	⊓	⊔
↓	↓	H	⊓	⊔
L	X	↑	⊓	⊔
X	L	↑	⊓	⊔

X = irrelevant

74121 Pin Configuration

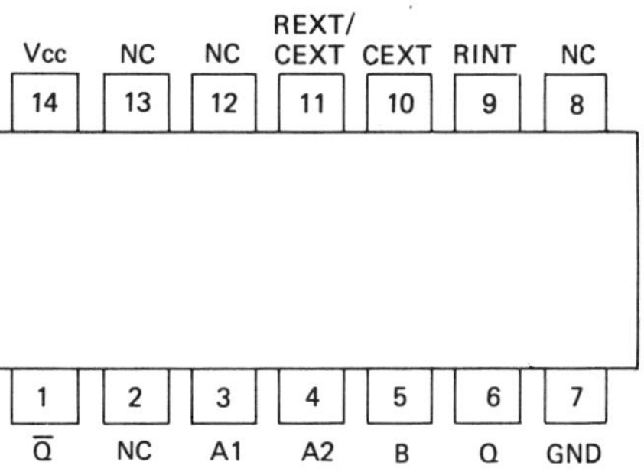
Vcc
NC
NC
REXT/
CEXT
CEXT
RINT
NC
14
13
12
11
10
9
8
1
2
3
4
5
6
7
$\overline{Q}$
NC
A1
A2
B
Q
GND

NC = NO CONNECTION

```
         CLR    $8005         ACCESS DATA DIRECTION REGISTER
         CLR    $8004         MAKE PORT A INPUTS
         LDAA   #%00000100    ACCESS DATA REGISTER
         STAA   $8005
WAITC    LDAA   $8004         GET INPUT DATA
         CMPA   #$FF          ARE ANY SWITCHES CLOSED?
         BEQ    WAITC         NO, WAIT
         LDAB   #$67          DELAY 1 MS TO DEBOUNCE
DLY      DECB
         BNE    DLY
```

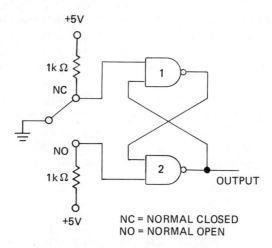

FIGURE 4-4. Debouncing a switch with cross-coupled NAND gates.

```
WAITO    LDAA   $8004        GET INPUT DATA
         CMPA   #$FF         ARE ANY SWITCHES CLOSED?
         BNE    WAITO        YES, WAIT
         SWI
```

Program 4-3 contains the required hexadecimal additions to Program 4-1; the initialization of the PIA and the recognition of the switch closure are unchanged.

PROGRAM 4-3

MEMORY ADDRESS (HEX)	MEMORY CONTENTS (HEX)	INSTRUCTION (MNEMONIC)	
0012	C6		LDAB #$67
0013	67		
0014	5A	DLY	DECB
0015	26		BNE DLY
0016	FD		
0017	B6	WAITO	LDAA $8004
0018	80		
0019	04		
001A	81		CMPA #$FF
001B	FF		
001C	26		BNE WAITO
001D	F9		
001E	3F		SWI

PROBLEM 4-4

Run Programs 4-1 and 4-3 with shorter delays and determine whether you can still see the bounce. Divide the contents of memory location 0013 in half after each trial (an approximate sequence is 67, 34, 1A, 0D, 07, 04, 02, 01).

The various debouncing methods represent a tradeoff between hardware and software. The software delay costs very little, since the program is simple and requires only a few bytes of memory. On the other hand, it occupies the processor completely, preventing it from performing other tasks. Hardware debouncing frees the processor for other work but requires an additional part and more connections. Note that either the hardware or the software may be shared by several different tasks.

COUNTING CLOSURES

We can keep a running count (in memory location 0040) of the number of switches closed as follows:

1)   Add the instructions

```
        INC     $40         INCREMENT NUMBER OF CLOSURES
        LDAB    #$67        DELAY 1 MS TO DEBOUNCE OPENING
DLY1    DECB
        BNE     DLY1
        BRA     WAITC       WAIT FOR NEXT CLOSURE
```

to the end of the program as shown in Program 4-4.

2)   Clear memory location 0040 before executing the program.

PROGRAM 4-4

MEMORY ADDRESS (HEX)	MEMORY CONTENTS (HEX)		INSTRUCTION (MNEMONIC)	
001E	7C		INC	$40
001F	00			
0020	40			
0021	C6		LDAB	#$67
0022	67			
0023	5A	DLY1	DECB	
0024	26		BNE	DLY1
0025	FD			
0026	20		BRA	WAITC
0027	E3			

Note that this program never returns control to the monitor. You will have to reset the computer to examine memory location 0040.

PROBLEM 4-5

Write a program that returns control to the monitor after counting the number of switch closures initially entered into memory location 0040. Assume that only one switch is ever closed at a time.

PROBLEM 4-6

Write a program that counts the number of times that a switch attached to bit 5 of port A of the user PIA is closed. Use memory location 0041 for the counter.

PROBLEM 4-7

Write a program that counts the number of times that switches attached to bit positions 2 and 5 are closed. Use memory location 0040 as the counter for bit position 2 and memory location 0041 as the counter for bit position 5. Assume that only one switch is ever closed at a time, so that the program simply has to wait for all switches to be open rather than waiting specifically for the opening of the switch that was closed.

If you find that the count is erratic, try lengthening the delay by using a 16-bit counter (either the index register or two memory locations). Remember to delay both after the switch is closed and after it is opened. You can use the 16-bit instruction DEX to decrement the index register.

You may have noticed that there is no direct addressing mode for the instruction INC. That is, you must use the extended addressing mode even when the eight most significant bits of the address are all zeros (as in INC $40). This is the case with all 6800 single-operand instructions, such as shifts, CLR, COM, DEC, INC, NEG, and TST. You might want to look at the binary forms of the various addressing modes for INC and compare these forms to the ones used for an instruction such as LDA. Can you see why the designers of the 6800 chip omitted the direct addressing mode for the single-operand instructions? (*Hint:* Note that the single-operand instructions can be applied to either accumulator.)

IDENTIFYING THE SWITCH

Remember that Table 4-1 contains the binary inputs formed when individual switches are closed. What are the inputs when several switches are closed at once? In Table 4-1, the bit that is zero is the one that identifies the switch (i.e., bit 0 is 0 for switch 0, bit 1 for switch 1, and so on). The problem is how to determine which bit is zero. A simple method is as follows (see Figure 4-5 for a flowchart).

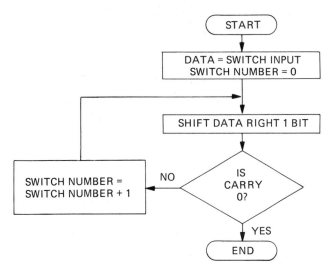

FIGURE 4-5. Flowchart for switch identification.

Step 1) SWITCH NUMBER = 0
         DATA = input from switches
Step 2) Shift DATA right one bit. If the CARRY is zero, the
         program is finished.
Step 3) SWITCH NUMBER = SWITCH NUMBER + 1
         Go to step 2.

A program to implement this method is

```
        CLRB            SWITCH NUMBER = ZERO
SRCHS   LSRA            IS NEXT SWITCH CLOSED?
        BCC    DONE     YES, DONE
        INCB            NO, SWITCH NUMBER = SWITCH NUMBER + 1
        BRA    SRCHS
DONE    SWI
```

Accumulator B contains the switch number at the end of the program.
An alternative approach uses somewhat different initial conditions
to eliminate one jump instruction; that is,

```
        LDAB   #$FF     SWITCH NUMBER = −1
SRCHS   INCB            SWITCH NUMBER = SWITCH NUMBER + 1
        LSRA            IS NEXT SWITCH CLOSED?
        BCS    SRCHS    NO, KEEP LOOKING
        SWI
```

Which approach do you prefer, and why?

The entire program for identifying a switch consists of the following sections:

1) Wait for any switch to be closed.
2) Wait 1 ms to debounce the switch.
3) Identify the switch by shifting the input and counting until a zero bit is found.

The assembly language program is

```
        CLR    $8005          ACCESS DATA DIRECTION REGISTER
        CLR    $8004          MAKE PORT A INPUTS
        LDAA   #%00000100     ACCESS DATA REGISTER
        STAA   $8005
WAITC   LDAA   $8004          GET INPUT DATA
        CMPA   #$FF           ARE ANY SWITCHES CLOSED?
        BEQ    WAITC          NO, WAIT
        LDAB   #$67           YES, DELAY 1 MS TO DEBOUNCE
DLY     DECB
        BNE    DLY
        LDAB   #$FF           SWITCH NUMBER = −1
SRCHS   INCB                  SWITCH NUMBER = SWITCH NUMBER + 1
        LSRA                  IS NEXT SWITCH CLOSED?
        BCS    SRCHS          NO, KEEP LOOKING
        STAB   $41            YES, SAVE SWITCH NUMBER
        SWI
```

You can see the switch number by examining memory location 0041 (or accumulator B) after executing the program. Program 4-5 is a complete hexadecimal version of this program, but note that memory locations 0000 through 0016 are the same as in Programs 4-3 and 4-4.

PROGRAM 4-5

MEMORY ADDRESS (HEX)	MEMORY CONTENTS (HEX)	INSTRUCTION (MNEMONIC)	
0000	7F	CLR	$8005
0001	80		
0002	05		
0003	7F	CLR	$8004
0004	80		
0005	04		
0006	86	LDAA	#%00000100

MEMORY ADDRESS (HEX)	MEMORY CONTENTS (HEX)	INSTRUCTION (MNEMONIC)	
0007	04		
0008	B7	STAA	$8005
0009	80		
000A	05		
000B	B6	WAITC LDAA	$8004
000C	80		
000D	04		
000E	81	CMPA	#$FF
000F	FF		
0010	27	BEQ	WAITC
0011	F9		
0012	C6	LDAB	#$67
0013	67		
0014	5A	DLY DECB	
0015	26	BNE	DLY
0016	FD		
0017	C6	LDAB	#$FF
0018	FF		
0019	5C	SRCHS INCB	
001A	44	LSRA	
001B	25	BCS	SRCHS
001C	FC		
001D	D7	STAB	$41
001E	41		
001F	3F	SWI	

Enter Program 4-5 and try it for all the switches. If two switches are closed, what is the result?

PROBLEM 4-8

Rewrite Program 4-5 so that it always identifies the highest numbered switch that is closed. *Hint:* Shift left and decrement the counter instead of shifting right and incrementing, but remember to change the initial conditions appropriately.

PROBLEM 4-9

Revise Program 4-5 so that it checks the switches only once, identifies the highest numbered switch that is closed if it finds any closed, and places FF in memory location 0041 if it finds none closed. What would happen if this program checked the switches while one was bouncing? How could you solve this problem?

(*Hint:* If the program finds all the switches open, have it wait for 1 ms and examine the switches again.)

Write a general program that only accepts the input from the switches if it remains the same after a 1-ms delay. That is, the program should keep checking the switches until two readings separated by 1 ms produce the same input.

Table 4-2

FUNCTION TABLE FOR 74148 ENCODER*

INPUTS (X = irrelevant)										OUTPUTS				
EI	0	1	2	3	4	5	6	7	A_2	A_1	A_0	GS	EO
H	X	X	X	X	X	X	X	X	H	H	H	H	H
L	H	H	H	H	H	H	H	H	H	H	H	H	L
L	X	X	X	X	X	X	X	L	L	L	L	L	H
L	X	X	X	X	X	X	L	H	L	L	H	L	H
L	X	X	X	X	X	L	H	H	L	H	L	L	H
L	X	X	X	X	L	H	H	H	L	H	H	L	H
L	X	X	X	L	H	H	H	H	H	L	L	L	H
L	X	X	L	H	H	H	H	H	H	L	H	L	H
L	X	L	H	H	H	H	H	H	H	H	L	L	H
L	L	H	H	H	H	H	H	H	H	H	H	L	H

*H = high or logic 1, L = low or logic 0.

USING A HARDWARE ENCODER

The 74148 8-to-3 priority encoder produces a 3-bit active-low output that identifies the highest priority input that is active-low. Table 4-2 is a function table for the device and Figure 4-6 contains its pin configuration. Note the following features of the 74148 encoder:

1)   The outputs (A_2, A_1, A_0) are the logical complement of the highest-priority input that is active. For example, the outputs are 0, 1, 0 if input 5 is the highest-priority input that is low.

2)   The ENABLE IN (EI) input and the ENABLE OUT (EO) output are used to combine encoders to handle more than eight inputs. If EI is high (indicating activity at a level higher than the entire encoder), all the outputs are high. If EI is low (indicating no higher activity) but there is no active input to this encoder, EO is low, thus enabling encoders of lower priority.

3)   The GROUP SELECT (GS) output is low if the encoder is enabled and has an active input. GS thus differentiates between the case in which only input 0 is active and the case in which the entire

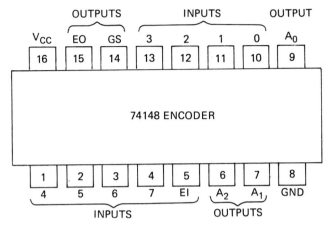

FIGURE 4-6. Pin configuration of 74148 encoder.

encoder is inactive or disabled (compare the top and bottom lines of Table 4-2).

Connect the encoder as described in Table 4-3. The following program will identify the highest numbered switch that is closed before the program is executed (the switch number ends up in accumulator A and in memory location 0041).

Table 4-3

**CONNECTIONS FOR 74148
ENCODER**

PIN NUMBER	DESIGNATION	CONNECTION
1	Input 4	Switch 4
2	Input 5	Switch 5
3	Input 6	Switch 6
4	Input 7	Switch 7
5 (EI)	Enable in	Ground
6 (A_2)	Output 2	User PIA pin PA2
7 (A_1)	Output 1	User PIA pin PA1
8	Ground	Ground
9 (A_0)	Output 0	User PIA pin PA0
10	Input 0	Switch 0
11	Input 1	Switch 1
12	Input 2	Switch 2
13	Input 3	Switch 3
14 (GS)	Group select	User PIA pin PA7
15 (EO)	Enable out	No connection
16	V_{cc}	+5 V

```
CLR     $8005           ACCESS DATA DIRECTION REGISTER
CLR     $8004           MAKE PORT A INPUTS
LDAA    #%00000100      ACCESS DATA REGISTER
STAA    $8005
LDAA    $8004           GET SWITCH DATA
COMA                    INVERT LOGIC
ANDA    #%00000111      MASK SWITCH BITS
STAA    $41             SAVE SWITCH NUMBER
SWI
```

The hexadecimal version of this program is given as Program 4-6. Enter and run Program 4-6. Try it for several different cases.

PROGRAM 4-6

MEMORY ADDRESS (HEX)	MEMORY CONTENTS (HEX)	INSTRUCTION (MNEMONIC)	
0000	7F	CLR	$8005
0001	80		
0002	05		
0003	7F	CLR	$8004
0004	80		
0005	04		
0006	86	LDAA	#%00000100
0007	04		
0008	B7	STAA	$8005
0009	80		
000A	05		
000B	B6	LDAA	$8004
000C	80		
000D	04		
000E	43	COMA	
000F	84	ANDA	#%00000111
0010	07		
0011	97	STAA	$41
0012	41		
0013	3F	SWI	

PROBLEM 4-10

To determine if any switches are closed, the program must examine the GS line attached to bit position 7. Revise Program 4-6 so that it examines the GS line, stores the switch number in memory location 0041 if it finds any switches closed, and stores FF in that location if it finds none closed.

PROBLEM 4-11

What would the input be if you inverted the switch connections (i.e., connected switch 7 to encoder input 0, and so on)? Write a program that places the switch number in memory location 0041 in this case. How does the inversion affect the priority of the switches?

Obviously, a hardware encoder makes the software simpler and faster and saves input bits (since it uses 4 rather than 8). On the other hand, the encoder adds to the parts count, dissipates power, requires extra connections (which further reduce reliability), and uses board space. In low-volume applications, the cost of extra hardware may be justifiable if the software is greatly simplified. In high-volume applications, repeated hardware costs must be kept as low as possible.

KEY POINT SUMMARY

1)   A mechanical switch requires a relatively long time to settle into a new position. You can either introduce a delay during which the processor does not examine the switch or you can add hardware that smooths the transition. Mechanical components typically have much longer time constants than do electrical components. The interface between the components must account for this difference.

2)   Inputs must usually be converted into a convenient form before they can be processed. Either hardware or software can perform this conversion.

3)   Timing and code conversion are two common functions that can be performed either in hardware or in software. Hardware implementations reduce the amount and complexity of the required software; this usually simplifies system development, particularly if the designer is more familiar with hardware than with software. Software implementations reduce the number of parts, save board space, and increase reliability.

4)   Many factors affect tradeoffs between software and hardware. Among these are the cost and availability of parts, designer experience, product volume, amount of memory available, amount of board space, and performance requirements. Remember the following considerations:

a)   Software costs are incurred only once, whereas hardware costs are repeated for each system produced. Thus, high-volume products should have more software and less hardware than low-volume products.

b)   A single processor can perform many tasks, particularly if they involve slow mechanical components. Hardware, on the other hand, is more difficult to share, even among similar tasks.

c)   Certain tasks, such as switch and keyboard encoding, display decoding, and serial/parallel interfacing, are so common that special hardware is available to handle them at very low cost. Hardware for less common tasks, even if their complexity is comparable, may be far more expensive.

☐ *Laboratory* **5**

Processing Data Outputs

PURPOSE

To learn how to process data outputs using the MEK6800D2 micro-computer.

PARTS REQUIRED

None.

REFERENCE MATERIALS

L. A. Leventhal, *Introduction to Microprocessors: Software, Hardware, Programming,* Prentice-Hall, Englewood Cliffs, NJ, 1978, pp. 205-208, 377-378, 414-417.

L. A. Leventhal, *6800 Assembly Language Programming,* Osborne/McGraw-Hill, Berkeley, CA, 1978, pp. 7-3 through 7-5, 11-39 through 11-47.

W. J. Weller, *Practical Microcomputer Programming: The M6800,* Northern Technology Books, Evanston, IL, 1977, Chapters 9 and 14.

MEK6800D2 Evaluation Kit II Manual, Motorola Semiconductor Products Inc., Austin, TX, 1977, pp. 2-3 through 2-4 (keyboard/display), 3-3 through 3-4 (display routine).

TTL Data Book for Design Engineers, 2nd ed., Texas Instruments, Inc., Dallas, TX, 1976, pp. 7-22 through 7-34 (7447 through 7449 seven-segment decoder/drivers).

L. A. Leventhal, "Cut Your Processor's Computation Time," *Electronic Design,* August 16, 1977, pp. 82-86.

WHAT YOU SHOULD LEARN

1) How seven-segment displays are organized and connected.
2) How to activate the MEK6800D2 displays and light the segments.
3) How to turn the displays on or off for specified periods of time.
4) How to convert data into the seven-segment code required to form characters on the displays.
5) How and when to use lookup tables.
6) How to count on displays.
7) The advantages and disadvantages of lookup tables.
8) The tradeoffs between hardware and software approaches to decoding.

TERMS

Array—a collection of related data items, usually stored in consecutive memory locations (also called a *block*).

Base address—the address in memory at which an array or table starts. Also called *starting address* or *base*.

Blanking input—an input that turns off the elements in a display.

Common-anode display—a multiple display in which signals are applied to the cathodes of the individual displays and the anodes are tied together to the power supply; uses negative logic (i.e., a logic 0 lights a display).

Common-cathode display—a multiple display in which signals are applied to the anodes of the individual displays and the cathodes are tied together to ground; uses positive logic (i.e., a logic 1 lights a display).

Decoder—a device that produces unencoded outputs from coded inputs.

Endless loop (or **jump-to-self**) **instruction**—an instruction that transfers control to itself, thus executing indefinitely (or until a hardware signal interrupts it).

Index—a data item used to identify a particular element of an array or table.

Indexed addressing—an addressing method in which the address included in the instruction is modified by the contents of an index register to find the actual address used.

Index register—a register that can be used to modify memory addresses.

Lookup table—an array of data organized so that the answer to a problem may be determined merely by obtaining the correct entry (without any calculations).

Ripple blanking—blanking all leading or trailing displays by having each one indicate to its successor whether it is blank.

Seven-segment code—the code required to form decimal digits or other characters on a seven-segment display.

Seven-segment display—a display made up of seven separately controlled elements that can form decimal digits or other characters.

6800 INSTRUCTIONS

CPX—compare index register; subtract the contents of the specified memory location and the next consecutive location from the contents of the index register, but leave the contents of the index register unchanged. The only flag that CPX sets properly is the ZERO flag. Therefore, only the ZERO flag can be used for branching afterward (i.e., either CPX, BNE or CPX, BEQ produces predictable results; sequences using the CARRY, NEGATIVE, or OVERFLOW flags do not). This problem has been corrected in the 6801 microprocessor.

PROCESSING OUTPUTS

As with inputs, we would like the microprocessor to do more than merely determine the value of a particular binary output. Rather, we want the processor to produce a series of outputs and convert the output data into the forms that the peripherals require. The processor should also be able to provide the proper timing.

Here, again, either software or hardware can perform these tasks. The designer must make tradeoffs based on the characteristics of a particular application. Furthermore, the designer may be able to make tradeoffs between time and memory. One simple way to perform a calculation is to store all the possible results in memory and find the correct one just as you would obtain a function value from a book of mathematical tables.

This method (called *table lookup*) is fast and easy to implement but usually requires more memory than an explicit calculation.

USING THE ON-BOARD SEVEN-SEGMENT DISPLAYS

We will use the on-board MEK6800D2 seven-segment displays as a simple example of an output device that requires parallel data, timing, and code conversion. The displays are organized as shown in Figure 5-1. The LEDs are common-cathode (see Figure 5-2a) with inverting drivers so that a logic 0 lights a segment. Figure 5-3 shows how the segments are connected, and Figure 5-4 shows how the six displays are numbered. The display numbering corresponds with that used in the schematic of the MEK6800D2 Keyboard/Display Module (see Figure A3-a of the *MEK6800D2 Evaluation Kit II Manual*).

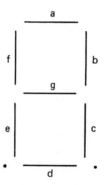

FIGURE 5-1. A seven-segment display.

The seven-segment displays on the MEK6800D2 Keyboard/Display Module are connected to the CPU through a Peripheral Interface Adapter that occupies memory addresses 8020 through 8023. The segments are connected to port A (memory address 8020) as shown in Figure 5-3; bit 7 is not used. The commons on the various displays are connected to port B (memory address 8022) as shown in Figure 5-5; bits 6 and 7 are not used. The commons are connected so that a logic 1 activates a particular display (remember that a logic 0 lights a segment). So, using the numbering system of Figure 5-4 and Table 5-1, the outputs in Table 5-2 will activate particular displays. The following sequence of instructions sends data to a digit in the display. The monitor program initializes the Keyboard/Display PIA, so the user does not have to load its data direction and control registers.

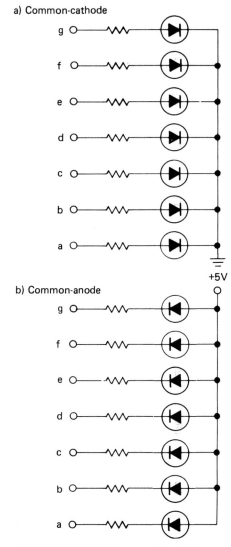

FIGURE 5-2. Display configurations.

	b$_7$	b$_6$	b$_5$	b$_4$	b$_3$	b$_2$	b$_1$	b$_0$
Memory Location 8020 (hex)	Not Used	g	f	e	d	c	b	a

FIGURE 5-3. Segment connections for the MEK6800D2 displays.

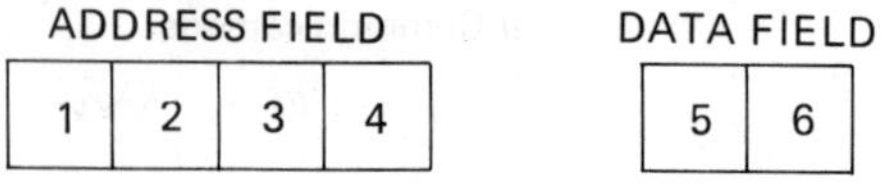

ADDRESS FIELD   DATA FIELD

| 1 | 2 | 3 | 4 | | 5 | 6 |

FIGURE 5-4. Numbering of the MEK6800D2 displays.

	b_7	b_6	b_5	b_4	b_3	b_2	b_1	b_0
Memory Location 8022 (hex)	Not Used	Not Used	D_1	D_2	D_3	D_4	D_5	D_6

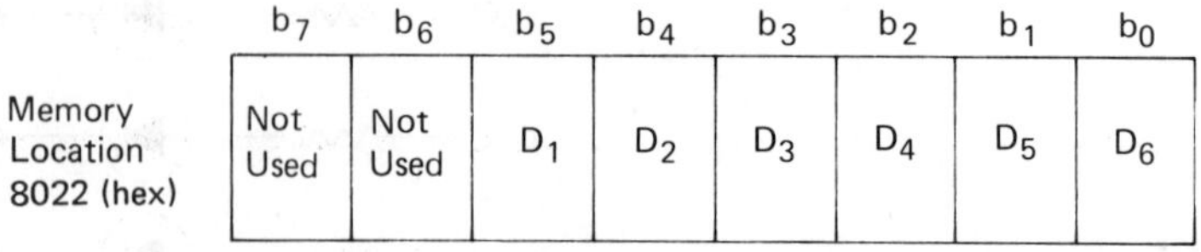

FIGURE 5-5. Common connections for the MEK6800D2 displays.

```
LDAA     ACTIVE          ACTIVATE A DISPLAY
STAA     $8022
LDAA     DATA            SEND IT DATA
STAA     $8020
```

Table 5-1

NUMBERING OF THE MEK6800D2 DISPLAYS

DISPLAY	NUMBER
Address Digit 1 (MSD)	1
Address Digit 2	2
Address Digit 3	3
Address Digit 4 (LSD)	4
Data Digit 1 (MSD)	5
Data Digit 2 (LSD)	6

Table 5-2

OUTPUTS FOR ACTIVATING DISPLAYS
(MEMORY LOCATION 8022)

DISPLAY NUMBER	OUTPUT (BINARY)	OUTPUT (HEX)
1	00100000	20
2	00010000	10
3	00001000	08
4	00000100	04
5	00000010	02
6	00000001	01

Note the following:

1) You must activate the proper display before sending it data. The activation involves storing a value from Table 5-2 in memory location 8022. You can activate more than one display at a time by setting more than one bit position. For example:

DISPLAY NUMBERS	OUTPUT (BINARY)	OUTPUT (HEX)
1 and 2	00110000	30
3 and 4	00001100	0C
5 and 6	00000011	03
1, 2, and 3	00111000	38
4, 5, and 6	00000111	07

2) You can send data to the activated displays by storing the data in memory location 8020.

Table 5-3 contains the hexadecimal outputs required to light the various segments individually. Remember that a logic 0 lights a segment. For example, the following program will light segment d on the leftmost address display (display number 1):

Table 5-3

**OUTPUTS FOR LIGHTING SEGMENTS
(MEMORY LOCATION 8020)**

SEGMENT	OUTPUT (BINARY)	OUTPUT (HEX)
g	10111111	BF
f	11011111	DF
e	11101111	EF
d	11110111	F7
c	11111011	FB
b	11111101	FD
a	11111110	FE

```
LDAA    #$20        ACTIVATE LEFTMOST DISPLAY
STAA    $8022
LDAA    #$F7        LIGHT SEGMENT D
```

```
STAA        $8020
SWI
```

Program 5-1 is the hexadecimal version. We have arbitrarily cleared both unused bit positions in the outputs that activate the displays and set the unused bit position in the outputs that light the segments. Active levels thus only appear in the bit positions that are actually in use.

To light several segments at the same time, simply clear all the corresponding bit positions. For example:

SEGMENTS	OUTPUT (BINARY)	OUTPUT (HEX)
f and g	10011111	9F
d and e	11100111	E7
a and b	11111100	FC
a, b, and c	11111000	F8
a, d, and f	11010110	D6

PROGRAM 5-1

MEMORY ADDRESS (HEX)	MEMORY CONTENTS (HEX)	INSTRUCTION (MNEMONIC)	
0000	86	LDAA	#$20
0001	20		
0002	B7	STAA	$8022
0003	80		
0004	22		
0005	86	LDAA	#$F7
0006	F7		
0007	B7	STAA	$8020
0008	80		
0009	20		
000A	3F	SWI	

Enter and run Program 5-1. What happens? The problem is that the monitor immediately uses the displays for its own purposes (to show the last address executed and its contents). You can retain control of the displays by placing an endless loop (i.e., an instruction that jumps to itself) at the end of Program 5-1.

000A	20	HERE	BRA	HERE
000B	FE			

This program will run forever, so you will have to press RESET or the blue E key to return control to the monitor.

PROBLEM 5-1

Write a program that lights segment g of the leftmost address display (display 1).

PROBLEM 5-2

Write a program that lights segment g of the rightmost address display (display 4).

PROBLEM 5-3

Write a program that lights segments e and g of the rightmost data display (display 6). What letter is formed?

ADDING A DELAY

We can easily leave the display on for a specified amount of time by using a delay program:

	LDAA	#CT1
DLY1	LDAB	#CT2
DLY2	DECB	
	BNE	DLY2
	DECA	
	BNE	DLY1

Program 5-2 is the hexadecimal version with the delay at the end. Enter and run this program with CT1 = CT2 = 0.

PROGRAM 5-2

MEMORY ADDRESS (HEX)	MEMORY CONTENTS (HEX)	INSTRUCTION (MNEMONIC)	
0000	86	LDAA	#$20
0001	20		
0002	B7	STAA	$8022
0003	80		
0004	22		
0005	86	LDAA	#$F7
0006	F7		
0007	B7	STAA	$8020
0008	80		

MEMORY ADDRESS (HEX)	MEMORY CONTENTS (HEX)	INSTRUCTION (MNEMONIC)	
0009	20		
000A	86	LDAA	#CT1
000B	CT1		
000C	C6	DLY1 LDAB	#CT2
000D	CT2		
000E	5A	DLY2 DECB	
000F	26	BNE	DLY2
0010	FD		
0011	4A	DECA	
0012	26	BNE	DLY1
0013	F8		
0014	3F	SWI	

PROBLEM 5-4

Run the program for the following sequence of values for CT1: 80, 40, 20, 10, 08, 04, 02, 01. When can you no longer see the display light?

PROBLEM 5-5

Make the program show the letter H on the rightmost display (display 6).

SEVEN-SEGMENT CODE CONVERSION

We can form any decimal digit on a seven-segment display. Table 5-4 contains the required codes. The problem is how to convert a decimal digit to a seven-segment code. Certainly, the values in Table 5-4 do not appear to be related in any obvious way.

One approach would be to use Boolean algebra to simplify Table 5-4. We could then perform the conversion as a series of logical ANDs and ORs. This is how we would implement the conversion with logic gates.

A simpler approach, however, is to place Table 5-4 in memory and use it as a lookup table. The program can then perform the conversion as follows:

1) Calculate the address of the desired code by adding the starting (or *base*) address of the table to the element number (or *index*).

2) Use the calculated address to obtain the code.

Table 5-4

DECIMAL-TO-SEVEN-SEGMENT CONVERSION TABLE
FOR MEK6800D2 DISPLAYS

	SEVEN-SEGMENT CODE	
DECIMAL DIGIT	(HEX)	(BINARY)
0	C0	11000000
1	F9	11111001
2	A4	10100100
3	B0	10110000
4	99	10011001
5	92	10010010
6	82	10000010
7	F8	11111000
8	80	10000000
9	98	10011000

One would think that you could simply use indexed addressing to perform the address-length addition. The obvious approach would be to place the starting address of the table in the index register and the index in the offset, and then use indexed addressing to find the entry. However, if you try this approach, you will find that it does not work because the offset is part of the program memory (ROM in most applications) and cannot be changed as the data changes. Nor can you interchange the starting address and index, since the starting address is 16 bits long and cannot fit in an 8-bit offset.

There is no good solution to this problem. One approach is to load the index register with the 8 most significant bits of the starting address and the index. The 8 least significant bits of the starting address can then be used as the offset. Two memory locations are needed as temporary storage to assemble the misfit for loading into the index register, since the 6800 does not allow direct transfers between the accumulators and the index register. The following program converts a decimal digit in memory location 0040 into a seven-segment code in memory location 0041, using memory locations 0042 and 0043 for temporary storage:

```
LDAA    #$A0      GET MSB'S OF STARTING ADDRESS
STAA    $42
LDAA    $40       GET DATA
STAA    $43
LDX     $42       MOVE OFFSET ADDRESS TO INDEX REGISTER
LDAA    $50,X     GET SEVEN-SEGMENT CODE
STAA    $41       SAVE RESULT
SWI
```

This program assumes that we have placed the seven-segment code table in memory starting at address A050. The table thus does not inter fere with any of our programs or with the area used by the JBUG monitor for temporary storage (see page A1-16 of the *MEK6800D2 Evaluation Kit II Manual*). Note that you must enter both Program 5-3 (starting at address 0000) and Table 5-4 (starting at address A050) into memory. The 6801 microprocessor simplifies table lookup by providing the instruction ABX, which adds the contents of accumulator B to the contents of the index register and saves the 16-bit sum in the index register. How could you use ABX in Program 5-3?

PROGRAM 5-3

MEMORY ADDRESS (HEX)	MEMORY CONTENTS (HEX)	INSTRUCTION (MNEMONIC)	
0000	86	LDAA	#$A0
0001	A0		
0002	97	STAA	$42
0003	42		
0004	96	LDAA	$40
0005	40		
0006	97	STAA	$43
0007	43		
0008	DE	LDX	$42
0009	42		
000A	A6	LDAA	$50,X
000B	50		
000C	97	STAA	$41
000D	41		
000E	3F	SWI	

MEMORY ADDRESS (HEX)	MEMORY CONTENTS (HEX)	ENTRY
A050	C0	0
A051	F9	1
A052	A4	2
A053	B0	3
A054	99	4
A055	92	5
A056	82	6
A057	F8	7
A058	80	8
A059	98	9

Note that you can use the short direct addressing mode with the instruction LDX, even though this instruction loads the 16-bit index register. LDX $42 loads the index register from memory locations 0042 (MSBs) and 0043 (LSBs). Be careful of the fact that LDX requires three words of memory when used with immediate addressing, but only two when used with direct addressing.

Program 5-3 works as follows (assuming that memory location 0040 contains 03):

1) LDAA #$A0 and STAA $42 place A0 (the MSBs of the starting address of the lookup table) in memory location 0042.

2) LDAA $40 and STAA $43 place the data (03) in memory location 0043.

3) LDX $42 loads the index register with the MSBs of the starting address of the table and the data; the index register thus contains A003. This method is general; it does not depend on the table and the data being close together or being located anywhere particular in memory.

4) LDAA $50,X loads accumulator A from the effective address calculated by adding the offset (the LSBs of the starting address of the table) to the index register (MSBs of starting address and data). The effective address is therefore 50 + A003 = A053. So accumulator A is loaded from address A053, which contains B0, the code that forms a 3 on the seven-segment display.

To make the result easier to see, add the following instructions that show it on the leftmost display:

```
        STAA    $8020       PLACE RESULT ON DISPLAY
        LDAA    #$20        ACTIVATE LEFTMOST DISPLAY
        STAA    $8022
HERE    BRA     HERE
```

The required hexadecimal additions are:

MEMORY ADDRESS (HEX)	MEMORY CONTENTS (HEX)	INSTRUCTION (MNEMONIC)	
000E	B7	STAA	$8020
000F	80		
0010	20		
0011	86	LDAA	#$20
0012	20		
0013	B7	STAA	$8022
0014	80		

(Continued)

MEMORY ADDRESS (HEX)	MEMORY CONTENTS (HEX)	INSTRUCTION (MNEMONIC)		
0015	22			
0016	20	HERE	BRA	HERE
0017	FE			

Table 5-5

**SEVEN-SEGMENT CODES
FOR LETTERS AND OTHER CHARACTERS**

SYMBOL	SEVEN-SEGMENT CODE (HEX)
Capital letters	
A	88
C	C6
E	86
F	8E
H	89
J	E1
L	C7
O	C0
P	8C
U	C1
Y	91
Lowercase letters	
b	83
c	A7
d	A1
h	8B
n	AB
o	A3
r	AF
u	E3
Other characters	
?	AC
- (hyphen)	BF
_ (underscore)	F7

It does not matter if you activate the display after storing the data in the PIA port, as long as the lag is too short to be visible. Note that you can form some letters as well as decimal digits on seven-segment displays (see Table 5-5). If you run the program with the additions, you will

Table 5-6

**HEXADECIMAL-TO-SEVEN-SEGMENT
CONVERSION TABLE FOR MEK6800D2 DISPLAYS**

HEXADECIMAL DIGIT	SEVEN-SEGMENT CODE (HEX)
0	C0
1	F9
2	A4
3	B0
4	99
5	92
6	82
7	F8
8	80
9	98
A	88
b (lowercase)	83
C	C6
d (lowercase)	A1
E	86
F	8E

probably notice that the displays are much brighter than usual. Explain the increased brightness. (*Hint:* Remember the results of Problem 3-14.)

PROBLEM 5-6

Extend Program 5-3 so that it converts hexadecimal digits into seven-segment codes using Table 5-6.

PROBLEM 5-7

Of course, the JBUG monitor uses a table to form hexadecimal digits on the displays, Revise Program 5-3 to use the JBUG conversion table starting at memory location E3CA. This table is in ROM, so you do not have to enter it. How does the JBUG table differ from Table 5-6?

COUNTING ON THE DISPLAYS

We can use Table 5-6 to count in hexadecimal on the displays. The following program will count up on the leftmost address display (display 1):

```
LDX     #$A050     START THE COUNT AT ZERO
LDAA    #$20       ACTIVATE LEFTMOST DISPLAY
```

```
              STAA    $8022
DSPLY         LDAA    0,X           GET SEVEN-SEGMENT CODE FOR
*                                     CURRENT COUNT
              STAA    $8020         DISPLAY THE CURRENT COUNT
              LDAA    #CT1          WASTE SOME TIME
DLY1          LDAB    #CT2
DLY2          DECB
              BNE     DLY2
              DECA
              BNE     DLY1
              INX                   ADD 1 TO COUNT BY POINTING
*                                     TO NEXT DIGIT
              CPX     #$A060        HAS THE COUNT BEEN COMPLETED?
              BNE     DSPLY         NO, CONTINUE
              SWI
```

Program 5-4 is the hexadecimal version. Remember that you must also enter Table 5-6 into memory addresses A050 through A05F. The instruction CPX subtracts the contents of the specified memory address (and the next consecutive address) from the index register; no result is saved but the flags are affected. Be careful—the 6800 microprocessor does not set the NEGATIVE (SIGN) or CARRY flag correctly when executing CPX, so only the ZERO flag may be used afterward for branching (with BNE or BEQ). The newer 6801 microprocessor sets all flags properly when executing CPX. Note that the operand in the CPX instruction (A060) is one larger than the highest address in the table, since the program increments the index register (with INX) before checking its value.

PROBLEM 5-8

Make Program 5-4 use the rightmost display (display 6) instead of the leftmost display (display 1). How could you revise the program so that it fetches the display number (assumed to be between 1 and 6 inclusive) from memory location 0040?

Example:

(0040) = 02 causes the program to count on display #2, the next to most significant digit of the address display.

PROBLEM 5-9

Make Program 5-4 start over at zero after it reaches F.

PROBLEM 5-10

Make Program 5-4 start counting at F and count down to zero.

PROGRAM 5-4

MEMORY ADDRESS (HEX)	MEMORY CONTENTS (HEX)		INSTRUCTION (MNEMONIC)	
0000	CE		LDX	#$A050
0001	A0			
0002	50			
0003	86		LDAA	#$20
0004	20			
0005	B7		STAA	$8022
0006	80			
0007	22			
0008	A6	DSPLY	LDAA	0,X
0009	00			
000A	B7		STAA	$8020
000B	80			
000C	20			
000D	86		LDAA	#CT1
000E	CT1			
000F	C6	DLY1	LDAB	#CT2
0010	CT2			
0011	5A	DLY2	DECB	
0012	26		BNE	DLY2
0013	FD			
0014	4A		DECA	
0015	26		BNE	DLY1
0016	F8			
0017	08		INX	
0018	8C		CPX	#$A060
0019	A0			
001A	60			
001B	26		BNE	DSPLY
001C	EB			
001D	3F		SWI	

PROBLEM 5-11

Implement the counting program with the following nonstandard hexadecimal digit set used by Hewlett-Packard in their 5001 Signature Analyzer, a piece of test equipment that can detect faults in microprocessor-based systems. Hewlett-Packard uses this set rather than the normal one because its digits are easy to tell apart and can be read upside down; both of these characteristics are necessary in service instruments. Besides, this set can be formed on seven-segment displays without using any lowercase letters.

NORMAL HEXADECIMAL DIGIT	HP5001 HEXADECIMAL DIGIT
0	0
1	1
2	2
3	3
4	4
5	5
6	6
7	7
8	8
9	9
A	A
B or b	C
C	F
D or d	H
E	P
F	U

PROBLEM 5-12

Revise the continuous counting program (Problem 5-9) so that it continues only as long as the switch attached to bit position 0 of port A of the user PIA is open. Write one version that checks the switch after each digit is displayed and one version that only checks the switch when it reaches the end of the table (i.e., after displaying F).

SWITCH AND LIGHT PROGRAM

We can also use the table to display the number of the last switch closed.

PROBLEM 5-13

Combine the switch identification program of Laboratory 4 (Program 4-5) with the seven-segment conversion program (Program 5-3) to wait for a switch closure at port A of the user PIA and report its number on the leftmost seven-segment display.

ADVANTAGES AND DISADVANTAGES OF LOOKUP TABLES

By now, you have seen many of the advantages and disadvantages of lookup tables. Among the advantages are:

- No computation has to be performed, so tables are faster than calculations unless the calculations are very simple.

- No program is required beyond the basic lookup routine. Lookup tables are thus easy to implement.
- The same lookup routine can be used for many different tables. Changes and extensions are simple and additional tables involve almost no programming at all.
- Table entries are available for other purposes (such as counting) in a convenient order.
- The table-lookup procedure is the same for all values. There are no boundary problems or variations in execution time.

Among the disadvantages of tables are:

- They require extra memory, particularly if the range of input values is large or great accuracy is necessary.
- They may be difficult to organize unless the input data is simple.
- The table-lookup procedure cannot distinguish common or simple cases that might be handled easily.
- Programs that use tables may be very difficult to understand, since no calculations are performed explicitly.

HARDWARE/SOFTWARE TRADEOFFS

As with inputs, hardware can do part of the output processing. For example, a 7447 decoder (see Table 5-7 and Figure 5-6) will automatically convert decimal inputs into common-anode seven-segment code. Neither a table nor a conversion routine is necessary.

In fact, the 7447 device is more than just a decoder. It also has

1) A LAMP TEST input that lights all the segments to show if they are working.

2) A blanking input (BI) that turns all the segments off.

3) A ripple blanking input and output (RBI and RBO) that can be used to blank leading or trailing 0's (i.e., display 37 instead of 0037 or 37.00). If the ripple blanking input is low, a zero data input will not be displayed and the ripple blanking output will be low. If the display is not blanked, the ripple blanking output will be high. This output is then attached to the ripple blanking input of the next digit.

A decoder such as the 7447 can replace a large amount of software. Like an encoder, the decoder also increases the number of parts and con-

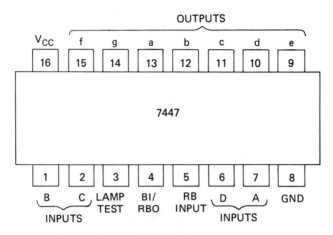

FIGURE 5-6. Pin configuration for the 7447 seven-segment decoder/driver.

Table 5-7

**FUNCTION TABLE FOR THE
7447 SEVEN-SEGMENT
DECODER/DRIVER**

DECIMAL OR FUNCTION	INPUTS							OUTPUTS						
	LT	RBI	D	C	B	A	BI/RBO	a	b	c	d	e	f	g
0	1	1	0	0	0	0	1	0	0	0	0	0	0	1
1	1	X	0	0	0	1	1	1	0	0	1	1	1	1
2	1	X	0	0	1	0	1	0	0	1	0	0	1	0
3	1	X	0	0	1	1	1	0	0	0	0	1	1	0
4	1	X	0	1	0	0	1	1	0	0	1	1	0	0
5	1	X	0	1	0	1	1	0	1	0	0	1	0	0
6	1	X	0	1	1	0	1	1	1	0	0	0	0	0
7	1	X	0	1	1	1	1	0	0	0	1	1	1	1
8	1	X	1	0	0	0	1	0	0	0	0	0	0	0
9	1	X	1	0	0	1	1	0	0	0	1	1	0	0
10	1	X	1	0	1	0	1	1	1	1	0	0	1	0
11	1	X	1	0	1	1	1	1	1	0	0	1	1	0
12	1	X	1	1	0	0	1	1	0	1	1	1	0	0
13	1	X	1	1	0	1	1	0	1	1	0	1	0	0
14	1	X	1	1	1	0	1	1	1	1	0	0	0	0
15	1	X	1	1	1	1	1	1	1	1	1	1	1	1
BI	X	X	X	X	X	X	0	1	1	1	1	1	1	1
RBI	1	0	0	0	0	0	0	1	1	1	1	1	1	1
LT	0	X	X	X	X	X	1	0	0	0	0	0	0	0

nections, decreases reliability, uses board space, and adds to the per-unit cost.

PROBLEM 5-14

> Change the program for Problem 5-13 so that it displays a blank instead of a zero. Do not change the conversion table. How would you blank a zero if you were using a 7447 decoder?

KEY POINT SUMMARY

1)   Most output devices (and observers) require that data be available for a relatively long time by processor standards. The I/O ports must latch the data and the processor must not change it too frequently.

2)   Outputs must usually be converted into the forms required by peripherals. Either hardware (decoders) or software can be used to perform the conversions.

3)   Output transfers generally involve control signals as well as data. These control signals may be used for multiplexing or for controlling peripheral operations.

4)   Lookup tables are a convenient way to perform code conversions if the functions are complex. Such tables simply contain all the codes organized in some convenient manner. They are easy and quick to use but may occupy a large amount of memory.

5)   A microprocessor can usually update operator displays while performing other tasks, since the displays change slowly.

□ Laboratory 6

Processing Data Arrays

PURPOSE

To learn how to process arrays or blocks of data using the MEK6800D2 microcomputer.

PARTS REQUIRED

None.

REFERENCE MATERIALS

L. A. Leventhal, *Introduction to Microprocessors: Software, Hardware, Programming,* Prentice-Hall, Englewood Cliffs, NJ, 1978, pp. 179-198.

L. A. Leventhal, *6800 Assembly Language Programming,* Osborne/McGraw-Hill, Berkeley, CA, 1978, Chapter 5.

W.J. Weller, *Practical Microcomputer Programming: The M6800,* Northern Technology Books, Evanston, IL, 1977, Chapters 4, 5, and 9.

MEK6800D2 Evaluation Kit II Manual, Motorola Semiconductor Products Inc., Austin, TX, 1977, pp. 2-3 through 2-4 (keyboard/display), 3-3 through 3-4 (display routine).

M6800 Programming Reference Manual, Motorola Semiconductor Products Inc., Phoenix, AZ, 1976, pp. 4-4 through 4-6 (indexed addressing).

WHAT YOU SHOULD LEARN

1) What identifies elements of an array or block of data.
2) Why flexible addressing methods are important.
3) How to conveniently process arrays using the 6800 microprocessor.
4) How to perform a summation.
5) How to use a terminator.
6) How to display a block of data.
7) How to place messages on the displays.
8) How to make programs more general and more flexible.

TERMS

Array—a collection of related data items, usually stored in consecutive memory locations (also called a *block*).

Block—*see* Array.

Checksum—a logical sum of data used to guard against errors.

Logical sum—a binary sum with no carries between bit positions.

Object code (or **object program**)—the program that is the output of a translator program, such as an assembler. Usually, a machine language program ready for execution.

Offset—distance from a starting point or base address.

Pointer—a register or memory location that contains an address rather than data.

Source code (or **source program**)—computer program written in an assembly language or high-level language.

Terminator—a data item that has no function other than to mark the end of an array.

6800 INSTRUCTIONS

ABA—add accumulator B to accumulator A; add the contents of accumulator B to the contents of accumulator A and place the result in accumulator A.

ADC—add with carry; add the contents of the specified memory location and the CARRY flag to the contents of an accumulator.

The result is placed in the accumulator. ADCA #0 adds the CARRY flag to accumulator A.

TST—test zero or minus; subtract zero from the contents of the specified accumulator or memory location and change the flags accordingly. This instruction affects only the flags. TSTA or TSTB sets the flags according to the contents of the specified accumulator.

DATA ARRAYS

Most computer tasks involve applying the same instructions to an entire collection of data. Such a collection of data may be referred to as an *array* or *block*. Typical operations on arrays are calculating averages, finding the largest element for scaling, organizing data for storage on tape or disk, editing strings of characters, sorting, arranging sequences of operations, performing statistical analysis, and searching for particular commands or other inputs.

The elements of arrays are most often stored in successive memory locations. Two items are then necessary to identify a particular element of the array:

1) The starting address of the entire array or *base address*.

2) The element number or *index*.

We often refer mathematically to an element of an array as A_i, where A identifies the array as a whole (i.e., base address), and i identifies the particular element (i.e., index). Note that once you have determined the starting address of an array, you may refer to all elements relative to it (i.e., you may refer to "the seventh element" or "the fifteenth element"). Programs that handle arrays in this way need only be told where the arrays start; the data need not be moved to particular memory locations.

Note how important a flexible addressing method is to programs that process arrays. Such programs should not depend on exactly where in memory the arrays are located or how long they are. Otherwise, minor changes in the locations, lengths, or other characteristics of the arrays will require major revisions in the programs.

PROBLEM 6-1

Which of these instructions could you use to handle any element of an array? Why?

a) LDAA $40

b) LDAB #$A3

c)   LDAA $20,X

d)   LDX $40

Which instructions can be used to transfer data from several different memory locations even if the program is stored in read-only memory?

PROBLEM 6-2

If an array starts at base address B and each element occupies one memory location, what is the address of the second element? Assume that memory location B contains the "zeroth" element. What is the address of the jth element, where j is an arbitrary integer? How are these addresses affected if we refer to the element in B as the "first" element? This variation is similar to the alternative numbering of floors in a building as Ground (0), 1, 2, 3, etc., or as 1, 2, 3, 4, etc.

PROBLEM 6-3

How are the answers to Problem 6-2 affected if each element occupies two memory locations? What if each element occupies k memory locations, where k is an arbitrary integer?

PROBLEM 6-4

If the arrays are two-dimensional, we can store them by row (or by column) in the linear memory of the computer. For example, we can refer to an element as A_{jk}, where j is the row number and k is the column number. We can store the elements in memory in the following order, starting with the zeroth row: A_{00}, $A_{01}, A_{02}, \ldots, A_{0n}, A_{10}, A_{11}, A_{12}, \ldots, A_{m0}, A_{m1}, A_{m2}, \ldots, A_{mn}$, where m is the number of the last row and n is the number of the last column (the array has a total of $m + 1$ rows and $n + 1$ columns, since we have started each dimension at zero). If we store element A_{00} in the base address B, what is the address of A_{12}? What is the address of element A_{jk}, where j and k are arbitrary integers? How are these addresses affected if the elements each occupy more than one memory location?

PROBLEM 6-5

The following program places the contents of memory locations 0040 and 0041 in descending order (i.e., larger element first). How many changes would you have to make if the addresses had to be changed to 0050 and 0051? How about A050 and A051? Try running the program and making the required changes. Write a version that would require only one change to handle any two consecutive memory locations. Which version would be more useful, and why? Which version could be used more easily in sorting an entire block of data?

Source Program:

```
        LDAA    $40     GET FIRST ELEMENT
        CMPA    $41     IS SECOND ELEMENT SMALLER?
        BCC     DONE    YES, DONE
        LDAB    $41     NO, REORDER ELEMENTS
        STAA    $41
        STAB    $40
DONE    SWI
```

Object Program:

MEMORY ADDRESS (HEX)	MEMORY CONTENTS (HEX)		INSTRUCTION (MNEMONIC)	
0000	96		LDAA	$40
0001	40			
0002	91		CMPA	$41
0003	41			
0004	24		BCC	DONE
0005	06			
0006	D6		LDAB	$41
0007	41			
0008	97		STAA	$41
0009	41			
000A	D7		STAB	$40
000B	40			
000C	3F	DONE	SWI	

Examples:

1) (0040) = 3A
    (0041) = 6B
    Result: (0040) = 6B
             (0041) = 3A

2) (0040) = 59
    (0041) = 2F
    Result: (0040) = 59
             (0041) = 2F

PROCESSING ARRAYS WITH THE 6800 MICROPROCESSOR

You will find it most convenient to process arrays with the 6800 micro-processor as follows (see Figure 6-1 for a flowchart):

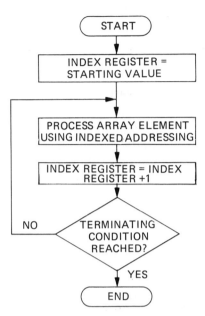

FIGURE 6-1. Array processing with the 6800 microprocessor.

1) Place the starting address of the array in the index register using the instruction LDX. The index register serves as a *pointer*, since it contains an address rather than data.

2) Refer to a particular element of the array (the one addressed by the index register) using indexed addressing with a zero offset (e.g., ADDA 0,X or ADDA X).

3) Refer to other elements in the array using indexed addressing with nonzero offsets. Note that you can only access elements at higher addresses (since the offset is always positive) and that you can only reach 256 elements in this way (since the offset is only 8 bits long). You must access elements that are further away by performing an explicit 16-bit addition using the accumulators (the 6800 has no instructions that add to the index register except INX).

4) Proceed to the next element of the array with the instruction INX (or the previous element with DEX).

Note some of the features of this approach:

1) Once you have placed a starting address in the index register, the remaining instructions do not depend on where the array is located in memory.

2) You can perform operations directly on the element addressed by the index register and on the 255 following elements: for example,

117

LDAA 0,X—load the element addressed by the index register into accumulator A.

ADDA $10,X—add the element sixteen (10 hex) beyond the one addressed by the index register to accumulator A.

3)   You can move the accessible part of the block up one with INX or down one with DEX.

4)   You can access an arbitrary element (with a 16-bit index) by performing the required addition, assuming that the index is in INDXL (LSBs) and INDXM (MSBs) and that the base address is BASEL (LSBs) and BASEM (MSBs):

```
LDAA    INDXL      CALCULATE LSB'S OF INDEXED ADDRESS
ADDA    #BASEL
STAA    INDXL
LDAA    INDXM      CALCULATE MSB'S OF INDEXED ADDRESS
ADCA    #BASEM
STAA    INDXM
LDX     INDXM      GET INDEXED ADDRESS
LDAA    0,X        GET ELEMENT FROM INDEXED ADDRESS
```

We have assumed that INDXM and INDXL are two consecutive memory addresses (INDXM is the lower address) that can be used for temporary storage of the indexed address. Note that ADC adds in the carry from the 8 least significant bits.

PROBLEM 6-6

Write a program that subtracts from accumulator A the contents of the memory location nine beyond the one addressed by the index register and stores the result back in that location.

Example:

$$(X) = 0040$$

Result:

$$(0049) = (A) - (0049)$$

Remember that the parentheses indicate "contents of."

PROBLEM 6-7

Write a program that moves the contents of the memory location immediately before the one addressed by the index register to the memory location immediately after the one addressed by the index register.

Example:

$$(X) = 0043$$

Result:

$$(0044) = (0042)$$

PROBLEM 6-8

Write a program that adds 3 to the contents of the index register. Write one version that uses INX and one version that performs the addition in the accumulators, using memory locations 0040 and 0041 for temporary storage. Which version is shorter? Which one executes more quickly? Which version is better if you have to add 9 to the contents of the index register? How could you add the contents of memory locations 0042 and 0043 (MSBs in 0042) to the index register?

Examples:

$$(X) = A0FE$$
$$(0042) = 02$$
$$(0043) = 6E$$

Results:

a)   After adding 3 to the index register

$$(X) = A101$$

b)   After adding 9 to the index register

$$(X) = A107$$

c)   After adding (0042) and (0043) to the index register

$$(X) = A0FE + 026E$$
$$= A36C$$

Note that none of the results (in X) is an actual memory address in the MEK6800D2 microcomputer.

SUM OF DATA

A simple example of array processing is finding the sum of the elements. This task is part of calculating an average, a summation, or a numerical integral. The following program assumes that there are four elements in memory locations 0042 through 0045 (see Figure 6-2 for a flowchart):

	LDAB	#4	COUNT = 4
	LDX	#$42	POINT TO START OF ARRAY
	CLRA		CLEAR THE SUM INITIALLY
ADDELM	ADDA	0,X	ADD AN ELEMENT TO THE SUM
	INX		
	DECB		
	BNE	ADDELM	
	STAA	$40	SAVE SUM
	SWI		

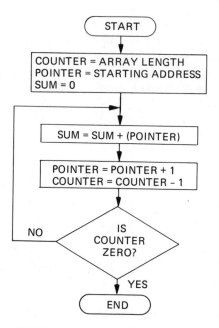

FIGURE 6-2. Flowchart of summation program.

Program 6-1 is the hexadecimal version.

PROGRAM 6-1

MEMORY ADDRESS (HEX)	MEMORY CONTENTS (HEX)	INSTRUCTION (MNEMONIC)	
0000	C6	LDAB	#4
0001	04		
0002	CE	LDX	#$42
0003	00		
0004	42		
0005	4F	CLRA	

MEMORY ADDRESS (HEX)	MEMORY CONTENTS (HEX)		INSTRUCTION (MNEMONIC)	
0006	AB	ADDELM	ADDA	0,X
0007	00			
0008	08		INX	
0009	5A		DECB	
000A	26		BNE	ADDELM
000B	FA			
000C	97		STAA	$40
000D	40			
000E	3F		SWI	

Run Program 6-1 with the following data:

$$(0042) = 07$$

$$(0043) = 23$$

$$(0044) = 31$$

$$(0045) = 20$$

Result:

$$(0040) = 7B$$

Remember that all the numbers are hexadecimal. Replace (0042) with F1. What is the result, and why?

Implement the following variations.

PROBLEM 6-9

Add six numbers starting with memory location 0042.

Sample Problem:

$$(0042) = 07$$

$$(0043) = 23$$

$$(0044) = 31$$

$$(0045) = 20$$

$$(0046) = 16$$

$$(0047) = 38$$

Result:

$$(0040) = C9$$

PROBLEM 6-10

Get the number of elements in the array from memory location 0041.

Sample Problem:

$$(0041) = 05 \quad \text{(i.e., the array has five elements)}$$
$$(0042) = 07$$
$$(0043) = 23$$
$$(0044) = 31$$
$$(0045) = 20$$
$$(0046) = 16$$

Result:

$$(0040) = 91$$

PROBLEM 6-11

Change Program 6-1 so that it EXCLUSIVE ORs the numbers together instead of adding them. The result is called a *logical sum* or *checksum* and is often used to detect errors in tape or disk records.

Sample Problem (four data items starting with memory location 0042, result in 0040):

$$(0042) = 07$$
$$(0043) = 23$$
$$(0044) = 31$$
$$(0045) = 20$$

Result:

$$(0040) = 35$$

PROBLEM 6-12

Extend Program 6-1 so that it saves the carries and stores the 16-bit sum in memory locations 0040 and 0041 (MSBs in 0040).

Sample Problem:

$$(0042) = F7$$
$$(0043) = 23$$
$$(0044) = 31$$
$$(0045) = 20$$
$$(0046) = 16$$

Result:

$$(0040) = 01 \text{ (MSBs of sum)}$$
$$(0041) = 81 \text{ (LSBs of sum)}$$

USING A TERMINATOR

If you are not sure how long the array is (or do not want to count the elements each time), you can end the array with a special marker or terminator. Note that the terminator must have a value that cannot be confused with a real element. In the case of a sum, zero is a good choice because it does not affect the sum anyway. The program using the terminator is (see Figure 6-3 for a flowchart)

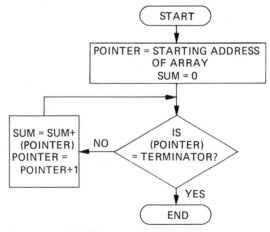

FIGURE 6-3. Flowchart of summation program with terminator.

```
LDX     #$42       POINT TO START OF ARRAY
CLRA               CLEAR THE SUM INITIALLY
```

```
ADDELM    TST     0,X      IS ELEMENT = TERMINATOR (ZERO)?
          BEQ     DONE     YES, DONE
          ADDA    0,X      NO, SUM = SUM + ELEMENT
          INX
          BRA     ADDELM
DONE      STAA    $40      SAVE SUM
          SWI
```

Program 6-2 contains the hexadecimal version. The instruction TST subtracts zero from the contents of the specified memory location or accumulator, thus setting the flags according to those contents without changing any registers or memory locations.

PROGRAM 6-2

MEMORY ADDRESS (HEX)	MEMORY CONTENTS (HEX)		INSTRUCTION (MNEMONIC)	
0000	CE		LDX	#$42
0001	00			
0002	42			
0003	4F		CLRA	
0004	6D	ADDELM	TST	0,X
0005	00			
0006	27		BEQ	DONE
0007	05			
0008	AB		ADDA	0,X
0009	00			
000A	08		INX	
000B	20		BRA	ADDELM
000C	F7			
000D	97	DONE	STAA	$40
000E	40			
000F	3F		SWI	

Run Program 6-2 with the following data:

$$(0042) = 07$$

$$(0043) = 23$$

$$(0044) = 31$$

$$(0045) = 20$$

$$(0046) = 16$$

$$(0047) = 38$$
$$(0048) = 00$$

Result:

$$(0040) = C9$$

What happens if you set (0045) = 00?

What are the advantages and disadvantages of using a terminator as compared to counting the number of elements? Which approach results in faster executing programs? Which approach makes data entry simpler?

Try the following variations.

PROBLEM 6-13

Revise Program 6-2 so that it loads the current element into accumulator B. Use the instruction ABA (add accumulator B to accumulator A and place the sum in accumulator A). Write a version that requires only one branch instruction. (*Hint:* Use TSTB to set the flags according to the current contents of accumulator B.)

PROBLEM 6-14

If some elements in the array could be zero, a different terminator must be used. Revise Program 6-2 to use FF as a terminator. Would this approach be better than the one in Program 6-2 if the data values were the numbers of characters received from a teletypewriter [10 characters per second (cps)] in 1 s? Which approach would be better if the values were the time delays between characters? Assume that the processor must wait one time unit before it checks for the next character and will end the search if the next character does not appear before 256 time units have elapsed.

DISPLAYING AN ARRAY

We can also use this method to place different data on each of the six seven-segment displays: that is (see Figure 6-4 for a flowchart),

```
START      LDAA    '#%00100000      START WITH LEFTMOST DISPLAY
           STAA    $8022
           LDX     #$42             POINT TO START OF ARRAY
DSPLY      LDAA    0,X              GET DATA
           STAA    $8020            SEND DATA TO DISPLAY
           LDAA    #CT1             DELAY A WHILE
DLY1       LDAB    #CT2
DLY2       DECB
           BNE     DLY2
           DECA
           BNE     DLY1
```

```
INX                      POINT TO NEXT DATA
LSR     $8022            ACTIVATE NEXT DISPLAY
BNE     DSPLY            IF ANY ARE LEFT
BRA     START            OTHERWISE, START OVER
```

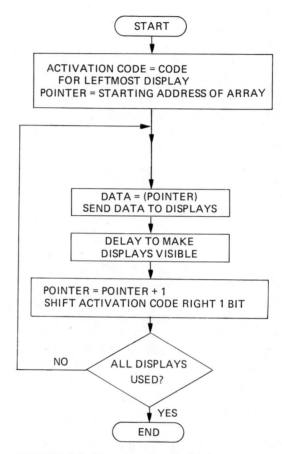

FIGURE 6-4. Flowchart for displaying an array.

The hexadecimal version is Program 6-3.

PROGRAM 6-3

MEMORY ADDRESS (HEX)	MEMORY CONTENTS (HEX)	INSTRUCTION (MNEMONIC)		
0000	86	START	LDAA	#%00100000
0001	20			

MEMORY ADDRESS (HEX)	MEMORY CONTENTS (HEX)	INSTRUCTION (MNEMONIC)	
0002	B7	STAA	$8022
0003	80		
0004	22		
0005	CE	LDX	#$42
0006	00		
0007	42		
0008	A6	DSPLY LDAA	0,X
0009	00		
000A	B7	STAA	$8020
000B	80		
000C	20		
000D	86	LDAA	#CT1
000E	CT1		
000F	C6	DLY1 LDAB	#CT2
0010	CT2		
0011	5A	DLY2 DECB	
0012	26	BNE	DLY2
0013	FD		
0014	4A	DECA	
0015	26	BNE	DLY1
0016	F8		
0017	08	INX	
0018	74	LSR	$8022
0019	80		
001A	22		
001B	26	BNE	DSPLY
001C	EB		
001D	20	BRA	START
001E	E1		

Set CT1 = CT2 = 0 and run Program 6-3 with the following data:

$$(0042) = 89$$
$$(0043) = 86$$
$$(0044) = C7$$
$$(0045) = C7$$
$$(0046) = C0$$
$$(0047) = FF$$

PROBLEM 6-15

Set CT2 = 0. Try the following series of hexadecimal values for CT1: 80, 40, 20, 10, 08, 04, 02, 01. Explain what happens. How could you make the program produce a "newspanel"-type display in which the message appears to move to the left?

PROBLEM 6-16

Change the program so that it uses the following data:

$$(0052) = 86$$
$$(0053) = AF$$
$$(0054) = AF$$
$$(0055) = A3$$
$$(0056) = AF$$
$$(0057) = FF$$

Could you make this change if the program were in ROM? Replace LDX #$42 with LDX $40. What must you place in memory locations 0040 and 0041? Now how do you switch messages? Which approach do you think is better?

KEY POINT SUMMARY

1)   Arrays are collections of data items that have similar meanings or purposes. An element of an array is characterized by its position or index; the entire array is characterized by its starting address. Thus, to reach a particular element of an array, you must know the starting address of the array and the index of the element.

2)   The keys to processing arrays are:

- A pointer that holds the address of the element being processed.

- A flexible addressing method that allows a single set of instructions to handle any or all of the elements.

- A counter or terminator that can be used to determine the length of the array.

3) To process arrays with the 6800 microprocessor, you can use the index register to hold the pointer, indexed addressing to reach the data in memory, and an accumulator or memory location to hold the counter or terminator. The other registers or memory locations can be used to hold other pointers or counters.

4) Loops within loops (i.e., nested loops) and variable pointers and counters can be used to handle multidimensional arrays and to provide greater flexibility.

☐ Laboratory 7

Forming Data Arrays

PURPOSE

To learn how to form arrays of data using the MEK6800D2 microcomputer.

PARTS REQUIRED

Eight switches or pushbuttons attached as shown in Figure 2-1.

REFERENCE MATERIALS

L. A. Leventhal, *Introduction to Microprocessors: Software, Hardware, Programming,* Prentice-Hall, Englewood Cliffs, NJ, 1978, pp. 179-198.

L. A. Leventhal, *6800 Assembly Language Programming,* Osborne/McGraw-Hill, Berkeley, CA, 1978, Chapter 5.

W. J. Weller, *Practical Microcomputer Programming: The M6800,* Northern Technology Books, Evanston, IL, 1977, Chapters 4, 5, and 9.

MEK6800D2 Evaluation Kit II Manual, Motorola Semiconductor Products Inc., Austin, TX, 1977, p. 2-3 (I/O devices), Appendix 3 (schematic diagrams).

M6800 Programming Reference Manual, Motorola Semiconductor Products Inc., Phoenix, AZ, 1976, pp. 4-4 through 4-6 (indexed addressing).

L. A. Leventhal, "Take Advantage of 8080 and 6800 Data-Manipulation Capabilities," *Electronic Design,* April 12, 1977, pp. 90-97. Note the corrections in *Electronic Design,* August 2, 1977, p. 8.

WHAT YOU SHOULD LEARN

1) How to use pointers and counters to form arrays.

2) How to terminate array formation.

3) How to clear an area of memory.

4) How to place starting values in an area of memory.

5) How to enter input data into an array.

6) How to access a specific element in an array.

7) How to keep counts or running totals in an array.

TERMS

Arithmetic shift—a shift operation that preserves the value of the sign bit (most significant bit). In a right shift, this results in the sign bit being copied into the succeeding bit positions (called *sign extension*).

Clear—set to zero.

Logical shift—a shift operation that places 0's in the empty bits.

6800 INSTRUCTIONS

ASR—arithmetic shift right; shift each bit of an accumulator or memory location right one bit, retaining the value of the sign or most significant bit (bit 7).

BHI—branch if higher; jump over the specified number of memory locations if both the CARRY flag and the ZERO flag are 0; otherwise, proceed to the next instruction in sequence. Note that, after a CMP instruction, BCC and BHI are identical, except that BCC causes a branch if the operands were equal (setting the ZERO flag to 1), whereas BHI does not. Thus BCC is an unsigned "branch if Accumulator greater than or equal to memory" and BHI is an unsigned "branch if Accumulator greater than memory."

BLS—branch if lower or same; jump over the specified number of memory locations if either the CARRY flag or the ZERO flag is 1; otherwise, proceed to the next instruction in sequence. Note that, after a CMP instruction, BCS and BLS are identical, except that BLS causes a branch if the operands were equal (setting the CARRY flag to 0 and the ZERO flag to 1), whereas BCS does not. Thus BLS is an unsigned "branch if Accumulator less than or equal to memory" and BCS is an unsigned "branch if Accumulator less than memory."

LSR—logical shift right; shift each bit of an accumulator or memory location right one bit and clear the most significant bit.

NOP—no operation; do nothing except increment the program counter. NOP is a space filler used to allow later insertions or to replace erroneous instructions.

FORMING DATA ARRAYS

The arrays that we used in Laboratory 6 do not, of course, simply appear in the computer's memory. In real applications, the program must form the array before processing it. Typically, array formation requires two variables:

1) A pointer that contains the address of the next empty location in the array.

2) A counter that contains the length of the array.

Remember that on processors such as the 6800, addresses are 16 bits long and data is 8 bits long. So the pointer will occupy either a 16 bit register or two memory locations, and the counter may occupy an 8-bit register or one memory location if the array is less than 256 elements long.

The basic procedure for forming an array is (see Figure 7-1) as follows:

1) Initialization.

POINTER = STARTING ADDRESS OF ARRAY

COUNTER = 0

LENGTH = LENGTH OF ARRAY (if known)

2) Entering an element.

(POINTER) = DATA

POINTER = POINTER + 1

COUNTER = COUNTER + 1

Remember that the parentheses around POINTER mean "contents of." The data may be a constant, the result of a calculation, or an external input.

3) Conclusion.

    a) Maximum count.
       If COUNTER = LENGTH then DONE; otherwise, return to step 2.

    b) Terminator.
       If DATA = TERMINATOR then DONE; otherwise, return to step 2.

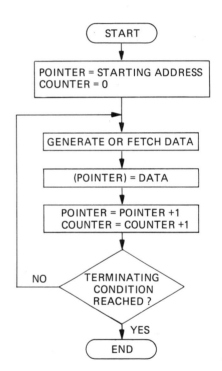

FIGURE 7-1. Flowchart for array formation.

A variety of methods can be used to conclude array formation.

CLEARING AN ARRAY

A simple way to form an array is to start with all elements equal to zero. This is a natural starting point for accumulating totals or test results. Note that you cannot assume that an unused RAM location contains zero; it could start in any state whatsoever when power is applied. The following program clears memory locations 0042 through 0049:

```
        CLRA                DATA = ZERO
        NOP
        LDX     #$42        POINT TO START OF ARRAY
        LDAB    #8          NUMBER OF BYTES = 8
CLR1    STAA    0,X         CLEAR A BYTE
        INX
        DECB
        BNE     CLR1
        SWI
```

The NOP (no operation) does nothing except make the program easier to change. Program 7-1 is the hexadecimal version.

PROGRAM 7-1

MEMORY ADDRESS (HEX)	MEMORY CONTENTS (HEX)		INSTRUCTION (MNEMONIC)	
0000	4F		CLRA	
0001	01		NOP	
0002	CE		LDX	#$42
0003	00			
0004	42			
0005	C6		LDAB	#8
0006	08			
0007	A7	CLR1	STAA	0,X
0008	00			
0009	08		INX	
000A	5A		DECB	
000B	26		BNE	CLR1
000C	FA			
000D	3F		SWI	

Enter and run Program 7-1. Implement the following variations.

PROBLEM 7-1

Clear memory locations 0042 through 0051.

PROBLEM 7-2

Clear memory locations 0052 through 0061.

PROBLEM 7-3

Place 80 hex in memory locations 0042 through 0049.

PROBLEM 7-4

Place the value from memory location 0040 in memory locations starting with 0042 and continuing through a number of locations given by the contents of memory location 0041. Does your program work properly if (0041) = 0?

Example:

$$(0040) = 3F \qquad \text{(value to be stored)}$$
$$(0041) = 03 \qquad \text{(number of locations to be changed)}$$

Result:

$$(0042) = 3F$$
$$(0043) = 3F$$
$$(0044) = 3F$$

The program should not change any memory locations if (0041) = 00.

PLACING VALUES IN AN ARRAY

The next step is to place a different value in each element of the array. The following program places the element number or index in each element (see Figure 7-2 for a flowchart). Program 7-2 is the hexadecimal version.

```
        CLRA              ELEMENT NUMBER = ZERO
        NOP
        LDX    #$42       POINT TO START OF ARRAY
        LDAB   #8         NUMBER OF ELEMENTS = 8
LDNUM   STAA   0,X        ELEMENT = ELEMENT NUMBER
        INCA              ELEMENT NUMBER = ELEMENT NUMBER + 1
        INX
        DECB
        BNE    LDNUM
        SWI
```

PROGRAM 7-2

MEMORY ADDRESS (HEX)	MEMORY CONTENTS (HEX)	INSTRUCTION (MNEMONIC)		
0000	4F		CLRA	
0001	01		NOP	
0002	CE		LDX	#$42
0003	00			
0004	42			
0005	C6		LDAB	#8
0006	08			
0007	A7	LDNUM	STAA	0,X
0008	00			
0009	4C		INCA	
000A	08		INX	
000B	5A		DECB	
000C	26		BNE	LDNUM
000D	F9			
000E	3F		SWI	

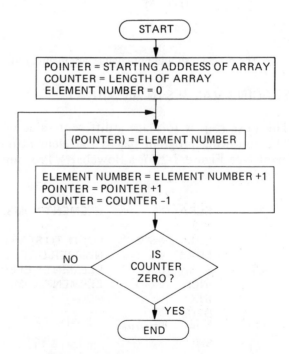

FIGURE 7-2. Flowchart for placing the element numbers in an array.

Enter and run this program. Note that this program is more than just an academic exercise, since it produces an array of identification numbers. For example, assume that you have another corresponding array with test results or totals. You could sort that array into increasing or decreasing order while using the identification numbers to keep track of the original positions (or meanings) of the elements. For instance, you could start with

IDENTIFICATION ARRAY	RESULT ARRAY
0	40
1	27
2	66
3	59

and end up with (in decreasing order of results)

IDENTIFICATION ARRAY	RESULT ARRAY
2	66
3	59
0	40
1	27

Try the following variations.

PROBLEM 7-5

Reverse the order of the elements; that is, start with (0042) = 07 and end with (0049) = 00.

PROBLEM 7-6

Start with 1 and let each subsequent element have twice the value of the previous element; that is,

$$(0042) = 01$$

$$(0043) = 02$$

$$(0044) = 04$$

$$(0045) = 08$$

$$(0046) = 10$$

$$(0047) = 20$$
$$(0048) = 40$$
$$(0049) = 80$$

Do you need a counter in your program? The operation that is involved is a *logical shift,* since the empty bit is cleared.

PROBLEM 7-7

Create the following sequence:

$$(0042) = 80 \quad (10000000 \text{ binary})$$
$$(0043) = C0 \quad (11000000 \text{ binary})$$
$$(0044) = E0 \quad (11100000 \text{ binary})$$
$$(0045) = F0 \quad (11110000 \text{ binary})$$
$$(0046) = F8 \quad (11111000 \text{ binary})$$
$$(0047) = FC \quad (11111100 \text{ binary})$$
$$(0048) = FE \quad (11111110 \text{ binary})$$
$$(0049) = FF \quad (11111111 \text{ binary})$$

What are the values of these numbers if they are in the two's-complement form? The operation shown is a right *arithmetic shift,* since it does not change the sign bit.

ENTERING INPUT DATA INTO AN ARRAY

The next task will be to form an array from switch entries. The steps will be (see Figure 7-3) as follows:

1) Initialize the array.

    POINTER = BASE ADDRESS

    COUNTER = LENGTH OF ARRAY (4)

2) Wait for a switch to be closed.
3) Debounce the switch closure.
4) Identify the switch.
5) Enter the switch number into the array.

    (POINTER) = SWITCH NUMBER

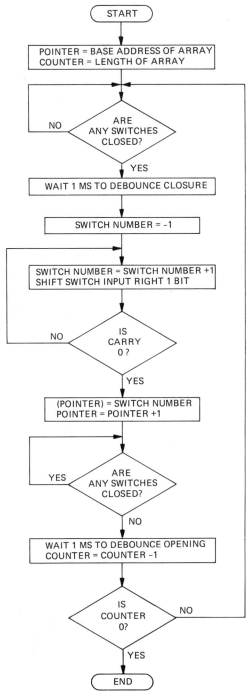

FIGURE 7-3. Flowchart for forming an array from the switches.

$$\text{POINTER} = \text{POINTER} + 1$$

$$\text{COUNTER} = \text{COUNTER} - 1$$

6) Wait for all switches to be open.

7) Debounce the switch opening.

8) If COUNTER $\neq$ 0, return to step 2.

The following program forms an array starting in memory location A050 from 4 switch closures (all switches must be opened between closures).

```
*
*    SET UP USER PIA PORT A FOR INPUT
*
        CLR    $8005          ACCESS DATA DIRECTION REGISTER
        CLR    $8004          MAKE PORT A LINES INTO INPUTS
        LDAA   #%00000100     ENABLE DATA TRANSFERS
        STAA   $8005
*
*    INITIALIZE COUNTER AND POINTER FOR ARRAY FORMATION
*
        LDX    #$A050         POINT TO START OF ARRAY
        LDAA   #4             COUNTER = ARRAY LENGTH
        STAA   $60
*
*    WAIT FOR SWITCH TO BE CLOSED
*
WAITC   LDAA   $8004          GET SWITCH DATA
        CMPA   #$FF           ARE ANY SWITCHES CLOSED?
        BEQ    WAITC          NO, WAIT
*
*    DEBOUNCE SWITCH CLOSURE WITH 1 MS DELAY
*
        LDAB   #$67           DELAY 1 MS AFTER CLOSURE
DLYC    DECB
        BNE    DLYC
*
*    IDENTIFY SWITCH BY SHIFTING INPUT
*
        LDAB   #$FF           SWITCH NUMBER = −1
IDSW    INCB                  ADD 1 TO SWITCH NUMBER
        LSRA                  SWITCH POSITION FOUND?
        BCS    IDSW           NO, KEEP SHIFTING INPUT
*
*    ENTER SWITCH NUMBER INTO ARRAY
*
```

```
        STAB    0,X             PUT SWITCH NUMBER IN ARRAY
        INX                     MOVE POINTER TO NEXT ARRAY LOCATION
*
*   WAIT FOR ALL SWITCHES TO OPEN
*
WAITO   LDAA    $8004           GET SWITCH DATA
        CMPA    #$FF            ARE ANY SWITCHES CLOSED?
        BNE     WAITO           YES, WAIT
*
*   DEBOUNCE SWITCH OPENING WITH 1 MS DELAY
*
        LDAB    #$67            DELAY 1 MS AFTER OPENING
DLYO    DECB
        BNE     DLYO
*
*   COUNT SWITCH CLOSURES
*
        DEC     $60
        BNE     WAITC
        SWI
```

Remember that an * indicates an entire line of comments in 6800 assembler notation. Program 7-3 is the hexadecimal version; enter and run the program. Use the following sequence of switch closures: 5, 7, 0, 3. Remember to open all switches after each closure. The results should be

$$(A050) = 05$$

$$(A051) = 07$$

$$(A052) = 00$$

$$(A053) = 03$$

PROGRAM 7-3

MEMORY ADDRESS (HEX)	MEMORY CONTENTS (HEX)	INSTRUCTION (MNEMONIC)	
0000	7F	CLR	$8005
0001	80		
0002	05		
0003	7F	CLR	$8004
0004	80		
0005	04		
0006	86	LDAA	#%00000100
0007	04		

MEMORY ADDRESS (HEX)	MEMORY CONTENTS (HEX)	INSTRUCTION (MNEMONIC)	
0008	B7	STAA	$8005
0009	80		
000A	05		
000B	CE	LDX	#$A050
000C	A0		
000D	50		
000E	86	LDAA	#4
000F	04		
0010	97	STAA	$60
0011	60		
0012	B6	WAITC LDAA	$8004
0013	80		
0014	04		
0015	81	CMPA	#$FF
0016	FF		
0017	27	BEQ	WAITC
0018	F9		
0019	C6	LDAB	#$67
001A	67		
001B	5A	DLYC DECB	
001C	26	BNE	DLYC
001D	FD		
001E	C6	LDAB	#$FF
001F	FF		
0020	5C	IDSW INCB	
0021	44	LSRA	
0022	25	BCS	IDSW
0023	FC		
0024	E7	STAB	0,X
0025	00		
0026	08	INX	
0027	B6	WAITO LDAA	$8004
0028	80		
0029	04		
002A	81	CMPA	#$FF
002B	FF		
002C	26	BNE	WAITO
002D	F9		
002E	C6	LDAB	#$67
002F	67		
0030	5A	DLYO DECB	
0031	26	BNE	DLYO
0032	FD		

MEMORY ADDRESS (HEX)	MEMORY CONTENTS (HEX)	INSTRUCTION (MNEMONIC)	
0033	7A	DEC	$60
0034	00		
0035	60		
0036	26	BNE	WAIT
0037	DA		
0038	3F	SWI	

Revise Program 7-3 to perform the following tasks:

PROBLEM 7-8

Enter eight switch closures into an array starting at memory location 0061.

PROBLEM 7-9

Use switch 0 as a terminator (i.e., the entry procedure concludes when switch 0 is closed). Can you ever get a data entry of zero?

Hint: If you have to insert a few instructions into the program, a simple procedure is to replace a 2-byte instruction with a BRA (branch unconditionally) to an unused area. In the unused area, place the insert plus the instruction that you replaced. Then complete the patch with a BRA back to the instruction following the one that you replaced. You can replace a 3-byte instruction with a JMP or with a BRA plus an NOP.

PROBLEM 7-10

Take the four entries in memory locations A050 through A053 and combine them to form two two-digit numbers in memory locations 0061 and 0062. Load memory location 0061 with the contents of memory locations A050 (4 MSBs) and A051 (4 LSBs); load memory location 0062 with the contents of memory locations A052 (4 MSBs) and A053 (4 LSBs).

Example:

Switches closed are 6, 3, 4, 2

$$(A050) = 06$$

$$(A051) = 03$$

$$(A052) = 04$$

$$(A053) = 02$$

Result:

$$(0061) = 63$$

$$(0062) = 42$$

Note the obvious similarity between this process and the entry of a four-digit hexadecimal address from the MEK6800D2 keyboard. Remember that the keys are simply binary switches.

ACCESSING SPECIFIC ELEMENTS

Still another problem is how to find a specific element of the array. This is essential when the program must count events (number of transactions of a particular type or number of activations of a particular sensor) or must accumulate data properly (e.g., total for a particular account, test point, or station). For example, the following program clears a particular element of an array starting at address A050. Memory location 0041 contains the element number.

Examples:

1) $(0041) = 02$
   Result: $\{A050 + (0041)\} = (A052) = 00$
2) $(0041) = 07$
   Result: $\{A050 + (0041)\} = (A057) = 00$

```
LDAA    #$A0      GET MSB'S OF STARTING ADDRESS
STAA    $40
LDX     $40       MOVE OFFSET ADDRESS TO INDEX REGISTER
CLR     $50,X     CLEAR ELEMENT
SWI
```

Program 7-4 is the hexadecimal version; enter it and run the two examples. Note the obvious similarity between Program 7-3 and the seven-segment code conversion routine (Program 5-3). Here again, we have allowed the array or table to be located anywhere in memory. Program 7-4 does not depend on the array and the data being close together or being located in the lowest 256 bytes of memory (which can be reached using direct addressing).

Note that the instruction CLR $50,X clears the indexed address (i.e., a memory location); it has no effect on the index register. Be particularly careful of instructions like CLR X and DEC X in which the zero offset is assumed; these instructions affect the memory location addressed by the index register, not the index register itself. Note the difference between DEC X and DEX.

PROGRAM 7-4

MEMORY ADDRESS (HEX)	MEMORY CONTENTS (HEX)	INSTRUCTION (MNEMONIC)	
0000	86	LDAA	#$A0
0001	A0		
0002	97	STAA	$40
0003	40		
0004	DE	LDX	$40
0005	40		
0006	6F	CLR	$50,X
0007	50		
0008	3F	SWI	

Try the following variations of Program 7-4.

PROBLEM 7-11

Place 80 hex in the accessed memory location.

Example:

$$(0041) = 02$$

Result:

$$\{A050 + (0041)\} = (A052) = 80$$

PROBLEM 7-12

Add 1 to the contents of the accessed memory location.

Example:

$$(0041) = 04$$
$$(A054) = CF$$

Result:

$$\{A050 + (0041)\} = (A054) = (A054) + 1 = D0$$

How would you change your program to add 10 (hex) instead of 1? That is, the result should now be (starting from the original example)

$$\{A050 + (0041)\} = (A054) = (A054) + 10 = DF$$

PROBLEM 7-13

Place the value from memory location 0042 in the accessed memory location.

Example:

$$(0041) = 06 \quad (index)$$
$$(0042) = 3F \quad (value)$$

Result:

$$\{A050 + (0041)\} = (A056) = (0042) = 3F$$

How would you make your program only replace the old value in the accessed memory location if the new one is larger? Assume that the numbers are unsigned. This procedure would be necessary if the results represented the worst cases for a set of tests or scaling values for a set of plots.

PROBLEM 7-14

Assume that each element of the array is 2 bytes long and clear the appropriate element.

Example:

$$(0041) = 03$$

Result:

$$\{A050 + 2 \times (0041)\} \quad = (A056) = 00$$
$$\{A050 + 2 \times (0041) + 1\} = (A057) = 00$$

Hint: You will have to double the element number in memory location 0041 (use ASL) and clear the indexed address and the next higher address. Remember the answer to Problem 6-3.

PROBLEM 7-15

Assume that each element of the array is 2 bytes long and place the contents of memory locations 0042 and 0043 in the appropriate element (0042 in the byte at the lower address).

Example:

$$(0041) = 03 \quad \text{(index)}$$
$$(0042) = 3F \quad \text{(8 MSBs of value)}$$
$$(0043) = D1 \quad \text{(8 LSBs of value)}$$

Result:

$$\{(A050 + 2 \times (0041)\} \quad = (A056) = (0042) = 3F$$
$$\{(A050 + 2 \times (0041) + 1\} = (A057) = (0043) = D1$$

COUNTING SWITCH CLOSURES

PROBLEM 7-16

Write a program that counts how many times each switch attached to port A of the user PIA is closed. Only consider single switch closures and assume that all switches must be opened between closures. The steps required are (see Figure 7-4):

1)   Initialize the array of counts by clearing all the elements.

2)   Wait for a switch to be closed.

3)   Debounce the switch closure.

4)   Identify the switch.

5)   Add 1 to the count for that switch.

6)   Wait for all switches to be open.

7)   Debounce the switch opening.

8)   Return to step 2.

Use addresses A050 through A057 for the number of times switches 0 through 7 are closed.

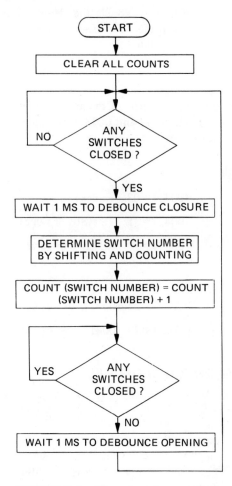

FIGURE 7-4. Flowchart for cumulative counts program.

KEY POINT SUMMARY

1)   Arrays can be formed by using a pointer to hold the address of the next element and a counter to hold the length of the array. Either a maximum length or a terminator can be used to conclude array formation.

2)   On the 6800 microprocessor, the index register can be used conveniently as the pointer while an accumulator or memory location can be used as the counter. You can form an array by using indexed addressing to store the elements and incrementing the pointer in the index register after each storage operation.

3)   To access a particular element in an array, you must know the starting address of the array and the element number or index. The access procedure on the 6800 microprocessor is very similar to the table-lookup procedure: load the index register with the MSBs of the starting address and the element number and use indexed addressing with the LSBs of the starting address as the offset.

4)   You can handle an array with multibyte entries by multiplying the element number times the length of the element and then adding the result to the starting address. Multiplication by a small integer can be implemented as a series of additions. An arithmetic left shift is equivalent to a multiplication by 2.

☐ Laboratory 8

Designing and Debugging Programs

PURPOSE

To learn the fundamental approaches to program design and debugging.

PARTS REQUIRED

None.

REFERENCE MATERIALS

L. A. Leventhal, *Introduction to Microprocessors: Software, Hardware, Programming,* Prentice-Hall, Englewood Cliffs, NJ, 1978, Chapter 6.

L. A. Leventhal, *6800 Assembly Language Programming,* Osborne/McGraw-Hill, Berkeley, CA, 1978, Chapters 13-15.

W. J. Weller, *Practical Microcomputer Programming: The M6800,* Northern Technology Books, Evanston, IL, 1977, Chapter 16, Appendixes A and B.

MEK6800D2 Evaluation Kit II Manual, Motorola Semiconductor Products Inc., Austin, TX, 1977, pp. 1-10 and 1-11 (breakpoint and single-step), 1-11 through 1-17 (operating example), 2-6 (hardware implementation of single-step command).

M6800 Programming Reference Manual, Motorola Semiconductor Products Inc., Phoenix, AZ, 1976, pp. 3-3 through 3-5 (effects of SWI instruction), pp. A-67 through A-68 (SWI instruction).

J. K. Hughes and J. I. Michtom, *A Structured Approach to Programming,* Prentice-Hall, Englewood Cliffs, NJ, 1977.

WHAT YOU SHOULD LEARN

1) The stages of software development.

2) The standard flowcharting symbols.

3) How to use flowcharting as a design tool.

4) How to draw flowcharts.

5) The common debugging tools.

6) How to insert breakpoints on the MEK6800D2 micro-computer.

7) How to use the MEK6800D2 single-step (trace one instruction) mode.

8) How to debug simple programs systematically.

9) Some common errors in 6800 machine language programs.

TERMS

Breakpoint—a condition specified by the user under which execution is to end temporarily, used as an aid in program debugging. The specification of the conditions under which execution will end is referred to as *setting breakpoints* and the deactivation of those conditions is referred to as *clearing breakpoints.*

Bug—error or flaw.

Coding—writing instructions in a computer language.

Data flowchart—a flowchart that traces the path of a particular type of data through the program.

Debugger—a program that helps in finding and correcting errors in a user program. Some versions are referred to as dynamic debugging tools or DDT after the famous insecticide.

Debugging—locating and correcting errors in a system.

Dump—a facility that displays the contents of an entire section of memory or group of registers on an output device.

Editor—a program that manipulates text material and allows the user to make corrections, additions, deletions, and other changes.

File—a collection of related information that is treated as a unit for purposes of storage or retrieval.

Flowchart—a graphic representation of a procedure or computer program.

Modular programming—a programming method whereby the over-all program is divided into logically separate sections or *modules.*

Murphy's Law—the famous maxim that "Whatever can go wrong, will." No one has ever doubted its applicability to computer programming.

No-op (or **no operation**)—an instruction that does nothing other than increment the program counter.

Problem definition—the determination of exactly what requirements a system must meet.

Program design—the design of a computer program to meet the requirements specified in the problem definition.

Program flowchart—a flowchart that traces the operation of the program.

Single step—a facility that allows a program to be executed one step at a time.

Structured programming—a programming method whereby all programs consist of structures from a limited but complete set; each structure should have a single entry and a single exit.

Testing—checking a system to ensure that it meets the requirements specified in the problem definition.

Text file—a file consisting of symbolic characters rather than numbers (a *data file*) or computer instructions (a *program file*).

Top-down design—a design method whereby the overall structure is designed first and parts of the structure are subsequently defined in greater detail.

Trace—a facility that displays all or part of the status of a computer at specified points while a program is being executed.

Unsigned number—a number in which all the bits are used to represent magnitude.

6800 INSTRUCTIONS

NOP—no operation; do nothing except increment the program counter. The hexadecimal code is 01.

STAGES OF SOFTWARE DEVELOPMENT

So far, we have dealt with short programs and we have started with initial versions. In real applications, of course, programming is far more difficult and uncertain. We will not (and cannot) deal with all its aspects here, but we will discuss design and debugging in enough detail so that you should be able to write and run short programs.

In fact, software development consists of a series of stages:

1) *Problem definition,* in which you determine exactly what requirements the program must meet.

2) *Program design,* in which you provide a "blueprint" for the program that will meet those requirements.

3) *Coding,* in which you translate the program design into computer instructions. Note that writing instructions is only one of many stages.

4) *Debugging,* in which you locate and correct errors in the program.

5) *Testing,* in which you ensure that the program meets the requirements of the problem definition.

6) *Documentation,* in which you describe the progam so that it can be used, maintained, and extended.

7) *Maintenance,* in which you correct and upgrade the program to handle problems found in field use.

8) *Extension* and *redesign,* in which you upgrade the program to handle new requirements or new tasks.

The life history of a computer program is thus similar to the life history of other engineering projects. As usual, definition, design, debugging, testing, documentation, and maintenance typically require far more time and effort than does the writing of a program (or the construction of a hardware prototype). As with most projects, you should spend an adequate amount of time in the definition and design stages and proceed cautiously and systematically through the debugging and testing stages.

We will concentrate here on simple problems in which

1) The problem definition is specified.

2) The program can be designed with a flowchart.

3) Debugging and testing are virtually the same.

4) The later stages (e.g., documentation, maintenance) can be ignored. This is certainly not the case in actual practice; maintenance is often the most time consuming and costly stage of all.

FLOWCHARTING

Flowcharting is the traditional program design method. Its advantages are that it shows the structure of the program in a pictorial form, it has a set of standard symbols (see Figure 8-1), and it is well understood even by those who are unfamiliar with computer programming.

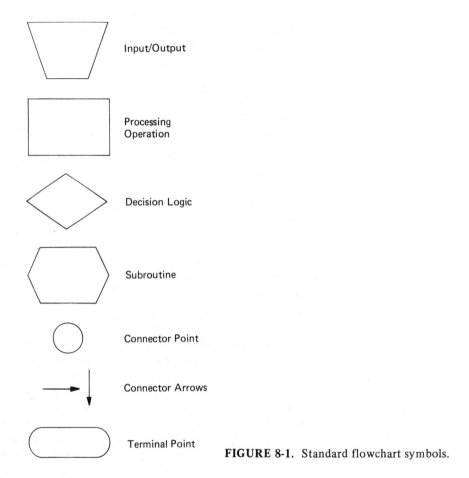

FIGURE 8-1. Standard flowchart symbols.

We strongly recommend the following approach to flowcharting:

1)   Start by drawing a rough flowchart. Don't worry about how artistic it is or whether it is a complete representation of the program.

2)   Check the flowchart for obvious errors and possible improvements. Be sure that all branches lead somewhere, all variables are initialized or derived, and all decisions make sense (try a simple case if you are not sure).

3)   Now draw a revised flowchart. Again, do not worry about the details or the appearance.

4)   When you finish coding, debugging, and testing the program, draw a clear, current flowchart as part of the final documentation.

Don't let the flowchart become a burden. There is no systematic way to debug a flowchart or to code from it. You might as well write an initial program. If the logic of the program is complex, flowcharting is not a satisfactory design method. You must then consider such methods as modular programming, structured programming, and top-down design, which are described in the references.

FLOWCHARTING EXAMPLE 1—COUNTING ZEROS

Purpose:

Count the number of 0's in memory locations 0041 through 0048 and place the result in memory location 0040.

Sample Case:

$$(0041) = 37$$
$$(0042) = 40$$
$$(0043) = 00$$
$$(0044) = 5E$$
$$(0045) = 00$$
$$(0046) = D1$$
$$(0047) = 39$$
$$(0048) = 00$$

Result:

(0040) = 03, since there are 0's in memory locations 0043, 0045, and 0048.

Our initial flowchart is Figure 8-2. A hand check shows that we forgot to initialize NZERO and that we inverted the branches after deciding whether the memory location contains zero. Figure 8-3 shows the improved flowchart which we will use as a guide in writing the program. We have not checked the flowchart in detail; we will describe how to debug the actual program later.

PROBLEM 8-1

Draw a flowchart for a program that counts the number of values in memory locations 0042 through 0049 that exceed the value in memory location 0041. Place the result in memory location 0040. Assume that all numbers are unsigned.

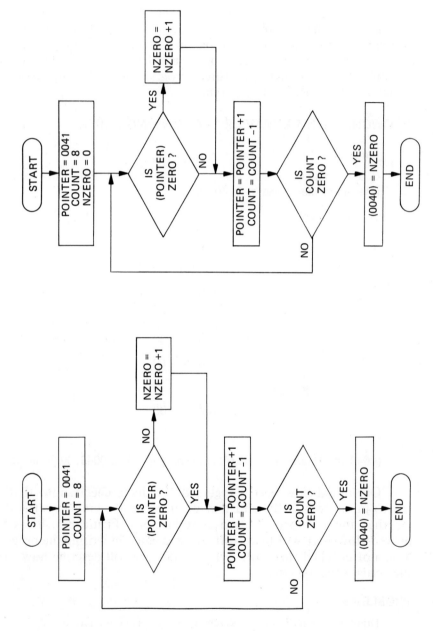

FIGURE 8-2. Initial flowchart for the zero counting program.

FIGURE 8-3. Improved flowchart for the zero counting program.

Example:

$$(0041) = 67 \text{ (threshold)}$$
$$(0042) = 35 \text{ (first value)}$$
$$(0043) = 4A$$
$$(0044) = A9$$
$$(0045) = 67$$
$$(0046) = B3$$
$$(0047) = 69$$
$$(0048) = 14 \text{ (last value)}$$

Result:

(0040) = 03, since memory locations 0044, 0046, and 0047 contain values larger than the one in memory location 0041.

PROBLEM 8-2

Draw a flowchart for a program that searches an array in memory locations 0042 through 0049 for a nonzero value. If one is found, the search terminates, the value is placed in memory location 0041, and the memory location from which it was taken is cleared. If no nonzero value is found, memory location 0041 is cleared.

Example 1:

$$(0042) = 00$$
$$(0043) = 00$$
$$(0044) = 06$$
$$(0045) = 13$$
$$(0046) = 00$$
$$(0047) = 12$$
$$(0048) = 04$$
$$(0049) = 07$$

Result:

(0041) = 06, since that is the first nonzero value encountered. (0044) = 00, since the element removed from the array is then cleared.

Example 2:

$$(0042) \text{ through } (0049) = 00$$

Result:

(0041) = 00, since all the elements of the array are zero.

FLOWCHARTING EXAMPLE 2—FINDING A MAXIMUM VALUE

Purpose:

Find the maximum unsigned binary number in memory locations 0041 through 0048 and store it in memory location 0040.

Sample Case:

$$(0041) = 37$$

$$(0042) = 40$$

$$(0043) = 88$$

$$(0044) = 5E$$

$$(0045) = 2B$$

$$(0046) = D1$$

$$(0047) = 39$$

$$(0048) = AE$$

Result:

(0040) = D1, since that is the largest unsigned binary number.

Our initial flowchart is Figure 8-4. A simple hand check shows that we forgot to initialize MAX and that we forgot to save the new maximum. In fact, as you will probably see if you implement the program, even the flowchart of Figure 8-5 is far from optimal.

PROBLEM 8-3

Draw a flowchart for a program that finds the minimum unsigned binary number in memory locations 0041 through 0048 and stores it in memory location 0040.

Example:

$$(0041) = 37$$

$$(0042) = 40$$

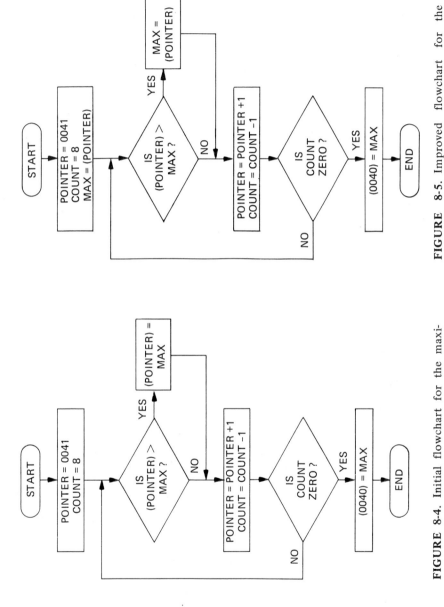

FIGURE 8-4. Initial flowchart for the maximum program.

FIGURE 8-5. Improved flowchart for the maximum program.

$$(0043) = 88$$
$$(0044) = 5E$$
$$(0045) = 2B$$
$$(0046) = D1$$
$$(0047) = 39$$
$$(0048) = AE$$

Result:

(0040) = 2B, since that is the smallest unsigned binary number.

PROBLEM 8-4

Draw a flowchart for a program that finds the maximum unsigned 16-bit binary number in memory locations 0042 through 0049 and stores it in memory locations 0040 and 0041. All numbers are stored in the Motorola style with the most significant bits first (i.e., at the lower address).

Example:

(0042) = 88 (MSBs of first number)
(0043) = 40 (LSBs of first number)
(0044) = 2B (MSBs of second number)
(0045) = 5E (LSBs of second number)
(0046) = 39 (MSBs of third number)
(0047) = D1 (LSBs of third number)
(0048) = A6 (MSBs of fourth number)
(0049) = AE (LSBs of fourth number)

Result:

(0040) = A6 (MSBs of maximum)
(0041) = AE (LSBs of maximum)

since A6AE is the maximum unsigned 16-bit binary number (A6AE is larger than 39D1, 2B5E, or 8840).

FLOWCHARTING EXAMPLE 3—PRODUCE A SPECIFIED DELAY

Purpose: A switch attached to bit 7 of port A of the user PIA acts as a DELAY switch. When the switch is closed, the processor waits for the number of seconds (0 through 63) specified by the switches attached to bits 0 through 5 of port A of the user PIA.

Sample Case:

The switches attached to bit positions 0 through 5 of user PIA port A produce a reading of 011110 (1 = open, 0 = closed). When the switch attached to bit 7 of port A is closed, the processor will wait for 30 s (011110 binary = 1E hex = 30 decimal). Figure 8-6 contains the initial flowchart. A check shows that the flowchart is incorrect if the length of the delay is zero. (Why?) Figure 8-7 contains the revised flowchart.

PROBLEM 8-5

Draw a flowchart for an extended program that uses the switch attached to bit 6 of port A to determine if the delay is to be in seconds (switch open) or in milliseconds (switch closed).

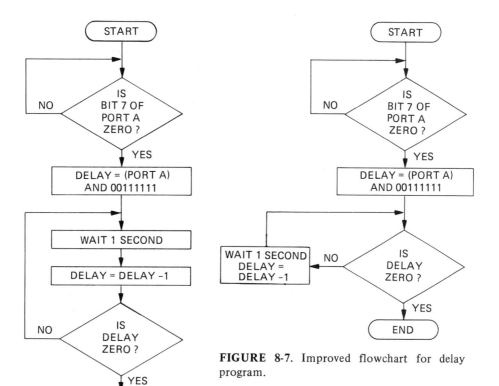

FIGURE 8-7. Improved flowchart for delay program.

FIGURE 8-6. Initial flowchart for delay program.

PROBLEM 8-6

Draw a flowchart for an extended program that uses the switch attached to bit 6 of port A to escape from the delay. The program should check that switch every tenth of a second to see if the delay should be continued. If that switch is closed, the delay is immediately ended.

DEBUGGING TOOLS

There are several important debugging tools, most of which are available in the JBUG monitor. The tools are:

1) A *breakpoint*, which allows the user to stop the program and examine the current status. Breakpoints allow you to localize an error within a section of a program and pass through sections that are known to be correct.

2) A *single-step* facility, which allows the user to execute the program one step at a time. The JBUG monitor provides this capability. A single-step mode allows you to pinpoint an error.

3) A *dump*, which displays the contents of an entire section of memory on an output device. The MIKBUG and MINIBUG teletypewriter monitors have this capability. A dump allows you to examine many values simultaneously. The JBUG monitor can only show you the contents of one register or memory location at a time.

4) A *trace*, which displays the current contents of registers and memory locations while the program is executing. Traces provide a detailed accounting of the operation of the program. The JBUG monitor provides tracing in conjunction with the single-step mode (referred to in the *Evaluation Kit II Manual* as the ability to "Trace One Instruction"). This is a simple tracing capability that the operator must activate with the G key as described earlier.

BREAKPOINTS

You can insert a breakpoint in a MEK6800D2 program by placing the SWI instruction (3F) in the appropriate memory location. This instruction returns control to the monitor while saving the current status of the program. You may then examine the registers by using the G key (see Table 1-1 for the order). You can also exit from the register display by pressing the blue E key. You can then examine memory locations and perform other functions. The only problem is that you must add 1 to the program counter (using the addresses in Table 1-2) before pressing G to resume the program; the increment is necessary because JBUG decrements the program counter by 1 so that it contains the address of the SWI instruction.

The JBUG monitor allows you to insert (or set) and remove (or clear) breakpoints automatically by merely specifying the addresses. The procedures are as follows:

1) To set a breakpoint, enter the hexadecimal address at which you want it placed and press the V key (top row, rightmost column). Then press the E key to exit from the entry procedure.

2) To clear all breakpoints, simply press V (i.e., without entering a hexadecimal address) while the JBUG prompt is displayed.

The JBUG monitor allows up to five breakpoints. Once you have set the breakpoints, the monitor takes charge. When you enter a starting address and press G to execute a program, the monitor replaces the operation codes in the specified memory addresses with SWI instructions. When the program reaches a breakpoint, it returns control to the monitor and the monitor restores the original operation codes before displaying the breakpoint address and the contents of that address. When you resume the program by pressing G (without entering a new address), the monitor program executes the instruction that was replaced by SWI before restoring the breakpoints.

Some points to watch are:

1) The program stops before the address in which you place the breakpoint; the computer does not execute the instruction in that address until you resume the program by pressing G.

2) You must set breakpoints only at addresses that contain operation codes. Replacing data or parts of addresses with SWI instructions will obviously result in chaos.

3) If you insert SWI instructions yourself, replace only operation codes and do not let the computer return to your program in the middle of an instruction. You may, of course, leave extra locations in which you can place either SWI or NOP instructions. Remember to increment the program counter in the stack before resuming the program (as we noted, JBUG handles this problem if you use its breakpointing facility).

We should note that development systems usually have far more extensive breakpoint facilities than the MEK6800D2 microcomputer has. Useful features include the ability to clear individual breakpoints, set an arbitrary number of breakpoints, and set breakpoints on the following conditions:

1) Whenever a particular operation code is executed. The usual ones selected are those that perform input or output operations.

2)   Whenever a particular memory address is referenced.

3)   Whenever a particular sequence of instructions is executed.

4)   Whenever the instruction at a particular ROM address is executed. Obviously, neither you nor the monitor program can replace an instruction in ROM.

5)   Whenever a particular signal or combination of signals occurs. This is a purely hardware breakpoint.

Still more advanced features include the ability to combine the simpler features and to count the number of occurrences. Note the parallels between the ways in which one can set breakpoints and the ways in which one can specify triggering events on an oscilloscope.

SINGLE-STEP MODE

You can put the MEK6800D2 microcomputer into a single-step mode by:

1)   Setting a breakpoint at the start of the program (or section of a program) with the V key.

2)   Starting program execution at the specified address with the G key.

3)   Executing the program one step at a time by pressing the N key repeatedly. Note that pressing N also removes all the breakpoints.

You can trace the registers by pressing the G key after the execution of an instruction. The first two steps in this procedure simply establish a starting address for the single-step mode and are unnecessary if the starting address already exists. Each time you press N, the MEK6800D2 will execute one instruction (which may occupy one to three memory locations) and will display the next operation code and its address. You can, of course, return to the prompt by pressing the blue E key. Remember that the MEK6800D2 displays the next operation code, not the one that it has just executed.

Important Note: Remember that Table 1-1 contains the order in which registers are displayed after the execution of SWI or the pressing of the R key. That order is:

Program Counter and contents of address in Program Counter

Index Register

Accumulator A

Accumulator B

Condition Code Register

Stack Pointer

You can move down the list (in a circular manner) by pressing the G key. Table 1-2 specifies the memory locations that you must change if you wish to alter the contents of a register before resuming the program. The locations are:

(A008 and A009)—Stack Pointer (S)

S+1—Condition Code Register

S+2—Accumulator B

S+3—Accumulator A

S+4—High-order (most significant) byte of Index Register

S+5—Low-order (least significant) byte of Index Register

S+6—High-order (most significant) byte of Program Counter

S+7—Low-order (least significant) byte of Program Counter

DEBUGGING EXAMPLE—COUNTING ZEROS

From the flowchart in Figure 8-3, we code the following program for counting zeros:

```
              LDX      $41
              LDAB     8
              CLRA
              LDAA     X
CNTZ          BEQ      CHCNT
              INCA
CHCNT         INC      X
              DECB
              BEQ      CNTZ
              STAA     $40
              SWI
```

Program 8-1 is the hexadecimal version.

PROGRAM 8-1

MEMORY ADDRESS (HEX)	MEMORY CONTENTS (HEX)	INSTRUCTION (MNEMONIC)	
0000	CE	LDX	#$41
0001	41		

MEMORY ADDRESS (HEX)	MEMORY CONTENTS (HEX)		INSTRUCTION (MNEMONIC)	
0002	D6		LDAB	8
0003	08			
0004	4F		CLRA	
0005	A6		LDAA	X
0006	00			
0007	27	CNTZ	BEQ	CHCNT
0008	01			
0009	4C		INCA	
000A	6C	CHCNT	INC	X
000B	5A		DECB	
000C	26		BNE	CNTZ
000D	F9			
000E	96		LDAA	$40
000F	3F		SWI	

Enter this program but *don't run it. Important rule:* Never just let a program run the first time. The program may easily write over itself or cause other problems. Expect errors and plan for them.

Let us first place a breakpoint at the end of the initialization (i.e., in memory location 0005). The way to do this is to press 0, 0, 0, 5 (the breakpoint address), V (set breakpoint), and (blue) E (exit from breakpoint entry function). When the program reaches the breakpoint, the registers should contain the following values:

(A) = 00　　(number of zeros found)

(B) = 08　　(counter)

(X) = 0041　(starting address of array)

Run the program with the breakpoint in it. What are your results? Ours were

(A) = 00

(B) = F9

(X) = 41D8

Obviously, the program is far from correct.

Let us go back and try the single-step mode. We press

blue　E　(escape from register display)

0

```
          0
          0
          0
          V    (set breakpoint at address 0000)
  blue    E    (escape from breakpoint entry)
          0
          0
          0
          0
          G    (start program execution at address 0000)
```

The processor immediately reaches the breakpoint and stops, displaying the program counter (0000) and the contents of that address (CE). We now press N and the processor executes the first instruction in the program. To examine the registers, simply press G and the registers will appear in the order described in Table 1-1. The register contents should be

$$(X) = 0041$$

Instead, they are

$$(X) = 41D6$$

Obviously, we have the wrong instruction. We cannot observe the actual execution of the instruction—all we see are the results. To see more would require a logic analyzer or a control panel that would display the contents of the address and data buses and the states of the various control signals.

The problem here is that the index register is 16 bits long and cannot be loaded with 41 alone. Instead, we must load it with 0041, which should occupy the two memory locations following the operation code. This is a great source of confusion in 6800 programs—maintaining the distinctions among 8-bit data items, 16-bit complete addresses, and 8-bit direct (page-zero) addresses in which the 8 most significant bits are assumed to be zero.

To correct the error, we must load address 0001 with 00 and 0002 with 41. We must then move the remaining instructions down one position in memory. This change forces us to reload the entire program. Obviously, a long program would require a different approach, since reloading thousands of locations would be impractical. The usual approach is to prepare the assembly language program using an editor that allows insertions, deletions, replacements, and other changes. The output of the editor program is a *text file* which can then be assembled. If there are errors in the assembly or in the execution of the program, we can correct them by returning to the editor, making the appropriate changes in the text file (which has been saved in memory, on cassette, or on disk), and reassembling the program. Of course, this approach requires a more elaborate computer (with better peripherals) than the MEK6800D2.

After making the correction (according to Murphy's Law, it was bound to be in the first instruction), we can return to the single-step procedure. We reenter the breakpoint at 0000 (all breakpoints are automatically removed in the single-step mode), start program execution at address 0000, press N to execute the first instruction, and finally check the contents of the index register. The contents are now 0041, just as they should be.

We continue by pressing N to execute the second instruction. Note that you can press N at any time; you do not have to press the blue E key first to exit from the register display.

The results after the second instruction are

$$(X) = 0041$$

$$(B) = 27$$

Thus LDAB 8 is wrong, but why? The simplest alternative would be LDAB #8. This is, in fact, the instruction that we want, since our aim is to load accumulator B with the number 8, not the contents of memory location 0008. Always be careful of the distinction between immediate and direct addressing (i.e., between an address and the contents of that address). The correction is to replace D6 in memory location 0003 with C6.

We can now try the entire initialization routine. First, we must reenter the breakpoint in memory location 0006 (remember that we moved everything down one) and execute the program. The results are correct; that is,

$$(A) = 00$$

$$(B) = 08$$

$$(X) = 0041$$

Note the key points of this debugging exercise:

1)   A breakpoint can tell you if an entire section of a program is correct or not.

2)   A single-step mode (particularly if it allows you to trace the registers) can show you precisely what is wrong.

3)   Inserting instructions or additional words into machine language programs is very difficult because the entire program must be moved. The use of an editor program is the common way to overcome this problem. Note that one can always delete instructions or extra words

since you can replace them with NOP instructions. NOPs have no effect on the program other than to increase its execution time slightly.

A SECOND BREAKPOINT

Now let us remove the first breakpoint and place a second breakpoint at the end of the loop:

1) Press blue E, V, and blue E again to clear the original breakpoint (remember to remove breakpoints that you no longer need).

2) Press 0, 0, 0, D, V, blue E to set a breakpoint in memory location 000D and exit from the breakpoint entry procedure.

Program 8-2 is the current hexadecimal version of the program.

PROGRAM 8-2

MEMORY ADDRESS (HEX)	MEMORY CONTENTS (HEX)		INSTRUCTION (MNEMONIC)	
0000	CE		LDX	#$41
0001	00			
0002	41			
0003	C6		LDAB	#8
0004	08			
0005	4F		CLRA	
0006	A6		LDAA	X
0007	00			
0008	27	CNTZ	BEQ	CHCNT
0009	01			
000A	4C		INCA	
000B	6C	CHCNT	INC	X
000C	5A		DECB	
000D	26		BNE	CHCNT
000E	F9			
000F	96		LDAA	$40
0010	3F		SWI	

We now need some data. Clearly, the alternatives are to make memory location 0041 zero or nonzero. Let us first try

$$(0041) = 00$$

The results at the breakpoint should be

$$(A) = 01$$
$$(B) = 07$$
$$(X) = 0042$$

The results actually are

$$(A) = 00$$
$$(B) = 08$$
$$(X) = 0041$$

We have a clean sweep—all the registers are wrong. The number of zeros in accumulator A and the pointer in the index register have not been incremented and the counter in accumulator B has not been decremented.

Let us restore the breakpoint in memory location 0006 and try the single-step mode again. The procedure is:

1) Press 0, 0, 0, 6, V to set a breakpoint in memory location 0006 and blue E to exit from the breakpoint entry.
2) Press 0, 0, 0, 0, G to start program execution in memory location 0000.
3) Press N to execute the instruction in memory location 0006.

After LDAA X is executed, we should have

$$(A) = ((X)) = (0041) = 00$$

Examining accumulator A shows that its contents are, in fact, correct. We then press N to execute the instruction in memory location 0008.

We can see an error immediately. The BEQ instruction causes a branch around the instruction (INCA) which is supposed to increment the number of zeros. It is not difficult to see that we have inverted the condition logic—that is, we have BEQ (BRANCH IF EQUAL TO ZERO) when we should have BNE (BRANCH IF NOT EQUAL TO ZERO). Inverting decision logic is a common error, particularly when the ZERO flag is involved. Remember that BEQ causes a branch if the ZERO flag is 1 (i.e., the previous result was zero). Fortunately, this error is easy to correct—all that we have to do is change the 27 in memory location 0008 to 26.

After changing memory location 0008 and pressing the blue E key to restore the JBUG prompt, we can then press N to execute the INC X instruction. Clearly, there is another error in that instruction. In the first place, the program counter is increased by 2 instead of by 1, so its final value is 000D. Furthermore, the index register is not incremented. The problem here is that the instruction INC X is not what we want at all— that instruction increments the memory location addressed via indexing.

This is the reason why the program counter was increased by 2—the processor thinks that the 5A in memory location 000C is an indexed offset, not a new instruction. What we need in memory location 000B is INX (08 hex). Note the confusion between the 16-bit index register and the 8-bit memory location that is addressed using the index register.

After making that correction, we can restore the second breakpoint (note again that all breakpoints are cleared in the single-step mode) and try the program again. We will use (0041) = (0042) = 00.

The results after the first iteration are correct, but the number of zeros counted after the second iteration is 1 instead of 2. A hand check of the program shows that we are branching incorrectly and not reloading accumulator A. The label CNTZ should come one instruction earlier. But this change will not solve the problem—now when we reload accumulator A, we will lose the count that is being saved in that register. The solution here is to replace LDAA X with TST X since TST X sets the flags according to the contents of memory without changing any registers. The corrections are (0006) = 6D and (000E) = F7.

Now try the program on some test data, such as

   1)   (0041) − (0048) = 00.

   2)   Same as (1) except that (0041) = 01.

   3)   Same as (1) except that (0048) = 01.

The final version of the program is

```
              LDX     #$41      POINT TO START OF ARRAY
              LDAB    #8        NUMBER OF ELEMENTS = 8
              CLRA              NUMBER OF ZEROS FOUND = ZERO
CNTZ          TST     X         IS NEXT ELEMENT ZERO?
              BNE     CHCNT
              INCA              YES, INCREMENT NUMBER OF ZEROS FOUND
CHCNT         INX
              DECB
              BNE     CNTZ
              LDAA    $40       SAVE NUMBER OF ZEROS FOUND
              SWI
```

Program 8-3 is the hexadecimal program with the corrections that we have discussed.

PROBLEM 8-7

What errors still remain in Program 8-3? Correct them and run the final version for the three test cases that we just described.

PROGRAM 8-3

MEMORY ADDRESS (HEX)	MEMORY CONTENTS (HEX)		INSTRUCTION (MNEMONIC)	
0000	CE		LDX	#$41
0001	00			
0002	41			
0003	C6		LDAB	#8
0004	08			
0005	4F		CLRA	
0006	6D	CNTZ	TST	X
0007	00			
0008	26		BNE	CHCNT
0009	01			
000A	4C		INCA	
000B	08	CHCNT	INX	
000C	5A		DECB	
000D	26		BNE	CNTZ
000E	F7			
000F	96		LDAA	$40
0010	3F		SWI	

PROBLEM 8-8

Revise Program 8-3 so that it counts the number of positive elements in memory locations 0041 through 0048 and stores that number in memory location 0040. An element is positive if its most significant bit (bit 7) is zero, but its value is not zero.

Example:

$$(0041) = 01$$
$$(0042) = 80$$
$$(0043) = 7F$$
$$(0044) = FF$$
$$(0045) = 00$$
$$(0046) = 00$$
$$(0047) = 00$$
$$(0048) = 00$$

Result:

(0040) = 02 since there are positive elements in memory locations 0041 and 0043.

PROBLEM 8-9

Code, debug, and test Flowcharting Example 2, the maximum-value program.

PROBLEM 8-10

Code, debug, and test Flowcharting Example 3, the program that produces a specified delay. The following routine uses accumulator B and the index register to provide a 1-s wait:

```
          LDAB      #2           WAIT 1 SECOND
DLY1      LDX       #$95FE
DLY2      DEX
          BNE       DLY2
          DECB
          BNE       DLY1
```

You may want to check the delay constants for yourself to see that they are approximately correct.

PROBLEM 8-11

Code, debug, and test Problem 8-4, the 16-bit maximum.

COMMON PROGRAMMING ERRORS

You should note the following common errors in 6800 machine language programs:

1) Confusing data and addresses. Watch the difference between immediate and direct addressing; immediate addressing means that the data follows the operation code "immediately" while direct addressing means that the address of the data follows the operation code. Remember that the value stored in a memory location that is addressed directly or through indexing is not related to the address or offset.

2) Inverting the order of two-word addresses. Remember that the 6800 expects the most significant bits first.

3) Copying operation codes incorrectly. You should check programs before executing them.

4) Confusing 8- and 16-bit instructions and operands. Watch the difference between INX and INC X, LDAA X and LDX. Remember that the index register and all complete addresses are 16 bits long, whereas data and short direct addresses are 8 bits long. Be particularly careful of the fact that it takes two memory locations to load or store the 16-bit index register.

5) Inverting the logic of conditional jump instructions (e.g., using BCC instead of BCS or BNE instead of BEQ). Be particularly careful after a comparison or test such as CMP, CPX, or TST.

6) Jumping to the wrong address. This often results in including or not including initialization instructions or instructions that update counters and pointers.

7) Calculating relative offsets incorrectly. You should use the program in the JBUG monitor rather than calculating offsets by hand. If you must change an offset, check the new value carefully.

8) Omitting addresses, offsets, or data. Watch for instructions such as LDX #, which requires 16 bits of data in the next two words (most significant bits first); LDX $40, which requires only an 8-bit direct address; and INC X, which requires an 8-bit offset (00).

Some of these errors (e.g., 2, 3, and 7) will not occur if you use an assembler.

Other common errors are:

9) Failing to initialize counters and pointers.

10) Branching incorrectly when operands are equal (i.e., neither is larger).

11) Overlooking trivial cases such as zero or one element in an array or table, no inputs, and so on.

12) Forgetting that instructions such as LDA, STA, and LDX affect the ZERO and NEGATIVE flags. Remember also that INC, DEC, INX, and DEX do not affect the CARRY, whereas CLR clears the CARRY and COM sets it.

13) Trying to use the same register for several different purposes at the same time. You should use the lower 256 bytes of memory (address 0000-00FF) as extra scratchpad registers, since they can be addressed quickly and efficiently (using the direct mode).

14) Confusing the contents of the index register with the contents of the memory location addressed by that register. Note that CLR X clears an 8-bit memory location, not the 16-bit index register (you need LDX #0—a 3-byte instruction—to clear the index register).

You will undoubtedly make and discover errors that we have not mentioned, but this list should at least suggest some possibilities. Unfortunately, debugging computer programs is more of an art than a science.

KEY POINT SUMMARY

1) The writing of software, like the building of hardware, consists of many stages. Writing the actual computer instructions (or *coding*) is one of the easiest stages.

2)   Flowcharting is a simple graphic technique for designing and documenting programs. A set of standard flowchart symbols is in widespread use.

3)   A flowchart is a good starting point for a program, but it should not become a burden all by itself.

4)   Breakpoints are stopping places in programs that you can use to determine whether sections are correct or to pass through sections that are known to be correct. The MEK6800D2 monitor (JBUG) allows the user to automatically set up to five breakpoints with the V key.

5)   You can use the single-step mode to pinpoint an error, usually after you have used breakpoints to localize it.

6)   Common programming errors include confusing data and addresses, inverting logic or reversing the direction of operations, failing to initialize variables or save results, omitting operands, forgetting how instructions affect flags, ignoring trivial cases, and branching incorrectly.

☐ *Laboratory* **9**

Arithmetic

PURPOSE

To learn to perform arithmetic calculations using the 6800 microprocessor.

PARTS REQUIRED

None.

REFERENCE MATERIALS

L. A. Leventhal, *Introduction to Microprocessors: Software, Hardware, Programming,* Prentice-Hall, Englewood Cliffs, NJ, 1978, pp. 198-210.

L. A. Leventhal, *6800 Assembly Language Programming,* Osborne/McGraw-Hill, Berkeley, CA, 1978, Chapter 8.

W. J. Weller, *Practical Microcomputer Programming: The M6800,* Northern Technology Books, Evanston, IL, 1977, Chapters 5-7, 9-11.

H. Schmid, *Decimal Computation,* John Wiley, New York, 1974.

J. F. Hart et al., *Computer Approximations,* John Wiley, New York, 1968.

Y. L. Luke, *Mathematical Functions and Their Approximations*, Academic Press, New York, 1975.

K. Hwang, *Computer Arithmetic*, John Wiley, New York, 1979.

WHAT YOU SHOULD LEARN

1) The standard BCD representation.

2) How to choose between the binary and BCD representations.

3) What the DAA (DECIMAL ADJUST) instruction does.

4) How to add decimal numbers.

5) How to add 16-bit binary numbers.

6) How to round binary and decimal numbers.

7) How to perform multiple-precision binary and decimal addition.

8) How to use lookup tables to perform arithmetic.

TERMS

BCD (binary-coded-decimal)—a representation of decimal numbers in which each decimal digit is separately coded into a binary number.

Carry—a bit which is 1 if an addition overflows into the succeeding digit position.

Half (or auxiliary) carry—a flag used in 8-bit computers to indicate whether there was a carry from the less significant 4 bits or less significant digit.

Pseudo-operation (or pseudo-op or pseudo-instruction)—an assembly language operation code that directs the assembler to perform some action but does not result in the generation of a machine language instruction.

Rounding—approximating a number by the closest whole number.

Standard (or 8, 4, 2, 1) BCD—a BCD representation in which the bit positions have the same weights as in ordinary binary numbers.

Truncation—dropping the less significant part of a number.

6800 INSTRUCTIONS

ADC—add with carry; add the contents of the specified memory location and the CARRY flag to an accumulator. The result is placed in the accumulator.

CLC—clear carry; set the CARRY flag to zero.

DAA—decimal adjust accumulator A; correct the binary sum in accumulator A to a proper BCD sum using the CARRY (C) and HALF-CARRY (H) flags.

SBC—subtract with carry; subtract the contents of the specified memory location and the CARRY flag from an accumulator. The result is placed in the accumulator.

SEC—set carry; set the CARRY flag to one.

TAB—transfer accumulator A to accumulator B; place the contents of accumulator A in accumulator B. Accumulator A is unchanged.

TBA—transfer accumulator B to accumulator A; place the contents of accumulator B in accumulator A. Accumulator B is unchanged.

6800 ASSEMBLER PSEUDO-OPERATIONS

FCB—form constant byte; place the specified byte-length data (8 bits per item) in the next available memory locations. The items in the list of data should be separated by commas. This pseudo-operation loads memory with fixed data (such as tables, messages, and numerical constants) that is necessary for the proper execution of the program.

FDB—form double-byte constant; place the specified double-byte length data (16 bits per item) in the next available memory locations. The items in the list of data should be separated by commas. This pseudo-operation loads memory with 16-bit fixed data (or addresses).

ORG—set origin; assign the object code generated from the subsequent assembly language statements to memory addresses starting with the one specified. The ORG pseudo-operation allows the assembly language programmer to assign a starting place for the program and to assign subsequent sections of the program to different areas of memory as required.

ARITHMETIC

The processing of data almost always involves arithmetic. Typical operations are the averaging of data readings, scaling, linearization of inputs, calculation of numerical integrals and derivatives, determination of frequency responses, statistical analysis, and preparation of plots. Simple applications require only binary or decimal addition and subtraction. Decimal arithmetic is necessary in calculators, business equipment, terminals, instruments, appliances, and games.

Earlier we showed how to add 8-bit binary numbers and perform an 8-bit binary summation. Here we will describe binary subtraction, decimal addition and subtraction, rounding, multiword binary and decimal addition and subtraction, and the use of lookup tables.

AN 8-BIT SUM

The following program (remember Program 1-3) adds two unsigned binary numbers from memory locations 0040 and 0041 and stores the sum in memory location 0042, ignoring any carry that might be generated.

```
LDX     #$40
LDAA    0,X          GET FIRST NUMBER
ADDA    1,X          ADD SECOND NUMBER
NOP
STAA    2,X          SAVE SUM
SWI
```

The hexadecimal version of this program is Program 9-1.

PROGRAM 9-1

MEMORY ADDRESS (HEX)	MEMORY CONTENTS (HEX)	INSTRUCTION (MNEMONIC)	
0000	CE	LDX	#$40
0001	00		
0002	40		
0003	A6	LDAA	0,X
0004	00		
0005	AB	ADDA	1,X
0006	01		
0007	01	NOP	
0008	A7	STAA	2,X
0009	02		
000A	3F	SWI	

We have included a NOP to simplify the later implementation of a decimal version. Enter Program 9-1 and run it with the following sample data:

1) (0040) = 32
    (0041) = 25
    Result: (0042) = 57

    2)   (0040) = 38
         (0041) = 25
         Result: (0042) = 5D

PROBLEM 9-1

Extend Program 9-1 so that it sets memory location 0043 to 0 if there is no carry from the addition and to 1 if there is. Use the following sample data:

    1)   (0040) = 38
         (0041) = 25
         Result: (0042) = 5D
                 (0043) = 00
    2)   (0040) = 98
         (0041) = 89
         Result: (0042) = 21
                 (0043) = 01

PROBLEM 9-2

Revise Program 9-1 so that it performs binary subtraction instead of binary addition. Run the program with the following sample data:

    1)   (0040) = 32
         (0041) = 25
         Result: (0042) = 0D
    2)   (0040) = 32
         (0041) = 58
         Result: (0042) = DA

PROBLEM 9-3

What is the value of CARRY at the end of each sample run of the binary subtraction program? Is CARRY equal to the actual carry from the two's-complement addition? Remember that the microprocessor performs subtraction by adding the two's complement of the number to be subtracted. Draw a circuit that could form CARRY from the carry output of the arithmetic-logic unit and a status line that differentiates between addition and subtraction instructions. Assume that the status line (SUBTRACT/$\overline{\text{ADD}}$) is 0 if an addition is being performed and 1 if a subtraction is being performed.

THE BINARY-CODED-DECIMAL (BCD) REPRESENTATION

Numbers that are entered, processed, and displayed in decimal form are most conveniently represented in a BCD code, in which each decimal digit is separately coded into 4 bits. In the most popular BCD code (see Table

9-1), the numbers 0 through 9 are the same as in binary. However, numbers above 9 are different because of the separate coding of the decimal digits (see Table 9-2 for some examples). Note the following features of BCD as compared to binary:

1) Each decimal digit is coded separately in BCD. This is not the case in binary, since 10 is not an integral power of 2. Computers will surely correct this situation when they take over the world—people will be required to have either 8 or 16 fingers.

2) The BCD representation is always greater than or equal to the binary representation of the same number.

3) The BCD representation requires more memory than the binary representation. For example, 8 bits can represent a binary number as large as 255 but only 99 in BCD. The number 999 requires three BCD digits (12 bits) but only 10 bits in binary (since $2^{10} = 1024$).

Table 9-1

STANDARD BCD REPRESENTATION

DECIMAL DIGIT	BCD REPRESENTATION
0	0000
1	0001
2	0010
3	0011
4	0100
5	0101
6	0110
7	0111
8	1000
9	1001

Table 9-2

STANDARD BCD REPRESENTATIONS OF SOME DECIMAL NUMBERS

DECIMAL NUMBER	BCD REPRESENTATION	BINARY REPRESENTATION
10	00010000	00001010
11	00010001	00001011
12	00010010	00001100
13	00010011	00001101
16	00010110	00010000
25	00100101	00011001
50	01010000	00110010
66	01100110	01000010
83	10000011	01010011

4)   Some binary numbers are not valid BCD numbers. In the standard BCD code, no digit can have a value between 1010 and 1111 inclusive.

One problem with BCD numbers is that they cannot be processed in binary arithmetic units. This is because the BCD representation of 10 (00010000) is not one larger than the BCD representation of 9 (00001001)—it is, in fact, seven larger. (Try it!) Thus, when you add BCD numbers in a binary adder, you have to include an extra factor of six whenever the sum of two digits is 10 or more.

Example 1:

$$
\begin{array}{r}
33\ (\text{BCD}) \ = \ 00110011 \\
+\,25\ (\text{BCD}) \ = \ \underline{00100101} \\
01011000 \ = \ 58\ (\text{BCD})
\end{array}
$$

There is no problem here, since neither sum of digits is 10 or more.

Example 2:

$$
\begin{array}{r}
38\ (\text{BCD}) \ = \ 00111000 \\
+\,25\ (\text{BCD}) \ = \ \underline{00100101} \\
01011101 \ = \ 5D
\end{array}
$$

Here we need an extra factor of 6, since 8 + 5 produces a carry in ordinary decimal arithmetic.

$$
\begin{array}{r}
5D \\
+06 \\
\hline
63
\end{array}
$$

Example 3:

$$
\begin{array}{r}
98\ (\text{BCD}) \ = \ 10011000 \\
+\,25\ (\text{BCD}) \ = \ \underline{00100101} \\
10111101 \ = \ BD
\end{array}
$$

Here we need extra factors of 6 for both digits.

$$
\begin{array}{r}
BD \\
+66 \\
\hline
123
\end{array}
$$

Obviously, the programmer would find it very difficult to decide when to add 6. You have to examine each sum of digits; this is particularly difficult when the computer is handling more than one digit at a time. Since BCD arithmetic is common in microprocessor applications (such as games and point-of-sale terminals), most processors have a special instruction to solve this problem. On the 6800, the instruction is DAA or DECIMAL ADJUST ACCUMULATOR A. This instruction corrects a binary sum in accumulator A (the result of an ADCA or ADDA instruction) to a decimal sum (i.e., DAA adds 6 in all the right places).

AN 8-BIT DECIMAL SUM

The following program adds two BCD numbers from memory locations 0040 and 0041 and stores the sum in memory location 0042, ignoring any carry that might be generated.

```
LDX      #$40
LDAA     0,X          GET FIRST NUMBER
ADDA     1,X          ADD SECOND NUMBER
DAA                   MAKE ADDITION DECIMAL
STAA     2,X          SAVE SUM
SWI
```

The only change from the binary addition program is that memory location 0007 contains DAA (19) instead of NOP (01). Note that DAA only works after an addition instruction; it does not work correctly after subtraction, increment, or decrement instructions.

PROBLEM 9-4

Determine the values of accumulator A, CARRY (C), and HALF-CARRY (H) after the ADDA 1,X instruction for the following examples:

a)   (0040) = 38
     (0041) = 25
b)   (0040) = 98
     (0041) = 25
c)   (0040) = 98
     (0041) = 89
d)   (0040) = 90
     (0041) = 91

The HALF-CARRY (H) is bit 5 of the condition code register and the CARRY is bit 0. Why is the HALF-CARRY necessary? (*Hint:* Examine the results of examples c and d.)

PROBLEM 9-5

Add a continuation to the decimal addition program that shows the least significant digit of the sum on the rightmost seven-segment display. Using the examples from Problem 9-4, the rightmost display should show 3 for example a (least significant digit of 63), 3 for example b (least significant digit of 123), 7 for example c (least significant digit of 187), and 1 for example d (least significant digit of 181). Use the JBUG seven-segment code table that starts in memory location E3CA.

PROBLEM 9-6

Make the program perform decimal subtraction instead of decimal addition. Be careful—DAA works properly only after an addition instruction (ADCA or ADDA); however, remember that

$$X - Y = X + 99 - Y + 1 - 100$$

99 − Y is always a valid BCD number if Y is a BCD number; you can add the extra 1 by subtracting Y from 9A (hex). Try this program for the examples in Problem 9-4. What is the value of CARRY at the end of each example? What does CARRY mean at the end of this program?

DECIMAL SUMMATION

We have already shown (in Laboratory 6) how to perform a binary summation (see Program 6-1). The following program adds an array of unsigned binary numbers starting in memory location 0043 and places the sum in memory location 0040, ignoring any carries. The length of the array is assumed to be in memory location 0042. Program 9-2 is the hexadecimal version.

```
          LDX     #$42
          LDAB    0,X         GET ARRAY LENGTH
          CLRA                SUM = ZERO INITIALLY
ADDELM    INX
          ADDA    0,X         ADD AN ELEMENT TO THE SUM
          NOP
          DECB
          BNE     ADDELM
          STAA    $40         SAVE SUM
          SWI
```

PROGRAM 9-2

MEMORY ADDRESS (HEX)	MEMORY CONTENTS (HEX)	INSTRUCTION (MNEMONIC)	
0000	CE	LDX	#$42
0001	00		
0002	42		
0003	E6	LDAB	0,X
0004	00		
0005	4F	CLRA	
0006	08	ADDELM INX	
0007	AB	ADDA	0,X
0008	00		
0009	01	NOP	
000A	5A	DECB	
000B	26	BNE	ADDELM
000C	F9		
000D	97	STAA	$40
000E	40		
000F	3F	SWI	

We have included a NOP again to make the decimal version easy to implement. Enter Program 9-2 and run it with the following sample data:

$$(0042) = 03$$
$$(0043) = 35$$
$$(0044) = 47$$
$$(0045) = 28$$

Result:

$$(0040) = A4$$

Change the program so the summation is decimal (BCD) rather than binary. Run the revised program with the same sample data. The answer now should be

Result:

$$(0040) = 10$$

16-BIT BINARY ARITHMETIC

We may extend the original binary addition program to handle 16-bit numbers. However, 16-bit addition involves more than just two 8-bit additions even though the 6800 has two 8-bit accumulators. Now there is the problem of carries from the least significant 8 bits to the most significant 8 bits.

We can handle the carries as follows:

1) Add the least significant bits using the ordinary ADD instruction.

2) Add the most significant bits using ADC (ADD WITH CARRY), which produces the result

$$(AC) = (AC) + (M) + (CARRY)$$

where AC is an accumulator and M is the addressed memory location.

The following program adds an array of 16-bit binary numbers starting in memory location 0043 and places the sum in memory locations 0040 and 0041. Each number is stored in two 8-bit words, with the most significant bits first. The length of the array (how many 16-bit numbers there are) is in memory location 0042. The program uses memory location 0042 as a counter, since it needs both accumulators to hold the 16-bit sum.

```
            LDX     #$43        POINT TO START OF ARRAY
            CLRA                SUM = ZERO INITIALLY
            CLRB
ADDELM      ADDB    1,X         ADD IN 8 LSB'S OF ELEMENT
            ADCA    0,X         ADD IN 8 MSB'S OF ELEMENT
            INX
            INX
            DEC     $42
            BNE     ADDELM
            STAA    $40         SAVE 16-BIT SUM
            STAB    $41
            SWI
```

Program 9-3 is the hexadecimal version of this program. Enter and run Program 9-3 with the following data:

PROGRAM 9-3

MEMORY ADDRESS (HEX)	MEMORY CONTENTS (HEX)	INSTRUCTION (MNEMONIC)		
0000	CE		LDX	#$43
0001	00			
0002	43			
0003	4F		CLRA	
0004	5F		CLRB	
0005	EB	ADDELM	ADDB	1,X
0006	01			
0007	A9		ADCA	X
0008	00			
0009	08		INX	
000A	08		INX	
000B	7A		DEC	$42
000C	00			
000D	42			
000E	26		BNE	ADDELM
000F	F5			
0010	97		STAA	$40
0011	40			
0012	D7		STAB	$41
0013	41			
0014	3F		SWI	

(0042) = 02 (number of 16-bit elements)

(0043) = 47 (MSBs of first element)

(0044) = 3E (LSBs of first element)

(0045) = 2A (MSBs of second element)

(0046) = F5 (LSBs of second element)

Result:

(0040) = 72 (MSBs of sum)

(0041) = 33 (LSBs of sum)

that is,

$$\begin{array}{r} 473E \\ + 2AF5 \\ \hline 7233 \end{array}$$

PROBLEM 9-7

Revise Program 9-3 so that the 16-bit elements and the sum are stored with the least significant bits first (at the lower address). This format is used in many computers. Remember to rearrange the data before executing the revised program.

PROBLEM 9-8

Make Program 9-3 perform decimal (BCD) addition rather than binary addition. Be careful—the instruction DAA only operates on accumulator A; use memory locations 0040 and 0041 for temporary storage if you need them. Try the decimal program on the following sample data:

(0042) = 02 (number of 4-digit elements)

(0043) = 21 (MSDs of first element)

(0044) = 36 (LSDs of first element)

(0045) = 18 (MSDs of second element)

(0046) = 97 (LSDs of second element)

Result:

(0040) = 40 (MSDs of sum)

(0041) = 33 (LSDs of sum)

that is,

$$\begin{array}{r} 2136 \\ + 1897 \\ \hline 4033 \end{array}$$

PROBLEM 9-9

Extend the BCD addition program of Problem 9-8 so that it concludes with the carries saved in memory location 003F. Use the following sample data:

(0042) = 02

(0043) = 21

(0044) = 36

(0045) = 98

(0046) = 97

Remember to keep the carries in decimal form (i.e., you cannot just use INC to increment the register or memory location in which the carries are being saved).

Result:

$$(003F) = 01$$
$$(0040) = 20$$
$$(0041) = 33$$

that is,

$$\begin{array}{r} 2136 \\ +9897 \\ \hline 12033 \end{array}$$

ROUNDING

Rounding binary numbers is simple because each bit is either 0 or 1. So all that you must do is look at the most significant bit of the part of the number that you plan to drop. The procedure is as follows:

1) If MSB = 1, round up by adding 1 to the remaining bits.
2) If MSB = 0, leave the remaining bits unchanged.

The following program will round a 16-bit number in memory locations 0041 and 0042 (MSBs in 0041) to an 8-bit number in memory location 0040.

```
        LDX     #$40
        LDAB    1,X         GET MSB'S
        LDAA    2,X         DO LSB'S REQUIRE ROUNDING UP?
        BPL     DONE        NO, DONE
        INCB                YES, ADD 1 TO MSB'S
DONE    STAB    0,X         STORE ROUNDED RESULT
        SWI
```

Clearly, we could replace LDAA 2,X with TST 2,X. The program would then not use accumulator A at all.

Program 9-4 is the hexadecimal version of the binary rounding program. Try it for the following cases:

1)   (0041) = 69
      (0042) = 61
      Result: (0040) = 69

2)   (0041) = 69
      (0042) = D1
      Result: (0040) = 6A

PROGRAM 9-4

MEMORY ADDRESS (HEX)	MEMORY CONTENTS (HEX)		INSTRUCTION (MNEMONIC)	
0000	CE		LDX	#$40
0001	00			
0002	40			
0003	E6		LDAB	1,X
0004	01			
0005	A6		LDAA	2,X
0006	02			
0007	2A		BPL	DONE
0008	01			
0009	5C		INCB	
000A	E7	DONE	STAB	0,X
000B	00			
000C	3F		SWI	

Decimal rounding is somewhat more difficult because:

1)   You must determine if the most significant digit to be truncated is 5 or more. If so, the remaining digits must be rounded up.

2)   All additions must be decimal. You cannot use the INC instruction to add 1. (Why not?) Instead, you must use a pair of instructions such as

ADDA   #1
DAA

PROBLEM 9-10

Write a program that rounds a four-digit BCD number in memory locations 0041 and 0042 (most significant digits in 0041) to a two-digit BCD number in memory location 0040. Try the program for the following cases:

1) (0041) = 69
   (0042) = 61
   Result: (0040) = 70

2) (0041) = 69
   (0042) = 28
   Result: (0040) = 69

PROBLEM 9-11

Write a program that rounds a 24-bit binary number in memory locations 0040, 0041, and 0042 (most significant bits in 0040) to a 16-bit binary number in memory locations 0040 and 0041 (MSBs in 0040). Try the program for the following test cases:

1) (0040) = 93
   (0041) = 6F
   (0042) = 75
   Result: (0040) = 93
            (0041) = 6F

2) (0040) = 93
   (0041) = 6F
   (0042) = D5
   Result: (0040) = 93
            (0041) = 70

3) (0040) = 93
   (0041) = FF
   (0042) = D5
   Result: (0040) = 94
            (0041) = 00

Be careful of the fact that INC does not affect the CARRY flag; it does, however, affect the ZERO flag.

MULTIPLE-PRECISION ARITHMETIC

We can extend the previous programs to handle numbers of any bit length. The procedure for adding binary numbers of arbitrary length is (see Figure 9-1) as follows:

1) Initialization.

COUNT = LENGTH OF NUMBERS (IN BYTES)

POINTER 1 = STARTING ADDRESS OF NUMBER 1

POINTER 2 = STARTING ADDRESS OF NUMBER 2

CARRY = 0, since there is never a carry into the least significant bits

2)   Add 8 bits.

(POINTER 1) = (POINTER 1) + (POINTER 2) + CARRY

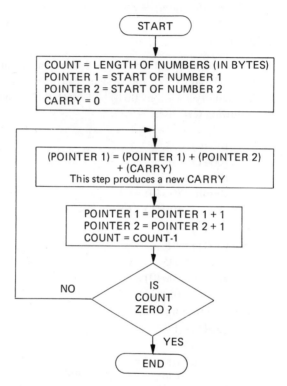

FIGURE 9-1. Flowchart for multiple-precision arithmetic program.

This step produces a new CARRY.

3)   Update counter and pointers.

POINTER 1 = POINTER 1 + 1

POINTER 2 = POINTER 2 + 1

COUNT = COUNT − 1

If COUNT ≠ 0, return to 2.

One problem is that this program uses two pointers. Clearly, we cannot place both in the index register at the same time. For now, we will simply assume that the two arrays are less than 256 elements apart and that POINTER 2 – POINTER 1 is therefore a constant value that can be held in an 8-bit indexed offset. A more general approach would require the use of memory locations to hold the additional address. The 6809 microprocessor (an advanced version of the 6800) solves this problem by having two 16-bit index registers.

If the length of the numbers is in memory location 0040, the numbers start (least significant bits first) in memory locations 0041 and 0061, and the result replaces the number starting in memory location 0041, the required program is

```
        LDX     #$41        POINT TO START OF FIRST NUMBER, SUM
        LDAB    $40         GET LENGTH OF NUMBERS
        CLC                 CLEAR CARRY TO START
ADDELM  LDAA    0,X         GET 8 BITS OF FIRST NUMBER
        ADCA    $20,X       ADD 8 BITS OF SECOND NUMBER
        STAA    0,X         STORE RESULT AS FIRST NUMBER
        INX
        DECB
        BNE     ADDELM
        SWI
```

Program 9-5 is the hexadecimal version. Note that neither INX nor DEC affects the CARRY flag (neither would DEX or INC) so that its value is available for the next iteration. How would you revise Program 9-5 so that it stored the sum as the second number instead of as the first number.

PROGRAM 9-5

MEMORY ADDRESS (HEX)	MEMORY CONTENTS (HEX)	INSTRUCTION (MNEMONIC)		
0000	CE		LDX	#$41
0001	00			
0002	41			
0003	D6		LDAB	$40
0004	40			
0005	0C		CLC	
0006	A6	ADDELM	LDAA	0,X
0007	00			
0008	A9		ADCA	$20,X
0009	20			
000A	A7		STAA	0,X
000B	00			
000C	08		INX	

MEMORY ADDRESS (HEX)	MEMORY CONTENTS (HEX)	INSTRUCTION (MNEMONIC)	
000D	5A	DECB	
000E	26	BNE	ADDELM
000F	F6		
0010	3F	SWI	

Try Program 9-5 on the following 48-bit problem:

$(0040) = 06$ (length of numbers in bytes)

$(0041) = C7$ (LSBs of first number)

$(0042) = 59$

$(0043) = F0$

$(0044) = AB$

$(0045) = 3E$

$(0046) = 29$ (MSBs of first number)

$(0061) = EA$ (LSBs of second number)

$(0062) = 93$

$(0063) = A1$

$(0064) = 28$

$(0065) = D0$

$(0066) = 19$ (MSBs of second number)

Result:

$(0041) = B1$ (LSBs of sum)

$(0042) = ED$

$(0043) = 91$

$(0044) = D4$

$(0045) = 0E$

$(0046) = 43$ (MSBs of sum)

that is,

$$
\begin{array}{r}
293EABF059C7 \\
+\,\underline{19D028A193EA} \\
430ED491EDB1
\end{array}
$$

PROBLEM 9-12

Change Program 9-5 so the two numbers can be located anywhere in memory. Run the revised program with the same data as before except that the second number starts in memory location A051; that is,

(A051) = EA   (LSBs of second number)

(A052) = 93

(A053) = A1

(A054) = 28

(A055) = D0

(A056) = 19   (MSBs of second number)

Use memory locations 0030 through 0033 as temporary storage for the two pointers.

PROBLEM 9-13

Write a program that adds decimal numbers of arbitrary length. Assume the same conditions as in the binary addition example. Try the program on the following 12-digit sample case:

(0040) = 06   (length of numbers in bytes)

(0041) = 87   (least significant digits of first number)

(0042) = 59

(0043) = 60

(0044) = 71

(0045) = 34

(0046) = 29   (most significant digits of first number)

(0061) = 15   (least significant digits of second number)

(0062) = 93

(0063) = 81

(0064) = 28

(0065) = 60

(0066) = 19   (most significant digits of second number)

Result:

(0041) = 02   (least significant digits of sum)

(0042) = 53

(0043) = 42

(0044) = 00

(0045) = 95

(0046) = 48   (most significant digits of sum)

that is,

$$
\begin{array}{r}
293471605987 \\
+\ 196028819315 \\
\hline
489500425302
\end{array}
$$

PROBLEM 9-14

Write a program that subtracts decimal numbers of arbitrary length. Assume the same conditions as in the binary addition example. The number starting in memory location 0061 is to be subtracted from the number starting in memory location 0041. Try the program on the following 12-digit sample case. Be careful of the fact that the CARRY is an inverted borrow in this situation (remember Problem 9-6). That is, CARRY = 1 if no borrow is generated from the subtraction, and CARRY = 0 if a borrow is generated.

(0040) = 06   (length of numbers in bytes)

(0041) = 87   (least significant digits of minuend)

(0042) = 59

(0043) = 60

(0044) = 71

(0045) = 34

(0046) = 29   (most significant digits of minuend)

(0061) = 15   (least significant digits of subtrahend)

(0062) = 93

(0063) = 81

(0064) = 28

(0065) = 60

(0066) = 19   (most significant digits of subtrahend)

Result:

(0041) = 72   (least significant digits of difference)

(0042) = 66

(0043) = 78

(0044) = 42

(0045) = 74

(0046) = 09   (most significant digits of difference)

that is,

$$
\begin{array}{r}
293471605987 \\
-\ 196028819315 \\
\hline
097442786672
\end{array}
$$

ARITHMETIC WITH LOOKUP TABLES

More complex arithmetic can often be performed by using lookup tables. Such tables simply contain all the possible answers organized in a convenient manner. Now all that you have to do is locate the desired answer, just as we did in the seven-segment code conversion presented earlier.

For example, we could form a table from the squares of the numbers between 0 and 7 inclusive. The following program uses the table to find the square of the number in memory location 0041 and places the result in memory location 0042. The lookup procedure is the same one that we used in Programs 5-3 (seven-segment code conversion) and 7-4 (accessing a specific element of an array). One of the major advantages of the tabular approach is that the same lookup program can be used in many different applications, thus saving time, effort, and money.

```
LDAA   #$A0              GET MSB'S OF STARTING ADDRESS
STAA   $40
LDX    $40               MOVE OFFSET ADDRESS TO INDEX REGISTER
LDAA   $50,X             GET SQUARE OF DATA
STAA   $42
SWI

ORG    $A050
FCB    0,1,4,9,16,25,36,49
```

ORG (Origin or Set Origin) is a directive to the assembler (often called a *pseudo-operation* or *pseudo-op*) which indicates that the statements following the directive are to be placed in memory beginning at the specified address. FCB (Form Constant Byte) is another pseudo-operation which indicates that the specified 8-bit data is to be placed in the succeeding memory locations. Program 9-6 is the hexadecimal version.

PROGRAM 9-6

MEMORY ADDRESS (HEX)	MEMORY CONTENTS (HEX)	INSTRUCTION (MNEMONIC)	
0000	86	LDAA	#$A0
0001	A0		
0002	97	STAA	$40
0003	40		
0004	DE	LDX	$40
0005	40		
0006	A6	LDAA	$50,X
0007	50		
0008	97	STAA	$42
0009	42		
000A	3F	SWI	
A050	00	FCB	0
A051	01		1
A052	04		4
A053	09		9
A054	10		16
A055	19		25
A056	24		36
A057	31		49

Run Program 9-6 with the following sample data:

1) (0041) = 04
   Result: (0042) = 10
2) (0041) = 07
   Result: (0042) = 31

PROBLEM 9-15

Write a program that uses the square table of Program 9-6 to add the squares of the contents of memory locations 0041 and 0043 and places the result in memory location 0044.

Example:

$$(0041) = 03$$
$$(0043) = 06$$

Result:

$(0044) = 2D$ (hex), since $2D = 09$ (3^2) + 24 (6^2) in hexadecimal.

PROBLEM 9-16

Write a program that uses a table to calculate the BCD square of a single BCD digit in memory location 0041 and places the result in memory location 0042.

Examples:

1) $(0041) = 06$
   Result: $(0042) = 36$
2) $(0041) = 09$
   Result: $(0042) = 81$

The answers are BCD numbers.

PROBLEM 9-17

Write a program that uses a table to calculate the cube of a BCD digit. Be careful of the fact that $7^3 = 343$, which is too large for a single 8-bit word. Assume that the data is in memory location 0041 and that the answer is placed in memory locations 0042 and 0043 (MSBs in 0042).

Examples:

1) $(0041) = 03$
   Result: $(0042) = 00$
            $(0043) = 1B$
2) $(0041) = 07$
   Result: $(0042) = 01$
            $(0043) = 57$

Remember that the results are hexadecimal numbers.

PROBLEM 9-18

Write a program that converts a single decimal digit in memory location 0041 into a four-digit square root in memory locations 0042 and 0043 (most significant digits in 0042). Use the following table; place it in memory starting at

A050 and indicate its placement in your assembly language program with an FDB (FORM DOUBLE-BYTE CONSTANT) pseudo-operation.

SQUARE ROOT TABLE

VALUE	SQUARE ROOT
0	00.00
1	01.00
2	01.41
3	01.73
4	02.00
5	02.24
6	02.45
7	02.65
8	02.83
9	03.00

Examples:

1)   (0041) = 03
    Result: (0042) = 01
                 (0043) = 73

2)   (0041) = 07
    Result: (0042) = 02
                 (0043) = 65

PROBLEM 9-19

Extend the answer to Problem 9-18 so that it converts the decimal digit in memory location 0041 into a six-digit square root in memory locations 0042, 0043, and 0044 (most significant digits in 0042). Use the following table:

SQUARE ROOT TABLE

VALUE	SQUARE ROOT
0	00.0000
1	01.0000
2	01.4142
3	01.7321
4	02.0000
5	02.2361
6	02.4495
7	02.6458
8	02.8284
9	03.0000

Examples:

1) (0041) = 02
    Result: (0042) = 01
             (0043) = 41
             (0044) = 42

2) (0041) = 06
    Result: (0042) = 02
             (0043) = 44
             (0044) = 95

If the table is very long, you can save memory by storing only some of the entries and interpolating to obtain intermediate values. This method is discussed in T.A. Seim, "Numerical Interpolation for Microprocessor-Based Systems," *Computer Design,* February 1978, pp. 111-116.

KEY POINT SUMMARY

1) The BCD representation is a convenient way to handle decimal numbers, since each decimal digit is coded separately. This representation does, however, require more memory and processing instructions than the ordinary binary representation.

2) Most microprocessors have special decimal arithmetic instructions. The 6800 DECIMAL ADJUST ACCUMULATOR A instruction (DAA) corrects the result of a binary addition to the proper BCD sum.

3) Multiple-precision arithmetic requires a succession of 8-bit operations. Extra instructions are needed to update counters and pointers and to move data to and from the 8-bit accumulators.

4) The CARRY flag transfers information (carries or borrows) between 8-bit operations; ADD WITH CARRY and SUBTRACT WITH CARRY instructions handle the carries or borrows appropriately.

5) Rounding simply requires an examination of the most significant bit or digit that is to be dropped. Rounding may be a multiple-precision operation involving carries.

6) Using lookup tables is a simple way to perform complex arithmetic at the cost of extra memory. The lookup procedure depends only on the organization of the table and the length of the elements; it does not depend on the data values or the function involved.

Subroutines and the Stack

PURPOSE

To learn how to use subroutines on the MEK6800D2 microcomputer.

REFERENCE MATERIALS

L. A. Leventhal, *Introduction to Microprocessors: Software, Hardware, Programming,* Prentice-Hall, Englewood Cliffs, NJ, 1978, pp. 57-60, 97-100, 113-115, 120, 220-229.

L. A. Leventhal, *6800 Assembly Language Programming,* Osborne/McGraw-Hill, Berkeley, CA, 1978, Chapters 10 and 15.

W. J. Weller, *Practical Microcomputer Programming: The M6800,* Northern Technology Books, Evanston, IL, 1977, Chapters 8 and 9.

MEK6800D2 Evaluation Kit II Manual, Motorola Semiconductor Products Inc., Austin, TX, 1977, Chapter 3 (JBUG Monitor) and Appendix 1 (Assembly Listing of JBUG Monitor).

M6800 Programming Reference Manual, Motorola Semiconductor Products Inc., Phoenix, AZ, 1976, pp. 3-8 through 3-10 (Subroutine linkage and stack usage), A-44 (JSR instruction), A-57 (RTS instruction).

1) Why subroutines are useful.

2) How to transfer control to and from subroutines using the JUMP TO SUBROUTINE and RETURN FROM SUBROUTINE instructions.

3) How to call subroutines from other subroutines.

4) How to use the stack and stack pointer in simple programs.

5) How to use the stack for temporary data storage.

6) How to use a delay subroutine.

7) How to use I/O routines as subroutines.

8) How to use the JBUG monitor subroutines.

TERMS

Hardware stack—a stack that the computer manages automatically as part of executing instructions that use it.

Information-hiding principle—a principle of program development whereby one part of a program cannot use information about another part of a program that is not essential to its function. Incidental information is thus hidden in a single part or module.

Library program—a program that is part of a collection of programs and is written and documented according to a standard format.

LIFO (last-in, first-out) memory—a memory that is organized according to the order in which elements are entered and from which elements can only be retrieved in an order opposite to that in which they were entered.

Nesting—constructing programs, subroutines, or interrupt service routines so that one level is contained within another and so on. The *nesting level* is the number of transfers of control required to reach a particular routine without returning.

Nibble—a unit of 4 bits. A byte (8 bits) may be described as consisting of a high nibble (4 most significant bits) and a low nibble (4 least significant bits).

Overflow (of a stack)—exceeding the amount of memory allocated to a stack.

Parameter—an item that must be provided to a subroutine or program in order for it to be executed.

Passing parameters—making the required parameters available to a subroutine.

Pop (or pull)—to remove an operand from a stack.

Push—to store an operand in a stack.

Reentrant—a program that can be executed correctly even while the same program is being interrupted or preempted.

Software stack—a stack that is managed by means of specific instructions, as opposed to a hardware stack which the computer manages automatically.

Stack—a section of memory that can be accessed in a last-in, first-out manner in which the last data entered is the first to be removed, and so on.

Stack pointer—a register or memory location that is used to address a stack.

Subroutine—a subprogram that can be reached from more than one place in a main program.

Subroutine call—the process whereby control is passed from a main program to a subroutine.

Subroutine linkage—the mechanism that is used to transfer control from a main program to a subroutine and back.

Underflow (of a stack)—attempting to remove more data from a stack than has been entered into it.

6800 INSTRUCTIONS

BSR—branch to subroutine; branch over the specified number of memory locations and save the old value of the program counter (after the BSR instruction has been fetched) in the stack.

JSR—jump to subroutine; jump to the specified address (using either extended or direct addressing) and save the old value of the program counter (after the JSR instruction has been fetched) in the stack.

LDS—load stack pointer; load the stack pointer from the specified memory location and the following location. Note that two memory locations are required to load the 16-bit stack pointer.

PSH—store accumulator in stack; store the contents of the specified accumulator in the next location in the stack (i.e., at the address in the stack pointer). The stack pointer is decremented after the data is stored.

PUL—load accumulator from stack; load the specified accumulator from the top location in the stack (i.e., from the address obtained by incrementing the stack pointer). The stack pointer is incremented before the accumulator is loaded.

RTS—return from subroutine; jump to the address contained in the top two locations in the stack.

STS—store stack pointer; store the contents of the stack pointer in the specified memory address and the following address. Note that two memory locations are required to store the 16-bit stack pointer.

STX—store index register; store the contents of the index register in the specified memory address and the following address. Note that two memory locations are required to store the 16-bit index register.

TAP—transfer accumulator A to condition code (P) register; transfer the contents of accumulator A to the condition code register. Accumulator A is not affected.

TPA—transfer condition code (P) register to accumulator A; transfer the contents of the condition code register to accumulator A. The condition code register is not affected.

TXS—transfer index register to stack pointer; place the contents of the index register minus 1 in the stack pointer. The index register is unchanged.

SUBROUTINES

Clearly, we will want to reuse many of the short programs that we have written. The input and output routines, software delay, switch identification, seven-segment code conversion, and arithmetic programs will be useful in many tasks. The idea, then, is to have a way to incorporate the short programs into longer programs.

The easiest method is to place the short programs in separate areas of memory. Then we need a way to transfer control from the main program to the short program and back again. Note that this method allows us to use the same short program at several different points in the main program.

We use the following terminology:

- The program that is subordinate to the main program is called a *subroutine.*
- The process of transferring control to the subroutine is referred to as a *subroutine call.*
- A piece of data or an address that a subroutine needs to perform its tasks is called a *parameter.*
- The process of transferring parameters to the subroutine is referred to as *passing parameters.*

- The method whereby control is transferred to the subroutine and back to the main program is called a *subroutine linkage.*

The 6800 microprocessor has two instructions that are essential in the implementation of subroutines. These instructions work as follows:

- JUMP TO SUBROUTINE (JSR) places the contents of the specified address (either indexed or extended addressing may be used) in the program counter and saves the old value of the program counter (the address following the JUMP TO SUB-ROUTINE instruction) in the stack. BRANCH TO SUB-ROUTINE (BSR) is similar, except that it uses a relative offset just like the conditional branch instructions.
- RETURN FROM SUBROUTINE (RTS) fetches a new value for the program counter from the top two locations in the stack.

So a JSR (JUMP TO SUBROUTINE) instruction in the main program transfers control to the subroutine that starts at the specified address. You can use either extended or indexed addressing with JSR. An RTS (RETURN FROM SUBROUTINE) instruction at the end of the subroutine causes the CPU to resume executing the main program where it left off. The subroutine linkage is thus in the stack—the JSR instruction saves the return address there and the RTS instruction picks it up.

THE RAM STACK

The 6800's JUMP TO SUBROUTINE and RETURN FROM SUB-ROUTINE instructions use the stack and stack pointer. The processor transfers data to and from the stack as follows:

1) It places data in the stack by first storing the data at the address in the stack pointer and then decrementing the stack pointer (Figure A-1).

2) It removes data from the stack by first incrementing the stack pointer and then loading the data from the address in the stack pointer (Figure A-2).

The CPU increments or decrements the stack pointer automatically when executing instructions that use the stack. We could produce the same effects with the index register (resulting in what is called a *software stack*), but the increment or decrement instructions (INX or DEX) would require extra time and memory.

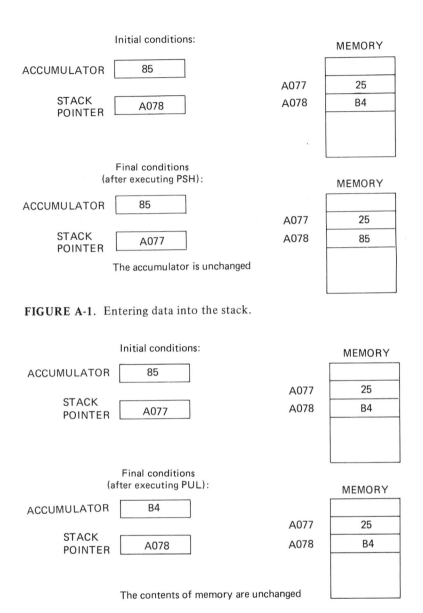

FIGURE A-1. Entering data into the stack.

FIGURE A-2. Removing data from the stack.

Note the following features of the stack:

1) The stack is just an ordinary area of read/write memory. The only thing that moves is the address in the stack pointer (examine Figures A-1 and A-2 carefully).

2)   The programmer (or the monitor program) assigns an area to the stack by placing an initial value in the 16-bit stack pointer. The instructions LDS (LOAD STACK POINTER) or TXS (TRANSFER INDEX REGISTER TO STACK POINTER) can be used for this purpose. The JBUG monitor starts its stack at address A078. We will start our stack at address 00FF so that it will not interfere with the monitor or with our programs. Programs usually do not explicitly change the stack pointer once it has been initialized.

3)   The stack grows down in memory (i.e., from higher addresses to lower addresses). If you feel uneasy about this, just try standing on your head and everything will be all right.

4)   The stack pointer always contains the next available (empty) stack address. That is, the item most recently entered into the stack is at an address one higher than the contents of the stack pointer.

5)   The instructions BSR, JSR, and RTS transfer 16-bit addresses to or from the stack. The 8 most significant bits are obtained first and stored last in accordance with the usual Motorola method for storing addresses. Be careful—the most significant bits are stored last but the stack is growing down, so they end up at the lower address.

Examples:

1)   (SP) = 00BE
   (00BF) = 00
   (00C0) = 28

After RTS is executed,

   (SP) = 00C0
   (PC) = 0028

2)   (SP) = 00D8
   (PC) = 001C

After JSR $0038 (occupying addresses 001C through 001E) is executed,

   (SP) = 00D6
  (00D7) = 00
  (00D8) = 1F

6)   The instructions PUL (REMOVE DATA FROM THE STACK) and PSH (STORE DATA IN THE STACK) transfer 8 bits of data between the top of the stack and an accumulator. There is no way to directly transfer data between the stack and the index register on the 6800; this problem has been solved on the 6801 microprocessor by the addition of PSHX

(PUSH INDEX REGISTER) and PULX (PULL INDEX REGISTER) instructions.

Examples:

1)   (SP) = 00C7
        (A)   = F2

After PSHA is executed,

        (SP)   = 00C6
    (00C7) = F2
2)   (SP)   = 00E4
    (00E5) = 3B

After PULB is executed,

        (SP) = 00E5
        (B)   = 3B

Note that the contents of memory location 00E5 are unchanged.

GUIDELINES FOR STACK MANAGEMENT

Most beginners find the stack confusing and even frightening. However, you will have no problems with the stack if you follow these guidelines:

1) Load the stack pointer during system initialization. Start the stack at the highest available RAM address.

2) Always balance stack operations. Each JUMP TO SUB-ROUTINE should be balanced by a RETURN FROM SUBROUTINE and each PSH by a PUL. This is just like balancing left and right parentheses in arithmetic or in sentences. Be careful that there are no unbalanced paths through the program.

3) Don't be fancy. Leave the stack and the stack pointer alone except for JSR, RTS, PUL, and PSH instructions. Simple programs rarely need more than 20 RAM locations for the stack. Leave yourself lots of room so that you never have overflow problems.

Note that the stack pointer must contain a RAM address if the stack is to be used. Occasionally on the MEK6800D2, executing incorrect instructions will place a ROM, I/O, or unassigned address in the stack pointer. Then many of the commands will not work properly because they use the stack. You can solve this problem by resetting the computer (thus loading A078 into the stack pointer) or by explicitly loading the stack pointer with a RAM address (such as 00FF).

SUBROUTINE LINKAGES IN THE STACK

Let us see how the JSR and RTS instructions work in a simple situation. Enter the following program into memory:

STARTING AT $0000

LDS	#$00FF	INITIALIZE USER STACK POINTER
JSR	$0060	GO TO SUBROUTINE
SWI		

STARTING AT $0060

STS	$40	SAVE STACK POINTER
SWI		

Program A-1 is the hexadecimal version; enter and execute it.

PROGRAM A-1

MEMORY ADDRESS (HEX)	MEMORY CONTENTS (HEX)	INSTRUCTION (MNEMONIC)	
0000	8E	LDS	#$00FF
0001	00		
0002	FF		
0003	BD	JSR	$0060
0004	00		
0005	60		
0006	3F	SWI	
0060	9F	STS	$40
0061	40		
0062	3F	SWI	

PROBLEM A-1

What are the final values of the stack pointer and memory locations 00FE and 00FF? What are the values of memory locations 0040 and 0041? Explain why these values differ from the final value of the stack pointer.

Note that SWI is itself a subroutine call instruction. It stores the current program counter (and all the other registers) in the stack and gets the new program counter from two fixed memory locations (E3FA and E3FB in the JBUG monitor). Those memory locations, in turn, contain the address E032 (verify this!). You can see clearly how SWI works by executing it in the single-step mode.

Be careful not to press RESET after running Program A-1. What happens if you do? Note also that the JBUG register display routine always shows a stack pointer value seven less than the actual value (can you suggest a reason why?).

PROBLEM A-2

What are the final values of the stack pointer and memory locations 00FE and 00FF if you replace the SWI (3F) in memory location 0062 with RTS (39)? Explain what has happened. You may want to place another STS instruction at the end of the main program so that you can easily check the final value of the stack pointer; that is,

0006	9F	STS	$42
0007	42		
0008	3F	SWI	

PROBLEM A-3

What are the final values of the stack pointer and memory locations 00FC through 00FF if you place the following instructions in memory? Remember to execute the main program starting in memory location 0000. Note again that JSR has no direct addressing mode. Can you suggest why that mode is not provided?

0060	9F	STS	$40
0061	40		
0062	BD	JSR	$80
0063	00		
0064	80		
0065	39	RTS	
0080	9F	STS	$42
0081	42		
0082	3F	SWI	

What are the values of the stack pointer in memory locations 0040 and 0041 and in 0042 and 0043? What happens if you change the program as follows?

0060	9F	STS	$40
0061	40		
0062	BD	JSR	$80
0063	00		
0064	80		
0065	9F	STS	$44
0066	44		
0067	3F	SWI	
0080	9F	STS	$42
0081	42		
0082	39	RTS	

Why is it essential that the stack be organized in a last-in, first-out manner? A subroutine that is called by another subroutine is said to be *nested* within that subroutine.

SAVING REGISTERS IN THE STACK

You can use the stack to save registers before calling a subroutine. Now you need not worry about which registers the subroutine uses. Remember the following:

    1)   You can save the accumulators with the instructions PSHA and PSHB; you can restore the old values with the instructions PULA and PULB.

    2)   You can save the condition code register (Figure 2-4) with the instruction sequence

```
TPA              MOVE FLAGS TO ACCUMULATOR
PSHA             SAVE FLAGS IN STACK
```

The instruction TPA transfers the condition code or P register to accumulator A. Note that you cannot store the condition code register in the stack directly.

    You can reload the condition code register with the instruction sequence

```
PULA             REMOVE FLAGS FROM STACK
TAP              RESTORE FLAGS
```

The instruction TAP transfers accumulator A to the condition code or P register.

3)   You can only save the index register in the stack by transferring it via memory and the accumulators. A typical sequence is

```
STX     TEMP        SAVE INDEX REGISTER IN MEMORY
LDAA    TEMP+1      MOVE INDEX REGISTER TO STACK
PSHA
LDAA    TEMP
PSHA
```

We store the least significant bits in the stack first so that they end up at the higher address in the usual 6800 arrangement.

You can restore the index register from the stack with a sequence like

```
PULA                REMOVE INDEX REGISTER FROM STACK
STAA    TEMP
PULA
STAA    TEMP+1
LDX     TEMP        RESTORE INDEX REGISTER FROM MEMORY
```

Because this procedure is so awkward, many 6800 subroutines simply save the index register in two assigned memory locations.

4)   You must restore register values in the opposite order from that in which they were saved. If they are saved in the order

```
PSHA
PSHB
TPA
PSHA
```

they must be restored in the order

```
PULA
TAP
PULB
PULA
```

For example, let us assume that the subroutine performs a table access using the index in accumulator A and the base address in the index register; that is,

```
STX     $40         SAVE BASE ADDRESS IN MEMORY
ADDA    $41         ADD BASE ADDRESS TO INDEX
STAA    $41
```

```
            BCC      ACCTB    WITH CARRY
            INC      $40
   ACCTB    LDX      $40      GET INDEXED ADDRESS
            LDAA     0,X      GET ELEMENT FROM TABLE
            RTS
```

Here both the index and the base address are variables and neither can be placed in the indexed offset. The 6809 microprocessor has a special indexing mode that performs this entire operation automatically during an instruction cycle.

The following program will fetch a seven-segment code from the JBUG table that starts in memory location E3CA. You must place the data in memory location 0042. We have loaded the condition code register and index register from memory initially and stored their final contents in memory to make their initial and final values easy to observe and change. Otherwise, we would have to use the cumbersome methods described in Laboratory 1. Program A-2 contains the hexadecimal versions of the main program and the subroutine.

```
LDS      #$00FF     INITIALIZE USER STACK POINTER
LDAA     $50        INITIALIZE CONDITION CODE REGISTER
TAP
LDX      $52        INITIALIZE INDEX REGISTER
LDAA     $42        GET DATA
LDX      #$E3CA     GET BASE ADDRESS OF TABLE
JSR      $60        ACCESS ELEMENT OF TABLE
STAA     $43        SAVE RESULT
TPA                 SAVE FINAL VALUE OF CONDITION CODE REGISTER
STAA     $51
STX      $54        SAVE FINAL VALUE OF INDEX REGISTER
SWI
```

We have used the following memory locations for temporary storage:

ADDRESS	CONTENTS
0050	Initial value of condition code register
0051	Final value of condition code register
0052	Initial value of MSBs of index register
0053	Initial value of LSBs of index register
0054	Final value of MSBs of index register
0055	Final value of LSBs of index register

PROGRAM A-2

MEMORY ADDRESS (HEX)	MEMORY CONTENTS (HEX)		INSTRUCTION (MNEMONIC)	
Main Program				
0000	8E		LDS	#$00FF
0001	00			
0002	FF			
0003	96		LDAA	$50
0004	50			
0005	06		TAP	
0006	DE		LDX	$52
0007	52			
0008	96		LDAA	$42
0009	42			
000A	CE		LDX	#$E3CA
000B	E3			
000C	CA			
000D	BD		JSR	$60
000E	00			
000F	60			
0010	97		STAA	$43
0011	43			
0012	07		TPA	
0013	97		STAA	$51
0014	51			
0015	DF		STX	$54
0016	54			
0017	3F		SWI	
Subroutine				
0060	DF		STX	$40
0061	40			
0062	9B		ADDA	$41
0063	41			
0064	97		STAA	$41
0065	41			
0066	24		BCC	ACCTB
0067	03			
0068	7C		INC	$40
0069	00			
006A	40			
006B	DE	ACCTB	LDX	$40
006C	40			
006D	A6		LDAA	0,X
006E	00			
006F	39		RTS	

Run Program A-2 for the following test cases:

1) (0042) = 03
    Result: (0043) = 30
2) (0042) = 0D
    Result: (0043) = 21

Run each test case four times with the following conditions:

1) (0050) = D0
    (0052) = 00
    (0053) = 00
2) (0050) = FF
    (0052) = 00
    (0053) = 00
3) (0050) = D0
    (0052) = FF
    (0053) = FF
4) (0050) = FF
    (0052) = FF
    (0053) = FF

Remember that the unused bits in the condition code register (bits 6 and 7) are always 1's.

Do the initial values that we place in the condition code register and index register affect their final values? Note that the JSR instruction does not affect the condition code register or the index register, but the subroutine does. Forgetting the effects of subroutines is a common source of errors in programs; a subroutine call may result in the execution of many instructions and may change the values of registers, flags, and memory locations.

We can easily revise the main program so that it saves the initial value of the condition code register in the stack. The revised program is

```
LDS     #$00FF       INITIALIZE USER STACK POINTER
LDAA    $50          INITIALIZE CONDITION CODE REGISTER
TAP
TPA                  SAVE FLAGS IN STACK
PSHA
LDX     $52          INITIALIZE INDEX REGISTER
LDAA    $42          GET DATA
LDX     #$E3CA       GET BASE ADDRESS OF TABLE
JSR     $60          ACCESS ELEMENT OF TABLE
STAA    $43          SAVE RESULT
```

```
PULA                    RESTORE FLAGS FROM STACK
TAP
TPA
STAA        $51         SAVE CONDITION CODE REGISTER
STX         $54         SAVE INDEX REGISTER
SWI
```

Program A-3 is the hexadecimal version of the revised main program.

PROGRAM A-3

MEMORY ADDRESS (HEX)	MEMORY CONTENTS (HEX)	INSTRUCTION (MNEMONIC)	
0000	8E	LDS	#$00FF
0001	00		
0002	FF		
0003	96	LDAA	$50
0004	50		
0005	06	TAP	
0006	07	TPA	
0007	36	PSHA	
0008	DE	LDX	$52
0009	52		
000A	96	LDAA	$42
000B	42		
000C	CE	LDX	#$E3CA
000D	E3		
000E	CA		
000F	BD	JSR	$60
0010	00		
0011	60		
0012	97	STAA	$43
0013	43		
0014	32	PULA	
0015	06	TAP	
0016	07	TPA	
0017	97	STAA	$51
0018	51		
0019	DF	STX	$54
001A	54		
001B	3F	SWI	

Repeat the various test cases with the revised program and show that it preserves the flags.

PROBLEM A-4

Change the main program so that it saves and restores the index register (save the index register after saving the condition code register). Determine the final values of the stack pointer and memory locations 00FB through 00FF if you replace the RTS instruction at the end of the subroutine (memory location 006F) with SWI and set the initial conditions as follows:

(0050) = 10   (initial value of condition code register)

(0052) = 12   (initial value of MSBs of index register)

(0053) = 34   (initial value of LSBs of index register)

Saving incidental registers in the stack limits the flow of information between the main program and the subroutine. The way in which the subroutine uses those registers will not affect the operation of the main program. The programmer need not understand the details of the subroutine and need not change the main program if the subroutine is revised or replaced.

A DELAY SUBROUTINE

The following subroutine from Laboratory 4 provides a 1-ms delay:

```
DLYMS      LDAB      #$67      DELAY 1 MS
DLY        DECB
           BNE       DLY
           RTS
```

We can use it in a main program as follows:

```
           LDS       #$00FF    INITIALIZE USER STACK POINTER
           JSR       DLYMS     WAIT 1 MS
           SWI
```

The hexadecimal version of the main program and subroutine are given in Program A-4. Enter and run this program.

PROGRAM A-4

MEMORY ADDRESS (HEX)	MEMORY CONTENTS (HEX)	INSTRUCTION (MNEMONIC)	
0000	8E	LDS	#$00FF
0001	00		

MEMORY ADDRESS (HEX)	MEMORY CONTENTS (HEX)		INSTRUCTION (MNEMONIC)	
0002	FF			
0003	BD		JSR	$60
0004	00			
0005	60			
0006	3F		SWI	
0060	C6	DLYMS	LDAB	#$67
0061	67			
0062	5A		DECB	
0063	26		BNE	DLY
0064	FD			
0065	39		RTS	

PROBLEM A-5

How could you make the subroutine preserve the original value of the condition code register? How much do the additional instructions affect the timing?

PROBLEM A-6

How could you make the main program produce a delay of length in milliseconds specified by the contents of memory location 0040? How could you make the subroutine produce a delay of length in milliseconds specified by the contents of accumulator A? What are the advantages and disadvantages of each approach?

Example:

(0040) = 07 results in a delay of 7 ms.

PROBLEM A-7

Revise the subroutine so that the delay is in seconds rather than in milliseconds. Have the subroutine preserve the original values of the index register and condition code register. Use accumulator B for the count in seconds and use the 1-s delay program given in Problem 8-10.

Example:

(B) = 05 results in a delay of 5 s. Use memory locations 0042 and 0043 as temporary storage for the index register. Note how much easier it is to save the index register in those locations rather than in the stack.

AN INPUT SUBROUTINE

The following subroutine identifies which of the eight switches attached to a port has been closed. The data from the port is assumed to be available in accumulator A.

```
IDSW     LDAB    #$FF         SWITCH NUMBER = -1
SRCHS    INCB                 INCREMENT SWITCH NUMBER
         LSRA                 IS NEXT SWITCH CLOSED?
         BCS     SRCHS        NO, KEEP LOOKING
         RTS
```

Program A-5 is the hexadecimal version. We have used memory locations starting with 0070 to avoid interfering with the 1-ms delay routine in Program A-4. The following program uses Program A-5 to identify a switch that is closed at port A of the user PIA:

```
         LDS     #$00FF       INITIALIZE USER STACK POINTER
         CLR     $8005        MAKE PORT A LINES INPUTS
         CLR     $8004
         LDAA    #%00000100   ENABLE DATA TRANSFERS
         STAA    $8005
WAITC    LDAA    $8004        EXAMINE SWITCHES
         CMPA    #$FF         ARE ANY SWITCHES CLOSED?
         BEQ     WAITC        NO, WAIT
         JSR     IDSW         YES, IDENTIFY CLOSED SWITCH
         STAB    $40          SAVE SWITCH NUMBER
         SWI
```

PROGRAM A-5

MEMORY ADDRESS (HEX)	MEMORY CONTENTS (HEX)		INSTRUCTION (MNEMONIC)	
0070	C6	IDSW	LDAB	#$FF
0071	FF			
0072	5C	SRCHS	INCB	
0073	44		LSRA	
0074	25		BCS	SRCHS
0075	FC			
0076	39		RTS	

The hexadecimal version of the main program is given in Program A-6. Enter and run this program. Where does the subroutine place the switch number?

PROGRAM A-6

MEMORY ADDRESS (HEX)	MEMORY CONTENTS (HEX)		INSTRUCTION (MNEMONIC)	
0000	8E		LDS	#$00FF
0001	00			
0002	FF			
0003	7F		CLR	$8005
0004	80			
0005	05			
0006	7F		CLR	$8004
0007	80			
0008	04			
0009	86		LDAA	#%00000100
000A	04			
000B	B7		STAA	$8005
000C	80			
000D	05			
000E	B6	WAITC	LDAA	$8004
000F	80			
0010	04			
0011	81		CMPA	#$FF
0012	FF			
0013	27		BEQ	WAITC
0014	F9			
0015	BD		JSR	IDSW
0016	00			
0017	70			
0018	D7		STAB	$40
0019	40			
001A	3F		SWI	

PROBLEM A-8

How would you make Program A-6 examine the switches once and conclude with either the switch number or FF (if no switches are closed) in memory location 0040? How would you use subroutine DLYMS to write a version that waits until two readings taken 1 ms apart give the same result? Remember that DLYMS affects accumulator B but not accumulator A.

PROBLEM A-9

Modify Program A-6 so that it waits for the number of separate switch closures specified in memory location 00A0 and stores the identification numbers starting in memory location 00A1. Use subroutine DLYMS to provide a 1 ms delay for debouncing.

Example:

If (00A0) = 03 and you close switches 0, 3, and 5 in that order, the results should be

$$(00A1) = 00$$

$$(00A2) = 03$$

$$(00A3) = 05$$

Assume that you must open all switches between closures.

AN OUTPUT SUBROUTINE

The following subroutine loads a decimal digit from the address in the index register, converts it to a seven-segment code, and shows it on the rightmost display. Program A-7 is the hexadecimal version.

```
        ORG    $60
DSP1    LDAB   #$FF          GET BLANK CODE
        LDAA   0,X           GET DATA
        CMPA   #10           IS DATA A DECIMAL DIGIT?
        BCC    DONE          NO, NO CONVERSION NECESSARY
        JSR    CNVSS         YES, CONVERT DATA TO SEVEN-
*                              SEGMENT CODE
DONE    LDAA   #%00000001    ACTIVATE RIGHTMOST DISPLAY
        STAA   $8022
        STAB   $8020         SEND CODE TO DISPLAY
        RTS


        ORG    $90
CNVSS   LDAB   #$A0          GET MSB'S OF STARTING
*                              ADDRESS
        STAB   $40
        STAA   $41
        LDX    $40           MOVE OFFSET ADDRESS TO
*                              INDEX REGISTER
        LDAB   $50,X         GET SEVEN-SEGMENT CODE
        RTS


        ORG    $A050
        FCB    $C0,$F9,$A4,$B0,
               $99,$92,$82,$F8,
               $80,$98
```

PROGRAM A-7

MEMORY ADDRESS (HEX)	MEMORY CONTENTS (HEX)	INSTRUCTION (MNEMONIC)		
0060	C6	DSP1	LDAB	#$FF
0061	FF			
0062	A6		LDAA	0,X
0063	00			
0064	81		CMPA	#10
0065	0A			
0066	24		BCC	DONE
0067	03			
0068	BD		JSR	CNVSS
0069	00			
006A	90			
006B	86	DONE	LDAA	#%00000001
006C	01			
006D	B7		STAA	$8022
006E	80			
006F	22			
0070	F7		STAB	$8020
0071	80			
0072	20			
0073	39		RTS	
0090	C6	CNVSS	LDAB	#$A0
0091	A0			
0092	D7		STAB	$40
0093	40			
0094	97		STAA	$41
0095	41			
0096	DE		LDX	$40
0097	40			
0098	E6		LDAB	$50,X
0099	50			
009A	39		RTS	
A050	C0		FCB	$C0,
A051	F9			$F9,
A052	A4			$A4,
A053	B0			$B0,
A054	99			$99,
A055	92			$92,
A056	82			$82,
A057	F8			$F8,
A058	80			$80,
A059	98			$98

PROBLEM A-10

Write a main program that uses the subroutines in Program A-7 and the 1-s delay routine (Problem A-7) to show the contents of memory location 00A0 on the rightmost display for 1 s.

PROBLEM A-11

Modify the display subroutine so that it uses the JBUG seven-segment code table starting in memory location E3CA. The new routine should accept any hexadecimal digit as valid data.

PROBLEM A-12

Make the display subroutine use accumulator B to determine the display that will be activated. The main program should provide the display number (1 to 6) as a parameter for the subroutine.

Examples:

(B) = 01 activates the leftmost display.
(B) = 06 activates the rightmost display.

PROBLEM A-13

Make the display subroutine from Problem A-12 return immediately with (B) = FF if B originally contains an invalid display number (something other than 1 through 6).

Example:

(B) = 7C causes an immediate return with (B) = FF.

Note how the table access subroutine in Program A-7 differs from the one in Program A-2. In Program A-2, both the table address and the element number are parameters. In Program A-7 only the element number is a parameter and the table is part of the program. The choice of parameters is very important because it determines the flexibility of the subroutine and how it is used. Note the tradeoffs we can make. The earlier subroutine requires two parameters and an external table but can handle any function with one-word input and output. The later subroutine requires only a single parameter but can perform only a specific table lookup.

USING THE MONITOR SUBROUTINES

The JSR instruction also allows us to use subroutines that are part of a monitor or operating system. For example, the JBUG monitor includes subroutines that handle input and output, perform code conversions, and generate time delays. Using these subroutines can save a large amount of time and effort.

Remember that we have already utilized a code conversion table in the monitor ROM—now we shall investigate the use of entire routines. An easy one to employ is the time-delay routine DLY1, which starts in address E0E0. This routine counts the contents of the index register down to zero and then returns control to the calling program. We can use it as follows:

```
LDS       #$00FF        INITIALIZE USER STACK POINTER
LDX       #COUNT        GET COUNT FOR DELAY
JSR       DLY1          WAIT A WHILE
SWI
```

The hexadecimal version of this program is given in Program A-8.

PROGRAM A-8

MEMORY ADDRESS (HEX)	MEMORY CONTENTS (HEX)	INSTRUCTION (MNEMONIC)	
0000	8E	LDS	#$00FF
0001	00		
0002	FF		
0003	CE	LDX	#COUNT
0004	COUNT		
0005			
0006	BD	JSR	DLY1
0007	E0		
0008	E0		
0009	3F	SWI	

Place zero in memory location 0005 and try the following sequence of values in 0004: 00, 80, 40, 20, 10, 08, 04, 02, 01. When can you no longer see the delay?

Even though JSR does not affect the accumulators or flags, the subroutine may affect them. In general, you must preserve any values that you need by saving them in the stack before calling the subroutine. Note the importance of knowing which registers a subroutine affects.

PROBLEM A-14

Determine which of the following registers and flags subroutine DLY1 affects by placing breakpoints immediately before and immediately after it is called.

1) Accumulator A

2) Accumulator B

3) NEGATIVE flag

4) ZERO flag

5) CARRY flag

PROBLEM A-15

Use subroutine DLY1 to write a program that waits for you to close and then open a switch attached to bit 0 of port A of the user PIA. A parameter value of 0050 will be sufficient to debounce most switches.

PROBLEM A-16

Use subroutine DLY1 to write a program that flashes the center bar (segment g) of the leftmost display (display #1). Vary the parameter of DLY1 until the result is satisfactory.

USING THE OUTPUT ROUTINES

Subroutine OUTDS (starting address E0FE) shows the contents of memory locations A00C through A011 (referred to as the *display buffer*) on the displays from left to right, providing a 1-ms delay between digits. So the following program will show the current contents of memory locations A050 through A055 on the displays. The idea is to move the data from those locations to the display buffer and then call subroutine OUTDS. The only problem with this procedure is that OUTDS is tightly coupled to the keyboard scan and provides no return, so you will have to reset the computer (or press the blue E key) to regain control.

```
         LDS     #$00FF      INITIALIZE USER STACK POINTER
         LDAB    #6          COUNT = NUMBER OF DISPLAYS
         LDX     #$A00C      POINT TO START OF DISPLAY BUFFER
MOVE1    LDAA    $44,X       GET 1 DIGIT OF DATA
         STAA    0,X         MOVE DIGIT TO DISPLAY BUFFER
         INX
         DECB
         BNE     MOVE1
         JSR     OUTDS       DISPLAY DATA CONTINUOUSLY
```

The offset of 44 (hexadecimal) is the distance from the starting address of the display buffer to the starting address of the data. Note that although subroutine OUTDS only displays each digit for 1 ms, it is automatically repeated to produce a continuous display. Program A-9 is the hexadecimal version; enter and run the program with the following data:

$$(A050) = 00$$

$$(A051) = 01$$

$$(A052) = 02$$

$$(A053) = 03$$

$$(A054) = 04$$

$$(A055) = 05$$

PROGRAM A-9

MEMORY ADDRESS (HEX)	MEMORY CONTENTS (HEX)		INSTRUCTION (MNEMONIC)	
0000	8E		LDS	#$00FF
0001	00			
0002	FF			
0003	C6		LDAB	#6
0004	06			
0005	CE		LDX	#$A00C
0006	A0			
0007	0C			
0008	A6	MOVE1	LDAA	$44,X
0009	44			
000A	A7		STAA	0,X
000B	00			
000C	08		INX	
000D	5A		DECB	
000E	26		BNE	MOVE1
000F	F8			
0010	BD		JSR	OUTDS
0011	E0			
0012	FE			

A final SWI is not necessary, since OUTDS does not return control anyway.

PROBLEM A-17

What happens if you place an invalid hexadecimal digit in memory location A050? Try the values 10, 11, 12, 38, and DC. Change Program A-9 so that it displays all invalid hexadecimal digits as blanks.

PROBLEM A-18

Use the results from Problem A-17 to write a program that places dashes (the JBUG prompt character) on all the displays.

PROBLEM A-19

Use the results from Problem A-17 to write a program that places the JBUG prompt message on the displays—that is, a dash on the leftmost display and all the others blank.

Table A-1 lists some of the JBUG monitor routines with their functions and entry points. Unfortunately, many of the routines are tightly coupled to save memory space so they are not very general.

Table A-1

JBUG MONITOR SUBROUTINES*

NAME	CALLING ADDRESS (HEX)	FUNCTION
BLDX (BUILD TWO BYTE ADDRESS)	E0E4	Builds a 2-byte address from the first four locations of DISBUF.
CLFLG	E0B2	Clears display buffer and all flags.
CLRDS	E0C4	Clears display buffer and blanks display.
DISNMI (DISABLE NMI INTERRUPTS)	E084	Disables nonmaskable interrupt from keyboard/display PIA.
DLY1	E0E0	Provides a time delay by counting the index register down to zero.
DLY20	E0DD	Delays 20 ms using index register.
HDR	E0D7	Places prompt (−) in first entry of display buffer.
MDIS (MEMORY DISPLAY)	E269	Displays contents of memory location addressed by first four locations of DISBUF.
MDIS1 (MEMORY CHANGE)	E27E	Changes contents of memory location addressed by first four locations of DISBUF to digits in DISBUF + 6 and DISBUF + 7.
MDIS2 (MOVE NIBBLES)	E29A	Moves low nibble (4 bits) of A to B and high nibble of A to low nibble of A.
MINC (INCREMENT MEMORY)	E2A4	Increments memory address display.
OUTDS (OUTPUT DISPLAY BUFFER)	E0FE	Displays six digits in DISBUF. Waits 1 ms between digits. Operates continuously with no return unless a key is pressed.
REGST (DISPLAY REGISTERS)	E2C6	Displays registers on user stack.
REGST5 (MOVE A TO DISPLAY BUFFER)	E31C	Moves two digits in A to first two locations in display buffer.
SETBR (SET BREAKPOINT)	E06A	Makes an entry in the breakpoint table.

*Address DISBUF is A00C, the starting address of the display buffer.

PROBLEM A-20

Use JBUG subroutines CLRDS, REGST5, and OUTDS to write a program that displays the contents of memory location 0040 on the two leftmost displays when the switch attached to bit 0 of port A of the user PIA is closed.

Example:

$$(0040) = B3$$

Result:

When the switch attached to bit 0 of port A of the user PIA is closed, the leftmost displays show B3 (the four displays to the right are all blank).

KEY POINT SUMMARY

1)   You can make a particular function or procedure available from anywhere in a program by making it into a subroutine.

2)   On the 6800 microprocessor, a JUMP TO SUBROUTINE (JSR) instruction in the main program transfers control to a subroutine and saves the return address in the stack. A RETURN FROM SUBROUTINE (RTS) instruction at the end of the subroutine restores control to the main program by placing the return address back in the program counter.

3)   The programmer must initialize the stack pointer before calling any subroutines or using the stack for other purposes.

4)   You can use the stack for temporary storage. This is convenient since the stack is ordered and easy to expand.

5)   You can use monitor subroutines just like the ones you have written. But you must know what parameters they require, which registers they use, and where they place their results. The monitor subroutines are not guaranteed to be general or useful.

☐ *Laboratory* **B**

Input/Output Using Handshakes

PURPOSE

To learn how to perform input and output using handshake status and control signals on the MEK6800D2 microcomputer.

PARTS REQUIRED

- Two switches attached to lines CA1 and CB1 of the user PIA as shown in Figure B-1. These switches should be debounced with cross-coupled NAND gates.

- Two LEDs and two switches attached to lines CA2 and CB2 of the user PIA as shown in Figures B-2 and B-3. The switches should be debounced with cross-coupled NAND gates. The LEDs should be attached by their cathodes. Jumper wires can be used to select whether the LEDs or the switches are attached to the lines.

- This Laboratory also uses the switches attached to user PIA port A as shown in Figure 2-1 and the LEDs attached to user PIA port B as shown in Figure 3-1.

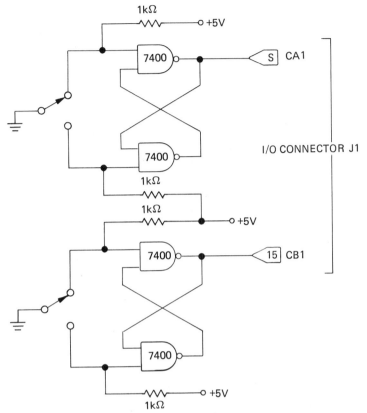

FIGURE B-1. Attachment of switches to user PIA control lines CA1 and CB1.

REFERENCE MATERIALS

L. A. Leventhal, *Introduction to Microprocessors: Software, Hardware, Programming,* Prentice-Hall, Englewood Cliffs, NJ, 1978, pp. 337-355, 363-369, 405-427.

L. A. Leventhal, *6800 Assembly Language Programming,* Osborne/McGraw-Hill, Berkeley, CA, 1978, Chapter 11.

W. J. Weller, *Practical Microcomputer Programming: The M6800,* Northern Technology Books, Evanston, IL, 1977, Chapter 14.

M6800 Programming Reference Manual, Motorola Semiconductor Products Inc., Phoenix, AZ, 1976, pp. 2-4 through 2-6.

J. B. Peatman, *Microcomputer-Based Design,* McGraw-Hill, New York, 1977, pp. 489-494.

G. J. Lipovski, *Microcomputer Interfacing,* D. C. Heath (Lexington Books), Lexington, MA, 1980, Chapter 3.

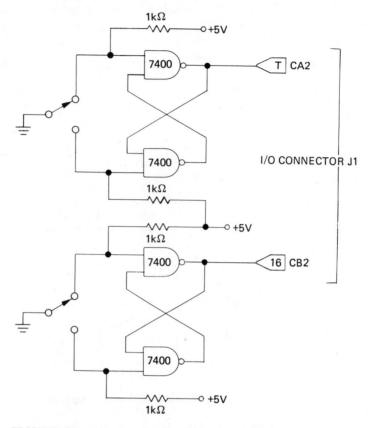

FIGURE B-2. Attachment of switches to user PIA control lines CA2 and CB2.

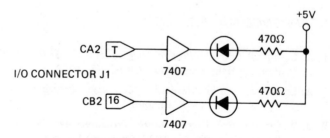

FIGURE B-3. Attachment of LEDs to user PIA control lines CA2 and CB2.

Note: Jumper wires are an easy way to select between the attachments in Figures B-2 and B-3; otherwise, using CA2 and CB2 as outputs could damage the AND gates in Figure B-2.

Note: The 6820 and 6821 Peripheral Interface Adapters have slightly different electrical characteristics, but they are identical from the software point of view and discussions of one apply equally well to the other. We will refer to either as a PIA; we have mentioned both of them here because the MEK6800D2 kit uses 6821 devices, while most of the references (including Motorola's manuals) describe only the 6820 device.

WHAT YOU SHOULD LEARN

1) The information required to complete a data transfer successfully.

2) How synchronous and asynchronous I/O are performed.

3) The status and control signals required by an asynchronous transfer.

4) The features of a 6820 or 6821 Peripheral Interface Adapter (PIA).

5) How to use PIA data lines for status and control signals.

6) How to select the operating mode of a PIA.

7) How to use the PIA control lines for handshaking.

8) How to make the PIA perform handshaking functions automatically.

9) The advantages and disadvantages of programmable I/O devices.

TERMS

Active transition—in a PIA, the edge on the control line that sets an interrupt flag.

Asynchronous—operating without reference to an overall timing source, that is, at irregular intervals.

Buffer—temporary storage area, generally used to hold data before it is transferred to its final destination.

Buffer empty—a signal that is active when a buffer or register is ready to accept data; that is, the most recent data has been transferred successfully.

Buffer full—a signal that is active when a buffer or register contains data that has not been transferred.

Clock—a regular series of pulses that controls transitions in a system.

Control (or command) register—a register whose contents determine the state of a transfer or the operating mode of a device.

Control signal—a signal that directs an I/O transfer or changes the operating mode of a peripheral.

Counter—a clocked device that enters a different state after each clock pulse (up to its capacity) and produces an output that reflects the total number of clock pulses it has received. Counters are also called *dividers,* since they divide the input frequency by *n,* where *n* is the capacity of the counter.

Data accepted—a signal that is active when the most recent data has been transferred successfully.

Data direction register—a register that determines whether I/O lines are inputs or outputs.

Data ready—a signal that is active when new data is available to the receiver. Same as *valid data.*

Data register—in a PIA, the actual input/output port. Also called an *output register* or a *peripheral register.*

Decoder—a device that produces unencoded outputs from coded inputs.

Handshake—a process whereby receiver and transmitter exchange predetermined signals to establish synchronization and to complete the data transfer.

Interrupt—a signal that temporarily suspends the computer's normal sequence of operations and transfers control to a special routine.

Interrupt flag—in a PIA, one of the bits in the control register that is set by active transitions on a control line.

Interrupt request—a signal that is active when a peripheral is requesting service, often used to cause a CPU interrupt.

Latch—a storage device controlled by a timing signal. The contents of the latch are fixed at their current values by a transition of the timing signal (or clock) and remain fixed until the next transition. A latch retains its contents until they are explicitly changed.

Multiplex—use one component or system for several different purposes on a shared basis.

Output register—in a PIA, the actual input/output port. Also called a *data register* or a *peripheral register.*

Peripheral ready—a signal that is active when a peripheral is ready to accept data from the computer.

Peripheral register—in a PIA, the actual input/output port. Also called a *data register* or an *output register.*

Programmable I/O device—an I/O device that can have its mode of operation determined by loading registers under program control.

Ready for data—a signal that is active when the receiver is ready to accept data.

Status register—a register whose contents show the state of a transfer or the operating mode of a device.

Status signal—a signal that describes the current state of a transfer or the operating mode of a device or peripheral.

Strobe—a signal that identifies or describes another set of signals and that can be used to control a buffer, latch, or register.

Synchronous—operating according to an overall timing source or clock, that is, at regular intervals.

Valid data—a signal that is active when new data is available to the receiver.

I/O REQUIREMENTS

So far we have been concerned with simple I/O. The only problems that we have encountered are the smoothing of irregular input transitions and the production of outputs that last long enough to satisfy a peripheral or an observer. Note some of the problems that we have not considered:

> 1)   Whether the peripheral is ready to receive data.

The displays are always ready for data. The only question is whether an observer can see it. This is not the case, however, for a printer, teletypewriter, or motor which may be turned off, malfunctioning, or still busy responding to the previous data.

> 2)   Whether new or valid data is available to the peripheral or the computer.

Brief changes on the output lines will not even be visible on the displays. Switch inputs can be disregarded during transition periods. Clearly, most input and output peripherals cannot be treated so casually.

> 3)   Whether the data has been transferred correctly.

Usually, there is no doubt that data sent to a display will appear there. Nor is there a problem with missing switch inputs if the computer checks them at a reasonable rate. Again, most peripherals transfer data more rapidly and cannot be treated so casually.

BASIC I/O METHODS

Note the features of a successful I/O transfer:

1) The receiver (computer or peripheral) must be ready.
2) The data must be available (or *valid*).
3) The receiver must take in the data before it changes.

So the sender must know whether the receiver is ready and whether it has accepted the data. The receiver must know whether new data is available.

One approach is to use a clock (i.e., a regular series of pulses) as a reference. The data transfers can then proceed at times determined by the clock. The receiver must be ready, the data must be available, and the data must be accepted at particular points in the clock cycle (e.g., 100 ns after the rising edge of the first pulse). Transitions on the clock line provide timing information. The only problem is to synchronize (i.e., line up) the receiver and the transmitter with the clock. This method is called *synchronous transfer*.

Synchronous transfers require no additional status or control signals. The clock determines the transfer rate. The disadvantages of synchronous transfers are their need for a clock and synchronization and their inflexibility. The only way one can change the data rate is by changing the clock. Thus synchronous transfers cannot easily accommodate peripherals that operate at varying data rates or that provide data irregularly.

An alternative approach is to use status signals to ensure a successful transfer. Typical signals are:

READY FOR DATA—active when the receiver is ready for a data transfer.

VALID DATA—active when new data is available.

DATA ACCEPTED—active when the receiver has accepted the most recent data.

Many variations of these signals are also used. The signals may be pulses or levels. The sender must provide the VALID DATA signal; the receiver must provide the READY FOR DATA and DATA ACCEPTED signals.

No clock is needed and transfers can proceed at any rate. This method is called *asynchronous transfer.*

The advantages of asynchronous transfer are its flexibility (since the devices determine the timing) and its simplicity (no clock or synchronization is necessary). The disadvantages of asynchronous transfer are the increased number of signals and reduced maximum data rates (since the signals must overlap properly).

THE PERIPHERAL INTERFACE ADAPTER (PIA)

Before we proceed, we must discuss the Peripheral Interface Adapter (PIA). We have briefly described this device in Laboratory 3. In fact, the PIA is a generalized input/output device that can operate in many different useful ways; the programmer selects the mode of operation for each port by storing data in the port's control register. This data activates a particular set of logic circuits in the PIA, much as an instruction does in the CPU. However, the circuits in the PIA are considerably simpler and oriented toward common input/output functions such as the transfer of status and control signals.

We will first examine the use of the PIA ports in simple I/O and we will then show how they can be used in asynchronous transfers. Laboratory D will deal with synchronous transfers.

As we said in Laboratory 3, each PIA (the 6820 and 6821 devices are the same as far as we are concerned) has two ports called A and B. These ports are almost identical, but the few differences (to be described later) make it preferable to use A as an input port and B as an output port. Each port contains:

- A data register (the actual I/O port, also called a peripheral register) used to transfer data to or from external I/O devices.

- A data direction register that determines whether the I/O lines are inputs or outputs. This register is inside the PIA and is not connected to the outside world.

- A control register that determines how the PIA operates. This register is also inside the PIA and is not connected to the outside world.

- Two control lines that can be used for status and control signals as determined by the contents of the control register. These lines, like the data lines, are connected to external devices (i.e., to the outside world).

Figure B-4 describes the 8-bit PIA control register. Remember that there is one of these for each port. The addresses for the various registers in the user PIA are repeated in Table B-1 for your convenience. The only bit in the control register that we have discussed so far is:

	7	6	5	4	3	2	1	0
CRA	IRQA1	IRQA2	CA2 Control			DDRA Access	CA1 Control	

	7	6	5	4	3	2	1	0
CRB	IRQB1	IRQB2	CB2 Control			DDRB Access	CB1 Control	

FIGURE B-4. Organization of the PIA control registers. (CRA is the control register for port A, CRB for port B.)

Table B-1

USER PIA MEMORY ADDRESSES

ADDRESS (HEX)	FUNCTION
8004	I/O port A or data direction register for port A*
8005	Control register for port A
8006	I/O port B or data direction register for port B*
8007	Control register for port B

*Bit 2 of PIA control register A (B) is 1 to activate the I/O port and 0 to activate the data direction register.

- Bit 2 selects either the data direction register or the I/O port (data or peripheral register) as the other address on one side of the PIA. Bit 2 = 0 to select the data direction register and 1 to select the I/O port.

Note the following features of the PIA:

1) You can make each bit of the I/O ports into an input or an output by setting the corresponding bit in the data direction register to a 0 (input) or 1 (output).

2)   The CPU can read and write the control registers with some limitations that will be described later.

3)   RESET clears the control and data direction registers, makes all the data lines inputs, and clears the output latches.

4)   The positions (and meanings) of the various bits in the control register are arbitrary and can only be determined from the manufacturer's specification sheets.

USING THE PIA DATA LINES FOR STATUS

We can simply use the PIA data lines for status and control signals. This is practical only when there are extra lines that are not needed for data. However, this approach does illustrate the use of status and control signals to govern data transfers. For the next few examples, we will use bit 7 of user PIA port A as an input status signal and bit 7 of user PIA port B as an output control signal. Remember that port A occupies memory address 8004 and port B address 8006.

Determining the operating mode of the PIA simply requires the combination of the initialization programs of Laboratories 2 and 3. That is, the following steps are necessary for each port of the PIA:

1)   Clear the control register to address the data direction register.

2)   Load the data direction register with a value that produces the appropriate arrangement of inputs and outputs (e.g., load it with zero for all inputs and FF for all outputs).

3)   Set bit 2 of the control register to address the I/O port and allow data transfers to and from the external world. Remember that the control register and data direction register are inside the PIA.

Program B-1 is the initialization routine that we will use throughout this Laboratory. The assembly language version is

```
CLR     $8005           ACCESS DATA DIRECTION REGISTERS
CLR     $8007
CLR     $8004           MAKE PORT A INPUTS
LDAA    #$FF            MAKE PORT B OUTPUTS
STAA    $8006
LDAA    #%00000100      ENABLE DATA TRANSFERS
STAA    $8005
STAA    $8007
```

PROGRAM B-1

MEMORY ADDRESS (HEX)	MEMORY CONTENTS (HEX)	INSTRUCTION (MNEMONIC)	
0000	7F	CLR	$8005
0001	80		
0002	05		
0003	7F	CLR	$8007
0004	80		
0005	07		
0006	7F	CLR	$8004
0007	80		
0008	04		
0009	86	LDAA	#$FF
000A	FF		
000B	B7	STAA	$8006
000C	80		
000D	06		
000E	86	LDAA	#%00000100
000F	04		
0010	B7	STAA	$8005
0011	80		
0012	05		
0013	B7	STAA	$8007
0014	80		
0015	07		

PROBLEM B-1

Enter Program B-1 into memory and add the following instructions:

LDAA	#%10101010	LIGHT EVERY OTHER LED
STAA	$8006	
SWI		

The hexadecimal additions are

0016	86	LDAA	#%10101010
0017	AA		
0018	B7	STAA	$8006
0019	80		
001A	06		
001B	3F	SWI	

Run the program. What happens? What happens when you press RESET? Remember that RESET makes all I/O lines inputs. What is the level of a PIA input when viewed from an output device?

Change memory location 000F from 04 to 00 and run the program again. What happens? Can you explain the difference?

Without pressing RESET, run the modified program again with a breakpoint in memory location 000E. What is the state of the LEDs at the breakpoint? Note that the PIA output port contains a latch. Does changing the data direction register affect the contents of that latch?

Does RESET affect the contents of the output latch? Describe a sequence of operations that will show whether your answer is correct.

PROBLEM B-2

Although we address PIA I/O ports as memory locations, we must remember that I/O devices behave differently from memories. For example, most I/O devices (e.g., printers, keyboards, and card readers) are either input or output devices but not both. Add the following instructions to Program B-1:

CLR	$8004
LDAA	$8004
STAA	$40

The hexadecimal additions are

0016	7F	CLR	$8004
0017	80		
0018	04		
0019	B6	LDAA	$8004
001A	80		
001B	04		
001C	97	STAA	$40
001D	40		
001E	3F	SWI	

What happens when you run the program? What are the final contents of memory location 0040? Explain what has happened. Do the positions of the switches attached to user PIA port A affect the result? What happens if you replace CLR with COM? How about NEG? What happens if you replace CLR with ASL? What is the final value of the CARRY flag (bit 0 of the condition code register)? What happens if you replace CLR with LSR?

In the case of the program with CLR, replace 8004 in the CLR and LDAA instructions with A050. Now what is the result? What happens if you replace

8004 with E285? Explain the differences. Which memory location acts more like user PIA port A? Why?

Note that instructions may look reasonable but may not make sense physically. The processor is unaware of the physical limitations of I/O devices. In fact, programmers who lack an engineering background are often equally unaware of those limitations and may write programs that conflict with physical realities.

Let us now use bit 7 of port A as a status signal. For an input port, this signal usually indicates that new data is available (e.g., the operator has pressed a key on a keyboard, a card reader has read another card, or a cassette recorder has advanced the tape to the next position). The following program waits for the switch attached to bit 7 of port A to be closed before reading the data from the port. It then displays the data on the LEDs attached to port B. Program B-1 initializes the PIA; we must explicitly turn the LEDs off each time since the PIA output port is latched (see Problem B-1). Program B-2 is the hexadecimal version of the program that waits for the status signal to become active (low) before reading the data from the switches.

```
              LDAA    #$FF       TURN OFF THE LEDS
              STAA    $8006
WAITR    TST     $8004      IS DATA READY?
              BMI     WAITR      NO, WAIT
              LDAA    $8004      YES, FETCH DATA
              COMA               AND SHOW IT ON THE LEDS
              STAA    $8006      WITH PROPER POLARITY (1 = ON)
              SWI
```

Open the switch attached to bit position 7 of user PIA port A and run Program B-2. What happens? Does it matter whether you open or close any of the switches attached to bit positions 0 through 6? Close all of those switches. Now close the switch attached to bit position 7. The only data that the processor accepts is the data that is present when the status signal becomes active. Changes that occur while the status signal is inactive are simply ignored.

PROGRAM B-2

MEMORY ADDRESS (HEX)	MEMORY CONTENTS (HEX)	INSTRUCTION (MNEMONIC)	
0016	86	LDAA	#$FF
0017	FF		
0018	B7	STAA	$8006
0019	80		
001A	06		

PROGRAM B-2 (continued)

MEMORY ADDRESS (HEX)	MEMORY CONTENTS (HEX)	INSTRUCTION (MNEMONIC)		
001B	7D	WAITR	TST	$8004
001C	80			
001D	04			
001E	2B		BMI	WAITR
001F	FB			
0020	B6		LDAA	$8004
0021	80			
0022	04			
0023	43		COMA	
0024	B7		STAA	$8006
0025	80			
0026	06			
0027	3F		SWI	

Note that we actually have only seven data lines available at user PIA port A, since we are using bit position 7 for status. A separate status port could hold 8 independent status bits, although we would have to mask the bits in the middle as in Laboratory 2. How would you change Program B-2 to use bit position 5 for status?

PROBLEM B-3

Change Program B-2 so that the status signal is active-high. Status signals in TTL logic are, in fact, usually active-low; can you suggest a reason for this choice? Change Program B-2 so that it waits for the status signal to go low and then back high. Remember to debounce the switch. Note that if the data is loaded during the bounce period, bit 7 may be read as a logic 1 even though it was a logic 0 when the TST instruction was executed.

PROBLEM B-4

Extend Program B-2 so that it loads data into an array starting at memory location 00A0. It should load an item from the switches into the array each time the status signal becomes active (low). Remember to debounce the switch.

PROBLEM B-5

Make the program of Problem B-4 load ten items into the array and stop. How would you make the program stop when it finds a zero entry?

For an output port, the status signal indicates that the output device is ready for more data (e.g., a printer has finished with the last character or a remote station has accepted the previous transmission).

The following program waits for the switch attached to bit 7 of port A to be closed before sending data from memory location 00A0 to port B. Program B-3 is the hexadecimal version. As before, Program B-1 is necessary to initialize the user PIA properly.

	LDAA	#$FF	TURN OFF THE LEDS
	STAA	$8006	
WAITR	TST	$8004	IS PERIPHERAL READY?
	BMI	WAITR	NO, WAIT
	LDAA	$A0	YES, SEND DATA
	COMA		
	STAA	$8006	
	SWI		

PROGRAM B-3

MEMORY ADDRESS (HEX)	MEMORY CONTENTS (HEX)	INSTRUCTION (MNEMONIC)	
0016	86		LDAA	#$FF
0017	FF		
0018	B7		STAA	$8006
0019	80		
001A	06		
001B	7D	WAITR	TST	$8004
001C	80		
001D	04		
001E	2B		BMI	WAITR
001F	FB		
0020	96		LDAA	$A0
0021	A0		
0022	43		COMA
0023	B7		STAA	$8006
0024	80		
0025	06		
0026	3F		SWI

Enter Program B-3 into memory and run it with (00A0) = FF. What happens before you close the switch attached to bit position 7 of user PIA port A? Does it matter what is in memory location 00A0? What happens when you close the status switch? Note that the old data remains on the output lines until the peripheral specifically requests new data or informs the computer that it is ready for new data.

PROBLEM B-6

Change Program B-3 so that the processor waits for the status signal to go high (i.e., the signal is active-high rather than active-low). Change the program so that it waits for the status signal to go low and then back high again. Remember to debounce the switch.

PROBLEM B-7

Make Program B-3 send data from an array starting at memory location 00A0. It should send a new item from the array to the lights each time the status signal becomes active (low). Remember to debounce the switch. Note that there are slight differences between the input and output procedures in that an output peripheral usually starts in the ready state (i.e., it can accept the first data item which is usually not available), whereas an input peripheral usually starts in the inactive state (i.e., it has no data available although the computer is ready to accept data).

Sample Data Arrays:

1) Single light moves from left to right, starting in bit position 7.

$$(00A0) = 80$$

$$(00A1) = 40$$

$$(00A2) = 20$$

$$(00A3) = 10$$

$$(00A4) = 08$$

$$(00A5) = 04$$

$$(00A6) = 02$$

$$(00A7) = 01$$

2) Start with all lights on and turn one more off each time, starting with the one in bit position 0.

$$(00A0) = FF$$

$$(00A1) = FE$$

$$(00A2) = FC$$

$$(00A3) = F8$$

$$(00A4) = F0$$

$$(00A5) = E0$$

$$(00A6) = C0$$

$$(00A7) = 80$$

$$(00A8) = 00$$

PROBLEM B-8

Make the program of Problem B-7 stop after sending eight items from the array.

USING THE PIA DATA LINES FOR CONTROL

We can also use the PIA data lines for control signals. In the case of an input port, the signal can indicate that the computer has accepted the previous data. The following program loads the data from the input port into memory location 00A0 and turns the control signal light on by clearing bit 7 of memory location 8006 (remember that a logic 0 lights an LED). Program B-4 is the hexadecimal version.

```
LDAA      #$FF            TURN OFF THE LEDS
STAA      $8006
LDAA      $8004           GET DATA FROM INPUT PORT
STAA      $A0             SAVE DATA
LDAA      #%01111111      TURN ON CONTROL LIGHT
STAA      $8006
SWI
```

PROGRAM B-4

MEMORY ADDRESS (HEX)	MEMORY CONTENTS (HEX)	INSTRUCTION (MNEMONIC)	
0016	86	LDAA	#$FF
0017	FF		
0018	B7	STAA	$8006
0019	80		
001A	06		
001B	B6	LDAA	$8004
001C	80		
001D	04		
001E	97	STAA	$A0
001F	A0		
0020	86	LDAA	#%01111111
0021	7F		
0022	B7	STAA	$8006
0023	80		

MEMORY ADDRESS (HEX)	MEMORY CONTENTS (HEX)	INSTRUCTION (MNEMONIC)
0024	06	
0025	3F	SWI

Enter and run Program B-4. Here the light indicates that the computer has accepted the data and is ready for more. This signal can be interpreted in many different ways—READY FOR DATA, DATA ACCEPTED, and DATA BUFFER EMPTY are some of the names and meanings that it may have.

PROBLEM B-9

Revise Program B-4 so that it only leaves the control light on long enough to be visible. Use monitor subroutine DLY1 to produce the delay; an initial value of 4000 hex in the index register will be adequate. Here the control signal is a pulse rather than a level.

We can combine Programs B-2 and B-4 to obtain a program that waits for the input status signal to become active before accepting the data and then sets the output control signal to indicate that the data has been accepted. Program B-5 is the hexadecimal version of the combined program. Here we have a complete handshake (see Figure B-5); the sender indicates the availability of new data and the receiver, in response, reads the data and indicates the successful completion of the transfer.

```
        LDAA    #$FF          TURN OFF THE LEDS
        STAA    $8006
WAITR   TST     $8004         IS DATA READY?
        BMI     WAITR         NO, WAIT
        LDAA    $8004         YES, GET DATA
        STAA    $A0           SAVE DATA
        LDAA    #%01111111    TURN ON CONTROL LIGHT
        STAA    $8006
        SWI
```

PROGRAM B-5

MEMORY ADDRESS (HEX)	MEMORY CONTENTS (HEX)	INSTRUCTION (MNEMONIC)	
0016	86	LDAA	#$FF
0017	FF		

PROGRAM B-5 (continued)

MEMORY ADDRESS (HEX)	MEMORY CONTENTS (HEX)	INSTRUCTION (MNEMONIC)	
0018	B7	STAA	$8006
0019	80		
001A	06		
001B	7D	WAITR TST	$8004
001C	80		
001D	04		
001E	2B	BMI	WAITR
001F	FB		
0020	B6	LDAA	$8004
0021	80		
0022	04		
0023	97	STAA	$A0
0024	A0		
0025	86	LDAA	#%01111111
0026	7F		
0027	B7	STAA	$8006
0028	80		
0029	06		
002A	3F	SWI	

Enter and run Program B-5. Here the status signal indicates that new data is available and the control signal indicates that the computer has accepted the data.

An obvious problem with Program B-5 is that the control signal stays active indefinitely. Clearly, we want to deactivate it eventually so that it can be used in the next transfer. There are several ways to determine how long the control signal stays active (on):

1) It can remain active only briefly, thus producing a pulse that can be counted or latched if necessary. The processor must turn the signal off as well as on.

2) It can go off when the status signal becomes active again, thus indicating the availability of new data. The control signal then indicates whether the processor has accepted the most recently sent data (i.e., it acts as a BUFFER FULL signal).

The processor must turn the control signal off when it finds the status signal active unless there is a hardware connection.

3) It can remain active for an amount of time determined by the program. This provides flexibility but requires more program intervention.

248

STEP 1
PERIPHERAL PROVIDES DATA AND ACTIVATES DATA READY.

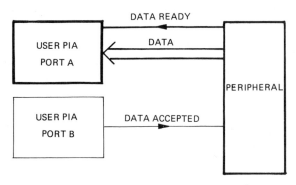

The peripheral provides both the data and an active DATA READY signal.

STEP 2
CPU RECOGNIZES THAT DATA READY IS ACTIVE AND READS THE DATA,
THUS PERFORMING THE ACTUAL DATA TRANSFER.

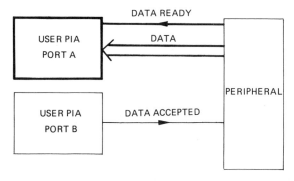

STEP 3
CPU ACTIVATES DATA ACCEPTED, INDICATING THE SUCCESSFUL
COMPLETION OF THE TRANSFER.

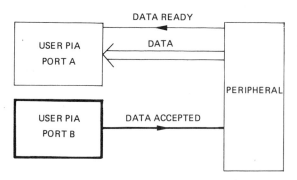

The peripheral can examine DATA ACCEPTED to determine when
it can send more data.

FIGURE B-5. Procedure for a complete input handshake.

As we shall see later, the PIA includes the hardware required to implement any of these alternatives. All the user must do is select the proper operating mode by storing the appropriate value in the control register.

PROBLEM B-10

> Change Program B-5 so that it starts with the control light lit and explicitly turns it off when it finds the status signal active. Set a breakpoint after the control light is turned off so that you can see it go on and off.

We can also combine Programs B-3 and B-4 to obtain a program that waits for the input status signal to become active before sending the data and then sets the output control signal to indicate that the data has been sent. Program B-6 is the hexadecimal version of the combined program. Here again we have a full handshake (see Figure B-6), although the order and meaning of the signals is somewhat different from the input case. The receiver indicates that it is ready to accept data; in response, the sender provides the data and an indication that it is available.

```
         LDAA    #$FF            TURN OFF THE LEDS
         STAA    $8006
WAITR    TST     $8004           IS PERIPHERAL READY?
         BMI     WAITR           NO, WAIT
         LDAA    $A0             YES, SEND DATA
         COMA
         ANDA    #%01111111      AND TURN ON CONTROL LIGHT
         STAA    $8006
         SWI
```

Enter and run Program B-6. Change it so that it only leaves the control light on long enough to be visible.

PROGRAM B-6

MEMORY ADDRESS (HEX)	MEMORY CONTENTS (HEX)	INSTRUCTION (MNEMONIC)	
0016	86	LDAA	#$FF
0017	FF		
0018	B7	STAA	$8006
0019	80		
001A	06		
001B	7D	WAITR TST	$8004
001C	80		
001D	04		
001E	2B	BMI	WAITR

PROGRAM B-6 (continued)

MEMORY ADDRESS (HEX)	MEMORY CONTENTS (HEX)	INSTRUCTION (MNEMONIC)	
001F	FB		
0020	96	LDAA	$A0
0021	A0		
0022	43	COMA	
0023	84	ANDA	#%01111111
0024	7F		
0025	B7	STAA	$8006
0026	80		
0027	06		
0028	3F	SWI	

STEP 1
PERIPHERAL ACTIVATES PERIPHERAL READY, INDICATING THAT IT
IS ABLE TO ACCEPT DATA.

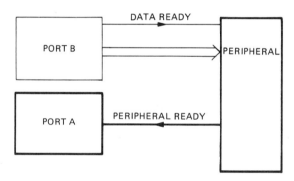

The output peripheral must provide the
input status signal PERIPHERAL READY.

STEP 2
CPU RECOGNIZES THAT PERIPHERAL READY IS ACTIVE AND SENDS
THE DATA, THUS PERFORMING THE ACTUAL DATA TRANSFER.

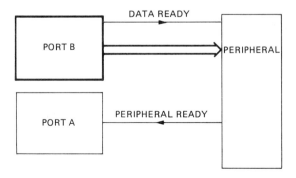

FIGURE B-6. Procedure for a complete output handshake.

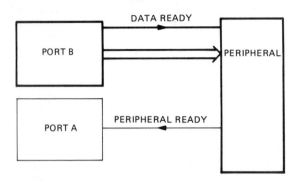

STEP 3
CPU ACTIVATES DATA READY, THUS INFORMING THE PERIPHERAL
THAT NEW DATA IS AVAILABLE.

The peripheral can examine DATA READY to determine
when new data is available.

FIGURE B-6. Continued.

PROBLEM B-11

Change Program B-6 so that it starts with the control light lit and explicitly turns the light off when the status signal becomes active. Set a breakpoint after the control light is turned off so that you can see it go on and off.

USING THE PIA INPUT CONTROL LINES

As we have noted, the PIA can automatically perform all the status and control functions that we have described so far. Let us now see how to use the PIA control lines to implement input and output handshakes.

The key features of the PIA are the following:

Bit 7 of the PIA control register is set (to 1) whenever an active transition occurs on control line 1. This bit is called an *interrupt flag*, since it is often used to generate interrupts as discussed in Laboratory C.

Bit 1 of the PIA control register determines whether the active transition is high-to-low (negative transition or trailing edge) or low-to-high (positive transition or leading edge). But 1 = 0 to make negative transitions active and 1 to make positive transitions active. Thus bit 7 of the PIA control register is actually a latch that is set by an active transition on control line 1. Bit 1 of the control register determines the active transition for the latch. A circuit like the one shown in Figure B-7 is inside the PIA. Note that reading the PIA data register clears bit 7 automatically; no further hardware or software is necessary. You should also note that the microprocessor cannot change bit 7 of the control register by storing a new value there (try this!); we will arbitrarily clear bit 7 of any control word that we use.

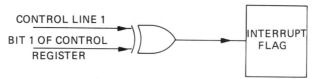

If bit 1 of the control register is 1, the EXCLUSIVE OR gate acts as an inverter.

FIGURE B-7. Possible internal implementation of the PIA edge control.

Thus the following program will wait until the switch attached to input control line CA1 is closed. The program will then read the data from user PIA port A and display it on the LEDs. As usual, Program B-1 is required to initialize the PIA. Program B-7 is the hexadecimal version of the input program using control line CA1 as the status signal. Note that a high-to-low transition on CA1 (i.e., closing the switch) sets bit 7 of the PIA control register, so we must check for a logic 1 even though the active state on CA1 is 0 (low).

```
           LDAA    #$FF      TURN OFF THE LEDS
           STAA    $8006
WAITR      TST     $8005     IS DATA READY?
           BPL     WAITR     NO, WAIT
           LDAA    $8004     YES, FETCH DATA
           COMA              AND SHOW IT ON THE LEDS
           STAA    $8006
           SWI
```

Enter and run Program B-7. What is the final value of memory location 8005 (hex)? Explain what has happened. Remember that the interrupt flag in bit position 7 of the control register is automatically cleared when the data register (I/O port) is read. Show that this actually happens by setting breakpoints at the LDAA $8004 instruction and at the COMA instruction; run the program and examine the contents of memory location 8005 at each breakpoint. What happens if you replace LDAA $8004 with STAA $8004? Reading the I/O port clears the interrupt flag, but writing data into the port does not. As we shall see later, this complicates the output handshake procedure.

We should note that the processor will occasionally exit from Program B-7 without waiting for you to close the switch. The usual reason is that bit 7 of the control register has been set inadvertently; you can clear it by examining memory location 8004, thus reading the I/O port.

PROGRAM B-7

MEMORY ADDRESS (HEX)	MEMORY CONTENTS (HEX)		INSTRUCTION (MNEMONIC)	
0016	86		LDAA	#$FF
0017	FF			
0018	B7		STAA	$8006
0019	80			
001A	06			
001B	7D	WAITR	TST	$8005
001C	80			
001D	05			
001E	2A		BPL	WAITR
001F	FB			
0020	B6		LDAA	$8004
0021	80			
0022	04			
0023	43		COMA	
0024	B7		STAA	$8006
0025	80			
0026	06			
0027	3F		SWI	

PROBLEM B-12

We have shown that LDAA $8004 clears the interrupt flag in bit position 7. In fact, any instruction that reads the I/O port clears the interrupt flag. Try the following instructions in place of LDAA $8004: ASL $8004, LSR $8004, TST $8004, CLR $8004, CLR $8006, CMPA $8004, BITA $8004, LDAA $8005. What is the effect of each on the interrupt flag? Note that the instruction must read the associated I/O port—writing into the I/O port, reading or writing the control register, or reading or writing some other address (such as the other port's data register) does not do the job.

PROBLEM B-13

Revise Program B-7 (and Program B-1) so that it responds to the opening of the switch attached to line CA1. Remember that the switch is debounced.

PROBLEM B-14

Make Program B-7 load data into an array starting at memory location 00A0. It should load an item from the switches into the array each time you close the status switch (attached to CA1).

Control line CA2 can be used in exactly the same way as CA1. The only differences are the bit positions in the control register. The bit positions for control line CA2 are:

Bit 6 of the PIA control register is set (to 1) whenever an active transition occurs on control line 2.

Bit 4 of the PIA control register determines whether the active transition is a trailing edge (0) or a leading edge (1).

As with bit 7, the microprocessor cannot change bit 6 of the PIA control register by storing a new value there; however, reading the PIA data register clears bit 6 automatically.

PROBLEM B-15

Make Program B-7 (and Program B-1) respond to the opening of the switch attached to line CA2.

PROBLEM B-16

Make Program B-7 load data into an array starting at memory location 00A0. It should load an item from the switches into the array each time you close the status switch (attached to CA2).

We can similarly use control line CB1 or CB2 as a PERIPHERAL READY input. The revised version of Program B-3 using control line CB1 is as follows (see Program B-8 for a hexadecimal version):

```
            LDAA      #$FF         TURN OFF THE LEDS
            STAA      $8006
WAITR       TST       $8007        IS PERIPHERAL READY?
            BPL       WAITR        NO, WAIT
            LDAA      $A0          YES, SEND DATA
            COMA
            STAA      $8006
            SWI
```

PROGRAM B-8

MEMORY ADDRESS (HEX)	MEMORY CONTENTS (HEX)	INSTRUCTION (MNEMONIC)	
0016	86	LDAA	#$FF
0017	FF		
0018	B7	STAA	$8006
0019	80		
001A	06		
001B	7D	WAITR TST	$8007
001C	80		
001D	07		
001E	2A	BPL	WAITR
001F	FB		
0020	96	LDAA	$A0

MEMORY ADDRESS (HEX)	MEMORY CONTENTS (HEX)	INSTRUCTION (MNEMONIC)	
0021	A0		
0022	43	COMA	
0023	B7	STAA	$8006
0024	80		
0025	06		
0026	3F	SWI	

Remember that a high-to-low transition on control line CB1 (i.e., closing the switch attached to that input) sets the interrupt flag (bit 7 of control register B). Enter Program B-8 into memory and run it with (00A0) = FF.

PROBLEM B-17

What is the value of memory location 8007 before you close the switch attached to control line CB1? What is its value immediately after the switch is closed (i.e., when the program exits from the status checking loop)? What is its value at the end of the program? What problem would this final value create if the program were sending a series of output data items to a peripheral and immediately returned to check the interrupt flag again (i.e., the program concluded with a BRA WAITR instruction after adjusting the address for the next data item)?

The difficulty illustrated in Problem B-17 is that storing data in a PIA I/O port does not clear the interrupt flag; only reading the I/O port clears the flag. However, this difficulty is easy to overcome—all that we must do is add a read instruction to Program B-8. This extra instruction should read the I/O port (thus clearing the interrupt flag) without affecting the operation of the program. For example, either a BIT instruction or a CMP instruction would read the I/O port without changing an accumulator. We will use BIT because it also leaves the CARRY flag unchanged. The revised program is as follows (see Program B-9 for hexadecimal version).

```
        LDAA    #$FF        TURN OFF THE LEDS
        STAA    $8006
WAITR   TST     $8007       IS PERIPHERAL READY?
        BPL     WAITR       NO, WAIT
        LDAA    $A0         YES, FETCH DATA
        COMA
        BITA    $8006       CLEAR PERIPHERAL READY
        STAA    $8006       SEND DATA
        SWI
```

Note that in Programs B-7 through B-9, the status input only has to be low long enough to set the interrupt flag. Thus the peripheral need only provide a READY pulse that is a few hundred nanoseconds long. If, as in Programs B-2, B-3, B-5, and B-6, the processor must recognize the active level, the pulse must be much longer or the processor could miss it. Obviously, there is far less danger of information being lost if the PIA latches the status signal.

PROGRAM B-9

MEMORY ADDRESS (HEX)	MEMORY CONTENTS (HEX)		INSTRUCTION (MNEMONIC)	
0016	86		LDAA	#$FF
0017	FF			
0018	B7		STAA	$8006
0019	80			
001A	06			
001B	7D	WAITR	TST	$8007
001C	80			
001D	07			
001E	2A		BPL	WAITR
001F	FB			
0020	96		LDAA	$A0
0021	A0			
0022	43		COMA	
0023	B5		BITA	$8006
0024	80			
0025	06			
0026	B7		STAA	$8006
0027	80			
0028	06			
0029	3F		SWI	

PROBLEM B-18

What is the value of memory location 8007 before you close the switch attached to control line CB1? What is its value before and after the BITA $8006 instruction? Does accumulator A change as a result of the execution of BITA $8006? Name some other instructions that would clear the interrupt flag without affecting the operation of the program.

PROBLEM B-19

Revise Program B-9 (and Program B-1) so that it responds to the opening of the switch attached to control line CB2.

PROBLEM B-20

Make Program B-9 send data from an array starting at memory location 00A0. It should send an item from the array to the LEDs each time the status signal goes low. How would you change the program to send an item each time the status signal goes high? How would you make the program respond to control line CB1? How would you make it respond to CA2? You can take advantage of unused control lines attached to other ports as long as you handle the status and control signals properly.

Note that you must be careful to document instructions such as the extra BITA $8006 instruction in Program B-9 (sometimes referred to as a "dummy read"), since a casual observer might otherwise think they are unnecessary and eliminate them. The problem with output operations is unique to the Peripheral Interface Adapter and would not necessarily occur with similar devices from other microprocessor families.

USING THE PIA OUTPUT CONTROL SIGNALS

Thus we have seen that the PIA control lines can be used to implement DATA READY or PERIPHERAL READY signals. This implementation does not use any of the data lines and provides features (such as latching of the transition on the status line and automatic clearing of the interrupt flag) that would otherwise require additional hardware or software.

Furthermore, we can use control line CA2 (or CB2) as an output control signal. The bits governing this mode of operation are (see Figure B-9):

Bit 5 of the PIA control register determines whether control line 2 is an input (0) or an output (1). Note that we have cleared this bit in all the previous examples.

If bit 5 = 1 (control line 2 is an output), bit 4 of the PIA control register determines whether control line 2 is pulsed automatically after an input or output operation (0) or is left at a fixed level (1).

If bit 5 = 1 and bit 4 = 0 (control line 2 is being pulsed automatically), bit 3 of the PIA control register determines whether the active-low pulse on control line 2 lasts until the next active transition on control line 1 (0) or for one clock cycle (1). The PIA can thus produce automatically either the long DATA ACCEPTED (or DATA BUFFER EMPTY) signal or the short multiplexing pulse that we discussed earlier.

If bit 5 = 1 and bit 4 = 1 (control line 2 is a fixed level), bit 3 of the PIA control register is the value of the level. This operating mode allows the program to manage the output control signal. The control signal may be a serial output that turns a peripheral on or off or selects its operating mode.

The easiest mode to use (and to explain) is the one that leaves control line 2 at the level given by bit 3 of the PIA control register. Now we can revise Program B-4 to use control line CA2 as the signal that indicates the acceptance of the data. The binary value that the program must store in control register A is 00111100 (3C hex), where

> bit 5 = 1 to make CA2 an output
>
> bit 4 = 1 to make CA2 a level
>
> bit 3 = 1 to make the level 1 (since we are driving the cathode of the LED, this turns the LED off)
>
> bit 2 = 1 to address the I/O port rather than the data direction register

So the revised program is as follows (see Program B-10 for a hexadecimal version):

```
LDAA      #$FF           TURN OFF THE LEDS
STAA      $8006
LDAA      $8004          GET DATA FROM INPUT PORT
COMA
STAA      $8006          SHOW DATA ON LIGHTS
LDAA      #%00110100     TURN ON CONTROL LIGHT
STAA      $8007
SWI
```

All the lights attached to user PIA port B are available for data, since we are using control line CA2 for the control signal. Enter and run Program B-10; you should set breakpoints before the second STAA $8006 and the STAA $8007 so that you can see the data appear on the lights and the control light change state. Note that we must set all the bits in the control register, even though we are only changing bit 3. Remember to change memory location 000F in the initialization routine (Program B-1) to 00111100 binary or 3C hexadecimal.

PROGRAM B-10

MEMORY ADDRESS (HEX)	MEMORY CONTENTS (HEX)	INSTRUCTION (MNEMONIC)	
0016	86	LDAA	#$FF
0017	FF		
0018	B7	STAA	$8006
0019	80		
001A	06		
001B	B6	LDAA	$8004
001C	80		
001D	04		
001E	43	COMA	

MEMORY ADDRESS (HEX)	MEMORY CONTENTS (HEX)	INSTRUCTION (MNEMONIC)	
001F	B7	STAA	$8006
0020	80		
0021	06		
0022	86	LDAA	#%00110100
0023	34		
0024	B7	STAA	$8007
0025	80		
0026	07		
0027	3F	SWI	

PROBLEM B-21

Make Program B-10 leave the control light on only long enough to be visible. As in Problem B-9, use monitor subroutine DLY1 (starting address E0E0) with an input parameter of 4000 hex to produce the delay.

We can also revise Program B-5 (the complete handshake input program) to use control line CA2. Here control line CA1 is the input status signal that indicates the availability of new data and control line CA2 is the output control signal that indicates the acceptance of the data (see Figure B-5). Program B-11 is the hexadecimal version.

```
        LDAA    #$FF            TURN OFF THE LEDS
        STAA    $8006
WAITR   TST     $8005           IS DATA READY?
        BPL     WAITR           NO, WAIT
        LDAA    $8004           YES, GET DATA FROM INPUT PORT
        COMA
        STAA    $8006           SHOW DATA ON LIGHTS
        LDAA    #%00110100      TURN ON CONTROL LIGHT
        STAA    $8005
        SWI
```

PROGRAM B-11

MEMORY ADDRESS (HEX)	MEMORY CONTENTS (HEX)	INSTRUCTION (MNEMONIC)	
0016	86	LDAA	#$FF
0017	FF		
0018	B7	STAA	$8006
0019	80		

MEMORY ADDRESS (HEX)	MEMORY CONTENTS (HEX)	INSTRUCTION (MNEMONIC)		
001A	06			
001B	7D	WAITR	TST	$8005
001C	80			
001D	05			
001E	2A		BPL	WAITR
001F	FB			
0020	B6		LDAA	$8004
0021	80			
0022	04			
0023	43		COMA	
0024	B7		STAA	$8006
0025	80			
0026	06			
0027	86		LDAA	#%00110100
0028	34			
0029	B7		STAA	$8005
002A	80			
002B	05			
002C	3F		SWI	

PROBLEM B-22

Make Program B-11 load input data into an array starting at memory location 00A0. The program should load an item from the switches into the array each time control line CA1 goes low. The control light (attached to control line CA2) should go on after each input operation and remain on long enough to be clearly visible (use monitor subroutine DLY1).

PROBLEM B-23

Make Program B-6 use control line CB1 as the status input and control line CB2 as the control output. Remember to clear the interrupt flag.

One difficulty in using the PIA operating mode in which we explicitly send control line 2 high or low is that we must not change any of the other bits in the PIA control register. Clearly, an output routine that changes the state of control line 2 should not depend on the value in the control register or change that value inadvertently. We can overcome this difficulty by using the logical functions just as in Laboratory 3:

1) To make control line 2 a logic 1, logically OR bit 3 of the control register with a 1.

```
LDAA      PIACR
ORAA      #%00001000          BRING CONTROL LINE 2 HIGH
STAA      PIACR
```

2)   To make control line 2 a logic 0, logically AND bit 3 of the control register with a 0.

```
LDAA      PIACR
ANDA      #%11110111          BRING CONTROL LINE 2 LOW
STAA      PIACR
```

These procedures leave the other bit positions in the control register unchanged.

PROBLEM B-24

Write a program that uses the logical functions to bring control line CB2 of the user PIA high, low, and then high again.

PIA AUTOMATIC CONTROL MODES

We can simplify Programs B-10 and B-11 even further by using the operating modes in which the PIA automatically generates a pulse on control line 2. For example, we can store the binary value 00100100 (24 hex) in user PIA control register A, where

bit 5 = 1 to make CA2 an output

bit 4 = 0 to make CA2 an automatic pulse

bit 3 = 0 to make CA2 go low after the I/O port has been read
and remain low until the next active transition occurs
on CA1 (CA2 is thus an INPUT BUFFER EMPTY signal)

bit 2 = 1 to address the I/O port rather than the data
direction register

The following program is equivalent to Program B-11 in that the processor waits for an active transition on control line CA1, reads the data, and then brings control line CA2 low to indicate that the data has been accepted. Remember that we must change memory location 000F in the initialization routine (the pattern loaded into the control registers) from 04 to 00100100 binary or 24 hexadecimal.

```
              LDAA    #$FF        TURN OFF THE LEDS
              STAA    $8006
      WAITR   TST     $8005       IS DATA READY?
              BPL     WAITR
              LDAA    $8004       YES, GET DATA FROM INPUT PONT
              COMA
              STAA    $8006       SHOW DATA ON LIGHTS
              SWI
```

Program B-12 is the hexadecimal version; enter and run the program, setting a breakpoint at the LDAA $8004 instruction. The LED attached to control line CA2 should remain off until you resume the program. When the CPU executes LDAA $8004 (thus reading the data port), the LED should light and remain lit until you open and close the switch attached to control line CA1, thus producing the next active transition. Note that we do not have to change the control register after the initialization; the PIA automatically brings the control output low and high. The mode in which we must actually clear and set the bit in the control register is sometimes called a *manual output mode.*

PROGRAM B-12

MEMORY ADDRESS (HEX)	MEMORY CONTENTS (HEX)	INSTRUCTION (MNEMONIC)	
0016	86		LDAA	#$FF
0017	FF			
0018	B7		STAA	$8006
0019	80			
001A	06			
001B	7D	WAITR	TST	$8005
001C	80			
001D	05			
001E	2A		BPL	WAITR
001F	FB			
0020	B6		LDAA	$8004
0021	80			
0022	04			
0023	43		COMA	
0024	B7		STAA	$8006
0025	80			
0026	06			
0027	3F		SWI	

PROBLEM B-25

Make Program B-6 use control line CB2 in the automatic mode as the control output.

PROBLEM B-26

Revise the answer to Problem B-25 so that it sends data from an array starting at memory location 00A0. It should send an item from the array to the lights each time the status input (control line CB1) goes low. Set a breakpoint after the status checking loop so that you can see the control light go on and off.

The other automatic mode (control register bit 3 = 1) generates a brief output control pulse lasting only one CPU clock cycle. This mode is most commonly used to multiplex displays as shown in Figure B-8, although other I/O devices such as converters may also require a brief clock pulse after each input or output operation. Change memory location 000F in the initialization routine to 00101100 binary or 2C hexadecimal and run Program B-12. You will not be able to see the control light come on since the pulse is so brief. One way to show that the PIA has produced a pulse is to tie CA2 to CB1 and check to see if bit 7 of control register B is set after you run the program.

We should note that the automatic modes act somewhat differently on port A than they do on port B. Port A produces the automatic pulses only after the I/O port is read, and port B produces the automatic pulses only after the I/O port is written. Of course, we can always fool the PIA by including an extra read or write instruction in the program; that is,

```
LDAA       PIADRB       GET DATA FROM PORT B
STAA       PIADRB       PRODUCE AUTOMATIC STROBE


STAA       PIADRA       SEND DATA TO PORT A
LDAA       PIADRA       PRODUCE AUTOMATIC STROBE
```

Remember that we said initially that port A was best suited for use as an input port and port B as an output port. Besides the differences in the automatic modes, port B is also buffered so that it has greater drive capability and can be read properly even when it is being used as an output port.

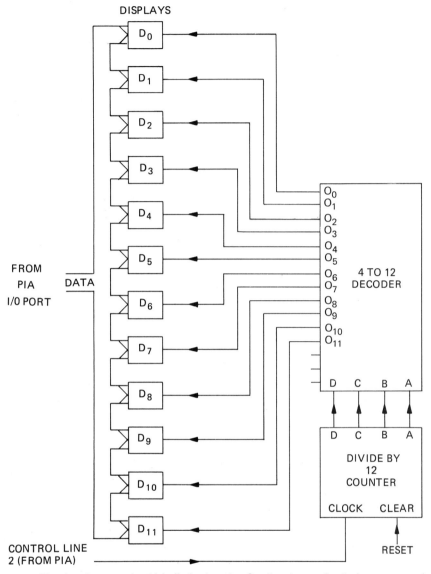

The decoder controls which display is active. Sending data to the display causes a pulse on control line 2 which clocks the counter.

FIGURE B-8. A 12-digit multiplexed display using a counter and a decoder.

PROGRAMMABLE I/O PORTS

The PIA has numerous operating modes (see the summary in Figure B-9). The programmability of this device means that it can operate in any of these modes, subject only to the program storing the appropriate value in the control register. The advantages of programmability are (as we noted also in Laboratory 3) that the same hardware can be used in many different applications and that changes or corrections can be made in software rather than in hardware. The disadvantages are that extra programming is necessary and that there are no standards for programmable devices. The options that are available and the ways in which they are selected are arbitrarily determined by the manufacturer and vary from device to device. For example, the functions and positions of the bits in the PIA control register are arbitrary. Similar devices from other manufacturers would have completely different registers.

However, the following features are typical of programmable I/O devices:

1) One or more command or control registers that determine how the device operates.

2) One or more status registers that contain information describing the current state of the device and the data transfer. The PIA control register is actually both a control and a status register.

3) Separate data and status or control inputs and outputs.

Many (if not all) of the bits in the command or control registers are set during initialization to implement a particular interface. The main program does not change those bits. In the case of the PIA, most applications programs would not change the arrangement of input and output lines or the operating mode.

Note that programmable I/O devices require careful documentation. The instructions that determine their operating modes and use them are arbitrary and are seldom described well in books or manuals. The programmer cannot expect that those who must read the documentation will understand how a specific programmable device works.

KEY POINT SUMMARY

1) Input and output transfers can only proceed properly if there is some way to determine when sender and receiver are ready, when data is actually available, and when the receiver has accepted the data.

2) Synchronous transfers proceed according to a clock reference, while asynchronous transfers proceed through the exchange of status and control signals. The exchange of these signals is called a *handshake*.

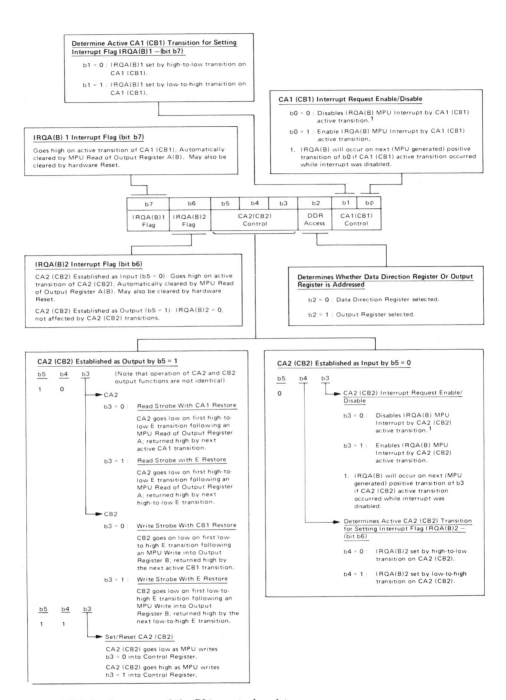

FIGURE B-9. Summary of the PIA control register.

3) Status and control signals can be implemented by using additional data ports. Such implementations are straightforward in theory, but require a large amount of software (and hardware) to coordinate the signals properly.

4) Each side of the PIA has two control lines. Both can be used as inputs. In that case, one bit of the control register (the interrupt flag) latches active transitions and one bit determines which transitions are active. Reading the data register clears the interrupt flags automatically. Output ports require an extra "dummy read" to clear the interrupt flags.

5) Control line 2 on each side can also be used as an output. Bit 5 of the control register determines whether this line is an input or an output. Several operating modes are available. In the automatic or pulse mode, control line 2 is automatically pulsed after each read operation on port A or write operation on port B. The active-low pulse lasts either until the next active transition on control line 1 or until the next clock cycle. In the manual or latched mode, the program can bring control line 2 high or low, thus producing pulses of any length or polarity. The automatic modes require less software but have limited applicability. Dummy read or write operations can produce pulses when normal operations do not.

6) Programmable I/O devices simplify hardware design. However, lack of standards for these devices makes careful program documentation essential. Each device has its own set of operating modes, ways to select those modes, and programming idiosyncrasies.

☐ Laboratory **C**

Interrupts

PURPOSE

To learn how and when to use interrupts.

PARTS REQUIRED

None.

REFERENCE MATERIALS

L. A. Leventhal, *Introduction to Microprocessors: Software, Hardware, Programming,* Prentice-Hall, Englewood Cliffs, NJ, 1978, pp. 337-355, 363-369, 405-427.

L. A. Leventhal, *6800 Assembly Language Programming,* Osborne/McGraw-Hill, Berkeley, CA, 1978, Chapter 11.

W. J. Weller, *Practical Microcomputer Programming: The M6800,* Northern Technology Books, Evanston, IL, 1977, Chapter 15.

MEK6800D2 Evaluation Kit II Manual, Motorola Semiconductor Products Inc., Austin, TX, 1977, pp. 1-10 through 1-11 (Trace One Instruction), 2-6 (Trace One Instruction), 3-11 through 3-14 (Interrupt Handling Routines).

M6800 Programming Reference Manual, Motorola Semiconductor Products Inc., Phoenix, AZ, 1976, pp. 2-4 through 2-6 (PIA), 3-3 through 3-8 (Saving MPU Status and Interrupt Pointers), A-56 (RTI instruction).

R. Grappel, "Technique Avoids Interrupt Dangers," *EDN,* May 5, 1979, p. 88.

G. J. Lipovski, *Microcomputer Interfacing,* D.C. Heath (Lexington Books), Lexington, MA, 1980, Chapter 4.

W. S. Holderby, "Designing a Microprocessor-Based Terminal for Factory Data Collection," *Computer Design,* March 1977, pp. 81-86.

WHAT YOU SHOULD LEARN

1) The uses, advantages, and disadvantages of interrupts.
2) The interrupt inputs available on the 6800 microprocessor and the responses they produce.
3) The special interrupt-related instructions available on the 6800 microprocessor.
4) How the MEK6800D2 microcomputer interrupts are implemented.
5) How to produce interrupts from PIAs.
6) How a simple interrupt service routine works and how to save and restore registers.
7) How to write a simple interrupt service routine utilizing the user PIA.
8) How to communicate between the main program and the interrupt service routines.
9) How to use interrupts to implement handshake input/output.
10) How to buffer data that is being transferred to or from input/output devices under interrupt control.
11) When and how to change register values that have been saved in the stack.
12) How to handle multiple sources of interrupts by means of vectoring and polling.
13) Guidelines for programming with interrupts.

TERMS

Disable (or **disarm**)—prohibit an activity from proceeding or a device from producing data outputs.

Enable (or **arm**)—allow an activity to proceed or a device to produce data outputs.

Interrupt–a signal that temporarily suspends the computer's normal sequence of operations and transfers control to a special routine.

Interrupt-driven–dependent on interrupts for its operation, may idle until it receives an interrupt.

Interrupt mask (or **interrupt enable**)–a mechanism that allows the program to determine whether interrupts will be accepted. A mask bit usually must be cleared to allow interrupts, whereas an enable bit must be set.

Interrupt service routine–a program that performs the actions required to respond to an interrupt.

Maskable interrupt–an interrupt that the system can disable.

Nonmaskable interrupt–an interrupt that cannot be disabled within the CPU.

Polling–determining the states of peripherals or other devices by examining each one in succession.

Power fail interrupt–an interrupt that informs the CPU of an impending loss of power.

Priority interrupt system–an interrupt system in which some interrupts have precedence over others–that is, will be serviced first or can interrupt the others' service routines.

Programmed input/output–input/output performed under program control without using interrupts or other special hardware techniques.

Reentrant–can be executed correctly while the same routine is being interrupted or otherwise held in abeyance.

Transparent routine–a routine that operates without interfering with the operations of other routines.

Trap (or **software interrupt**)–an instruction that forces a jump to a specific (CPU-dependent) address, often used to produce breakpoints or to indicate hardware or software errors.

Vectored interrupt–an interrupt that provides the CPU with an identification code (or *vector*) that the CPU can use to transfer control to the corresponding service routine. The process whereby control is transferred to the service routine is called *vectoring*.

6800 INSTRUCTIONS

CLI–clear interrupt mask (enable interrupts); set the INTERRUPT MASK (I) flag to zero, thus enabling the maskable interrupt ($\overline{\text{IRQ}}$ input).

RTI—return from interrupt; reload all the user registers from the stack in the order shown in Figure C-1.

SEI—set interrupt mask (disable interrupts); set the INTERRUPT MASK (I) flag to 1, thus disabling the maskable interrupt ($\overline{\text{IRQ}}$ input).

SWI—software interrupt; save all the user registers in the stack in the order shown in Figure C-1 and load the program counter from addresses FFFA and FFFB.

TSX—transfer stack pointer to index register; place the value of the stack pointer plus 1 in the index register.

WAI—wait for interrupt; save all the registers in the stack and suspend program execution until an interrupt occurs.

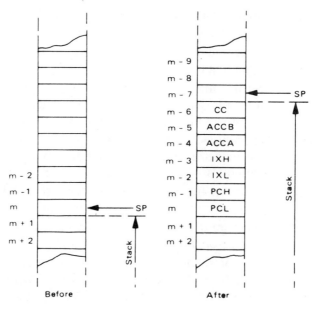

SP = Stack Pointer
CC = Condition Codes (Also called the Processor Status Byte)
ACCB = Accumulator B
ACCA = Accumulator A
IXH = Index Register, Higher Order 8 Bits
IXL = Index Register, Lower Order 8 Bits
PCH = Program Counter, Higher Order 8 Bits
PCL = Program Counter, Lower Order 8 Bits

FIGURE C-1. Saving the status of the Motorola 6800 microprocessor in the stack. (Courtesy of Motorola Semiconductor Products, Inc.)

INTERRUPTS

Interrupts are direct inputs to the CPU that can change its sequence of operations. An interrupt informs the CPU that something has happened, much as the ringing of a telephone informs a person that someone is on the line. The program then does not have to check READY flags or other status inputs. Instead, the inputs cause the CPU to suspend its normal operations and respond immediately.

The advantages of interrupts are:

- No need to check status inputs for fear of missing an event.
- Simple hardware implementation of time delays (see Laboratory D) without processor involvement.
- Faster response because of the direct hardware connection.

The disadvantages of interrupts are:

- Introduction of a random element into systems, since interrupts can occur at any time.
- Need for extra hardware to control interrupts and simplify their recognition (this hardware acts like a switchboard in a telephone system).
- Introduction of new programming problems, such as deciding when to allow interrupts and how to communicate between the main program and the interrupt service routines.

CHARACTERISTICS OF INTERRUPT SYSTEMS

Interrupt systems vary greatly from processor to processor. Typical characteristics are:

1) Number of inputs.

Each input can produce a different internal response.

2) Priority.

Some interrupts may take precedence over others (i.e., be recognized first or interrupt the others' service routines).

3) How sources are identified.

A system in which the CPU must examine sources until it finds the active one is called a *polling interrupt system;* one in which each source automatically directs the CPU to the proper service routine is called a *vectored interrupt system.*

4)   How control is transferred to and from the service routines.

Special CALL (or trap) and RETURN instructions are often involved.

5)   How interrupts are enabled and disabled.

Interrupts may have to be disabled during system initialization, critical functions, or service routines. Some events, such as power failure, may have to be nonmaskable, since they take priority over all other system functions.

6800 INTERRUPT SYSTEM

The 6800 microprocessor has two interrupt inputs:

$\overline{\text{NMI}}$ is a nonmaskable interrupt generally used to respond to power failure. The input is edge-sensitive, so that it will not interrupt its own service routine.

$\overline{\text{IRQ}}$ is a maskable interrupt generally used for input/output and other regular system functions. The input is level-sensitive.

The 6800 microprocessor responds to an interrupt by fetching a new value for the program counter from a fixed pair of memory locations. Table C-1 contains the addresses used by the interrupt inputs, RESET, and the SWI (SOFTWARE INTERRUPT) instruction. The processor automatically saves all its user registers in the stack in the order shown in Figure C-1 as part of the response to $\overline{\text{NMI}}$, $\overline{\text{IRQ}}$, or SWI.

Table C-1

MEMORY MAP FOR MOTOROLA 6800 INTERRUPT VECTORS (COURTESY OF MOTOROLA SEMICONDUCTOR PRODUCTS, INC.)

VECTOR ADDRESS		INPUT OR INSTRUCTION
MS	LS	
FFFE	FFFF	Reset
FFFC	FFFD	Nonmaskable Interrupt ($\overline{\text{NMI}}$)
FFFA	FFFB	Software Interrupt (SWI)
FFF8	FFF9	Interrupt Request ($\overline{\text{IRQ}}$)

The 6800 microprocessor also has an INTERRUPT MASK or I flag, which is bit 4 of the condition code register. If this flag is 1, the maskable interrupt is disabled; if this flag is 0, the maskable interrupt is enabled. The nonmaskable interrupt is always enabled into the processor, although external gates may disable it.

SPECIAL INTERRUPT-RELATED INSTRUCTIONS AND FEATURES

The 6800 microprocessor has several instructions intended for use with the interrupt system:

- CLI (CLEAR INTERRUPT MASK) clears the INTERRUPT MASK flag and thus enables maskable interrupts.
- RTI (RETURN FROM INTERRUPT) loads the registers from the stack in the order shown in Figure C-1. RTI thus restores the original states of all registers (including the condition code register and hence the INTERRUPT MASK flag) and returns control to the program that was interrupted. When you press the G key, the JBUG monitor transfers control to your program by executing an RTI instruction. The program therefore starts with the register values loaded from the stack.
- SEI (SET INTERRUPT MASK) sets the INTERRUPT MASK flag and thus disables maskable interrupts.
- SWI (SOFTWARE INTERRUPT) saves all the registers in the stack, disables the maskable interrupt, and loads the program counter from addresses FFFA and FFFB (see Table C-1). SWI thus produces almost the same response as an external interrupt (hence its name).
- WAI (WAIT FOR INTERRUPT) saves all the registers in the stack and halts the processor until an interrupt is received.

You should note the following features of the 6800 interrupt system:

1) $\overline{\text{RESET}}$ sets the INTERRUPT MASK flag and thus disables the maskable interrupt, allowing the program to initialize parameters before interrupts are accepted.

2) Accepting an interrupt sets the INTERRUPT MASK flag and thus disables the maskable interrupt. An interrupt will therefore not disturb its own service routine.

3) Accepting an interrupt automatically results in the saving of all user registers in the stack. Similarly, executing RTI automatically restores all the registers. No PSH or PUL instructions are necessary.

4) The $\overline{\text{NMI}}$ input is always enabled. It is most commonly used as a power-fail interrupt that saves essential data in a nonvolatile memory

(frequently, a low-power memory with battery backup). Loss of power clearly takes precedence over all other activities, since it will ultimately stop them from proceeding anyway.

MEK6800D2 INTERRUPTS

The MEK6800D2 microcomputer utilizes some of the interrupts and gives the user access to others. Table C-2 describes the MEK6800D2 interrupt system. The interrupts that we will use are:

- $\overline{\text{NMI}}$ is connected to the keyboard/display PIA and is vectored by JBUG through memory locations A006 and A007. This interrupt is used to provide the single-step facility. The startup routine places the address E14E in the specified locations so that $\overline{\text{NMI}}$ causes the processor to scan the keyboard.
- $\overline{\text{IRQ}}$ is connected to the user PIA and is vectored by JBUG through addresses A000 and A001.

Before you can use any of the interrupts, your program must:

1) Initialize the stack pointer, since an interrupt automatically causes the CPU to save all the user registers in the stack.
2) Load the address of the service routine into memory locations A000 and A001 ($\overline{\text{IRQ}}$) or A006 and A007 ($\overline{\text{NMI}}$).
3) Enable the maskable interrupt with the CLI instruction.

Table C-2

MEK6800D2 INTERRUPT ADDRESSES*

INPUT	FUNCTION	LOCATION OF SERVICE ROUTINE
$\overline{\text{RESET}}$	Reset switch	E08D (in JBUG ROM)
$\overline{\text{NMI}}$	Nonmaskable interrupt	Address in A006 and A007, monitor places E14E there
SWI	Software interrupt	E032 (in JBUG ROM)
$\overline{\text{IRQ}}$	Maskable interrupt	Address in A000 and A001

*Note that JBUG vectors $\overline{\text{NMI}}$ requests to address E019, saves the user stack pointer, and disables $\overline{\text{NMI}}$ interrupts by clearing the interrupt enables in the keyboard/display PIA control register before transferring control to the address in A006 and A007.

PIA INTERRUPTS

Most 6800 interrupts come from input/output devices attached to the processor through PIAs. Thus we must be concerned with how the PIA handles interrupts. The key control register bits are (see Tables C-3 and C-4):

- Control register bit 0 determines whether active transitions on control line 1 cause interrupts. Note that control register bit 0 must be 1 to enable interrupts; it is thus an INTERRUPT ENABLE, opposite in polarity to the microprocessor's INTERRUPT MASK flag. Remember that control register bit 1 determines which transitions on control line 1 are active.

Table C-3

CONTROL OF INTERRUPT INPUTS CA1 AND CB1

CRA-1 (CRB-1)	CRA-0 (CRB-0)	Interrupt Input CA1 (CB1)	Interrupt Flag CRA-7 (CRB-7)	MPU Interrupt Request $\overline{IRQA}$ ($\overline{IRQB}$)
0	0	↓ Active	Set high on ↓ of CA1 (CB1)	Disabled — $\overline{IRQ}$ remains high
0	1	↓ Active	Set high on ↓ of CA1 (CB1)	Goes low when the interrupt flag bit CRA-7 (CRB-7) goes high
1	0	↑ Active	Set high on ↑ of CA1 (CB1)	Disabled — $\overline{IRQ}$ remains high
1	1	↑ Active	Set high on ↑ of CA1 (CB1)	Goes low when the interrupt flag bit CRA-7 (CRB-7) goes high

Notes: 1. ↑ indicates positive transition (low to high)

2. ↓ indicates negative transition (high to low)

3. The Interrupt flag bit CRA-7 is cleared by an MPU Read of the A Data Register, and CRB-7 is cleared by an MPU Read of the B Data Register.

4. If CRA-0 (CRB-0) is low when an interrupt occurs (Interrupt disabled) and is later brought high, $\overline{IRQA}$ ($\overline{IRQB}$) occurs after CRA-0 (CRB-0) is written to a "one".

Table C-4

CONTROL OF CA2 AND CB2 AS INTERRUPT INPUTS
CRA5 (CRB5) is low

CRA-5 (CRB-5)	CRA-4 (CRB-4)	CRA-3 (CRB-3)	Interrupt Input CA2 (CB2)	Interrupt Flag CRA-6 (CRB-6)	MPU Interrupt Request $\overline{IRQA}$ ($\overline{IRQB}$)
0	0	0	↓ Active	Set high on ↓ of CA2 (CB2)	Disabled — $\overline{IRQ}$ remains high
0	0	1	↓ Active	Set high on ↓ of CA2 (CB2)	Goes low when the interrupt flag bit CRA-6 (CRB-6) goes high
0	1	0	↑ Active	Set high on ↑ of CA2 (CB2)	Disabled — $\overline{IRQ}$ remains high
0	1	1	↑ Active	Set high on ↑ of CA2 (CB2)	Goes low when the interrupt flag bit CRA-6 (CRB-6) goes high

Notes: 1. ↑ indicates positive transition (low to high)

2. ↓ indicates negative transition (high to low)

3. The Interrupt flag bit CRA-6 is cleared by an MPU Read of the A Data Register and CRB-6 is cleared by an MPU Read of the B Data Register.

4. If CRA-3 (CRB-3) is low when an interrupt occurs (Interrupt disabled) and is later brought high, $\overline{IRQA}$ ($\overline{IRQB}$) occurs after CRA-3 (CRB-3) is written to a "one".

- Control register bit 3 determines whether active transitions on control line 2 cause interrupts. Note that control register bit 3 must be 1 to enable interrupts. This bit only has an interrupt enabling function if control line 2 is an input (i.e., if control register bit 5 = 0). Remember that control register bit 4 determines which transitions on control line 2 are active.

MEK6800D2 KEYBOARD INTERRUPTS

The simplest interrupt to use is the keyboard (blue E key) interrupt, which is attached to $\overline{\text{NMI}}$ through the keyboard/display PIA. We do not have to enable either PIA or CPU interrupts, since the monitor routine that executes user programs enables the PIA interrupt and $\overline{\text{NMI}}$, of course, is always enabled into the CPU. This interrupt normally stops program execution and returns control to the JBUG monitor.

To see how the keyboard interrupt works, we will move the stack and the interrupt service address into user memory as follows:

1) Load 00FF into the stack pointer.
2) Load 0080 into memory locations A006 and A007 so that the nonmaskable interrupt will transfer control to that address. We will then start our service routine there.

The following program will wait for you to press the blue E key. We have changed the values in the user registers to make it easy to tell the values in the interrupt service routine from those in the main program. Program C-1 is the hexadecimal version.

```
        LDS     #$00FF       INITIALIZE USER STACK POINTER
        LDX     #$80         PLACE SERVICE ADDRESS IN USER RAM
        STX     $A006
        LDAA    #$EF         PLACE STARTING VALUES IN REGISTERS
        LDAB    #$CD
        LDX     #$89AB
HERE    BRA     HERE

        ORG     $80
        TST     $8022        CLEAR INTERRUPT FLAG IN KEYBOARD PIA
        LDAA    #$67         PLACE NEW VALUES IN REGISTERS
        LDAB    #$45
        LDX     #$0123
        RTI
```

PROGRAM C-1

MEMORY ADDRESS (HEX)	MEMORY CONTENTS (HEX)		INSTRUCTION (MNEMONIC)	
0000	8E		LDS	#$00FF
0001	00			
0002	FF			
0003	CE		LDX	#$80
0004	00			
0005	80			
0006	FF		STX	$A006
0007	A0			
0008	06			
0009	86		LDAA	#$EF
000A	EF			
000B	C6		LDAB	#$CD
000C	CD			
000D	CE		LDX	#$89AB
000E	89			
000F	AB			
0010	20	HERE	BRA	HERE
0011	FE			
0080	7D		TST	$8022
0081	80			
0082	22			
0083	86		LDAA	#$67
0084	67			
0085	C6		LDAB	#$45
0086	45			
0087	CE		LDX	#$0123
0088	01			
0089	23			
008A	3B		RTI	

PROBLEM C-1

Run Program C-1 with a breakpoint in address 008A. Press the blue E key. What are the values of the accumulators, index register, and condition code register? What is the current value of the stack pointer? What values did the processor place in the stack as a result of the interrupt? Remember that the processor stores those values immediately above the ones placed in the stack by SWI. Change memory location 0010 to 3F (SWI) and continue the program. What are the final values of the accumulators, index register, and condition code register? Explain what has happened.

Notes: If you press the blue E key more than momentarily, it will still be closed when the processor reaches the breakpoint. The closure will cause the computer to exit from the automatic register display and enter the prompt mode. You can return to the register display by pressing R.

You cannot use the single-step mode, since that mode depends on the non-maskable interrupt.

If you have trouble resuming the program because the microcomputer does not remove the breakpoint, simply replace the SWI by hand.

PROBLEM C-2

WAI (WAIT FOR INTERRUPT) is occasionally useful in working with interrupts. This instruction saves all the registers in the stack and halts the processor until an interrupt occurs. Replace memory locations 0010 and 0011 with

0010	3E	WAI
0011	3F	SWI

Does this change affect the execution of the program? To which memory location does RTI transfer control? What are the advantages and disadvantages of the two approaches?

When we use interrupts, the program does not have to check the interrupt flag in the PIA control register. The status checking (sometimes called *polling*) is replaced by a direct hardware connection through one of the microprocessor's interrupt inputs.

USER PIA INTERRUPTS

We can also produce interrupts from the user PIA. Its interrupt outputs are tied to the maskable interrupt or $\overline{\text{IRQ}}$, which is serviced at the address in memory locations A000 and A001. To employ the user PIA in this manner, we must enable its interrupts (the monitor did this automatically for the keyboard/display PIA) and we must clear the processor's INTERRUPT MASK flag (the keyboard/display PIA is tied to the nonmaskable interrupt). The required steps are as follows:

    1)   Place the interrupt service address in memory locations A000 and A001. You do not have to worry about this address changing since the monitor does not initialize it.

    2)   Enable one or more of the interrupts from the user PIA. Control register bit 0 must be 1 to enable interrupts from control line 1 and bit 1 determines which transitions cause those interrupts (bit 1 = 0 for

trailing edge interrupts, 1 for leading edge interrupts). Bits 3 and 4 have the same functions for control line 2 if that line is an input.

3) Enable the microprocessor's $\overline{\text{IRQ}}$ input by executing the CLI (CLEAR INTERRUPT MASK) instruction. You should normally disable the interrupt (by setting the INTERRUPT MASK flag) before returning control to the monitor.

The following program performs a series of initialization functions. It loads the stack pointer, initializes both ports of the PIA (with interrupts disabled), places 0080 in the interrupt service vector, reads both PIA I/O ports to clear spurious interrupts that may occur during startup, and turns off all the LEDs attached to user PIA port B. We will use this program (the hexadecimal version is Program C-2) throughout the rest of the current laboratory. Note that we leave the enabling of the CPU interrupt for last, since we must initialize all parameters before allowing interrupts.

```
LDS     #$00FF          INITIALIZE USER STACK POINTER
LDX     #$0080          ESTABLISH INTERRUPT SERVICE ADDRESS
STX     $A000
LDX     #$8004
CLR     1,X             ACCESS DATA DIRECTION REGISTERS
CLR     3,X
CLR     0,X             MAKE PORT A INPUTS
LDAA    #$FF            MAKE PORT B OUTPUTS
STAA    2,X
LDAB    #%00000100      ENABLE DATA TRANSFERS
STAB    1,X
STAB    3,X
BITA    0,X             CLEAR SPURIOUS INTERRUPTS
BITA    2,X
STAA    2,X             TURN OFF THE LEDS
```

PROGRAM C-2

MEMORY ADDRESS (HEX)	MEMORY CONTENTS (HEX)	INSTRUCTION (MNEMONIC)	
0000	8E	LDS	#$00FF
0001	00		
0002	FF		
0003	CE	LDX	#$0080
0004	00		
0005	80		
0006	FF	STX	$A000
0007	A0		
0008	00		

MEMORY ADDRESS (HEX)	MEMORY CONTENTS (HEX)	INSTRUCTION (MNEMONIC)	
0009	CE	LDX	#$8004
000A	80		
000B	04		
000C	6F	CLR	1,X
000D	01		
000E	6F	CLR	3,X
000F	03		
0010	6F	CLR	0,X
0011	00		
0012	86	LDAA	#$FF
0013	FF		
0014	A7	STAA	2,X
0015	02		
0016	C6	LDAB	#%00000100
0017	04		
0018	E7	STAB	1,X
0019	01		
001A	E7	STAB	3,X
001B	03		
001C	A5	BITA	0,X
001D	00		
001E	A5	BITA	2,X
001F	02		
0020	A7	STAA	2,X
0021	02		

The following program (see Program C-3 for a hexadecimal version) enables the interrupt from CA1 (on a high-to-low transition, i.e., when you close the switch), enables the CPU interrupt, and then simply counts in accumulator A. When the processor is interrupted, the interrupt service routine displays the count on the LEDs attached to user PIA port B. Thus closing the switch attached to CA1 causes the current count to be displayed. Program C-2 provides the proper initialization.

```
        LDAA    #%00000101    ENABLE CA1 INTERRUPT
        STAA    1,X
        CLRA                  START COUNT AT ZERO
        CLI                   ENABLE CPU INTERRUPT
COUNT   INCA                  KEEP INCREMENTING ACCUMU-
  *                             LATOR A
```

```
BRA      COUNT

ORG      $80
BITA     $8004          CLEAR INTERRUPT FLAG
COMA                    PLACE CURRENT COUNT ON LEDS
STAA     $8006
RTI
```

Enter and run Program C-3. Close the switch attached to CA1 several times and write down the series of counts that you observe. Does the COMA instruction in the interrupt service routine affect the count in the main program? Remember that RTI restores all the registers from the stack.

Since the interrupt enable for control line 1 is bit 0 of the PIA control register, you can disable that interrupt (if you know it is enabled) with the DEC instruction (DEC PIACR) or enable it (if you know it is disabled) with the INC instruction. This trick saves time and memory, but we will use the straightforward approach in the interest of clarity.

PROGRAM C-3

MEMORY ADDRESS (HEX)	MEMORY CONTENTS (HEX)		INSTRUCTION (MNEMONIC)	
0022	86		LDAA	#%00000101
0023	05			
0024	A7		STAA	1,X
0025	01			
0026	4F		CLRA	
0027	0E		CLI	
0028	4C	COUNT	INCA	
0029	20		BRA	COUNT
002A	FD			
0080	B5		BITA	$8004
0081	80			
0082	04			
0083	43		COMA	
0084	B7		STAA	$8006
0085	80			
0086	06			
0087	3B		RTI	

PROBLEM C-3

Change Program C-3 so that the interrupt input is CB1 instead of CA1.

PROBLEM C-4

Change Program C-3 so that opening the switch attached to CA2 causes an interrupt.

PROBLEM C-5

What is the value of the INTERRUPT MASK flag at the beginning of the service routine? Remember that I is bit 4 of the condition code register. What is the value of the INTERRUPT MASK flag at the end of the service routine? What is the value that is restored from the stack—how could you deduce this value?

PROBLEM C-6

Make Program C-3 keep a 16-bit count. Have the service routine store the current count in memory locations 00A0 and 00A1 (MSBs in 00A0) so you can easily examine it by setting a breakpoint. Why can't you use the index register to hold the counter? What is the value of the index register at the beginning of the service routine?

One occasional (but annoying and perplexing) problem is the occurrence of spurious interrupts. These may be caused by accidentally closing the wrong switch, by moving jumper wires, or by electrical noise either during startup or during operations. The way to clear interrupt flags that may have been set by spurious interrupts is (as we described in Laboratory B) to read the PIA data registers; that is, executing the following program will do the job.

```
BITA    $8004    CLEAR PORT A INTERRUPT
BITA    $8006    CLEAR PORT B INTERRUPT
SWI
```

You may want to keep this program somewhere in memory so that you can execute it and clear the interrupt flags if you find the computer caught in a loop. Most actual initialization routines include a sequence to clear spurious interrupts caused by startup.

COMMUNICATIONS BETWEEN MAIN PROGRAM AND SERVICE ROUTINE

We have not yet provided any way for the main program and the interrupt service routine to communicate. Of course, the interrupt service routine can examine the values that the main program placed in the registers. But it cannot place any results in the registers, since the RTI instruction restores their original contents. In fact, communicating through the registers is seldom a useful approach; the main program is generally using its registers for a variety of purposes and the interrupt service routine can seldom depend on specific values being there. Nor should the interrupt service routine change the registers. Such changes would make the main program and service routine implicitly dependent on each other, so one could not be revised or replaced without affecting the other. Programming is much simpler if the service routine is transparent to the main program; that is, the interaction should be explicit and thus easy to understand, correct, or change.

How, then, should the main program communicate with the interrupt service routine? The simplest way is to use assigned memory locations. The main program can then use those locations to provide data or accept results. The procedure works like the mail drops used in popular spy movies. The agent never sees the informant at all; all communications pass through the mail drop. The agent places orders, requests, and payments in the drop; the informant picks up inputs and provides the required information. This approach provides a well-defined means of communications. One of its advantages is that neither agent nor informant knows anything about the other and either one can be replaced without affecting the transfer of information.

For example, in the following program, the main program clears a memory location and waits for the interrupt service routine to change it. When that happens, the main program exits. Here the interrupt acts like a RUN command, causing the main program to proceed. We use memory location 00A0 for the READY flag (only one bit is really needed). Program C-4 is the hexadecimal version.

```
        LDAA    #%00000101    ENABLE CA1 INTERRUPT
        STAA    1,X
        CLR     $A0           CLEAR READY FLAG
        CLI                   ENABLE CPU INTERRUPT
WTRDY   LDAA    $A0           HAS READY FLAG BEEN SET?
        BEQ     WTRDY         NO, WAIT
        SEI                   YES, DISABLE CPU INTERRUPT
        SWI


        ORG     $80
        BITA    $8004         CLEAR INTERRUPT FLAG
        INC     $A0           SET READY FLAG
        RTI
```

Enter and run Program C-4. The flag values we have chosen are arbitrary; we could just as easily have the main program set the READY flag and the interrupt service routine clear it.

PROGRAM C-4

MEMORY ADDRESS (HEX)	MEMORY CONTENTS (HEX)		INSTRUCTION (MNEMONIC)	
0022	86		LDAA	#%00000101
0023	05			
0024	A7		STAA	1,X
0025	01			
0026	7F		CLR	$A0
0027	00			
0028	A0			
0029	0E		CLI	
002A	96	WTRDY	LDAA	$A0
002B	A0			
002C	27		BEQ	WTRDY
002D	FC			
002E	0F		SEI	
002F	3F		SWI	
0080	B5		BITA	$8004
0081	80			
0082	04			
0083	7C		INC	$A0
0084	00			
0085	A0			
0086	3B		RTI	

PROBLEM C-7

Make Program C-4 use bit 7 of memory location 00A0 as the READY flag. This approach leaves the 7 least significant bits of that location available for data.

PROBLEM C-8

Make Program C-4 wait until the value in location 00A0 is ten. How would you make the main program wait until memory location 00A0 has the same value as memory location 0040? This approach is useful when the computer must count a certain number of external events, such as pulses on a clock line or activations of a sensor.

We should note the disadvantages of using specified memory locations to communicate between the main program and the interrupt service routine. The locations are sometimes called a *mailbox,* since messages are transferred through a temporary storage place much as they are in standard postal services. The problems with this approach are:

1) The transfer is indirect and awkward. Everything has to be handled precisely so that the receiver can process the information without any direct communications (i.e., without asking questions or seeking clarification).

2) The mailbox must be checked often enough to avoid missing messages. The receiver may have to acknowledge each message to inform the sender that the information has been transferred properly.

3) The approach may involve a large amount of overhead. The sender must prepare the messages, the receiver must interpret them, and the sender must wait for the messages to be picked up. All of this slows the rate at which communications can proceed.

4) Other programs may accidentally use the mailbox, thus destroying the information in it. Imagine an agent who uses a park garbage can as a "drop" but finds that the garbage has been collected before the information could be retrieved.

HANDSHAKE INTERRUPTS

Interrupts are often used to implement handshake input/output, as described in Laboratory B. Here the input/output procedures of Figures B-5 and B-6 are initiated by interrupts which directly inform the microprocessor that data is available from an input peripheral or that an output peripheral is ready to receive data.

The following program (Program C-5 is the hexadecimal version) is the interrupt-driven equivalent of Program B-2. The main program clears the DATA READY flag (memory location 00A0) and waits for the interrupt service routine to set it. When an interrupt occurs on control line CA1, the service routine loads the data from the input port, displays the data, and sets the DATA READY flag. Note the extra overhead involved in this program as compared to Program B-2—the interrupts must be enabled and the DATA READY flag must be cleared, set, and tested. On the other hand, the main program need not examine the interrupt flag and the service routine can proceed independently when it is activated.

```
        LDAA    #%00000101      ENABLE CA1 INTERRUPT
        STAA    1,X
        CLR     $A0             CLEAR DATA READY FLAG
        CLI                     ENABLE CPU INTERRUPT
WTRDY   LDAA    $A0             IS DATA READY?
        BEQ     WTRDY           NO, WAIT
        SEI                     YES, DISABLE CPU INTERRUPT
```

```
        SWI

        ORG     $80
        LDAA    $8004           FETCH DATA FROM INPUT PORT
        STAA    $A1             SAVE INPUT DATA
        COMA
        STAA    $8006           AND SHOW IT ON THE LEDS
        INC     $A0             SET DATA READY FLAG
        RTI
```

PROGRAM C-5

MEMORY ADDRESS (HEX)	MEMORY CONTENTS (HEX)		INSTRUCTION (MNEMONIC)	
0022	86		LDAA	#%00000101
0023	05			
0024	A7		STAA	1,X
0025	01			
0026	7F		CLR	$A0
0027	00			
0028	A0			
0029	0E		CLI	
002A	96	WTRDY	LDAA	$A0
002B	A0			
002C	27		BEQ	WTRDY
002D	FC			
002E	0F		SEI	
002F	3F		SWI	
0080	B6		LDAA	$8004
0081	80			
0082	04			
0083	97		STAA	$A1
0084	A1			
0085	43		COMA	
0086	B7		STAA	$8006
0087	80			
0088	06			
0089	7C		INC	$A0
008A	00			
008B	A0			
008C	3B		RTI	

The main program knows that new data has been received because the DATA READY flag in memory location 00A0 has been set. In a real application, it would clear that flag and process the data. It might also disable the PIA interrupt so that new data would not be accepted until the old data had been processed. This is, in fact, how the MEK6800D2's keyboard works, since the JBUG monitor handles one entry at a time.

PROBLEM C-9

Change Program C-5 so that the main program disables the interrupt from port A of the user PIA instead of disabling the entire interrupt system. Make your program independent of the contents of the control register.

PROBLEM C-10

Make the main program in Program C-5 wait for a 7F input to be received. The 7F input is the synchronization character that we discussed in Laboratory 2. If the input is not 7F, the main program should clear the DATA READY flag and wait for the next input.

PROBLEM C-11

Write an interrupt-driven version of the output routine in Program B-3. The main program should clear memory location 00A0 to indicate that data is available for output. When CB1 causes an interrupt, the service routine should send the data from memory location 00A1 and set location 00A0 to indicate that the data has been transmitted. Remember to clear the interrupt flag in the service routine. Why was this not necessary in Program C-5?

PROBLEM C-12

Change the answer to Problem C-11 so that the service routine only sends the data if it is a synchronization character (7F hexadecimal). Otherwise, the service routine simply clears the CB1 interrupt flag. Note that all the LEDs will stay off unless (00A1) = 7F (hex).

BUFFERING INTERRUPTS

Program C-5 handles the input data one character at a time. Clearly, this creates problems if the data is coming in quickly or if only sequences of data are meaningful (as is commonly the case when the inputs are coming from a terminal or communications line). The obvious solution is to buffer the data in the computer's memory. Then the interrupt service routine can fill a buffer and the main program need not be concerned with each character separately.

In the following program (see Program C-6 for a hexadecimal version), the main program waits until the count in memory location 00A0 (originally set to 0) reaches 4. Memory locations 00A1 and 00A2 hold the address of the next available buffer location (the buffer starts at memory location 00B0).

```
            LDAA        #%00000101      ENABLE CA1 INTERRUPT
            STAA        1,X
            CLR         $A0             CLEAR BUFFER COUNT
     *                                    INITIALLY
            LDAA        #4              GET REQUIRED NUMBER OF
     *                                    INPUTS
            LDX         #$00B0          POINT TO START OF BUFFER
            STX         $A1
            CLI                         ENABLE CPU INTERRUPT
WTCNT       CMPA        $A0             HAVE ENOUGH INPUTS BEEN
     *                                    RECEIVED?
            BNE         WTCNT           NO, WAIT
            SEI                         YES, DISABLE CPU INTERRUPT
            SWI


            ORG         $80
            LDAA        $8004           FETCH DATA FROM INPUT PORT
            LDX         $A1
            STAA        0,X             SAVE DATA IN BUFFER
            INX                         INCREMENT BUFFER POINTER
            STX         $A1
            COMA                        SHOW DATA ON LEDS
            STAA        $8006
            INC         $A0             INCREMENT BUFFER COUNT
            RTI
```

PROGRAM C-6

MEMORY ADDRESS (HEX)	MEMORY CONTENTS (HEX)	INSTRUCTION (MNEMONIC)	
0022	86	LDAA	#%00000101
0023	05		
0024	A7	STAA	1,X
0025	01		
0026	7F	CLR	$A0
0027	00		
0028	A0		
0029	86	LDAA	#4
002A	04		
002B	CE	LDX	#$00B0
002C	00		
002D	B0		
002E	DF	STX	$A1
002F	A1		
0030	0E	CLI	

PROGRAM C-6 (continued)

MEMORY ADDRESS (HEX)	MEMORY CONTENTS (HEX)		INSTRUCTION (MNEMONIC)	
0031	91	WTCNT	CMPA	$A0
0032	A0			
0033	26		BNE	WTCNT
0034	FC			
0035	0F		SEI	
0036	3F		SWI	
0080	B6		LDAA	$8004
0081	80			
0082	04			
0083	DE		LDX	$A1
0084	A1			
0085	A7		STAA	0,X
0086	00			
0087	08		INX	
0088	DF		STX	$A1
0089	A1			
008A	43		COMA	
008B	B7		STAA	$8006
008C	80			
008D	06			
008E	7C		INC	$A0
008F	00			
0090	A0			
0091	3B		RTI	

Enter and run Program C-6. Set the switches to form the following array:

$$(00B0) = F0$$
$$(00B1) = 0F$$
$$(00B2) = AA$$
$$(00B3) = 55$$

PROBLEM C-13

Make Program C-6 fill the buffer until it receives an input of 0D (hex), the ASCII carriage return character. Use memory location 00A0 as an END OF LINE flag. The main program should clear the flag initially and then wait for it to be set. The service routine should set the flag when it receives a 0D input. A program like this handles input from a terminal one line at a time.

PROBLEM C-14

Make Program C-6 fill the buffer with a message that starts with an ASCII STX (Start of Text) character (02 hex) and ends with an ASCII ETX (End of Text) character (03 hex). All inputs before the STX are simply ignored. The STX and ETX characters themselves are omitted from the buffer. Such control characters are often used for synchronization.

Example:

If the inputs are (in order of receipt)

67	
B2	
02	ASCII STX
47	ASCII G
5F	ASCII O (letter)
0D	ASCII Carriage Return
03	ASCII ETX

The final buffer contents are

(00B0) = 47	ASCII G
(00B1) = 5F	ASCII O (letter)
(00B2) = 0D	ASCII Carriage Return

The two inputs preceding the STX are ignored and the STX and ETX characters do not appear in the buffer.

Hint: Use memory location 00A3 as a TRANSMISSION IN PROGRESS flag. The main program should clear that flag initially and the service routine should set the flag when it receives an STX input.

PROBLEM C-15

A common practice is to allow the interrupt service routine to fill one buffer while the main program processes another. This practice is known as *double buffering*, for obvious reasons. The advantage is that the main program and interrupt service routine can proceed independently, since each has its own buffer with which to work. Extend Program C-6 so that it first fills (with four inputs) the buffer starting at memory location 00B0 and then fills the buffer starting at memory location 00C0. Use memory location 00A3 as a flag that indicates whether the first buffer is full (0 means empty, 1 means full), and memory location 00A4 as a similar flag for the second buffer.

Example:

Initially, memory locations 00A3 and 00A4 are both cleared. If the inputs are (in order of receipt)

FE	(all switches open except #0)
FD	(all switches open except #1)
FB	(all switches open except #2)
F7	(all switches open except #3)
EF	(all switches open except #4)
DF	(all switches open except #5)
BF	(all switches open except #6)
7F	(all switches open except #7)

the first four values are placed in the first buffer and the second four values in the second buffer. Memory location 00A3 is set to 1 after the first four inputs have been received and memory location 00A4 is set to 1 after the second four inputs have been received.

The values in the first buffer are

$$(00B0) = FE$$
$$(00B1) = FD$$
$$(00B2) = FB$$
$$(00B3) = F7$$

The values in the second buffer are:

$$(00C0) = EF$$
$$(00C1) = DF$$
$$(00C2) = BF$$
$$(00C3) = 7F$$

PROBLEM C-16

In real applications of double buffering, the main program processes the data in one buffer, and the interrupt service routine fills the other buffer. When those operations have been completed, the main program switches buffers. Revise your answer to Problem C-15 so that the main program operates continuously, switching buffers whenever it finds that the interrupt service routine has filled one. We are thus essentially assuming that the main program always finishes processing the data in one buffer before the interrupt service routine fills the other buffer.

Use memory locations 00A5 and 00A6 to hold the starting address of the current input data buffer and memory locations 00A7 and 00A8 to hold the starting address of the current processing buffer.

Example:

We start with

$$(00A5) = 00$$

$$(00A6) = B0$$

After the first four inputs have been received (filling the first buffer), we have

$$(00A5) = 00$$

$$(00A6) = C0$$

$$(00A7) = 00$$

$$(00A8) = B0$$

After the second four inputs have been received (filling the second buffer), we have

$$(00A5) = 00$$

$$(00A6) = B0$$

$$(00A7) = 00$$

$$(00A8) = C0$$

We are assuming that the main program has processed the previous data by the time the next buffer has been filled.

PROBLEM C-17

Write an interrupt-driven output routine that transmits four values from a buffer starting at memory location 00B0.

Sample Problems:

1)   Single light moves one position to the right with each interrupt.

$$(00B0) = 80$$

$$(00B1) = 40$$

$$(00B2) = 20$$

$$(00B3) = 10$$

2)   Start with all lights on and turn one off with each interrupt, starting with the one attached to bit position 0.

$$(00B0) = FF$$

$$(00B1) = FE$$

$$(00B2) = FC$$

$$(00B3) = F8$$

Remember to complement the data before placing it on the LEDs.

PROBLEM C-18

Write an interrupt-driven output routine that continues transmitting data values from the buffer starting at memory location 00B0 until it encounters a value of 0D (hex), the ASCII carriage return.

Sample Data:

$$(00B0) = 80$$

$$(00B1) = 40$$

$$(00B2) = 20$$

$$(00B3) = 10$$

$$(00B4) = 08$$

$$(00B5) = 04$$

$$(00B6) = 02$$

$$(00B7) = 01$$

$$(00B8) = 0D$$

The output should appear as a single light that moves one position to the right with each interrupt. The program should exit with the displays showing 0D (hex), the carriage return character.

CHANGING VALUES IN THE STACK

Occasionally, the interrupt service routine must modify the main program's registers. The most common reasons are to change the return address or to disable the overall interrupt system. An example of a situation in which the return address must be changed is the response to an automatically inserted breakpoint. Here the service routine must decrement the return address by 1 so that it can replace the breakpoint and display the actual operation code and its address. Remember that the monitor has replaced the operation code in the specified address with an SWI instruction. The value of the program counter in the stack is the address immediately following the inserted SWI.

The key to changing register values in the stack is the TSX instruction, which places the current value of the stack pointer plus one in the index register. The extra one is necessary because the stack pointer contains the address of the next available (empty) stack location, which is one less than the first address that is actually occupied. You can then access the registers in the stack using indexed addressing with the offsets given in Table C-5.

This procedure should not be used as a primary communications mechanism between the main program and the interrupt service routine, since it changes the registers without informing the main program. However, it is handy in such special situations as the following:

1)   Handling breakpoints as we just described.

2)   Providing error exits for unusual conditions.

3)   Disabling all maskable interrupts when they might interfere with further activities. Remember that RTI automatically restores the interrupt mask (I) flag from the stack; that flag must have been 0 or else the maskable interrupt would not have been allowed.

As an example, the following program changes the return address to 0040 if the input is FF, thus providing a special exit in that situation. Program C-7 is the hexadecimal version.

Table C-5

INDEXED OFFSETS FOR ACCESSING DATA IN THE STACK

REGISTER	INDEXED OFFSET (AFTER TSX)
Condition Code (P) Register	0
Accumulator B	1
Accumulator A	2
8 MSBs of Index Register	3
8 LSBs of Index Register	4
8 MSBs of Program Counter	5
8 LSBs of Program Counter	6

```
         LDAA    #%00000101      ENABLE CA1 INTERRUPT
         STAA    1,X
         CLR     $A0             CLEAR DATA READY FLAG
         CLI                     ENABLE CPU INTERRUPT
WTRDY    LDAA    $A0             IS DATA READY?
         BEQ     WTRDY           NO, WAIT
         SEI                     YES, DISABLE INTERRUPT
```

```
            SWI

            ORG       $40
            SWI                                SPECIAL ERROR ROUTINE

            ORG       $80
            LDAA      $8004                    FETCH DATA FROM INPUT PORT
            STAA      $A1                      SAVE INPUT DATA
            CMPA      #$FF                     ARE ANY SWITCHES CLOSED?
            BEQ       EEXIT                    NO, TAKE ERROR EXIT
            COMA                               YES, SHOW DATA ON LEDS
            STAA      $8006
            INC       $A0                      SET DATA READY FLAG
            RTI
EEXIT       TSX                                SET RETURN TO ERROR ROUTINE
            LDAA      #$00
            STAA      5,X
            LDAA      #$40
            STAA      6,X
            RTI
```

A particularly important sequence is the one that disables the maskable interrupt, thus returning control to the main program with interrupts disabled. The main program can then change the parameters of the interrupt system or perform other uninterruptible functions. For example, when using buffered interrupt service routines as shown in the preceding section, we would normally disable interrupts after filling or emptying a buffer, thus giving the main program time to process the buffer, prepare another buffer, or switch buffers without interference. The PIA will latch interrupts that occur while the maskable interrupt is disabled, and those interrupts will be recognized as soon as the system is reenabled. Of course, we can simply disable the interrupts from a particular PIA port and allow other interrupts to occur.

PROGRAM C-7

MEMORY ADDRESS (HEX)	MEMORY CONTENTS (HEX)	INSTRUCTION (MNEMONIC)	
0022	86	LDAA	#%00000101
0023	05		
0024	A7	STAA	1,X
0025	01		
0026	7F	CLR	$A0
0027	00		
0028	A0		
0029	0E	CLI	

MEMORY ADDRESS (HEX)	MEMORY CONTENTS (HEX)	INSTRUCTION (MNEMONIC)		
002A	96	WTRDY	LDAA	$A0
002B	A0			
002C	27		BEQ	WTRDY
002D	FC			
002E	0F		SEI	
002F	3F			
0040	3F		SWI	
0080	B6		LDAA	$8004
0081	80			
0082	04			
0083	97		STAA	$A1
0084	A1			
0085	81		CMPA	#$FF
0086	FF			
0087	27		BEQ	EEXIT
0088	08			
0089	43		COMA	
008A	B7		STAA	$8006
008B	80			
008C	06			
008D	7C		INC	$A0
008E	00			
008F	A0			
0090	3B		RTI	
0091	30	EEXIT	TSX	
0092	86		LDAA	#$00
0093	00			
0094	A7		STAA	5,X
0095	05			
0096	86		LDAA	#$40
0097	40			
0098	A7		STAA	6,X
0099	06			
009A	3B		RTI	

The sequence that sets the INTERRUPT MASK flag in the stack and thus returns control with maskable interrupts disabled is

```
TSX
LDAA    0,X              ACCESS CONDITION CODE REGISTER
ORAA    #%00010000       SET INTERRUPT MASK FLAG
STAA    0,X
```

No other flags are affected. Remember that the INTERRUPT MASK flag is bit 4 of the condition code register.

PROBLEM C-19

Make the service routine in Program C-7 disable the maskable interrupt before returning if the input data is FF (hex).

PROBLEM C-20

Revise Program C-7 so that the main program simply executes a WAI instruction. The service routine should examine the input value and return to the WAI instruction if the value is not 7F (hex). Note that you can return to the WAI instruction by decrementing the program counter value in the stack by 1; use the following routine from the JBUG monitor (memory locations E037 through E03F):

```
          TSX              ACCESS REGISTERS ON STACK
          TST     6,X      ARE LSB'S OF PC ZERO?
          BNE     DECLSB
          DEC     5,X      YES, REDUCE MSB'S OF PC BY 1
DECLSB    DEC     6,X      REDUCE LSB'S OF PC BY 1
```

This is another approach to waiting for an initial synchronization character. The program should wait in place (servicing but essentially ignoring interrupts) until the service routine fetches a data input of 7F (hex) from the switches.

MULTIPLE INTERRUPT SOURCES

So far, we have always assumed that there is only a single source of interrupts in each situation. Real applications normally have multiple interrupts. At the very least, an interrupt-driven system will have both input and output devices producing interrupts. Still other sources may be present, such as alarms, timers, control panels, and remote stations. The problem is how to determine which source caused the interrupt. Once that has been done, the processor must execute the appropriate service routine.

One approach is to attach each source to its own interrupt input. Each interrupt input causes a transfer to a particular memory address at which the service routine for that source can begin. This is called a *vectored interrupt system*, since each source directs or *vectors* the processor to the appropriate service routine. In the case of the 6800 microprocessor, we could tie one source to $\overline{\text{IRQ}}$ (the maskable interrupt) and one to $\overline{\text{NMI}}$ (the nonmaskable interrupt). The 6809 microprocessor has one additional input—$\overline{\text{FIRQ}}$ (the fast maskable interrupt). Obviously, this approach suffices only when the number of interrupt sources is less than or equal to the number of separate interrupt inputs provided by the microprocessor.

If there are more sources, the simplest and least expensive approach is to examine the status of each source separately. This is analogous to answering a telephone that is connected to several different lines by trying one line at a time. The first source found to be active is serviced and the others are handled in the order of examination. This approach (called *polling*) is particularly simple for PIAs since the status of each source is readily available in a PIA control register. The next program waits for an interrupt on either control line CA1 or CB1 of the user PIA. The service routine examines the control registers and services the first interrupt that it finds active. If the input interrupt is active, the service routine loads the data from the switches into memory location 00A0 and returns. If the output interrupt is active, the service routine clears the interrupt flag (why?) and sends the data from memory location 00A1 to the LEDs. Program C-8 is the hexadecimal version.

Note that the main service routine in Program C-8 disables the maskable interrupt by setting the INTERRUPT MASK flag in the stack. If this is not done, you will not be able to observe how priority affects the servicing of the interrupts because the second interrupt will be serviced as soon as the first service routine is completed. With the disabling included, the lower-priority interrupt will not be serviced and its interrupt flag will remain set. You can check the interrupt flags by examining memory locations 8005 and 8007, but be careful not to clear them by examining memory location 8004 or 8006.

PROGRAM C-8

MEMORY ADDRESS (HEX)	MEMORY CONTENTS (HEX)	INSTRUCTION (MNEMONIC)	
0022	86	LDAA	#%00000101
0023	05		
0024	A7	STAA	1,X
0025	01		
0026	A7	STAA	3,X
0027	03		
0028	0E	CLI	
0029	3E	WAI	
002A	0F	SEI	
002B	3F	SWI	
0080	30	TSX	
0081	A6	LDAA	0,X
0082	00		
0083	8A	ORAA	#%00010000

MEMORY ADDRESS (HEX)	MEMORY CONTENTS (HEX)	INSTRUCTION (MNEMONIC)	
0084	10		
0085	A7	STAA	0,X
0086	00		
0087	7D	TST	$8005
0088	80		
0089	05		
008A	2B	BMI	SRVIN
008B	34		
008C	7D	TST	$8007
008D	80		
008E	07		
008F	2B	BMI	SRVOUT
0090	3F		
0091	3B	RTI	
00C0	B6	SRVIN LDAA	$8004
00C1	80		
00C2	04		
00C3	97	STAA	$A0
00C4	A0		
00C5	43	COMA	
00C6	B7	STAA	$8006
00C7	80		
00C8	06		
00C9	3B	RTI	
00D0	96	SRVOUT LDAA	$A1
00D1	A1		
00D2	B5	BITA	$8006
00D3	80		
00D4	06		
00D5	43	COMA	
00D6	B7	STAA	$8006
00D7	80		
00D8	06		
00D9	3B	RTI	

LDAA	#%00000101	
STAA	1,X	ENABLE CA1 INTERRUPT
STAA	3,X	ENABLE CB1 INTERRUPT
CLI		ENABLE CPU INTERRUPT
WAI		WAIT FOR AN INTERRUPT
SEI		DISABLE CPU INTERRUPT
SWI		

```
            ORG       $80
            TSX                        ACCESS REGISTERS IN STACK
            LDAA      0,X              GET CONDITION CODE REGISTER
            ORAA      #%00001000       SET INTERRUPT MASK FLAG
            STAA      0,X
            TST       $8005            IS INPUT INTERRUPT ACTIVE?
            BMI       SRVIN            YES, GO SERVICE IT
            TST       $8007            IS OUTPUT INTERRUPT ACTIVE?
            BMI       SRVOUT           YES, GO SERVICE IT
            RTI                        RETURN IF NEITHER ACTIVE

            ORG       $C0              INPUT INTERRUPT SERVICE
  SRVIN     LDAA      $8004            FETCH DATA FROM INPUT PORT
            STAA      $A0              SAVE DATA
            COMA                       AND SHOW IT ON THE LEDS
            STAA      $8006
            RTI

            ORG       $D0              OUTPUT INTERRUPT SERVICE
  SRVOUT    LDAA      $A1              GET OUTPUT DATA
            BITA      $8006            CLEAR INTERRUPT FLAG
            COMA                       SEND DATA TO LEDS
            STAA      $8006
            RTI
```

Enter and run Program C-8. Show that it responds appropriately to either interrupt. Set a breakpoint in memory location 0022, run the program, and set both interrupt flags (by closing the switches) when the program reaches the breakpoint. Which interrupt is serviced? The easiest way to determine this is to make the service routines produce noticeably different displays on the LEDs. For example, open all the input switches except the one attached to bit position 6 (the input data will then be BF hexadecimal). Set memory location 00A1 to 01 hexadecimal. Thus, if the input interrupt is serviced, all the LEDs will be lit except the one in bit position 6; if the output interrupt is serviced, all the LEDs will be off except the one in bit position 0.

PROBLEM C-21

Change the interrupt service routine in Program C-8 to invert the priority of the interrupt sources.

PROBLEM C-22

Some interrupt systems may ignore low-priority interrupts for a long time if there are many high-priority interrupts. One way to ensure that all interrupts get serviced is to rotate the priorities. Make Program C-8 invert the order in which interrupts are examined as part of each execution of the main service routine. Use memory location 00A2 as a flag that indicates the current order of examination (00 means "examine input interrupt first" and FF means "examine output interrupt first").

You can check your program by loading memory location 00A2 from the keyboard and showing that its value controls the priority of the interrupts. Also, the final value of that location should be the one's complement of its initial value.

PROBLEM C-23

Write a program for a complete interrupt-driven I/O system that initially enables only the input interrupt, waits for input data, disables the input interrupt and enables the output interrupt on receipt of data, waits for the output interrupt, and finally sends the input data, disables the output interrupt, and enables the input interrupt when the output interrupt occurs. Remember that the PIA latches transitions that occur while its interrupt outputs are disabled.

Be careful that you do not service a port where the interrupts have been disabled. Even if the interrupts from one port of a PIA have been disabled, an input on its control lines will still set an interrupt flag. The port will not cause an interrupt, but a polling routine that examines its control register will find an interrupt flag set. Thus, if you disable some PIA interrupts, you should only check the interrupt flags on the ports that are currently enabled. You can determine if a port is enabled by checking the enabling bits in the control register (bit 0 for control line 1, bit 3 for control line 2).

Polling is an adequate method for identifying interrupts as long as the number of sources is small and the required response time is long. Note that the only real difference between normal polling of PIAs and a polling interrupt system is that the latter is activated by an interrupt. As the number of inputs increases, polling becomes slow and cumbersome. If all sources are equally likely to produce an interrupt, then half of them will have to be polled on the average and the time required to identify the source will increase linearly with the number of sources. Therefore, polling cannot handle large interrupt systems. The alternative is to add external hardware in order to create a fully vectored system. For example, an encoder like the one described in Laboratory 4 could produce a numerical value that the processor could read from an input port. The processor could then use that value to determine which service routine to execute.

GUIDELINES FOR PROGRAMMING WITH INTERRUPTS

In writing programs for interrupt-based systems, the programmer should use the following guidelines:

1)   Initialize all parameters before enabling interrupts. In particular, the stack pointer must be loaded since the interrupt response utilizes the stack.

2)   Make all interrupt service routines transparent to the programs that they can interrupt. This means that service routines should not change any registers or flags (including interrupt masks and enables) unless such changes are essential and clearly understood. We have described some of the special conditions under which such changes are occasionally made.

3)   Provide a well-defined method for communicating between the main program and the interrupt service routines. This method should be flexible and should not depend on special characteristics of the main program or of the service routine.

There are many aspects of programming with interrupts that we have not discussed. Among these are the use of reentrant programs that can be interrupted and resumed later even if the same programs have been executed as part of the interrupt service. A reentrant program must use the registers and the stack for temporary storage, not specific memory addresses, since values stored in those addresses would be destroyed. Subroutines that are not reentrant cannot be called by interrupt service routines unless they are executed with the interrupts disabled. Even if the interrupts are disabled, the problem remains of whether to reenable them at the end of the subroutine. Grappel has discussed this problem in the brief article cited in the references at the beginning of the Laboratory. Other issues that we have not discussed include:

1)   When to use the nonmaskable interrupt. This input is most commonly used as a power-fail interrupt that causes the CPU to save essential data in a backup memory. Such an interrupt should be nonmaskable since all activities will be interrupted anyway by the impending loss of power.

2)   When to enable and disable interrupts. Interrupts must be disabled during activities that could not be resumed properly, such as delay loops, command sequences, and updating of multiple-word results that must be used during the interrupt service. If a program is changing data that occupies more than one word, it must complete the task if the interrupt service routine uses the data. Otherwise, the service routine could find the data only partially changed and interpret it incorrectly.

3)   How to implement interrupts from sources other than PIAs. Many other devices can be handled much like PIAs, although the specific details depend on the particular device. Other common sources of interrupts include serial interfaces, timers, converters, arithmetic chips, and peripheral controllers.

KEY POINT SUMMARY

1)   Interrupts provide a convenient way for the computer to respond to external events such as changes in the status of peripherals, alarms, requests for control or information, or the passage of time. The program does not have to check to see if events have occurred, since the occurrences cause changes in hardware inputs to the CPU. Interrupts provide fast response and simple logic but introduce a random element into programs that makes them difficult to debug and test.

2)   The 6800 microprocessor has two interrupt inputs, one that is maskable ($\overline{\text{IRQ}}$) and one that is nonmaskable ($\overline{\text{NMI}}$). In response to these inputs, the processor saves all its registers in the stack, disables the maskable interrupt, and fetches a new value for the program counter from a specified pair of memory locations. An RTI instruction at the end of the service routine restores the old register values from the stack.

3)   PIAs can be used in an interrupt-driven mode by setting the interrupt enable bits in the control register. Transitions on the control lines then cause interrupts as well as setting the interrupt flags.

4)   Before interrupts are enabled, the main program must load the stack pointer, determine the operating modes for the PIAs, and initialize all parameters that the service routines use. Since $\overline{\text{RESET}}$ disables all the PIA interrupts and the CPU interrupt, startup programs can perform the required initialization without interference.

5)   The registers cannot be used to communicate between the main program and the interrupt service routine because each generally needs the registers for its own purposes. A simple way to communicate is through assigned memory locations, which act like a mailbox. Either program can place information in those assigned memory locations to be picked up by the other program.

6)   Buffering allows interrupt-driven input/output to proceed independently of the main program. All that the main program must do is manage the buffers. A large buffer or multiple buffers (so-called double buffering) allows the main program more time to perform its management tasks and thus avoids the problems of data being lost or requests being ignored.

7)   Under special conditions, interrupt service routines may have to change the register values that are saved in the stack. The usual conditions are the need to provide special exits or to disable the entire interrupt system.

8)   If there is more than one source of interrupts, the program must have some way of differentiating among them. Vectoring means that each source provides a means of identification, either by being attached to

a separate interrupt input or by producing a data value that the processor can examine. Polling means that the processor must examine the status of each source separately until it finds one that is active.

9)   In polling interrupt systems, the priority of the sources depends on the order in which they are examined. This order can be changed or varied if necessary. However, the time required to identify a source increases linearly with the number of sources, so polling is reasonable only if the number of sources is small.

☐ *Laboratory* **D**

Timing Methods

PURPOSE

To learn how to handle timing on the MEK6800D2 microcomputer.

PARTS REQUIRED

A low-frequency clock input (5 to 200 Hz). One way to produce this input is to divide down the 4800-Hz clock that is available on pin 17 of I/O connector J2, as shown in Figure D-1. The 75- or 150-Hz clocks can then be tied with jumper wires to either pin PA7 (pin R of I/O connector J1) or CA1 (pin S of I/O connector J1). Any other clock source in the specified range, such as one obtained from the TTL output of a signal generator or from a 555 timer chip, will also be satisfactory. Figure D-2 shows the connection of the clock input (from whatever source) to user PIA port A.

REFERENCE MATERIALS

L. A. Leventhal, *Introduction to Microprocessors: Software, Hardware, Programming,* Prentice-Hall, Englewood Cliffs, NJ, 1978, pp. 343-345, 485-486.

L. A. Leventhal, *6800 Assembly Language Programming,* Osborne/McGraw-Hill, Berkeley, CA, 1978, pp. 11-8 through 11-11, 12-16 through 12-21.

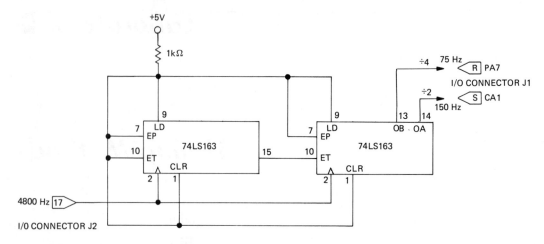

FIGURE D-1. A simple low-frequency clock generation circuit.

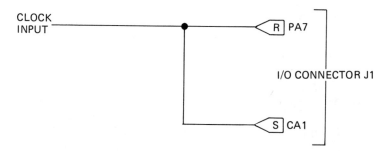

FIGURE D-2. Connection of clock input to user PIA port A (address 8004 hex).
(**Note:** Jumper wires can be used to select this configuration as opposed to those used in Laboratories B and C.)

W. J. Weller, *Practical Microcomputer Programming. The M6800,* Northern Technology Books, Evanston, IL, 1978, pp. 232-248.

MEK6800D2 Evaluation Kit II Manual, Motorola Semiconductor Products Inc., Austin, TX, p. 2-3 (System Clock).

M. Ferguson, "MIKBUG with Muscle," *Kilobaud,* July 1978, pp. 64-66 (description of Microware Systems Corporation's RT-68/MX real-time operating system for 6800-based microcomputers).

G. J. Lipovski, *Microcomputer Interfacing,* D.C. Heath (Lexington Books), Lexington, MA, 1980, Chapter 6.

G. Nash, "Microprocessor Software Programs Bit-Rate Generator," *EDN,* August 20, 1977, pp. 134-137.

A. Osborne, *An Introduction to Microcomputers, Volume 2: Some Real Micro-processors*, Osborne/McGraw-Hill, Berkeley, CA, 1978, pp. 9-78 through 9-106 (6840 programmable timer).

D. L. Ripps, "Help a Real-Time Multitasking OS," *Electronic Design*, June 21, 1979, pp. 86-91; continued September 13, 1979, pp. 146-151, and September 27, 1979, pp. 82-86 (description of the Industrial Programming Inc. Multi-Tasking Operating System, or MTOS, which is available for 6800 micro-processors).

W. S. Wagner, "12-Hour Clock Tells Time Out Loud," *Electronics*, August 16, 1979, pp. 132-133.

WHAT YOU SHOULD LEARN

1) The alternative ways to handle timing.
2) How to synchronize with an external clock.
3) How to determine the period of an external clock.
4) How to produce and use an elapsed time interrupt.
5) What a real-time clock is.
6) How to produce and use a simple real-time clock.
7) How to schedule tasks with the real-time clock.
8) How to keep calendar time with the real-time clock.
9) What a real-time operating system does.

TERMS

Dead time—a delay between events required to prevent errors caused by overlapping operations.

Multitasking—executing many tasks during a single period of time, usually by giving each a slice of time and suspending tasks that must wait for input/output, the completion of other tasks, or external events.

One-shot—a device that produces a single pulse of known length in response to a pulse input. Also called a *monostable multivibrator.*

Programmable timer—a device that can handle a variety of timing tasks, including the generation of delays, under program control.

Real-time—in synchronization with the actual occurrence of events.

Real-time clock—a device that interrupts a CPU at regular time intervals.

Real-time operating system—an operating system that can act as a supervisor for programs that have real-time requirements.

May also be referred to as a *real-time executive* or as a *real-time monitor.*

Scheduler—a program that determines when other programs should be started and terminated.

Suspend (a task)—halt execution and preserve the status of the task until some future time.

Task—an activity or subprogram.

Task status—the set of parameters that specify the current state of a task so that it can be suspended and resumed.

Timeout—a period during which no activity is allowed to proceed, an inactive period.

PROBLEMS OF TIMING

Timing is a continual problem in microprocessor applications. Inputs and outputs must be handled at the proper rate and timing information must be derived from external clocks. Delay programs can handle simple timing requirements but they occupy the processor and are inadequate for complex and varying timing needs.

Many applications have real-time requirements. Certain inputs and outputs must be handled at externally determined times. Such requirements are common in process and industrial control. Some applications, such as navigation systems and security systems, may even need to maintain calendar time.

We will explore the following methods of handling timing:

1) Varying the parameters of delay routines.
2) Measuring the periods of external clocks and adapting to their frequencies.
3) Using a programmable timer.
4) Using a real-time clock.

The aims of these methods are to provide more flexibility than fixed delay routines while occupying the processor as little as possible.

GENERALIZED DELAY ROUTINES

The simplest way to generalize a delay routine is to have an input parameter determine its length. The JBUG subroutine DLY1 (starting address E0E0) counts down the value that is placed in the index register. The routine is

```
DLY1    DEX
        BNE    DLY1
        RTS
```

The total time required by DLY1 is (in clock cycles)

- 9 for a JSR using extended addressing.
- 8 for each iteration (4 for DEX and 4 for BNE).
- 5 for the RTS instruction.

So the time used (including the requirements of a JSR instruction with extended addressing) is $14 + 8 \times N$ clock cycles, where N is the original contents of the index register (but note that the subroutine interprets an input value of 0000 as 10000 since it decrements the index register before checking the ZERO flag). Table D-1 contains some typical delays that can be obtained, with the length in milliseconds assuming the MEK6800D2 clock frequency of 614.4 kHz. You may find it instructive to derive some of these results on your own.

Table D-1

TIME INTERVALS USING JBUG SUBROUTINE DLY1

TIME INTERVAL		INITIAL COUNT (HEX)
Clock Cycles	Milliseconds (614.4-kHz clock)	
614	1	004B
1229	2	0098
1843	3	00E5
3072	5	017E
6144	10	02FE
12288	20	05FE
30720	50	0EFE
61440	100	1DFA
307200	500	95FE
524302	853.4	0000

The following program produces a delay specified by the contents of memory locations 0060 and 0061 (MSBs in 0060). Program D-1 is the hexadecimal version.

```
LDS    #$00FF    INITIALIZE USER STACK POINTER
LDX    $60       GET DELAY LENGTH
JSR    DLY1      WAIT
SWI
```

PROGRAM D-1

MEMORY ADDRESS (HEX)	MEMORY CONTENTS (HEX)	INSTRUCTION (MNEMONIC)	
0000	8E	LDS	#$00FF
0001	00		
0002	FF		
0003	DE	LDX	$60
0004	60		
0005	BD	JSR	DLY1
0006	E0		
0007	E0		
0008	3F	SWI	

Try running Program D-1 for various delay lengths in memory locations 0060 and 0061.

PROBLEM D-1

Write a subroutine that uses DLY1 to produce a delay of 100 ms without affecting any registers or flags. Save the condition code register in the stack and use memory locations 0062 and 0063 as temporary storage for the index register.

PROBLEM D-2

Write a subroutine that uses DLY1 to produce a delay of 1 ms times the original contents of accumulator A without affecting accumulator B or the index register.

Example:

$$(A) = 35 \text{ (hex)}$$

Result:

The routine should produce a delay of 35 (hex) ms without affecting accumulator B or the index register.

PROBLEM D-3

Write a subroutine that uses DLY1 to produce a delay of 1 s times the original contents of accumulator A without affecting accumulator B or the index register.

Example:

$$(A) = 03 \text{ (hex)}$$

Result:

The routine should produce a delay of 3 s without affecting accumulator B or the index register.

A generalized delay routine saves memory and programming time, as well as simplifying documentation. However, it still occupies the processor completely. This is acceptable if the system handles only one task at a time and does not operate in real time. Software delay routines (or *timeouts*) are often used to handle the initial response time of slow mechanical devices such as printers or motors.

WAITING FOR A CLOCK TRANSITION

We have not yet specified how to start the time interval and determine its length. Both starting procedures and interval lengths may be fixed either in hardware, or with ROM-based parameters. This approach simplifies the software and is compatible with non-computer-based systems, but it lacks flexibility. The resulting system will operate only in the specified environment and modifications must be made by changing hardware or by replacing ROMs. For example, a system of this type would only be able to handle I/O devices operating at fixed data rates under specified protocols. A different configuration of I/O devices would require a different system. Clearly, this lack of flexibility reduces the usefulness of the system and the size of its potential market.

An alternative approach is to have the program determine the parameter values required to handle a particular set of I/O devices. That is, the system adapts to its environment. For example, the system could establish synchronization by examining a clock input. Attach a low-frequency (5- to 200-Hz) clock source to bit 7 of user PIA port A. The following program waits for a low-to-high transition on the clock line. We will continue to use Program C-2 to load the stack pointer (with 00FF hex) and initialize the user PIA.

```
WAITL      LDAA      $8004      IS CLOCK LINE LOW?
           BMI       WAITL      NO, WAIT
WAITH      LDAA      $8004      IS CLOCK LINE HIGH?
           BPL       WAITH      NO, WAIT
           SWI
```

Program D-2 is the hexadecimal version. Note that the program first waits for the clock line to go low and then waits for it to go high (see Figure D-3 for a flowchart).

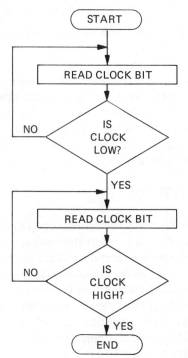

FIGURE D-3. Flowchart of clock synchronization program.

PROGRAM D-2

MEMORY ADDRESS (HEX)	MEMORY CONTENTS (HEX)		INSTRUCTION (MNEMONIC)	
0022	B6	WAITL	LDAA	$8004
0023	80			
0024	04			
0025	2B		BMI	WAITL
0026	FB			
0027	B6	WAITH	LDAA	$8004
0028	80			
0029	04			
002A	2A		BPL	WAITH
002B	FB			
002C	3F		SWI	

Enter and run Program D-2. Vary the clock rate. How would you make the program wait for a high-to-low transition rather than a low-to-high transition? You may find it easier to test this program and the following problems if you use a debounced switch (see Figure B-1) as the clock input. Then you can control the clock and check to see if your program is operating correctly.

PROBLEM D-4

Make Program D-2 handle a clock input attached to control line CA1. Remember to clear the interrupt flag by reading the I/O port after each active transition.

PROBLEM D-5

Make Program D-2 wait for the first full clock pulse (i.e., it should wait for a low-to-high transition followed by a high-to-low transition).

PROBLEM D-6

Make Program D-2 wait for 10 low-to-high transitions.

DETERMINING THE CLOCK PERIOD

We may extend Program D-2 to have the processor determine the length of the clock period. This involves:

1) Waiting for a transition.
2) Counting time intervals until the next transition.

Obviously, the period must be many CPU clock cycles in length for this method to be accurate.

The following program (see Figure D-4 for a flowchart) waits for a low-to-high clock transition and then counts the number of milliseconds that elapse until the next such transition:

```
        CLRB                  CLOCK COUNT = ZERO
WTLI    LDAA    $8004         IS CLOCK LINE LOW?
        BMI     WTL1          NO, WAIT
WTH1    LDAA    $8004         IS CLOCK LINE HIGH?
        BPL     WTH1          NO, WAIT
WTL2    INCB                  INCREMENT CLOCK COUNT
        LDX     #$4B          WAIT 1 MS
        JSR     DLY1
        LDAA    $8004         IS CLOCK LINE LOW?
        BMI     WTL2          NO, WAIT
WTH2    INCB                  INCREMENT CLOCK COUNT
        LDX     #$4B          WAIT 1 MS
        JSR     DLY1
        LDAA    $8004         IS CLOCK LINE HIGH?
        BPL     WTH2
        STAB    $60           SAVE CLOCK COUNT
        SWI
```

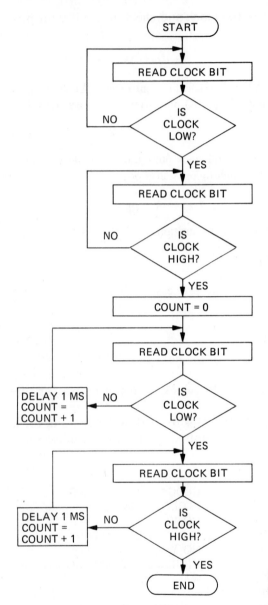

FIGURE D-4. Flowchart of clock period measurement program.

Program D-3 is the hexadecimal version; enter it into memory and run it. See how accurate it is for some low-frequency clock inputs. You should try inputs of 75 Hz and 150 Hz since these are easy to derive (see Figure D-1).

PROBLEM D-7

Make Program D-3 determine the width of the high phase of the clock.

PROGRAM D-3

MEMORY ADDRESS (HEX)	MEMORY CONTENTS (HEX)		INSTRUCTION (MNEMONIC)	
0022	5F		CLRB	
0023	B6	WTL1	LDAA	$8004
0024	80			
0025	04			
0026	2B		BMI	WTL1
0027	FB			
0028	B6	WTH1	LDAA	$8004
0029	80			
002A	04			
002B	2A		BPL	WTH1
002C	FB			
002D	5C	WTL2	INCB	
002E	CE		LDX	#$4B
002F	00			
0030	4B			
0031	BD		JSR	DLY1
0032	E0			
0033	E0			
0034	B6		LDAA	$8004
0035	80			
0036	04			
0037	2B		BMI	WTL2
0038	F4			
0039	5C	WTH2	INCB	
003A	CE		LDX	#$4B
003B	00			
003C	4B			
003D	BD		JSR	DLY1
003E	E0			
003F	E0			
0040	B6		LDAA	$8004
0041	80			
0042	04			
0043	2A		BPL	WTH2
0044	F4			
0045	D7		STAB	$60
0046	60			
0047	3F		SWI	

PROBLEM D-8

Determine the actual time between samples for the section of Program D-3 that measures the clock period. How could you make Program D-3 more accurate?

Once the processor has measured the clock period, it can then use that period to time input and output operations. The same program can handle I/O devices operating at different rates as long as it can determine what rate is being used. This approach is often employed to handle serial input/output with a terminal, since terminals may operate at any of a common set of data rates (10 or 30 characters per second for low-speed terminals, 1200 to 19,200 bits per second for higher-speed devices). A system that measures the clock period of the terminal can operate at any of the standard rates without hardware modification.

PROGRAMMABLE TIMERS

The previous methods still depend on the processor generating time intervals with delay routines. An alternative approach is to use a hardware timer under computer control. The processor then only has to determine how the timer will operate, start it, and wait for it to finish. The end of the time interval may cause an interrupt.

The simplest hardware timer is a one-shot (or monostable multivibrator) that produces a single pulse of fixed length in response to a pulsed input. More complex timers consist of dividers; input controls may determine how many stages are used. Programmable timers are the timing equivalent of the programmable input/output ports that we discussed in Laboratory B. These devices have a variety of operating modes that are selected by the contents of one or more control registers. The current state of the device can be determined from one or more status registers.

The 6840 device is the programmable timer intended for use in 6800-based microcomputers. It consists of three 16-bit counter/timers which can be loaded under program control. The 6840 timer can operate in a variety of ways to generate time intervals using these counters; three control registers determine the mode of operation. Among the alternatives are:

- Counting either the system clock or an externally supplied clock.
- Producing a single pulse or a continuous series of pulses. In the continuous mode, the counters are automatically reloaded after they have been decremented to zero.
- Optional output signals and interrupts.

The 6840 has many other features which we will not discuss here; the device is described fully in A. Osborne, *An Introduction to Microcomputers, Volume 2: Some Real Microprocessors,* Osborne/McGraw-Hill, Berkeley, CA, 1978, pp. 9-78 through 9-106.

Like programmable I/O devices, programmable timers simplify hardware design, save parts, and allow the development and use of a standard series of boards in many applications. On the other hand, programmable timers are expensive and difficult to use and document because of their arbitrary features and unique programming requirements.

AN ELAPSED TIME INTERRUPT

In order to utilize the processor efficiently, we still need a way of generating time intervals without processor intervention. The easiest way to accomplish this is to let the end of the time interval cause an interrupt. Now the processor can perform other tasks during the interval without any difficulties.

Attach a clock source to the CA1 input of the user PIA as shown in Figure D-2. We will assume henceforth that the input frequency is 150 Hz; you can obtain that frequency from a signal generator or by dividing down the 4800-Hz clock used in the MEK6800D2 cassette interface.

The following program clears memory location 0070, enables the interrupt system, and then waits for an interrupt. The interrupt service routine increments memory location 0070 and returns. We are using memory location 0070 because the 150-Hz clock is too fast to be observed directly. You can set a breakpoint in the service routine to observe the incrementing of memory location 0070. The program (see Program D-4 for a hexadecimal version) produces an interrupt on the falling edge of the clock pulse. Remember that Program C-2 loads a vector (0080) into the interrupt service address (A000 and A001) provided by the JBUG monitor.

MAIN PROGRAM

```
LDAA    #%00000101    SET CLOCK INTERRUPT ON FALLING EDGE
STAA    1,X
CLR     $70           CLEAR CLOCK COUNTER
CLI                   ENABLE CPU INTERRUPT
WAI                   DUMMY MAIN PROGRAM
SEI                   DISABLE CPU INTERRUPT
SWI
```

INTERRUPT SERVICE ROUTINE

```
ORG     $80
LDAA    $8004         CLEAR CLOCK INTERRUPT
INC     $70           INCREMENT CLOCK COUNTER
RTI
```

PROGRAM D-4

MEMORY ADDRESS (HEX)	MEMORY CONTENTS (HEX)	INSTRUCTION (MNEMONIC)	
0022	86	LDAA	#%00000101
0023	05		
0024	A7	STAA	1,X
0025	01		
0026	7F	CLR	$70
0027	00		
0028	70		
0029	0E	CLI	
002A	3E	WAI	
002B	0F	SEI	
002C	3F	SWI	
0080	B6	LDAA	$8004
0081	80		
0082	04		
0083	7C	INC	$70
0084	00		
0085	70		
0086	3B	RTI	

In a real application, you would have to synchronize the clock and the processor, perhaps by having the initialization routine start the clock as well as set up the interrupt system. Note that the interrupt service routine must clear the interrupt flag by reading the PIA I/O port even though no data transfer is necessary. Enter and run Program D-4. What happens if you omit the LDAA $8004 instruction?

PROBLEM D-9

Make Program D-4 wait for two clock interrupts. How would you modify Program D-4 so that memory location 0060 specifies the number of clock interrupts to wait?

Example:

(0060) = 50 means that that program waits for 50 hex (80 decimal) clock interrupts.

PROBLEM D-10

Write a program that waits for the number of clock interrupts specified by memory location 0060 and then lights the LEDs attached to user PIA port B for the number of clock interrupts specified by memory location 0061.

Example:

$$(0060) = 50$$

$$(0061) = 30$$

Result:

The program waits for 50 hex (80 decimal) clock interrupts and then lights the LEDs attached to user PIA port B for 30 hex (48 decimal) clock interrupts. Finally, it turns the LEDs off.

REAL-TIME CLOCK

A real-time clock simply produces continuous clock interrupts. The computer can keep time by counting them. For example, we can have Program D-4 keep an interrupt count in memory location 0070 by adding an endless loop to the main program. The changes are as follows:

002A	20	HERE	BRA	HERE
002B	FE			

Note that time is being kept in 1/150ths of a second in memory location 0070. Run the program a few times and see what values you find in that location.

PROBLEM D-11

Make the main program wait for one trailing edge of the clock before enabling the interrupt system. This delay synchronizes the operations of the program with the clock.

PROBLEM D-12

What percentage of the processor's time is being spent handling the real-time clock? Note that the 6800 processor requires 12 clock cycles to respond to an interrupt; the processor uses that time to save the registers in the stack and to load the new program counter value from memory.

We can now produce time intervals by using the count in memory location 0070. For example, to have the computer wait for five clock periods requires the following addition to the end of Program D-4.

```
           LDAA    #5
WAIT5      CMPA    $70        HAS CLOCK COUNTER REACHED 5?
```

```
            BNE        WAIT5      NO, WAIT
            SEI                   YES, DISABLE CPU INTERRUPTS
            SWI
```

The hexadecimal changes are as follows:

002A	86		LDAA	#5
002B	05			
002C	91	WAIT5	CMPA	$70
002D	70			
002E	26		BNE	WAIT5
002F	FC			
0030	0F		SEI	
0031	3F		SWI	

Enter and run this program. Make it wait for 10 clock periods.

PROBLEM D-13

Make the program wait for five clock periods and then light all the LEDs attached to user PIA port B for 10 clock periods. Change the program to produce the following on-off periods:

1)   OFF-10
     ON-5
2)   OFF-1
     ON-1

Make the program take the length of the off period from memory location 0060 and the length of the on period from memory location 0061.

PROBLEM D-14

Make the program from Problem D-12 operate continuously, turning the LEDs on and off according to the duty cycle specified by the contents of memory locations 0060 and 0061. To determine the count that marks the end of a time interval, add the length of the interval to the current value of the clock counter.

Run the program for the following test cases and describe what happens.

1)   OFF−(0060) = 01
     ON−(0061) = 01
2)   OFF−(0060) = 04
     ON−(0061) = 1C

3) OFF—(0060) = 10 (hex)
   ON—(0061) = 10 (hex)

4) OFF—(0060) = 1C
   ON—(0061) = 04

PROBLEM D-15

Make the program from Problem D-12 operate continuously, turning the LEDs on and off according to the following duty cycle for a single iteration:

OFF—10 (hex)

ON—20 (hex)

OFF—40 (hex)

ON—80 (hex)

Clearly, most industrial and process controllers involve rather complex duty cycles with numerous variations in length and amplitude.

To avoid having a very long program, you may want to place the ON-OFF values in a table. For example, use memory locations A050 through A053 as follows:

(A050) = 10 (first OFF period)

(A051) = 20 (first ON period)

(A052) = 40 (second OFF period)

(A053) = 80 (second ON period)

You can use the index register to hold the current address in the table and use the CPX instruction to determine when the program should stop.

EXTENDING PERIODS

We can extend the clock by using more memory locations for the counter. The following service routine uses memory locations 0070 and 0071. You must clear them either in the main program or by hand before executing the program.

```
ORG     $80
LDAA    $8004       CLEAR CLOCK INTERRUPT
LDX     $70         INCREMENT CLOCK COUNTER
INX
STX     $70
RTI
```

Remember that RTI automatically restores the value of the index register. The MSBs of the clock counter are in memory location 0070 in accordance with the usual Motorola method for storing 16-bit numbers. Enter and run this program (see Program D-5 for a hexadecimal version). Let it run for a while and see what values you find in memory locations 0070 and 0071. Remember to restore the endless loop instruction at the end of the main program.

PROGRAM D-5

MEMORY ADDRESS (HEX)	MEMORY CONTENTS (HEX)	INSTRUCTION (MNEMONIC)	
0080	B6	LDAA	$8004
0081	80		
0082	04		
0083	DE	LDX	$70
0084	70		
0085	08	INX	
0086	DF	STX	$70
0087	70		
0088	3B	RTI	

PROBLEM D-16

Write a program that uses the interrupt service routine of Program D-5 to wait for 300 clock periods before returning control to the monitor. Note that 300 decimal = 012C hex.

PROBLEM D-17

Write a program that uses the interrupt service routine of Program D-5 to turn all the LEDs attached to user PIA port B off for 300 clock periods and then on for 150 clock periods. Change the program to produce the following on-off periods:

1) OFF—150 (0096 hex)
   ON—300 (012C hex)

2) OFF—250 (00FA hex)
   ON—200 (00C8 hex)

PROBLEM D-18

Make the program from Problem D-17 operate continuously, turning the LEDs on and off according to the duty cycle specified by the contents of memory locations 0060 and 0061 (OFF period) and 0062 and 0063 (ON period). Try the following test cases:

1) (0060) = 01   (012C hex = 300 decimal)
    (0061) = 2C

    (0062) = 00   (0096 hex = 150 decimal)
    (0063) = 96

2) (0060) = 00   (00C8 hex = 200 decimal)
    (0061) = C8

    (0062) = 00   (00FA hex = 250 decimal)
    (0063) = FA

3) (0060) = 01   (01C2 hex = 450 decimal)
    (0061) = C2

    (0062) = 02   (0258 hex = 600 decimal)
    (0063) = 58

KEEPING TIME IN STANDARD UNITS

We can make the interrupt service routine keep time in seconds and minutes rather than in units determined by the computer's word length. The following interrupt service routine keeps the number of minutes in memory location 0070, the number of seconds in 0071, and the number of clock periods in 0072. As before, the main program must clear the counter locations initially.

```
        ORG     $80
        LDAA    $8004       CLEAR CLOCK INTERRUPT
        LDX     #$70
        INC     2,X         INCREMENT CLOCK COUNTER
        LDAA    2,X
        CMPA    #150        HAS 1 SECOND ELAPSED?
        BNE     DONE        NO, DONE
        CLR     2,X         YES, CLOCK COUNTER = ZERO
        INC     1,X         INCREMENT SECONDS
        LDAA    1,X
        CMPA    #60         HAS 1 MINUTE ELAPSED?
        BNE     DONE        NO, DONE
        CLR     1,X         YES, SECOND COUNT = ZERO
        INC     0,X         INCREMENT MINUTES
        LDAA    0,X
        CMPA    #60         HAS 1 HOUR ELAPSED?
        BNE     DONE        NO, DONE
        CLR     0,X         YES, MINUTE COUNT = ZERO
DONE    RTI
```

Program D-6 is the hexadecimal version.

PROGRAM D-6

MEMORY ADDRESS (HEX)	MEMORY CONTENTS (HEX)		INSTRUCTION (MNEMONIC)	
0080	B6		LDAA	$8004
0081	80			
0082	04			
0083	CE		LDX	#$70
0084	00			
0085	70			
0086	6C		INC	2,X
0087	02			
0088	A6		LDAA	2,X
0089	02			
008A	81		CMPA	#150
008B	96			
008C	26		BNE	DONE
008D	16			
008E	6F		CLR	2,X
008F	02			
0090	6C		INC	1,X
0091	01			
0092	A6		LDAA	1,X
0093	01			
0094	81		CMPA	#60
0095	3C			
0096	26		BNE	DONE
0097	0C			
0098	6F		CLR	1,X
0099	01			
009A	6C		INC	0,X
009B	00			
009C	A6		LDAA	0,X
009D	00			
009E	81		CMPA	#60
009F	3C			
00A0	26		BNE	DONE
00A1	02			
00A2	6F		CLR	0,X
00A3	00			
00A4	3B	DONE	RTI	

PROBLEM D-19

Use the service routine of Program D-6 to write a program that waits for 1 min and 45 s.

PROBLEM D-20

Modify Program D-6 to keep seconds as two decimal digits in memory location 0071 and minutes as two decimal digits in memory location 0070.

PROBLEM D-21

Modify Program D-6 to keep hours, minutes, seconds, and clock periods in memory locations 0070 through 0073, respectively. Hours, minutes, and seconds should be kept as pairs of decimal digits.

PROBLEM D-22

Use Program D-6 to write a program that turns all the LEDs attached to user PIA port B off for 1 min and 30 s and then on for 1 min and 15 s.

PROBLEM D-23

Make the program from Problem D-22 operate continuously, turning the LEDs off for 1 min and 30 s and then on for 1 min and 15 s.

PROBLEM D-24

We can handle more complex timing sequences by using tables. Write a program that turns the LEDs attached to user PIA port B on and off according to the following table in memory locations A050 through A058. Each entry is the length of a period in seconds and the final zero marks the end of the table.

(A050) = 02	(first OFF period)
(A051) = 03	(first ON period)
(A052) = 05	(second OFF period)
(A053) = 01	(second ON period)
(A054) = 06	(third OFF period)
(A055) = 04	(third ON period)
(A056) = 02	(fourth OFF period)
(A057) = 06	(fourth ON period)
(A058) = 00	(ending marker)

The LEDs should be off for 2 s, on for 3 s, off for 5 s, on for 1 s, off for 6 s, on for 4 s, off for 2 s, and finally on for 6 s.

PROBLEM D-25

We can easily extend the table of Problem D-24 to handle values besides ON and OFF. Write a program that operates the LEDs attached to user PIA port B according to the following table in memory locations A050 through A058. Each entry consists of a length in seconds followed by a data value to be sent to the LEDs. The final zero marks the end of the table. Turn all the LEDs off before concluding.

(A050) = 02   (first period)

(A051) = 00   (all LEDs on during first period)

(A052) = 04   (second period)

(A053) = 01   (all LEDs on except bit 0 during second period)

(A054) = 05   (third period)

(A055) = 03   (all LEDs on except bits 0 and 1 during third period)

(A056) = 04   (fourth period)

(A057) = 07   (all LEDs on except bits 0,1, and 2 during fourth period)

(A058) = 00   (ending marker)

REAL-TIME OPERATING SYSTEM

A real-time clock allows the programmer to satisfy many timing requirements. Tasks can be scheduled or suspended, delays can be produced, and real-time inputs and outputs can be handled. The programmer must, however, determine the order and priority of tasks and specify exactly how they are to use the real-time clock.

A real-time operating system removes much of this burden from the programmer. It schedules tasks, handles communications between tasks, generates time intervals, and provides real-time interrupt control for I/O devices. The programmer only has to learn how to use the operating system. Among the operating systems available for the Motorola 6800 are MTOS/68 from Industrial Programming, Inc. (9 Northern Blvd., Greenvale, NY 11548) and RT-68/MX from Microware Systems Corporation (PO Box 954, Des Moines, IA 50304). Both of these are described in the references. The obvious advantages of such operating systems are that they can be purchased rather than written, and that they provide standard procedures and formats. Both MTOS/68 and RT-68/MX are available in ROM for most 6800-based single-board computers.

KEY POINT SUMMARY

1) You can handle simple timing tasks with software delay routines. A standard routine that provides delays of varied lengths is often useful.

2) Programs can be made more flexible by allowing them to determine their own timing parameters from system inputs. The same program can then be used with peripherals operating at different data rates.

3) A program can easily examine a clock line, synchronize with it, and determine its period as long as its frequency is low compared to the CPU clock frequency.

4) A programmable timer can replace a delay routine. It simply provides an indication that a count loaded into it has been exhausted. Programmable timers add flexibility to systems because they can operate in a variety of different modes under program control. However, there are no standards for the functions or programming of these timers, so they require careful use and documentation.

5) Interrupts are a convenient way to handle timing. A real-time clock is a regular source of interrupts that can be counted to provide a basis for timing and scheduling. Time is specified in terms of the number of counts required.

6) A real-time operating system performs scheduling, coordination, and communications on a real-time basis. It provides a standard supervisor for applications with real-time requirements.

☐ *Laboratory* **E**

Serial Input/Output

PURPOSE

To learn how to handle serial input and output using the MEK6800D2 microcomputer.

PARTS REQUIRED

A connection between the 6850 ACIA's RECEIVED DATA (RXD) input and its TRANSMITTED DATA (TXD) output. This connection (see Figure E-1) echoes the data (i.e., it sends the data from the transmitter back into the receiver). If two MEK6800D2 microcomputers are available, the RECEIVED DATA inputs can be tied to the TRANSMITTED DATA outputs to form a full-duplex communications system. The microcomputers can then transmit messages to each other. Note that the RECEIVED DATA input of the ACIA is pin W of I/O connector J2 (the connector for the keyboard/display unit) and the TRANSMITTED DATA output is pin U of the same connector. You must remove integrated circuit U13 from its socket on the Keyboard/Display Module (this is a CMOS device, so handle it carefully) and jumper the ACIA Receive Clock (RXC–pin 19 of I/O connector J2) to the ACIA Transmit Clock (TXC–pin 17 of I/O

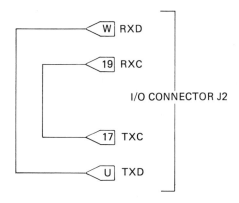

FIGURE E-1. Connections required to use the on-board ACIA in an echoing mode.

connector J2). This jumper is necessary because the MEK6800D2 cassette interface uses different Receive and Transmit Clocks, whereas we need the same clock to use the ACIA to communicate with itself or with another microcomputer. Of course, the cassette interface will not operate unless you remove the jumper and replace integrated circuit U13. Figure E-1 shows both connections that are required in the final section of this laboratory experiment.

REFERENCE MATERIALS

L. A. Leventhal, *Introduction to Microprocessors: Software, Hardware, Programming,* Prentice-Hall, Englewood Cliffs, NJ, 1978, pp. 360-363, 385-388, 420-427, 489-492.

L. A. Leventhal, *6800 Assembly Language Programming,* Osborne/McGraw-Hill, Berkeley, CA, 1978, pp. 11-69 through 11-80, 12-21 through 12-24.

W. J. Weller, *Practical Microcomputer Programming: The M6800,* Northern Technology Books, Evanston, IL, Chapter 14.

MEK6800D2 Evaluation Kit II Manual, Motorola Semiconductor Products Inc., Austin, TX, pp. 2-3 (INPUT/OUTPUT DEVICES), 2-4 through 2-10 (AUDIO CASSETTE INTERFACE), 3-9 through 3-11 (PUNCH AND LOAD ROUTINES).

M6800 Programming Reference Manual, Motorola Semiconductor Products Inc., Phoenix, AZ, 1976, pp. 2-6 through 2-8 (6850 ACIA).

J. E. McNamara, *Technical Aspects of Data Communication,* Educational Services Department, Digital Equipment Corp., Maynard, MA, 1977, Chapters 1-3, 5, 15.

G. J. Lipovski, *Microcomputer Interfacing,* D. C. Heath (Lexington Books), Lexington, MA, 1980, Chapter 7.

A. J. Weissberger, "Data-link Control Chips: Bringing Order to Data Protocols," *Electronics,* June 8, 1978, pp. 104-112.

J. Barnes and V. Gregory, "Use Microprocessors to Enhance Performance with Noisy Data," *EDN,* August 20, 1976, pp. 71-72.

J. Deal and R. Bass, "Program PROMs with a 6800," *EDN,* June 5, 1979, pp. 177-181.

K. Fronheiser, "Device Operation and System Implementation of the Asynchronous Communications Interface Adapter," Motorola Semiconductor Products Inc. Application Note AN-754, Phoenix, AZ, 1975.

J. Padmanabhan and M. S. Swaminathan, "Teleprinter Option Unites PROM Programmer to MC6800," *Electronics,* August 30, 1979, pp. 157-159.

K. Steiner, "Verify 6800 Data During Recovery," *EDN,* April 20, 1979, pp. 101-102.

J. Wong et al., "Software Error Checking Procedures for Data Communications Protocols," *Computer Design,* February 1979, pp. 122-125.

WHAT YOU SHOULD LEARN

1) What LSI chips are available to perform serial communications functions.
2) How to convert data between serial and parallel forms.
3) How to provide timing for serial data communications.
4) How to generate and recognize start and stop bits.
5) How to detect false start bits using majority logic.
6) How to generate and check parity.
7) How to use the 6850 Asynchronous Communications Interface Adapter (ACIA).

TERMS

ASCII—American Standard Code for Information Interchange, a 7-bit character code widely used in computers and communications.

Baud—a communications measure for serial data transmission, bits per second but including both data bits and bits used for synchronization, error checking, and other purposes. Common baud rates are 110, 300, 1200, 2400, 4800, and 9600.

Baud rate generator—a device that generates the proper time intervals between bits for serial data transmission.

BSC—Binary Synchronous Communications or BISYNC, an older line protocol often used by IBM computers and terminals.

Checksum—a logical sum of data that is included in a record as a guard against recording or transmission errors. Also referred to as longitudinal parity or longitudinal redundancy check (LRC).

Cyclic redundancy check (CRC)—an error-detecting code generated from a polynomial that can be added to a data record or sector.

Data-link control—a set of conventions governing the format and timing of data exchange between communicating systems. Also called a *protocol*.

DDCMP—Digital Data Communications Message Protocol, a widely used protocol that supports any method of physical data transfer (synchronous or asynchronous, serial or parallel).

Error-correcting code—a code that can be used by the receiver to correct errors in the messages to which the code is attached; the code itself does not contain any additional message.

Error-detecting code—a code that can be used by the receiver to detect errors in the messages to which the code is attached; the code itself does not contain any additional message.

False start bit—a start bit that does not last the minimum required amount of time, usually caused by noise on the transmission line.

Longitudinal parity—*see* Checksum.

Longitudinal redundancy check (LRC)—*see* Checksum.

Majority logic—a combinational logic function that is true when more than half the inputs are true.

Mark—the 1 state on a serial data communications line.

Modem—modulator/demodulator, a device that adds or removes a carrier frequency, thereby allowing data to be transmitted on a high-frequency channel or received from such a channel.

Parallel—more than one bit at a time.

Parity—a 1-bit code that makes the total number of 1 bits in the word, including the parity bit, odd (odd parity) or even (even parity). Also called vertical parity or vertical redundancy check (VRC).

Protocol—*see* Data-link control.

RS-232 (or EIA RS-232)—a standard interface for the transmission of serial digital data. It has been partially superseded by RS-449.

SDLC—Synchronous Data Link Control, the protocol successor to BSC for IBM computers and terminals.

Serial—one bit at a time.

Shift register—a clocked device that moves its contents 1 bit to the left or right during each clock cycle.

Space—the zero state on a serial data communications line.

Standard teletypewriter—a teletypewriter that operates asynchronously at a rate of 10 characters per second.

Start bit—a 1-bit signal that indicates the start of data transmission by an asynchronous device.

Stop bit—a 1-bit signal that indicates the end of data transmission by an asynchronous device.

Synchronization (or **sync**) **character**—a character that is used only to synchronize the transmitter and the receiver.

Teletypewriter—a device containing a keyboard and a serial printer that is often used in communications and with computers. Also referred to as a Teletype (a registered trademark of Teletype Corporation of Skokie, Illinois) or TTY.

Universal asynchronous receiver/transmitter (UART)—an LSI device that acts as an interface between systems that handle data in parallel and devices that handle data in asynchronous serial form.

Universal synchronous receiver/transmitter (USRT)—an LSI device that acts as an interface between systems that handle data in parallel and devices that handle data in synchronous serial form.

6800 INSTRUCTIONS

ROL—rotate left; shift each bit of an accumulator or memory location left one position as if the ends were connected through the CARRY flag (see Figure E-2).

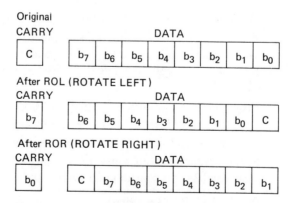

The other flags are not affected.

FIGURE E-2. 6800 shift instructions ROL and ROR.

ROR—rotate right; shift each bit of an accumulator or memory location right one position as if the ends were connected through the CARRY flag (see Figure E-2).

SERIAL INPUT/OUTPUT

Most I/O devices transfer data serially rather than in parallel. Serial data transmission greatly reduces hardware requirements, since only one data line is needed. However, since computers handle data in parallel, conversion is necessary on both input and output to interface a serial communications line.

This laboratory will describe how to perform such conversions and other interfacing tasks. We will show how to convert data between serial and parallel forms, how to provide timing, how to add start and stop bits, how to check and generate parity, and how to use the 6850 Asynchronous Communications Interface Adapter or ACIA, a programmable serial interface chip.

Serial I/O interfaces involve numerous hardware/software tradeoffs. We can perform all the tasks that we have mentioned in software. However, hardware serial interfaces are available for just a few dollars. These devices may be categorized as follows:

1) Asynchronous devices, generally called universal asynchronous receiver/transmitters or UARTs. UARTs perform the following functions:

- Serial/parallel conversion.
- Parity checking and generation.
- Start-bit recognition and generation.
- Stop-bit recognition and generation.
- Clocking.
- Buffering.

We will discuss the 6850 Asynchronous Communications Interface Adapter (ACIA), a UART specifically designed for use in 6800-based systems, later in this Laboratory.

2) Synchronous devices, generally called universal synchronous receiver/transmitters or USRTs. USRTs perform most of the UART functions under clock control and also generate and detect synchronization characters.

3) Data-link controllers. These devices perform all or most of the functions required by such advanced serial data communications methods as BSC, DDCMP, and SDLC. The book by J. E. McNamara (listed in the references) describes all these protocols.

The use of chips like the 6850 Asynchronous Communications Interface Adapter (a UART), the 6852 Synchronous Serial Data Adapter (a USRT), and the 6854 Advanced Data Link Controller greatly simplifies serial communications. Unless board space is unavailable or parts count must be minimized, their use is recommended in most applications. However, software methods for performing serial communications functions are occasionally useful as well as instructive.

SERIAL/PARALLEL CONVERSION

Converting data from parallel to serial requires a shift register. We can implement a shift register in software with the microprocessor's shift instructions. Since most serial data transmission starts with bit 0, we will use the LSR and ROR instructions in the following program to place bit 0 of memory location 0060 on the LED attached to bit 7 of user PIA port B. We will continue to use Program C-2 to provide the required initialization. Note the use of the ROTATE RIGHT instruction (ROR) to move one bit of data from the CARRY (where LSR $60 places it) to bit 7 of memory location 8006, which is the output port for the LEDs. Program E-1 is the hexadecimal version. We have complemented the data initially to make it easier to observe, since 0 bits light the LEDs. Remember that Program C-2 turns all the LEDs off as one of its initialization functions.

```
COM      $60          COMPLEMENT DATA TO SIMPLIFY OBSERVATION
LSR      $60          GET ONE BIT OF PARALLEL DATA
ROR      $8006        MOVE BIT TO SERIAL OUTPUT PORT
SWI
```

PROGRAM E-1

MEMORY ADDRESS (HEX)	MEMORY CONTENTS (HEX)	INSTRUCTION (MNEMONIC)	
0022	73	COM	$60
0023	00		
0024	60		
0025	74	LSR	$60
0026	00		
0027	60		
0028	76	ROR	$8006
0029	80		
002A	06		
002B	3F	SWI	

Program E-1 transmits one bit of data. Execute it eight times starting with (0060) = AA hex (10101010 binary). After the first execution, start the program in memory location 0025 to avoid repeating the initialization. The LED attached to bit position 7 should go off, on, off, on and so on, since the data consists of alternating 0 and 1 bits, starting with a 0 in bit position 0. The ROR $8006 instruction moves the previous serial outputs to the right so you can see all the bits that have been transmitted. What is the final value of memory location 0060? Why? Note how closely the program mimics the effects of a shift register on the LEDs.

PROBLEM E-1

Make Program E-1 transmit bit 7 of memory location 0060 first and use bit position 0 of user PIA port B as the serial output.

Converting inputs from serial to parallel is also simple. The following program (see Program E-2 for a hexadecimal version) fetches a serial input from bit position 7 of user PIA port A and combines it with the data in memory location 0061. Note that bit 0 is received first. The data is also shown in complemented form on the LEDs to simplify observation.

ASL	$8004	MOVE SERIAL INPUT TO CARRY
ROR	$61	AND COMBINE WITH PREVIOUS INPUTS
LDAA	$61	SHOW DATA ON LEDS
COMA		IN COMPLEMENTED FORM
STAA	$8006	
SWI		

PROGRAM E-2

MEMORY ADDRESS (HEX)	MEMORY CONTENTS (HEX)	INSTRUCTION (MNEMONIC)	
0022	78	ASL	$8004
0023	80		
0024	04		
0025	76	ROR	$61
0026	00		
0027	61		
0028	96	LDAA	$61
0029	61		
002A	43	COMA	
002B	B7	STAA	$8006
002C	80		

MEMORY ADDRESS (HEX)	MEMORY CONTENTS (HEX)	INSTRUCTION (MNEMONIC)
002D	06	
002E	3F	SWI

Clear memory location 0061 to start and execute Program E-2 eight times to assemble a byte of data. Set the switches so that the final result is (0061) = AA (hex).

PROBLEM E-2

Make Program E-2 start with bit 7 of the data and use bit position 0 of user PIA port A as the serial input.

TIMING

In real applications, the computer must provide the proper timing between bits. We can easily make the transmission program send the bits at a rate determined by a delay routine. The next example (see Program E-3 for a hexadecimal version) uses the maximum length of the monitor subroutine DLY1 (see Laboratory A and Table D-1). The data is originally in memory location 0060.

```
         LDAA    $60        GET PARALLEL DATA
         COMA               COMPLEMENT TO SIMPLIFY OBSERVATION
         LDAB    #8         NUMBER OF BITS = 8
OUTB     LSRA               MOVE SERIAL OUTPUT TO CARRY
         ROR     $8006      AND ON TO LEDS
         LDX     #0         WAIT A BIT TIME
         JSR     DLY1
         DECB               COUNT BITS
         BNE     OUTB
         SWI
```

PROGRAM E-3

MEMORY ADDRESS (HEX)	MEMORY CONTENTS (HEX)	INSTRUCTION (MNEMONIC)	
0022	96	LDAA	$60
0023	60		
0024	43	COMA	
0025	C6	LDAB	#8
0026	08		

338

MEMORY ADDRESS (HEX)	MEMORY CONTENTS (HEX)		INSTRUCTION (MNEMONIC)	
0027	44	OUTB	LSRA	
0028	76		ROR	$8006
0029	80			
002A	06			
002B	CE		LDX	#0
002C	00			
002D	00			
002E	BD		JSR	DLY1
002F	E0			
0030	E0			
0031	5A		DECB	
0032	26		BNE	OUTB
0033	F3			
0034	3F		SWI	

Run Program E-3 with (0060) = AA (hex) and with (0060) = 55 (hex). You can change the data rate by changing the parameter of the DLY1 routine. Try the following sequence of hexadecimal numbers in memory location 002C: 00, 80, 40, 20, 10, 08, 04, 02, 01. When can you no longer see the separate serial outputs? You can increase the data rate still further by clearing memory location 002C and reducing memory location 002D with a similar sequence.

PROBLEM E-3

Write a serial data reception program that waits between bits using the maximum length of subroutine DLY1. Assume that the serial data starts with bit 0 and is received through bit position 7 of user PIA port A. Run the program and set the input switch so that the final data value is (0061) = AA (hex). The delay subroutine will allow you about 1 s to move the input switch to the correct position; if you need more time, set a breakpoint at the end of the program.

USING THE REAL-TIME CLOCK

We can also use the real-time clock (see Laboratory D) to handle timing. The following program enables the real-time clock interrupt and transmits a bit each time the clock counter in memory location 0070 advances by 150 (i.e., at 1-s intervals, since the clock frequency is 150 Hz). The interrupt service routine is the same as in Program D-4. Program E-4 is the hexadecimal version. Remember that Program C-2 initializes the PIA and loads 0080 into the vector addresses (A000 and A001) provided by the JBUG monitor.

```
            LDAA      #%00000101    ENABLE CLOCK INTERRUPT
            STAA      1,X
            CLR       $70           CLEAR CLOCK COUNTER
            CLI                     ENABLE CPU INTERRUPT
            LDAB      #8            NUMBER OF BITS = 8
            LDAA      $60           GET PARALLEL DATA
            COMA                    COMPLEMENT TO SIMPLIFY
    *                                 OBSERVATION
OUTB        LSRA                    MOVE SERIAL OUTPUT TO CARRY
            ROR       $8006         AND ON TO LEDS
            PSHA                    SAVE PARALLEL DATA
            LDAA      $70           GET STARTING CLOCK COUNTER
            ADDA      #150          CALCULATE TARGET VALUE
WTCLK       CMPA      $70           TARGET VALUE REACHED?
            BNE       WTCLK         NO, WAIT
            PULA                    RESTORE PARALLEL DATA
            DECB                    COUNT BITS
            BNE       OUTB
            SEI                     DISABLE CPU INTERRUPT
            SWI

            ORG       $80
            LDAA      $8004         CLEAR CLOCK INTERRUPT
            INC       $70           INCREMENT CLOCK COUNTER
            RTI
```

PROGRAM E-4

MEMORY ADDRESS (HEX)	MEMORY CONTENTS (HEX)		INSTRUCTION (MNEMONIC)	
0022	86		LDAA	#%00000101
0023	05			
0024	A7		STAA	1,X
0025	01			
0026	7F		CLR	$70
0027	00			
0028	70			
0029	0E		CLI	
002A	C6		LDAB	#8
002B	08			
002C	96		LDAA	$60
002D	60			
002E	43		COMA	
002F	44	OUTB	LSRA	
0030	76		ROR	$8006
0031	80			
0032	06			

PROGRAM E-4 (continued)

MEMORY ADDRESS (HEX)	MEMORY CONTENTS (HEX)		INSTRUCTION (MNEMONIC)	
0033	36		PSHA	
0034	96		LDAA	$70
0035	70			
0036	8B		ADDA	#150
0037	96			
0038	91	WTCLK	CMPA	$70
0039	70			
003A	26		BNE	WTCLK
003B	FC			
003C	32		PULA	
003D	5A		DECB	
003E	26		BNE	OUTB
003F	EF			
0040	0F		SEI	
0041	3F		SWI	
0080	B6		LDAA	$8004
0081	80			
0082	04			
0083	7C		INC	$70
0084	00			
0085	70			
0086	3B		RTI	

Enter and run Program E-4 with (0060) = AA and with (0060) = 55. Note that the interrupt service routine does not affect any registers or flags. What happens if adding 150 to the current value of the clock counter produces a carry? This procedure works just like watching the minute hand on a clock while ignoring the hour hand.

PROBLEM E-4

Make Program E-4 wait for the number of clock interrupts given by the contents of memory location 0061 between bits. This change allows the same program to handle transmissions at different data rates. Of course, the system must determine the time between bits by a method such as the one described in Program D-3.

PROBLEM E-5

Make the serial reception program wait for 150 real-time clock interrupts between bits. Assume that the serial data starts with bit 0 and that the serial input is bit position 7 of user PIA port A.

Sample Cases

1) If the serial input switch is left open while the program executes, all the inputs will be 1's.
Result: (0061) = FF

2) If the serial input switch is left closed while the program executes, all the inputs will be 0's.
Result: (0061) = 00

Remember that you cannot use the single-step or Trace function when $\overline{IRQ}$ interrupts are enabled, because the nonmaskable interrupt used by the Trace function has higher priority than $\overline{IRQ}$ and will cause $\overline{IRQ}$ to be ignored. If you try to use the N key when $\overline{IRQ}$ interrupts are active, JBUG will continuously return with the same address.

PROBLEM E-6

Make Program E-4 use Program D-6 as the interrupt service routine. Now time is being kept in minutes, seconds, and clock counts. Make the time between bit outputs 1 s.

PROBLEM E-7

Make the answer to Problem E-5 use Program D-6 as the interrupt service routine. The time between serial input operations should be 1 s.

START AND STOP BITS

In the previous discussion, we have assumed that we can start and stop transmission and reception at any time. Of course, this is not generally the case, since external factors such as the availability of data or the rate at which an I/O device can handle data usually control the transfer. In real applications, the receiver must determine when data is available and must identify the beginning and ending of the transmission.

One simple way of marking the beginning and ending of the transmission is to place start and stop bits around the actual data. Figure E-3 shows the standard teletypewriter format in which a start bit (or logic 0) precedes the data and 2 stop bits (or logic 1's) follow the data and separate one character from the next. Note that the data line is normally in the 1 state (called the *mark* state on a teletypewriter). The transition to the 0 (or *space*) state signifies the start of transmission.

Note the advantages of this approach:

1) Transmission can start at any time. No clock is required.

2) The start and stop bits are easy to generate and detect.

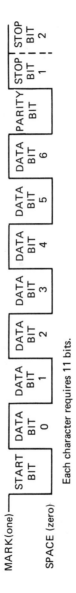

Each character requires 11 bits.

FIGURE E-3. The standard teletypewriter data format.

3)   The start bit can produce an interrupt.

4)   The stop bits separate characters.

Of course, the approach also has disadvantages:

1)   The start and stop bits reduce the actual data rate. If the format of Figure E-3 is used, 11 bits must be transmitted for each 8-bit character.

2)   Noise can produce false start bits. We will discuss methods for solving this problem later.

3)   Start and stop bits must be added to each character. This results in processing overhead, which can be reduced if the characters are grouped into blocks.

We can easily modify Program E-3 to produce an initial start bit. All that we must do is clear the CARRY flag initially (with the CLC instruction) and shift accumulator A at the end of the loop instead of at the beginning (so bit 0 of the data is actually the second bit transmitted instead of the first). Note that we have also increased the bit count by 1. Program E-5 is the hexadecimal version.

```
        LDAA    $60       GET PARALLEL DATA
        COMA              COMPLEMENT TO SIMPLIFY OBSERVATION
        LDAB    #9        NUMBER OF BITS = 9
        CLC               FORM START BIT
OUTB    ROR     $8006     MOVE SERIAL OUTPUT TO LEDS
        LDX     #0        WAIT A BIT TIME
        JSR     DLY1
        LSRA              MOVE NEXT SERIAL OUTPUT TO CARRY
        DECB              COUNT BITS
        BNE     OUTB
        SWI
```

PROGRAM E-5

MEMORY ADDRESS (HEX)	MEMORY CONTENTS (HEX)	INSTRUCTION (MNEMONIC)	
0022	96	LDAA	$60
0023	60		
0024	43	COMA	
0025	C6	LDAB	#9
0026	09		

MEMORY ADDRESS (HEX)	MEMORY CONTENTS (HEX)		INSTRUCTION (MNEMONIC)	
0027	0C		CLC	
0028	76	OUTB	ROR	$8006
0029	80			
002A	06			
002B	CE		LDX	#0
002C	00			
002D	00			
002E	BD		JSR	DLY1
002F	E0			
0030	E0			
0031	44		LSRA	
0032	5A		DECB	
0033	26		BNE	OUTB
0034	F3			
0035	3F		SWI	

Enter Program E-5 into memory and run it with (0060) = AA (hex) and with (0060) = 55 (hex). The start bit will appear as a light in front of the regular data, since a logic 0 lights an LED. By making the following changes to Program E-5, we can generate the stop bits as well.

1) Make the bit count 11 instead of 9.

2) Replace LSRA with the sequence SEC (SET CARRY), RORA so that 1's are automatically shifted in at the left as the data is shifted out at the right. The 1's will form the stop bits at the end.

PROBLEM E-8

Write and run the transmission program that generates a start bit and 2 stop bits. How would you modify your program to produce 1 stop bit instead of 2? Many 30-cps (characters per second) terminals (such as the popular Texas Instruments Silent 700) use a 10-bit data format with 1 stop bit.

PROBLEM E-9

A few older terminals use a data format with 1½ stop bits. Modify the program from Problem E-8 to produce data in that format. Assume that one bit time is given by the maximum length of the DLY1 subroutine as in Program E-5.

Receiving data with the start and stop bits included is more complex than transmitting the data. The program must detect the falling edge (a 1-to-0 or high-to-low transition), which signifies the beginning of a start bit. Remember that the line is normally in the 1 or *mark* state. The program must then wait half a bit time (after detecting the transition) to center the reception. This delay causes the computer to read the subsequent data bits near the centers of the pulses rather than at the edges. Reading near the centers avoids errors if the data changes as in Figure E-3. Centering also makes it unnecessary to generate highly accurate time intervals, since a little drift from the center does not matter. Program E-6 is the hexadecimal version of the following program.

WTSTB	LDAA	$8004	GET DATA
	BMI	WTSTB	WAIT FOR START BIT (ZERO INPUT)
	LDX	#$8000	CENTER WITH HALF BIT TIME DELAY
	JSR	DLY1	
	LDAB	#8	NUMBER OF BITS = 8
INBIT	LDX	#0	WAIT A BIT TIME
	JSR	DLY1	
	ASL	$8004	MOVE SERIAL INPUT TO CARRY
	RORA		AND COMBINE WITH PREVIOUS DATA
	DECB		COUNT BITS
	BNE	INBIT	
	STAA	$61	SAVE PARALLEL DATA
	SWI		

PROGRAM E-6

MEMORY ADDRESS (HEX)	MEMORY CONTENTS (HEX)		INSTRUCTION (MNEMONIC)	
0022	B6	WTSTB	LDAA	$8004
0023	80			
0024	04			
0025	2B		BMI	WTSTB
0026	FB			
0027	CE		LDX	#$8000
0028	80			
0029	00			
002A	BD		JSR	DLY1
002B	E0			
002C	E0			
002D	C6		LDAB	#8
002E	08			
002F	CE	INBIT	LDX	#0
0030	00			
0031	00			
0032	BD		JSR	DLY1

MEMORY ADDRESS (HEX)	MEMORY CONTENTS (HEX)	INSTRUCTION (MNEMONIC)	
0033	E0		
0034	E0		
0035	78	ASL	$8004
0036	80		
0037	04		
0038	46	RORA	
0039	5A	DECB	
003A	26	BNE	INBIT
003B	F3		
003C	97	STAA	$61
003D	61		
003E	3F	SWI	

The half-bit time delay requires half as large a starting value in the index register. Enter and run Program E-6; set a breakpoint in memory location 003A to give yourself time to move the serial input switch to the proper position for each data value. The program will not get past the initial loop until you close the input switch and form a start bit. Try the following cases:

1) Start with the input switch closed and change its position each time the breakpoint is reached.
   Result: (0061) = AA (hex)

2) Leave the input switch closed all the time.
   Result: (0061) = 00

3) Close the input switch to form the start bit and then immediately open it and leave it open.
   Result: (0061) = FF (hex)
   Note that the program waits 1½ bit times and reads the first serial input before it ever reaches the breakpoint.

PROBLEM E-10

Make Program E-6 check to see if there are 2 stop bits (logic 1s) at the end of the data. The revised program should set memory location 0062 to 00 if the two stop bits are present and to FF if they are not. Lack of the proper number of stop bits is called a *framing error*.

PROBLEM E-11

Make Program E-6 check for the number of stop bits specified by the contents of memory location 0063. Assume that the allowed values are 0, 1, and 2.

PROBLEM E-12

Make Program E-5 wait for 150 real-time clock interrupts between bit outputs. Use the interrupt service routine in Program E-4.

PROBLEM E-13

Make Program E-6 wait for 150 real-time clock interrupts between bit inputs. Use the interrupt service routine in Program E-4.

Of course, we can easily modify Program E-6 so that the start bit generates an interrupt on control line CB1 of the user PIA. The only new consideration is that the interrupt service routine must disable the CB1 interrupt after accepting it; otherwise, 1 to 0 transitions in the data will cause interrupts. The interrupt flag must be cleared and the interrupt re-enabled before the next character can be received. Remember that Program C-2 reads both I/O ports on the user PIA to clear spurious interrupts. Program E-7 is the hexadecimal version of the modified program.

PROGRAM E-7

MEMORY ADDRESS (HEX)	MEMORY CONTENTS (HEX)	INSTRUCTION (MNEMONIC)	
0022	86	LDAA	#%00000101
0023	05		
0024	A7	STAA	3,X
0025	03		
0026	0E	CLI	
0027	3E	WAI	
0028	CE	LDX	#$8000
0029	80		
002A	00		
002B	BD	JSR	DLY1
002C	E0		
002D	E0		
002E	C6	LDAB	#8
002F	08		
0030	CE	INBIT LDX	#0
0031	00		
0032	00		
0033	BD	JSR	DLY1
0034	E0		
0035	E0		
0036	78	ASL	$8004
0037	80		
0038	04		

MEMORY ADDRESS (HEX)	MEMORY CONTENTS (HEX)	INSTRUCTION (MNEMONIC)	
0039	46	RORA	
003A	5A	DECB	
003B	26	BNE	INBIT
003C	F3		
003D	97	STAA	$61
003E	61		
003F	3F	SWI	
0080	B6	LDAA	$8006
0081	80		
0082	06		
0083	B6	LDAA	$8007
0084	80		
0085	07		
0086	84	ANDA	#%11111110
0087	FE		
0088	B7	STAA	$8007
0089	80		
008A	07		
008B	3B	RTI	

```
        LDAA    #%00000101    ENABLE START BIT INTERRUPT
        STAA    3,X
        CLI                   ENABLE CPU INTERRUPT
        WAI                   WAIT FOR START BIT
        LDX     #$8000        CENTER WITH HALF BIT TIME DELAY
        JSR     DLY1
        LDAB    #8            NUMBER OF BITS = 8
INBIT   LDX     #0            WAIT A BIT TIME
        JSR     DLY1
        ASL     $8004         MOVE SERIAL INPUT TO CARRY
        RORA                  AND COMBINE WITH PREVIOUS DATA
        DECB                  COUNT BITS
        BNE     INBIT
        STAA    $61           SAVE PARALLEL DATA
        SWI

        ORG     $80
        LDAA    $8006         CLEAR START BIT INTERRUPT FLAG
        LDAA    $8007         DISABLE START BIT INTERRUPT
        ANDA    #$11111110
        STAA    $8007
        RTI
```

To produce the start bit interrupt as well as the regular data input, you can either tie the same debounced switch to both CB1 and PA7 or simulate the double connection by keeping separate switches in the same positions. As with Program E-6, a breakpoint will give you time to move the switches to the desired positions. Note that we have disabled the start bit interrupt in a way that is independent of the contents of the control register; we could also have used the single instruction DEC $8007.

PROBLEM E-14

Change Program E-7 (or E-6) so that you do not need the bit counter in accumulator B. (*Hint:* Load accumulator A initially with 10000000 (binary) or 80 hexadecimal and exit when the program has shifted the 1 bit from the leftmost position all the way over to the CARRY.)

PROBLEM E-15

Make Program E-7 use the real-time clock. Allow 150 real-time clock interrupts between bit outputs. Remember that there are now two independent sources of interrupts. Do not examine the interrupt flag set by the start bit if that interrupt is not enabled.

DETECTING FALSE START BITS

Many errors can occur in data communications, particularly if the connections are noisy (like the ordinary telephone network) or if the distances are long. One potential problem is noise that looks like a start bit to the receiver. Such noise is referred to as a *false start bit*. A way to reduce the frequency with which such bits are confused with real start bits is for the receiver to sample the line several times and use majority logic to determine the data value. This procedure will screen out short noise pulses.

The following program samples the data input at one-fourth, one-half, and three-fourths of a bit time after the initial detection of a start bit. It requires that at least two samples be 0's. Program E-8 is the hexadecimal version. At the end of Program E-8, the computer has used three-fourths of a bit time in the sampling process. So, a final delay of three-fourths of a bit time is necessary to reach the center of the first data bit.

Enter and run Program E-8. Set a breakpoint after the ¼-bit time delay so that you can move the serial input switch to either position and observe the sampling procedure. Note that majority logic works like voting; the value that is found most often "wins."

PROGRAM E-8

MEMORY ADDRESS (HEX)	MEMORY CONTENTS (HEX)	INSTRUCTION (MNEMONIC)		
0022	B6	WTSTB	LDAA	$8004
0023	80			
0024	04			
0025	2B		BMI	WTSTB
0026	FB			
0027	4F		CLRA	
0028	C6		LDAB	#3
0029	03			
002A	CE	CHBIT	LDX	#$4000
002B	40			
002C	00			
002D	BD		JSR	DLY1
002E	E0			
002F	E0			
0030	7D		TST	$8004
0031	80			
0032	04			
0033	2B		BMI	CSAMP
0034	01			
0035	4C		INCA	
0036	5A	CSAMP	DECB	
0037	26		BNE	CHBIT
0038	F1			
0039	81		CMPA	#2
003A	02			
003B	25		BCS	WTSTB
003C	E5			
003D	CE		LDX	#$C000
003E	C0			
003F	00			
0040	BD		JSR	DLY1
0041	E0			
0042	E0			
0043	3F		SWI	

WTSTB	LDAA	$8004	GET DATA
	BMI	WTSTB	WAIT FOR START BIT
	CLRA		ZERO COUNT = ZERO
	LDAB	#3	NUMBER OF SAMPLES = 3
CHBIT	LDX	#$4000	WAIT 1/4 BIT TIME

351

```
           JSR      DLY1
           TST      $8004        IS DATA BIT ZERO?
           BMI      CSAMP
           INCA                  YES, INCREMENT ZERO COUNT
  CSAMP    DECB                  COUNT SAMPLES
           BNE      CHBIT
           CMPA     #2           WAS MAJORITY OF SAMPLES ZERO?
           BCS      WTSTB        NO, FALSE START BIT
           LDX      #$C000       YES, WAIT 3/4 BIT TIME TO SAMPLE
           JSR      DLY1
           SWI
```

PROBLEM E-16

Rewrite Program E-8 to check the input at intervals of one-eighth of a bit time. Now, at least four of the six samples must be zero for the start bit to be accepted. Be sure to center the reception properly after accepting a start bit.

PROBLEM E-17

Write a reception program that checks each received bit at one-fourth, one-half, and three-fourths of a bit time and determines the actual value by majority logic. That is, the value of at least two of the samples is taken as the value of the data bit. Your program should start at the leading edge of the first data bit, assuming that the initialization routine has detected a start bit but has not centered the reception.

GENERATING AND CHECKING PARITY

Still another way to reduce the number of errors is to include error-detecting or correcting codes with the data. These codes show whether the data was received correctly and, if not, where the errors were; they contain no additional information and thus reduce the actual data rate.

Parity is a simple error-detecting code. This is a single bit added to each word, which makes the total number of 1 bits even (if even parity) or odd (if odd parity). Note the following examples:

1)   Data = 01101101: Even parity = 1, since the data contains an odd number (5) of 1 bits.

2)   Data = 00010001: Even parity = 0, since the data contains an even number (2) of 1 bits.

Parity has the following features:

1)   It can detect single but not double errors. Two bits received incorrectly will result in the same parity as that generated from the original data.

2) It does not allow for error correction. If the parity of the received data is wrong, there is no way of telling which bit is in error. All the receiver can do is request retransmission of the data.

3) Odd parity has the advantage over even parity that it will detect a string of 0's or 1's resulting from a break in transmission.

Parity is particularly convenient with the 7-bit ASCII character code, since the most significant bit can be used for parity. Most UARTs and other communications chips, as we have mentioned, will automatically generate parity for transmission and check it on reception. There are usually ways to choose whether a UART implements parity, whether it generates and checks even or odd parity, and how many bits it includes in each character.

The easiest way to generate parity using the 6800 microprocessor is to add all the bits together. The least significant bit of the sum will be 1 if the data contains an odd number of 1 bits and 0 if the data contains an even number. Thus the least significant bit of the sum is an even parity bit, since it makes the total number of 1 bits in the word (including the parity bit) even. The summation may be confusing at first, but remember that the sum of an even number of 1 bits is surely itself an even number and therefore has a least significant bit of 0. We can easily combine the addition process with the normal conversion between serial and parallel forms. The following program (Program E-9 is the hexadecimal version) generates even parity and sends it as the most significant bit of the data. We have assumed that the data is originally in memory location 0060. Note that we have not complemented the data in Program E-9 (because it would make parity generation confusing), so remember that the data will appear on the LEDs in negative logic (0 = light on, 1 = light off).

```
        LDAB    #8        NUMBER OF DATA BITS = 8
        STAB    $61
        CLRA              START PARITY AT ZERO
        LDAB    $60       GET PARALLEL DATA
OUTB    ABA               ADD DATA TO PARITY
        LSRB              MOVE SERIAL OUTPUT TO CARRY
        ROR     $8006     AND ON TO LEDS
        LDX     #0        WAIT A BIT TIME
        JSR     DLY1
        DEC     $61       COUNT BITS
        BNE     OUTB
        LSRA              FORM FINAL BIT FROM PARITY SUM
        ROR     $8006
        LDX     #0        WAIT A BIT TIME
        JSR     DLY1
        SWI
```

PROGRAM E-9

MEMORY ADDRESS (HEX)	MEMORY CONTENTS (HEX)	INSTRUCTION (MNEMONIC)		
0022	C6		LDAB	#8
0023	08			
0024	D7		STAB	$61
0025	61			
0026	4F		CLRA	
0027	D6		LDAB	$60
0028	60			
0029	1B	OUTB	ABA	
002A	54		LSRB	
002B	76		ROR	$8006
002C	80			
002D	06			
002E	CE		LDX	#0
002F	00			
0030	00			
0031	BD		JSR	DLY1
0032	E0			
0033	E0			
0034	7A		DEC	$61
0035	00			
0036	61			
0037	26		BNE	OUTB
0038	F0			
0039	44		LSRA	
003A	76		ROR	$8006
003B	80			
003C	06			
003D	CE		LDX	#0
003E	00			
003F	00			
0040	BD		JSR	DLY1
0041	E0			
0042	E0			
0043	3F		SWI	

Enter and run Program E-9 for the following examples:

1) (0060) = 41 ASCII A
    Result: Even parity bit = 0, since the data has two 1 bits (41 hex = 01000001 binary).

2) (0060) = 43 ASCII C

Result: Even parity bit = 1, since the data has three 1 bits (43 hex = 01000011 binary).

The results of Program E-9 are confusing, since the LEDs use negative logic. You can add a final COM instruction to produce positive logic; that is,

0043	73	COM	$8006
0044	80		
0045	06		
0046	3F	SWI	

Regardless, the final values on the LEDs should be (left to right or bit position 7 to bit position 0): even parity bit, data bit 7, data bit 6, data bit 5, data bit 4, data bit 3, data bit 2, and data bit 1. In example 1 above, the values will be 0, 0, 1, 0, 0, 0, 0, 0, since 41 hex = 01000001 binary. In example 2, the values will be 1, 0, 1, 0, 0, 0, 0, 1, since 43 hex = 01000011 binary.

PROBLEM E-18

Many computers and peripherals use a 7-bit ASCII character code and reserve the most significant bit (bit position 7) for parity. Make Program E-9 transmit 7 bit characters followed by an even parity bit.

Examples:

1) (0060) = 41 ASCII A

Result: Transmitted data should be 41, since its parity is even.

2) (0060) = 43 ASCII C

Result: Transmitted data should be C3, since the parity of 43 is odd.

PROBLEM E-19

Write a serial reception program that calculates the parity of the received data as it is being converted to parallel form. The program should place the parallel data in memory location 0061 and set memory location 0062 to 0 if the parity is even and to 1 if the parity is odd.

Examples:

1) Received data is 41 (hex) = 01000001 (binary).
   Result: (0061) = 41 (parallel data)
   (0062) = 00 since 41 hex has an even number of 1 bits.

2) Received data is C1 (hex) = 11000001 (binary).
   Result: (0061) = C1 (parallel data)
   (0062) = 01 since C1 hex has an odd number of 1 bits.

PROBLEM E-20

Make the answer to Problem E-19 check to see if bit 7 of the data is actually an odd parity bit. The program should place the parallel data in memory location 0061 and set memory location 0062 to 0 if the parity is correct and to 1 if the parity is wrong.

Examples:

1) Received data is FF (hex) = 11111111 (binary)
   Result: (0061) = FF (parallel data)
   (0062) = 01 since the parity of 11111111 is even.

2) Received data is C1 (hex) = 11000001 (binary)
   Result: (0061) = C1 (parallel data)
   (0062) = 00 since the parity of 11000001 is odd.

Example 1 shows why odd parity is more commonly used than even parity. The reason is that a string of 1's or 0's caused by a hardware fault shows up as an error if odd parity is being used, but not if even parity is being used. Think of what the data would be if the external input were open-circuited or short-circuited.

THE 6850 ASYNCHRONOUS COMMUNICATIONS INTERFACE ADAPTER (ACIA)

The 6850 Asynchronous Communications Interface Adapter is a UART specifically designed for use with the 6800 microprocessor. It occupies two memory locations and contains two read-only registers (received data and status) and two write-only registers (transmit data and control). Table E-1 defines the register contents and Table E-2 describes the control register bits (bit 7 is the receive interrupt enable bit).

The 6850 ACIA performs the following serial communications functions:

- It converts data between serial and parallel forms.
- It generates and detects start bits. The device also provides false start bit detection in the divide-by-16 and divide-by-64 clock modes.

Table E-1

DEFINITION OF ACIA REGISTER CONTENTS
(COURTESY OF MOTOROLA SEMICONDUCTOR PRODUCTS)

DATA BUS LINE NUMBER	BUFFER ADDRESS			
	RS · R/$\overline{W}$ TRANSMIT DATA REGISTER (WRITE-ONLY)	RS · R/W RECEIVE DATA REGISTER (READ-ONLY)	RS · R/$\overline{W}$ CONTROL REGISTER (WRITE-ONLY)	$\overline{RS}$ · R/W STATUS REGISTER (READ-ONLY)
0	Data bit 0*	Data bit 0	Counter Divide Select 1 (CR0)	Receive Data Register Full (RDRF)
1	Data bit 1	Data bit 1	Counter Divide Select 2 (CR1)	Transmit Data Register Empty (TDRE)
2	Data bit 2	Data bit 2	Word Select 1 (CR2)	Data Carrier Detect ($\overline{DCD}$)
3	Data bit 3	Data bit 3	Word Select 2 (CR3)	Clear-to-Send ($\overline{CTS}$)
4	Data bit 4	Data bit 4	Word Select 3 (CR4)	Framing Error (FE)
5	Data bit 5	Data bit 5	Transmit Control 1 (CR5)	Receiver Overrun (OVRN)
6	Data bit 6	Data bit 6	Transmit Control 2 (CR6)	Parity Error (PE)
7	Data bit 7†	Data bit 7‡	Receive Interrupt Enable (CR7)	Interrupt Request ($\overline{IRQ}$)

*Leading bit = LSB = bit 0.
†Data bit is "don't care" in 7-bit plus parity modes.
‡Data bit will be zero in 7-bit plus parity modes.

357

Table E-2

DESCRIPTION OF ACIA CONTROL REGISTER OPTIONS
(COURTESY OF MOTOROLA SEMICONDUCTOR PRODUCTS)*

CR1	CR0	Function
0	0	÷ 1
0	1	÷ 16
1	0	÷ 64
1	1	Master Reset

CR4	CR3	CR2	Function
0	0	0	7 Bits + Even Parity + 2 Stop Bits
0	0	1	7 Bits + Odd Parity + 2 Stop Bits
0	1	0	7 Bits + Even Parity + 1 Stop Bit
0	1	1	7 Bits + Odd Parity + 1 Stop Bit
1	0	0	8 Bits + 2 Stop Bits
1	0	1	8 Bits + 1 Stop Bit
1	1	0	8 Bits + Even Parity + 1 Stop Bit
1	1	1	8 Bits + Odd Parity + 1 Stop Bit

CR6	CR5	Function
0	0	$\overline{RTS}$ = low, Transmitting Interrupt Disabled.
0	1	$\overline{RTS}$ = low, Transmitting Interrupt Enabled.
1	0	$\overline{RTS}$ = high, Transmitting Interrupt Disabled.
1	1	$\overline{RTS}$ = low, Transmits a Break level on the Transmit Data Output. Transmitting Interrupt Disabled.

*Control register bit 7 is 1 to enable the receive interrupt, 0 to disable it.

- It generates and checks parity.
- It generates and checks stop bits.
- It provides an RS-232 interface with the required status and control signals.
- It produces receive and transmit interrupts.

The ACIA requires an externally supplied clock; it does not generate bit times, although some variations of the 6850 do (such as the Synertek 6551 device). One unusual feature of the ACIA is that it has no RESET input; the only way to reset an ACIA is to set bits 0 and 1 of its control register simultaneously. The ACIA does, however, provide power-on reset so that it comes up in an inactive mode with interrupts disabled.

The ACIA that is part of the MEK6800D2 microcomputer is supplied with a 4800-Hz transmit clock so that it can be used in the divide-by-16 mode at 300 Hz. It occupies addresses 8008 (control and status registers) and 8009 (transmit and receive data registers).

The following program (see Program E-10 for a hexadecimal version) resets the ACIA, puts it in the divide-by-16 clock mode with 8-bit data and 2 stop bits, waits for the transmit data register to be empty (bit 1 of the ACIA status register = 1), and then stores the contents of memory location 0060 in the transmit data register, thus initiating transmission. You may want to place this program in a loop (replacing SWI with BRA WAITE) and observe the TRANSMITTED DATA line on an oscilloscope.

```
         LDAA    #%00000011    RESET ACIA
         STAA    $8008
         LDAA    #%00010001    8-BIT DATA, 2 STOP BITS, NO PARITY
         STAA    $8008
WAITE    LDAA    $8008         IS TRANSMIT DATA REGISTER EMPTY?
         ANDA    #%00000010
         BEQ     WAITE         NO, WAIT
         LDAA    $60           YES, TRANSMIT DATA
         STAA    $8008
         SWI
```

PROGRAM E-10

MEMORY ADDRESS (HEX)	MEMORY CONTENTS (HEX)		INSTRUCTION (MNEMONIC)	
0000	86		LDAA	#%00000011
0001	03			
0002	B7		STAA	$8008
0003	80			
0004	08			
0005	86		LDAA	#%00010001
0006	11			
0007	B7		STAA	$8008
0008	80			
0009	08			
000A	B6	WAITE	LDAA	$8008
000B	80			
000C	08			
000D	84		ANDA	#%00000010
000E	02			
000F	27		BEQ	WAITE
0010	F9			
0011	96		LDAA	$60
0012	60			
0013	B7		STAA	$8009
0014	80			
0015	09			
0016	3F		SWI	

Receiving data from the ACIA is no more difficult than transmitting data through it. All that we must do is reset the ACIA, determine its operating mode, and then wait for the RECEIVE DATA REGISTER FULL bit (bit 0 of the status register—see Table E-1) to go high. When that bit goes high, the program simply reads the data from the Receive Data Register and saves it in memory.

The following program uses the divide-by-16 clock mode with 8-bit data and 2 stop bits. It places the received data in memory location 0061. Program E-11 is the hexadecimal version. The only special note of caution is to remember that reading and writing access physically distinct registers on an ACIA. Thus it makes no sense to use such instructions as shifts and complements on ACIA registers, since they would read the data from one register, operate on it, and write the result back into a completely different register. For example, we could not replace the sequence

LDAA	$8008
LSRA	

in the following program with the single instruction

LSR	$8008

because LSR $8008 would read the contents of the ACIA status register, shift it right logically one bit, and store the result in the ACIA control register. Clearly, the outcome of such an instruction would be unpredictable. This caution applies to many peripheral chips besides the ACIA; the programmer must read the specifications carefully. Note that the reason why reading and writing access different registers is that the READ/WRITE line is used for internal addressing.

PROGRAM E-11

MEMORY ADDRESS (HEX)	MEMORY CONTENTS (HEX)	INSTRUCTION (MNEMONIC)	
0000	86	LDAA	#%00000011
0001	03		
0002	B7	STAA	$8008
0003	80		
0004	08		
0005	86	LDAA	#%00010001
0006	11		

MEMORY ADDRESS (HEX)	MEMORY CONTENTS (HEX)	INSTRUCTION (MNEMONIC)	
0007	B7	STAA	$8008
0008	80		
0009	08		
000A	B6	WAITR LDAA	$8008
000B	80		
000C	08		
000D	44	LSRA	
000E	24	BCC	WAITR
000F	FA		
0010	B6	LDAA	$8009
0011	80		
0012	09		
0013	97	STAA	$61
0014	61		
0015	3F	SWI	

	LDAA	#%00000011	RESET ACIA
	STAA	$8008	
	LDAA	#%00010001	8-BIT DATA, 2 STOP BITS, NO PARITY
	STAA	$8008	
WAITR	LDAA	$8008	HAS DATA BEEN RECEIVED?
	LSRA		
	BCC	WAITR	NO, WAIT
	LDAA	$8009	YES, READ DATA
	STAA	$61	AND SAVE IT IN MEMORY
	SWI		

Note how easy it is to change the operating mode of the ACIA. You can change the number of bits in the data, the type of parity used, and the number of stop bits generated merely by changing one memory location in the object code or one data field in the source code. Clearly, a program that uses the UART is easier to change than is the software equivalent described in the earlier sections.

If, as shown in Figure E-1, we have the TRANSMITTED DATA output tied back to the RECEIVED DATA input of the ACIA, we can combine Programs E-10 and E-11 to echo the data back into the computer's memory. The combined program first transmits the data, then waits for it to be received, and finally stores it back in memory, Program E-12 is the hexadecimal version.

```
          LDAA    #%00000011    RESET ACIA
          STAA    $8008
          LDAA    #%00010001    8-BIT DATA, 2 STOP BITS, NO PARITY
          STAA    $8008
WAITE     LDAA    $8008         IS DATA REGISTER EMPTY?
          ANDA    #%00000010
          BEQ     WAITE         NO, WAIT
          LDAA    $60           YES, TRANSMIT DATA
          STAA    $8009
WAITR     LDAA    $8008         HAS DATA BEEN RECEIVED?
          LSRA
          BCC     WAITR         NO, WAIT
          LDAA    $8009         YES, READ DATA
          STAA    $61           AND SAVE IT IN MEMORY
          SWI
```

PROGRAM E-12

MEMORY ADDRESS (HEX)	MEMORY CONTENTS (HEX)	INSTRUCTION (MNEMONIC)		
0000	86		LDAA	#%00000011
0001	03			
0002	B7		STAA	$8008
0003	80			
0004	08			
0005	86		LDAA	#%00010001
0006	11			
0007	B7		STAA	$8008
0008	80			
0009	08			
000A	B6	WAITE	LDAA	$8008
000B	80			
000C	08			
000D	84		ANDA	#%00000010
000E	02			
000F	27		BEQ	WAITE
0010	F9			
0011	96		LDAA	$60
0012	60			
0013	B7		STAA	$8009
0014	80			
0015	09			
0016	B6	WAITR	LDAA	$8008
0017	80			
0018	08			
0019	44		LSRA	
001A	24		BCC	WAITR

MEMORY ADDRESS (HEX)	MEMORY CONTENTS (HEX)	INSTRUCTION (MNEMONIC)	
001B	FA		
001C	B6	LDAA	$8009
001D	80		
001E	09		
001F	97	STAA	$61
0020	61		
0021	3F	SWI	

Enter and run Program E-12. Try the following examples. Remember that the UART is handling 8-bit characters and is not generating or checking parity.

1)   (0060) = 41 ASCII A (01000001 binary)
     Result: (0061) = 41 ASCII A (01000001 binary)

2)   (0060) = C3 ASCII C with MSB of 1 (11000011 binary)
     Result: (0061) = C3 ASCII C with MSB of 1 (11000011 binary).

PROBLEM E-21

In its 7-bit modes, the UART generates and sends parity instead of bit 7 of the data. On reception, it checks parity and clears bit 7. Run Program E-12 using the 7-bit data mode with even parity and 2 stop bits.

Examples:

1)   (0060) = 41 ASCII A (01000001 binary)
     Result: (0061) = 41 ASCII A

2)   (0060) = C3 ASCII C with MSB of 1 (11000011 binary)
     Result: (0061) = 43 ASCII C

PROBLEM E-22

Extend the answer to Problem E-21 so that it checks for errors in the received data. It should report the errors in the following memory locations:

1)   (0062) = 01 if a framing error occurred.
     (0062) = 00 if no framing error occurred.

2)   (0063) = 01 if a receiver overrun occurred.
     (0063) = 00 if no receiver overrun occurred.

3)   (0064) = 01 if a parity error occurred.
      (0064) = 00 if no parity error occurred.

Table E-1 shows the positions of the various error bits in the ACIA status register. Remember that a framing error means that the proper number of stop bits was not present. A receiver overrun means that the computer failed to read the previous data before the current data was received.

PROBLEM E-23

Make Program E-12 transmit and receive four characters. Use memory locations 0060 through 0063 as the output buffer and memory locations 0070 through 0073 as the input buffer.

Example (7-bit characters, even parity, 2 stop bits):

(0060) = 48 ASCII H

(0061) = C5 ASCII E with MSB of 1

(0062) = CC ASCII L with MSB of 1

(0063) = 50 ASCII P

Result:

(0070) = 48 ASCII H

(0071) = 45 ASCII E

(0072) = 4C ASCII L

(0073) = 50 ASCII P

PROBLEM E-24

Make the answer to Problem E-23 continue transmitting and receiving until it transmits and receives an ASCII carriage return character (0D hexadecimal or 8D with even parity). The input buffer starts in memory location 0060 and the output buffer starts in memory location 0070.

Example (7-bit characters, even parity, 2 stop bits):

(0060) = 47 ASCII G

(0061) = CF ASCII O (letter) with MSB of 1

(0062) = 8D ASCII carriage return with MSB of 1

Result:

(0070) = 47 ASCII G

(0071) = 4F ASCII O (letter)

(0072) = 0D ASCII carriage return

We can also use the ACIA in an interrupt-driven mode. The governing bits are:

1) Control register bit 6 must be 0 and bit 5 must be 1 to enable the transmitting interrupt.

2) Control register bit 7 must be 1 to enable the receive interrupt.

3) Status register bit 7 is the interrupt flag or interrupt request bit. The RECEIVE DATA REGISTER FULL and TRANSMIT DATA REGISTER EMPTY bits differentiate between receive and transmitting interrupts.

The interrupt request bit is set whenever either a transmitting interrupt or a receive interrupt is active. It is cleared when the CPU either writes data into the transmit data register or reads data from the receive data register. There are no extra operations required on output as there are with the PIA (remember Laboratory B).

PROBLEM E-25

Make Program E-12 receive the data using an interrupt. To check this program, you will have to jumper a connection between pin 7 of the ACIA (its $\overline{\text{IRQ}}$ output) and either pin 4 of the CPU (its $\overline{\text{IRQ}}$ input) or pin D of the microcomputer's expansion connector ($\overline{\text{IRQ}}$).

KEY POINT SUMMARY

1) Serial I/O requires such interfacing functions as parallel/serial conversion, the addition and detection of start and stop bits, clocking, and parity generation and checking. Either hardware (UARTs, USRTs, and data-link control chips) or software can perform these functions.

2) Serial/parallel conversion can easily be performed with shift instructions. Only a few changes in the initial and final conditions are necessary to generate or detect start and stop bits.

3)   Serial data can be clocked in or out by any of the timing methods that have been discussed previously. Software delay loops, programmable timers, or a real-time clock can do the job.

4)   You can reduce the number of errors in serial communications by centering the reception, by sampling bits several times and using majority logic, or by including an error-detecting or correcting code such as parity. Parity can be generated by adding all the bits together; even parity is the least significant bit of the sum.

5)   The 6850 Asynchronous Communications Interface Adapter (ACIA) is a programmable UART specifically designed for use with the 6800 microprocessor. It will automatically detect or generate start bits, convert data between serial and parallel forms, check or add stop bits, check or generate parity, and provide the control signals required for an RS-232 interface. The programmability means that you can select the clock option, word length, type of parity, and other operating parameters by merely loading the ACIA's control register with the required value during initialization.

☐ Laboratory F

Microcomputer Timing and Control

PURPOSE

To show how the 6800 microprocessor generates timing and control signals and how these signals are used in the MEK6800D2 microcomputer.

PARTS REQUIRED

A dual-trace oscilloscope with a bandwidth of at least 5 MHz.

REFERENCE MATERIALS

L. A. Leventhal, *Introduction to Microprocessors: Software, Hardware, Programming,* Prentice-Hall, Englewood Cliffs, NJ, 1978, pp. 284-316, 325-332, 405-427.

A. Osborne, *An Introduction to Microcomputers, Volume 2: Some Real Microprocessors,* Osborne/McGraw-Hill, Berkeley, CA, 1978, Chapter 9.

J. B. Peatman, *Microcomputer-Based Design,* McGraw-Hill, New York, 1977, Chapter 3.

G. J. Lipovski, *Microcomputer Interfacing,* D. C. Heath (Lexington Books), Lexington, MA, 1980, Chapter 2.

N. Andreiev, "Special Report: Troubleshooting Instruments," *EDN*, October 5, 1978, pp. 89-99.

S. Lorentzen, "Troubleshooting Microprocessors with a Logic Analyzer System," *Computer Design*, March 1979, pp. 160-164.

M. J. Weisberg, "Designer's Guide to Testing and Troubleshooting Microprocessor-Based Products," *EDN*, March 20, 1980, pp. 177-214.

WHAT YOU SHOULD LEARN

1) Why a logic analyzer is necessary for troubleshooting micro-processor-based systems.

2) What kind of clock the 6800 microprocessor requires.

3) When the 6800 processor changes addresses and what the VALID MEMORY ADDRESS signal means.

4) How the 6800 microprocessor executes instructions.

5) What part of the 6800 instruction cycle is used to transfer data.

6) How the address lines are decoded to activate memories and I/O devices.

7) How to efficiently decode PIA addresses using linear selection.

TERMS

Access time—the delay between the time when a memory receives an address and the time when the data from that address is available at the outputs.

Address—the identification code that distinguishes one memory location or input/output port from another and that can be used to select a specific one.

Address bus—the bus that the CPU uses to select a particular element of the memory or input/output section.

Bidirectional—capable of transporting signals in either direction.

Bus—a group of parallel lines that connect two or more devices.

Bus contention—a situation in which two or more devices are trying to place data on a bus at the same time.

Clock—a regular timing signal that governs transitions in a system.

Decoder—a device that produces unencoded outputs from coded inputs. Also may refer to a device that converts data from one code to another.

Dual inline package (DIP or bug)—a semiconductor chip package having two rows of pins in a plane perpendicular to the edges of the package. Sometimes called a *bug,* since it appears to have legs.

Dynamic memory—a memory that loses its contents gradually without any external causes. The contents must be rewritten periodically if they are to be retained; the rewriting process is referred to as *refresh.*

Enable—allow an activity to proceed or a device to produce data outputs.

High-impedance state—*see* Tristate.

Hold time—the amount of time after the end of an activity signal during which some other signal must be stable (constant) to ensure the achievement of the correct final state.

Instruction—a group of bits that defines a computer operation and is part of the instruction set.

Instruction cycle—the process of fetching, decoding, and executing an instruction.

Instruction execution—the process of performing the operations indicated by an instruction.

Instruction execution time—the time required to fetch, decode, and execute an instruction.

Instruction fetch—the process of addressing memory and reading an instruction word into the CPU for decoding.

Instruction length—the number of words of memory needed to store a complete instruction.

Instruction set—the set of general-purpose instructions available with a given computer—that is, the set of inputs to which the CPU will produce a known response during an instruction fetch cycle.

Latch—a temporary storage device controlled by a timing signal. The contents of the latch are fixed at their current values by a transition of the timing signal (clock) and remain fixed until the next transition.

Linear select—using coded bus lines individually for selection purposes rather than decoding the lines. Linear select requires no decoders but allows only n separate devices to be connected rather than 2^n, where n is the number of lines.

Logic analyzer—a piece of test equipment that detects, stores, and displays the states of digital signals; usually has at least 8 and as many as 32 inputs.

Multiplex—to use one functional unit for several different purposes on a shared basis, to interleave two or more different signals on the same channel.

Refresh—the process of rewriting the contents of a dynamic memory before they are lost.

Tristate (or **three-state**)—logic outputs with three possible states—high, low, and an inactive (high-impedance or open-circuit) state that can be combined with other similar outputs in a busing structure.

Tristate enable—an input that, if not active, forces the outputs of a tristate device into the inactive or open-circuit state.

EXAMINING PROCESSOR SIGNALS

One problem with most microprocessor-based systems is that few simple signals are directly available to use in troubleshooting. Fortunately, the reliability of the chips is very high (an estimated mean lifetime of 500 years according to one report) and the number of chips in most systems is growing smaller. Thus simple replacement of chips or even boards is often a viable approach to maintenance and repair.

However, some understanding of how the microcomputer operates is both desirable and useful for the designer. This laboratory assumes that you have a dual-trace oscilloscope with a bandwidth of at least 5 MHz. Unfortunately, even a good oscilloscope is usually inadequate for troubleshooting. To diagnose problems in system operation, you must be able to simultaneously examine the clock, data bus, address bus, and control signals. This typically requires at least 8 to 16 lines, the states of which must be formatted and displayed in a comprehensible manner. Test instruments called *logic analyzers* provide the required features, but they are expensive. We will content ourselves here with examining signals on a less expensive oscilloscope. Figure F-1 contains the pinouts for the 6800 microprocessor.

TIMING AND CONTROL FUNCTIONS

Note some of the questions that we must answer in designing a microcomputer or in understanding its operations:

1) How does the processor transfer data to or from memory and I/O ports? Clearly timing is a critical factor here.

2) How does the processor decode and execute instructions? This is an internal processor function, but an understanding

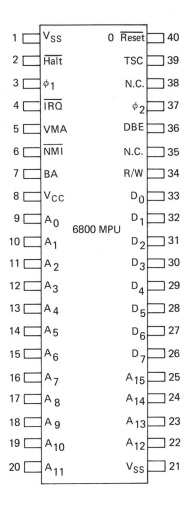

FIGURE F-1. Pin configuration for the 6800 microprocessor (MPU or microprocessing unit).

of it is important in microcomputer design, since the instruction cycle governs the operations of the computer.

3) How does the processor distinguish various types of cycles? The designer must use the signals that the processor provides to produce the proper external responses.

4) How are particular memory addresses or I/O ports selected? The address lines and control signals must be decoded to select the correct device.

5) How does the busing structure allow many memories, input/output devices, and other devices to share the same buses?

The designer must use the microprocessor's timing and control signals to construct a microcomputer that will meet the requirements of a particular application. Factors that the designer must consider are cost, speed, expandibility, consistency with other applications, testability, and ease of updating and maintenance.

THE SYSTEM CLOCK

Let us now look at some of the processor signals on the oscilloscope. Attach the oscilloscope ground to the expansion edge connector pad made up of pins $\overline{W}$, $\overline{X}$, $\overline{Y}$, 41, 42, and 43; this is a convenient ground point. The pad made up of pins A, B, C, 1, 2, and 3 is tied to +5 V. Put your oscilloscope in the CHOP mode so that it will maintain the timing relationships rather than retriggering when you switch channels; do not use the ALTERNATE mode.

Attach one of your probes to pin 3 of the 6800 CPU. This is one phase (ϕ_1) of the system clock (see Figure F-2) that controls the operations of the microprocessor. Remember that Figure F-1 contains the 6800's pin configuration. Attach your other probe to pin 37 of the 6800 CPU. This is the other phase (ϕ_2) of the clock. During clock phase 1, the processor changes addresses and determines the values of all the control signals. This phase is a setup period that is necessary because of the finite response (switching) time of the devices. During clock phase 2, the processor actually transfers data to or from the memory or I/O chips. All control and address signals must be constant (stable) during clock phase 2. Clock phase 2 is tied to the processor's DATA BUS ENABLE signal that activates the processor's bus drivers. In most systems, the designer also gates all inputs to the data bus (from memories and I/O ports) with clock phase 2 as shown in Figure F-3, so that these inputs only appear on the bus when clock phase 2 is active. This gating eliminates the problem of bus contention (two devices trying to control the same bus) that would otherwise occur when the processor changes addresses. Remember that finite switching times mean that both the old and the new address will try to control the bus for a brief time after the change.

PROBLEM F-1

Determine the frequency and pulse width of both phases of the processor clock.

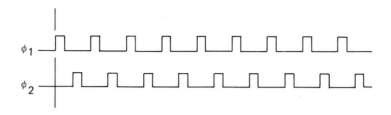

FIGURE F-2. The two-phase 6800 system clock.

Note: The output of the gate is always 0 except when clock phase 2 is high.

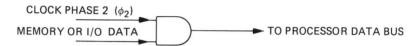

FIGURE F-3. Gating clock phase 2 with data from memories or I/O devices.

PROBLEM F-2

What are the minimum and maximum clock frequencies at which the 6800 processor can operate? These numbers are part of the processor specifications. The refresh requirements of the on-chip dynamic RAM determine the minimum frequency.

EXAMINING A SIMPLE PROGRAM

Now enter the following program in memory locations 0000 through 0002.

HERE   BRA   HERE

This is a single instruction that transfers control to itself continuously, thus producing a repetitive pattern of signals. Program F-1 is the hexadecimal version.

PROGRAM F-1

MEMORY ADDRESS (HEX)	MEMORY CONTENTS (HEX)	INSTRUCTION (MNEMONIC)		
0000	20	HERE	BRA	HERE
0001	FE			

Attach one of your probes to clock phase 2 (pin 37 of the CPU) and attach the other probe to VALID MEMORY ADDRESS (pin 5 of the CPU). This signal is high during cycles in which the processor is transferring data to or from memory or I/O devices and is low during cycles in which the processor is performing internal operations. Thus this signal is generally used to activate all external operations, since it indicates that the contents of the address bus is a meaningful address that will be used to transfer data. Note that this signal is high half the time and low half the time while Program F-1 is executing. Thus the processor is spending half its time transferring data to or from memory and half performing internal operations.

Now attach your second probe to address line A_0 (pin 9 of the 6800 CPU). This line goes high when memory address 0001 is being accessed. Note how the 6800 microprocessor executes instructions:

1) Each instruction is divided into a series of clock cycles that are used to transfer data to or from memory or I/O devices and execute internal operations.

2) Each clock cycle consists of one phase which is used to establish addresses and one phase which is used to transfer data.

The BRA instruction is executed in four clock cycles:

1)   During the first cycle, the CPU fetches the operation code (20 hex) and places it in the instruction register. The instruction register is inside the 6800 microprocessor and the user cannot access it. The processor fetches an instruction by placing the contents of the program counter (0000 hex) on the address bus and thus fetching the data from that address. The program counter is incremented as part of each cycle in which it is used.

2)   During the second cycle, the CPU fetches the relative offset (FE hex) and places it in a temporary register. Here again, the fetch is performed by placing the contents of the program counter (now 0001 hex) on the address bus and thus fetching the data from that address. The program counter is again incremented, so its final value is 0002.

3)   During the third and fourth cycles, the CPU adds the relative offset to the program counter. This takes two cycles, since a 16-bit addition must be performed. Note that no memory transfers are performed during these two cycles (hence VMA is low). The new program counter is calculated from

$$
\begin{array}{r}
0002 \\
+ \ \underline{FFFE} \\
0000
\end{array}
$$

Can you identify an instruction cycle on the oscilloscope? Note that VMA is high during the first two clock cycles.

PROBLEM F-3

Determine how long address line A_0 (CPU pin 9) remains high. Does address line A_1 (CPU pin 10) change value? Explain your result.

PROBLEM F-4

Determine how long VMA remains high. Can you suggest some ways in which this signal could be used? (*Hint:* Remember the gating control shown for clock phase 2 in Figure F-3.)

The CPU always reads data at the end of clock phase 2. The memory address is always stable before the end of clock phase 1. How much time does this allow for the memory access? Note that the only way to slow the memory cycle is to use a slower clock—some processors have a READY input that can keep the processor in a waiting state. Such processors can easily be synchronized with slow memories. However, the 6800 does not have a READY input.

MORE COMPLEX INSTRUCTION CYCLES

PROGRAM F-2

MEMORY ADDRESS (HEX)	MEMORY CONTENTS (HEX)	INSTRUCTION (MNEMONIC)	
0000	01	HERE	NOP
0001	20		BRA	HERE
0002	FD		

Examine VMA while Program F-2 is executing. Describe how VMA has changed from Program F-1.

The CPU executes the NOP instruction in two cycles:

1) In the first cycle, the CPU fetches the instruction from memory and places it in the instruction register. VMA is high since a memory access is being performed.

2) In the second cycle, the CPU executes the instruction. VMA is low since no memory access is performed.

PROBLEM F-5

What happens to address lines A_0 and A_1 during the execution of Program F-2? What happens if you place FE in memory location 0002 instead of FD?

PROBLEM F-6

What happens to the data lines during the execution of Program F-2? In particular, examine data lines D_0, D_1, and D_5. The other lines will all be identical (why?).

Change the program in memory to the following:

MEMORY ADDRESS (HEX)	MEMORY CONTENTS (HEX)	INSTRUCTION (MNEMONIC)		
0000	80	HERE	SUBA	#0
0001	00			
0002	20		BRA	HERE
0003	FC			

PROBLEM F-7

What does the VMA signal look like now? Can you explain its appearance?

The 6800 microprocessor executes all accumulator instructions using immediate addressing in two clock cycles:

1) During the first clock cycle, the processor fetches the operation code from memory using the program counter. The result is placed in the instruction register and the program counter is incremented.

2) During the second clock cycle, the processor fetches the data from memory using the program counter. The operation is performed and the program counter is incremented again.

VMA is high during both cycles since both involve memory accesses.

PROBLEM F-8

What happens to VMA if you replace the 80 (SUBA immediate) in memory location 0000 with 90 (SUBA direct)? Explain the result. What instruction is the processor executing?

The 6800 microprocessor performs all accumulator instructions using direct addressing in three clock cycles (except STA, which requires four cycles). The three cycle instructions are executed as follows:

1) During the first clock cycle, the processor fetches the operation code from memory using the program counter. The operation code is placed in the instruction register and the program counter is incremented.

2) During the second clock cycle, the processor fetches the address from memory using the program counter. The address is stored in a temporary register and the program counter is incremented. Note that there are really two temporary registers—one for the 8 MSBs of the address and one for the 8 LSBs. In the direct addressing mode, the processor clears the temporary register that holds the 8 MSBs.

3) During the third clock cycle, the processor fetches the data from memory using the address in the temporary registers. The operation is performed and the processor is then ready to fetch the next instruction. Note that the program counter is not used in the third cycle and is therefore not incremented.

PROBLEM F-9

What happens to VMA if you replace SUBA #0 with SUBA $A050? Describe the execution of an accumulator instruction using extended addressing in the same way that we described the execution of accumulator instructions using immediate and direct addressing.

PROBLEM F-10

What happens to VMA if you replace SUBA #0 with LDX #0? Describe the execution of an LDX instruction using immediate addressing.

Instructions that write data into memory must produce a signal that indicates the direction of data transfers and that can be used as a write pulse. The READ/WRITE line (CPU pin 34) serves this purpose. In the programs we have run so far, this line should always be in the READ state (a logic 1). Examine the READ/WRITE line during the execution of the last program and verify this.

PROBLEM F-11

What happens to VMA and R/W if you replace the 80 in memory location 0000 with 97 and the 00 in memory location 0001 with 40? What instruction is now in memory locations 0000 and 0001? Demonstrate that your answer is correct by loading accumulator A and memory location 0040 initially and showing that the instruction has the expected effects.

DECODING ADDRESS LINES

The MEK6800D2 microcomputer decodes address lines A_{15}, A_{14}, and A_{13} as described in Table F-1. A 74155 3-to-8 decoder (see Figure F-4 and Table F-2) performs the required logic function; the decoder is integrated circuit U11 on the Microcomputer Module. Execute Program F-2 and examine pin 4 of the decoder. How does the signal on this pin compare with VMA? Note that all the instructions in Program F-2 are being executed from RAM and VMA is being used to enable the entire decoder. Decoder pin 4 is the output signal used to enable (activate) the user RAM.

PROBLEM F-12

Some address lines are not tied to any memories in the MEK6800D2 microcomputer. For example, compare addresses 0000 and 0400. Try changing one and see what happens to the other. How about addresses 0800, 0C00, 1000, 1400, 1800, and 1C00? Why are these addresses not fully decoded, and how does the failure to fully decode the address lines affect the memory capacity of the microcomputer?

Table F-1

MEK6800D2 ADDRESS DECODING

A_{15}	A_{14}	A_{13}	DEVICE ACTIVATED
0	0	0	User RAM
0	0	1	Not used, available for expansion
0	1	0	Not used, available for expansion
0	1	1	Not used, available for PROM
1	0	0	I/O
1	0	1	Stack RAM
1	1	0	Not used, available for PROM
1	1	1	Monitor ROM

PROBLEM F-13

Try executing the following program:

```
            LDX     #$A000
   HERE     SUBA    0,X
            BRA     HERE
```

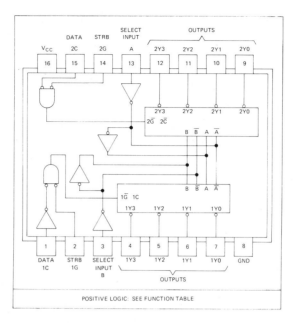

FIGURE F-4. Pin configuration for the 74155 decoder/demultiplexer.

In hexadecimal, this is

MEMORY ADDRESS (HEX)	MEMORY CONTENTS (HEX)	INSTRUCTION (MNEMONIC)	
0000	CE	LDX	#$A0000
0001	A0		
0002	00		
0003	A0	HERE SUBA	0,X
0004	00		
0005	20	BRA	HERE
0006	FC		

Examine decoder pin 11, the output signal used to activate the stack RAM starting at A000. How long is this signal active? Describe the execution of an accumulator instruction using indexed addressing. Describe the behavior of VMA.

PROBLEM F-14

Replace LDX #$A000 with LDX #$E000. Are there any changes on decoder pin 11? How about decoder pin 9? Explain what has happened.

Table F-2

Function Table for the 74155 Decoder/Demultiplexer Used as a 3-to-8 Decoder (Inputs 1C and 2C Connected Together and Inputs 1G and 2G Connected Together)*

INPUTS				OUTPUTS							
SELECT			STROBE OR DATA	(0)	(1)	(2)	(3)	(4)	(5)	(6)	(7)
$C^\dagger$	B	A	$G^\dagger$	2Y0	2Y1	2Y2	2Y3	1Y0	1Y1	1Y2	1Y3
X	X	X	H	H	H	H	H	H	H	H	H
L	L	L	L	L	H	H	H	H	H	H	H
L	L	H	L	H	L	H	H	H	H	H	H
L	H	L	L	H	H	L	H	H	H	H	H
L	H	H	L	H	H	H	L	H	H	H	H
H	L	L	L	H	H	H	H	L	H	H	H
H	L	H	L	H	H	H	H	H	L	H	H
H	H	L	L	H	H	H	H	H	H	L	H
H	H	H	L	H	H	H	H	H	H	H	L

*In the MEK6800D2 microcomputer, C is tied to $\overline{A}_{15}$, B to $\overline{A}_{14}$, A to $\overline{A}_{13}$, and G to $\overline{VMA}$ (so all decoder outputs are inactive when VMA is inactive). The MC8T97 drivers invert all the input address and control lines.

ADDRESSING I/O DEVICES

Run the program from Problem F-13 with the value 80 in memory location 0001. Watch the change on pin 12 of the decoder; this signal is used to activate all I/O devices. The I/O devices are therefore located in the address space between 8000 and 9FFF (hex).

Note that the I/O signal from the 74155 device only decodes address lines A_{15}, A_{14}, and A_{13}. Clearly, this leaves an 8K address space available for input/output devices (64K has been divided into eight sections). The problem now is how to activate individual I/O devices within the address space. Since each PIA occupies four addresses, we have enough address space for 2048 PIAs, far more than most systems need.

As long as we have so much address space available, there is no need to fully decode it. If, for example, we tried to fully decode 2048 PIA addresses with 74155 devices, we would need 256 chips (since each has eight outputs), not even considering the gates and control signals required to handle such a large number of devices. However, we can avoid these requirements by simply using each address line to select a single PIA. Figure F-5 shows the pin configuration of a PIA. The RS (Register Select) lines decode the internal registers of the PIA and are normally tied to address lines A_0 and A_1. The CS (Chip Select) lines can be used to

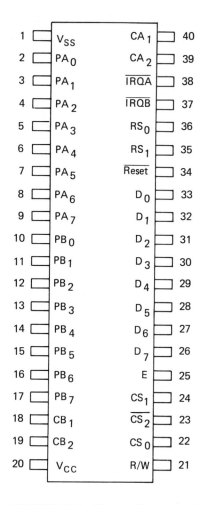

Pin	Signal	Signal	Pin
1	V_{SS}	CA_1	40
2	PA_0	CA_2	39
3	PA_1	$\overline{IRQA}$	38
4	PA_2	$\overline{IRQB}$	37
5	PA_3	RS_0	36
6	PA_4	RS_1	35
7	PA_5	$\overline{Reset}$	34
8	PA_6	D_0	33
9	PA_7	D_1	32
10	PB_0	D_2	31
11	PB_1	D_3	30
12	PB_2	D_4	29
13	PB_3	D_5	28
14	PB_4	D_6	27
15	PB_5	D_7	26
16	PB_6	E	25
17	PB_7	CS_1	24
18	CB_1	$\overline{CS_2}$	23
19	CB_2	CS_0	22
20	V_{CC}	R/W	21

FIGURE F-5. Pin configuration for the 6821 Peripheral Interface Adapter (PIA).

select a particular PIA. One is tied to the I/O signal from the 74155 device, so that the PIA is only selected when that signal is active. Another is tied directly to an address line—A_2 for the user PIA and A_5 for the keyboard/display PIA. The PIA is therefore activated when that address line is high. This kind of decoding (called *linear select*) allows a total of 11 PIAs (remember that address lines A_{15}, A_{14}, and A_{13} are tied to the 74155 decoder and A_1 and A_0 are used to select registers). Eleven PIAs are more than enough for most small controllers, since each PIA has 20 I/O lines (two 8-bit I/O ports and four control lines).

PROBLEM F-15

If we reserve the I/O signal from the 74155 device for activating PIAs and ACIAs, how much memory can we add to an MEK6800D2 microcomputer? Note the tradeoffs involved here—if we want to increase the memory capacity, we must use a larger decoder and limit the address space available for PIAs. If we replaced the 3-to-8 decoder with a 4-to-16 decoder and reserved one of the decoder outputs for I/O, how much memory could we address? How many PIAs would be allowed using linear select?

PROBLEM F-16

List the addresses that PIAs can occupy in the MEK6800D2 microcomputer using linear select. Remember that we can use address lines A_2 through A_{12} to select PIAs.

PROBLEM F-17

One problem with linear select is that it results in a curious, discontinuous set of addresses. Each 1 bit in the selection lines activates a PIA, so that only addresses with one 1 bit in those lines are really valid. What happens if the processor stores data in an address that has 1 bits in two selection lines? Check your answer by executing the following program and observing memory locations 0060 and 0061.

```
CLR      $8007              MAKE USER PIA PORT B OUTPUT
LDAA     #$FF
STAA     $8006
LDAB     #%00000100
STAB     $8007
STAA     $8006              PUT KNOWN VALUE (FF) IN  PIA PORTS
STAA     $8022
LDAA     #$06               NOW TRY BROADCASTING DATA TO BOTH
STAA     $8026                 PORTS AT ONCE
LDAA     $8006              SEE IF DATA GOT TO USER PIA PORT B
STAA     $60
LDAA     $8022              SEE IF DATA GOT TO KBD PIA PORT B
STAA     $61
SWI
```

Address 8006 (hex) is port B of the user PIA, and address 8022 is port B of the keyboard/display PIA. Remember that the monitor determines the operating mode of the keyboard/display PIA, so the program need not initialize that device. Try changing the broadcast data (memory address 0014) and see what happens. The analogy to a general broadcast on a communications network is obvious.

MEMORY ADDRESS (HEX)	MEMORY CONTENTS (HEX)	INSTRUCTION (MNEMONIC)	
0000	7F	CLR	$8007
0001	80		
0002	07		
0003	86	LDAA	#$FF
0004	FF		
0005	B7	STAA	$8006
0006	80		
0007	06		
0008	C6	LDAB	#%00000100
0009	04		
000A	F7	STAB	$8007
000B	80		
000C	07		
000D	B7	STAA	$8006
000E	80		
000F	06		
0010	B7	STAA	$8022
0011	80		
0012	22		
0013	86	LDAA	#$06
0014	06		
0015	B7	STAA	$8026
0016	80		
0017	26		
0018	B6	LDAA	$8006
0019	80		
001A	06		
001B	97	STAA	$60
001C	60		
001D	B6	LDAA	$8022
001E	80		
001F	22		
0020	97	STAA	$61
0021	61		
0022	3F	SWI	

The elaborate procedure is necessary because the monitor program is constantly using the keyboard/display PIA.

KEY POINT SUMMARY

1) A logic analyzer is necessary to fully understand or debug the hardware in microprocessor-based systems. The analyzer can display the states of many simultaneous signals in a comprehensible format.

2) The 6800 microprocessor executes its instructions as a series of clock cycles during which data is transferred to or from memory and internal operations are performed.

3) The 6800 microprocessor differentiates between internal and external cycles by means of the VALID MEMORY ADDRESS (VMA) signal. This signal is high when the contents of the address bus are an actual address that will be used to transfer data during that cycle.

4) The execution of an instruction involves at least two clock cycles. The first cycle is an instruction fetch in which the CPU places the program counter on the address bus and loads the contents of the accessed memory location into the instruction register. The CPU adds 1 to the program counter each time it is used.

5) The various addressing modes result in different methods of instruction execution. In immediate addressing, the program counter is used to fetch the data. In direct and extended addressing, the program counter is used to fetch the address and a subsequent memory access cycle utilizes that address. In indexed addressing, two cycles are used to perform the indexing before the calculated address is used to access memory.

6) The more significant address lines are generally decoded to form enabling signals. These signals allow particular memories or I/O devices to send or receive data. In general, only one memory or I/O device can send or receive data at a time.

7) The designer can make tradeoffs between the memory capacity of the microcomputer and the complexity of the decoding system. Full decoding of addresses maximizes memory capacity but increases parts count. Partial decoding of addresses is often sufficient in small systems.

Appendixes

APPENDIX 1—MOTOROLA 6800 INSTRUCTION SET[1]

MPU INSTRUCTION SET

The MC6800 has a set of 72 different instructions. Included are binary and decimal arithmetic, logical, shift, rotate, load, store, conditional or unconditional branch, interrupt and stack manipulation instructions (Tables 2 thru 6).

MPU ADDRESSING MODES

The MC6800 eight-bit microprocessing unit has seven address modes that can be used by a programmer, with the addressing mode a function of both the type of instruction and the coding within the instruction. A summary of the addressing modes for a particular instruction can be found in Table 7 along with the associated instruction execution time that is given in machine cycles. With a clock frequency of 1 MHz, these times would be microseconds.

Accumulator (ACCX) Addressing — In accumulator only addressing, either accumulator A or accumulator B is specified. These are one-byte instructions.

Immediate Addressing — In immediate addressing, the operand is contained in the second byte of the instruction except LDS and LDX which have the operand in the second and third bytes of the instruction. The MPU addresses this location when it fetches the immediate instruction for execution. These are two or three-byte instructions.

Direct Addressing — In direct addressing, the address of the operand is contained in the second byte of the instruction. Direct addressing allows the user to directly address the lowest 256 bytes in the machine i.e., locations zero through 255. Enhanced execution times are achieved by storing data in these locations. In most configurations, it should be a random access memory. These are two-byte instructions.

Extended Addressing — In extended addressing, the address contained in the second byte of the instruction is used as the higher eight-bits of the address of the operand. The third byte of the instruction is used as the lower eight-bits of the address for the operand. This is an absolute address in memory. These are three-byte instructions.

Indexed Addressing — In indexed addressing, the address contained in the second byte of the instruction is added to the index register's lowest eight bits in the MPU. The carry is then added to the higher order eight bits of the index register. This result is then used to address memory. The modified address is held in a temporary address register so there is no change to the index register. These are two-byte instructions.

Implied Addressing — In the implied addressing mode the instruction gives the address (i.e., stack pointer, index register, etc.). These are one-byte instructions.

Relative Addressing — In relative addressing, the address contained in the second byte of the instruction is added to the program counter's lowest eight bits plus two. The carry or borrow is then added to the high eight bits. This allows the user to address data within a range of -125 to +129 bytes of the present instruction. These are two-byte instructions.

[1]Courtesy of Motorola Semiconductor Products, Inc.

Table A1-1

MICROPROCESSOR INSTRUCTION SET—ALPHABETIC SEQUENCE

Mnemonic	Description	Mnemonic	Description	Mnemonic	Description
ABA	Add Accumulators	CLR	Clear	PUL	Pull Data
ADC	Add with Carry	CLV	Clear Overflow		
ADD	Add	CMP	Compare	ROL	Rotate Left
AND	Logical And	COM	Complement	ROR	Rotate Right
ASL	Arithmetic Shift Left	CPX	Compare Index Register	RTI	Return from Interrupt
ASR	Arithmetic Shift Right			RTS	Return from Subroutine
		DAA	Decimal Adjust		
BCC	Branch if Carry Clear	DEC	Decrement	SBA	Subtract Accumulators
BCS	Branch if Carry Set	DES	Decrement Stack Pointer	SBC	Subtract with Carry
BEQ	Branch if Equal to Zero	DEX	Decrement Index Register	SEC	Set Carry
BGE	Branch if Greater or Equal Zero			SEI	Set Interrupt Mask
BGT	Branch if Greater than Zero	EOR	Exclusive OR	SEV	Set Overflow
BHI	Branch if Higher			STA	Store Accumulator
BIT	Bit Test	INC	Increment	STS	Store Stack Register
BLE	Branch if Less or Equal	INS	Increment Stack Pointer	STX	Store Index Register
BLS	Branch if Lower or Same	INX	Increment Index Register	SUB	Subtract
BLT	Branch if Less than Zero			SWI	Software Interrupt
BMI	Branch if Minus	JMP	Jump		
BNE	Branch if Not Equal to Zero	JSR	Jump to Subroutine	TAB	Transfer Accumulators
BPL	Branch if Plus			TAP	Transfer Accumulators to Condition Code Reg.
BRA	Branch Always	LDA	Load Accumulator	TBA	Transfer Accumulators
BSR	Branch to Subroutine	LDS	Load Stack Pointer	TPA	Transfer Condition Code Reg. to Accumulator
BVC	Branch if Overflow Clear	LDX	Load Index Register	TST	Test
BVS	Branch if Overflow Set	LSR	Logical Shift Right	TSX	Transfer Stack Pointer to Index Register
				TXS	Transfer Index Register to Stack Pointer
CBA	Compare Accumulators	NEG	Negate		
CLC	Clear Carry	NOP	No Operation	WAI	Wait for Interrupt
CLI	Clear Interrupt Mask				
		ORA	Inclusive OR Accumulator		
		PSH	Push Data		

Table A1-2

ACCUMULATOR AND MEMORY INSTRUCTIONS

OPERATIONS	MNEMONIC	IMMED OP	~	=	DIRECT OP	~	=	INDEX OP	~	=	EXTND OP	~	=	IMPLIED OP	~	=	BOOLEAN/ARITHMETIC OPERATION (All register labels refer to contents)	H 5	I 4	N 3	Z 2	V 1	C 0
Add	ADDA	8B	2	2	9B	3	2	AB	5	2	BB	4	3				A + M → A	↕	●	↕	↕	↕	↕
	ADDB	CB	2	2	DB	3	2	EB	5	2	FB	4	3				B + M → B	↕	●	↕	↕	↕	↕
Add Acmltrs	ABA													1B	2	1	A + B → A	↕	●	↕	↕	↕	↕
Add with Carry	ADCA	89	2	2	99	3	2	A9	5	2	B9	4	3				A + M + C → A	↕	●	↕	↕	↕	↕
	ADCB	C9	2	2	D9	3	2	E9	5	2	F9	4	3				B + M + C → B	↕	●	↕	↕	↕	↕
And	ANDA	84	2	2	94	3	2	A4	5	2	B4	4	3				A · M → A	●	●	↕	↕	R	●
	ANDB	C4	2	2	D4	3	2	E4	5	2	F4	4	3				B · M → B	●	●	↕	↕	R	●
Bit Test	BITA	85	2	2	95	3	2	A5	5	2	B5	4	3				A · M	●	●	↕	↕	R	●
	BITB	C5	2	2	D5	3	2	E5	5	2	F5	4	3				B · M	●	●	↕	↕	R	●
Clear	CLR							6F	7	2	7F	6	3				00 → M	●	●	R	S	R	R
	CLRA													4F	2	1	00 → A	●	●	R	S	R	R
	CLRB													5F	2	1	00 → B	●	●	R	S	R	R
Compare	CMPA	81	2	2	91	3	2	A1	5	2	B1	4	3				A − M	●	●	↕	↕	↕	↕
	CMPB	C1	2	2	D1	3	2	E1	5	2	F1	4	3				B − M	●	●	↕	↕	↕	↕
Compare Acmltrs	CBA													11	2	1	A − B	●	●	↕	↕	↕	↕
Complement, 1's	COM							63	7	2	73	6	3				$\overline{M}$ → M	●	●	↕	↕	R	S
	COMA													43	2	1	$\overline{A}$ → A	●	●	↕	↕	R	S
	COMB													53	2	1	$\overline{B}$ → B	●	●	↕	↕	R	S
Complement, 2's	NEG							60	7	2	70	6	3				00 − M → M	●	●	↕	↕	①	②
(Negate)	NEGA													40	2	1	00 − A → A	●	●	↕	↕	①	②
	NEGB													50	2	1	00 − B → B	●	●	↕	↕	①	②
Decimal Adjust, A	DAA													19	2	1	Converts Binary Add. of BCD Characters into BCD Format	●	●	↕	↕	↕	③
Decrement	DEC							6A	7	2	7A	6	3				M − 1 → M	●	●	↕	↕	④	●
	DECA													4A	2	1	A − 1 → A	●	●	↕	↕	④	●
	DECB													5A	2	1	B − 1 → B	●	●	↕	↕	④	●
Exclusive OR	EORA	88	2	2	98	3	2	A8	5	2	B8	4	3				A ⊕ M → A	●	●	↕	↕	R	●
	EORB	C8	2	2	D8	3	2	E8	5	2	F8	4	3				B ⊕ M → B	●	●	↕	↕	R	●
Increment	INC							6C	7	2	7C	6	3				M + 1 → M	●	●	↕	↕	⑤	●
	INCA													4C	2	1	A + 1 → A	●	●	↕	↕	⑤	●
	INCB													5C	2	1	B + 1 → B	●	●	↕	↕	⑤	●
Load Acmltr	LDAA	86	2	2	96	3	2	A6	5	2	B6	4	3				M → A	●	●	↕	↕	R	●
	LDAB	C6	2	2	D6	3	2	E6	5	2	F6	4	3				M → B	●	●	↕	↕	R	●
Or, Inclusive	ORAA	8A	2	2	9A	3	2	AA	5	2	BA	4	3				A + M → A	●	●	↕	↕	R	●
	ORAB	CA	2	2	DA	3	2	EA	5	2	FA	4	3				B + M → B	●	●	↕	↕	R	●
Push Data	PSHA													36	4	1	A → M$_{SP}$, SP − 1 → SP	●	●	●	●	●	●
	PSHB													37	4	1	B → M$_{SP}$, SP − 1 → SP	●	●	●	●	●	●
Pull Data	PULA													32	4	1	SP + 1 → SP, M$_{SP}$ → A	●	●	●	●	●	●
	PULB													33	4	1	SP + 1 → SP, M$_{SP}$ → B	●	●	●	●	●	●
Rotate Left	ROL							69	7	2	79	6	3				M ⎫	●	●	↕	↕	⑥	⑥
	ROLA													49	2	1	A ⎬	●	●	↕	↕	⑥	⑥
	ROLB													59	2	1	B ⎭	●	●	↕	↕	⑥	⑥
Rotate Right	ROR							66	7	2	76	6	3				M ⎫	●	●	↕	↕	⑥	⑥
	RORA													46	2	1	A ⎬	●	●	↕	↕	⑥	⑥
	RORB													56	2	1	B ⎭	●	●	↕	↕	⑥	⑥
Shift Left, Arithmetic	ASL							68	7	2	78	6	3				M ⎫	●	●	↕	↕	⑥	⑥
	ASLA													48	2	1	A ⎬	●	●	↕	↕	⑥	⑥
	ASLB													58	2	1	B ⎭	●	●	↕	↕	⑥	⑥
Shift Right, Arithmetic	ASR							67	7	2	77	6	3				M ⎫	●	●	↕	↕	⑥	⑥
	ASRA													47	2	1	A ⎬	●	●	↕	↕	⑥	⑥
	ASRB													57	2	1	B ⎭	●	●	↕	↕	⑥	⑥
Shift Right, Logic	LSR							64	7	2	74	6	3				M ⎫	●	●	R	↕	⑥	⑥
	LSRA													44	2	1	A ⎬	●	●	R	↕	⑥	⑥
	LSRB													54	2	1	B ⎭	●	●	R	↕	⑥	⑥
Store Acmltr.	STAA				97	4	2	A7	6	2	B7	5	3				A → M	●	●	↕	↕	R	●
	STAB				D7	4	2	E7	6	2	F7	5	3				B → M	●	●	↕	↕	R	●
Subtract	SUBA	80	2	2	90	3	2	A0	5	2	B0	4	3				A − M → A	●	●	↕	↕	↕	↕
	SUBB	C0	2	2	D0	3	2	E0	5	2	F0	4	3				B − M → B	●	●	↕	↕	↕	↕
Subtract Acmltrs.	SBA													10	2	1	A − B → A	●	●	↕	↕	↕	↕
Subtr. with Carry	SBCA	82	2	2	92	3	2	A2	5	2	B2	4	3				A − M − C → A	●	●	↕	↕	↕	↕
	SBCB	C2	2	2	D2	3	2	E2	5	2	F2	4	3				B − M − C → B	●	●	↕	↕	↕	↕
Transfer Acmltrs	TAB													16	2	1	A → B	●	●	↕	↕	R	●
	TBA													17	2	1	B → A	●	●	↕	↕	R	●
Test, Zero or Minus	TST							6D	7	2	7D	6	3				M − 00	●	●	↕	↕	R	R
	TSTA													4D	2	1	A − 00	●	●	↕	↕	R	R
	TSTB													5D	2	1	B − 00	●	●	↕	↕	R	R
																		H	I	N	Z	V	C

LEGEND:

OP   Operation Code (Hexadecimal);
~   Number of MPU Cycles;
=   Number of Program Bytes;
+   Arithmetic Plus;
−   Arithmetic Minus;
·   Boolean AND;
M$_{SP}$ Contents of memory location pointed to be Stack Pointer;

+   Boolean Inclusive OR;
⊙   Boolean Exclusive OR;
$\overline{M}$ Complement of M;
→   Transfer Into;
0   Bit = Zero;
00   Byte = Zero;

CONDITION CODE SYMBOLS:

H   Half-carry from bit 3;
I   Interrupt mask
N   Negative (sign bit)
Z   Zero (byte)
V   Overflow, 2's complement
C   Carry from bit 7
R   Reset Always
S   Set Always
↕   Test and set if true, cleared otherwise
●   Not Affected

Note − Accumulator addressing mode instructions are included in the column for IMPLIED addressing

INDEX REGISTER AND STACK MANIPULATION INSTRUCTIONS

POINTER OPERATIONS	MNEMONIC	IMMED OP	~	#	DIRECT OP	~	#	INDEX OP	~	#	EXTND OP	~	#	IMPLIED OP	~	#	BOOLEAN/ARITHMETIC OPERATION	COND. CODE REG. 5 H	4 I	3 N	2 Z	1 V	0 C
Compare Index Reg	CPX	8C	3	3	9C	4	2	AC	6	2	BC	5	3				$X_H - M, X_L - (M+1)$	•	•	⑦	↕	⑧	•
Decrement Index Reg	DEX													09	4	1	$X - 1 \to X$	•	•	•	↕	•	•
Decrement Stack Pntr	DES													34	4	1	$SP - 1 \to SP$	•	•	•	•	•	•
Increment Index Reg	INX													08	4	1	$X + 1 \to X$	•	•	•	↕	•	•
Increment Stack Pntr	INS													31	4	1	$SP + 1 \to SP$	•	•	•	•	•	•
Load Index Reg	LDX	CE	3	3	DE	4	2	EE	6	2	FE	5	3				$M \to X_H, (M+1) \to X_L$	•	•	⑨	↕	R	•
Load Stack Pntr	LDS	8E	3	3	9E	4	2	AE	6	2	BE	5	3				$M \to SP_H, (M+1) \to SP_L$	•	•	⑨	↕	R	•
Store Index Reg	STX				DF	5	2	EF	7	2	FF	6	3				$X_H \to M, X_L \to (M+1)$	•	•	⑨	↕	R	•
Store Stack Pntr	STS				9F	5	2	AF	7	2	BF	6	3				$SP_H \to M, SP_L \to (M+1)$	•	•	⑨	↕	R	•
Indx Reg → Stack Pntr	TXS													35	4	1	$X - 1 \to SP$	•	•	•	•	•	•
Stack Pntr → Indx Reg	TSX													30	4	1	$SP + 1 \to X$	•	•	•	•	•	•

JUMP AND BRANCH INSTRUCTIONS

OPERATIONS	MNEMONIC	RELATIVE OP	~	#	INDEX OP	~	#	EXTND OP	~	#	IMPLIED OP	~	#	BRANCH TEST	COND. CODE REG. 5 H	4 I	3 N	2 Z	1 V	0 C
Branch Always	BRA	20	4	2										None	•	•	•	•	•	•
Branch If Carry Clear	BCC	24	4	2										C = 0	•	•	•	•	•	•
Branch If Carry Set	BCS	25	4	2										C = 1	•	•	•	•	•	•
Branch If = Zero	BEQ	27	4	2										Z = 1	•	•	•	•	•	•
Branch If ≥ Zero	BGE	2C	4	2										$N \oplus V = 0$	•	•	•	•	•	•
Branch If > Zero	BGT	2E	4	2										$Z + (N \oplus V) = 0$	•	•	•	•	•	•
Branch If Higher	BHI	22	4	2										C + Z = 0	•	•	•	•	•	•
Branch If ≤ Zero	BLE	2F	4	2										$Z + (N \oplus V) = 1$	•	•	•	•	•	•
Branch If Lower Or Same	BLS	23	4	2										C + Z = 1	•	•	•	•	•	•
Branch If < Zero	BLT	2D	4	2										$N \oplus V = 1$	•	•	•	•	•	•
Branch If Minus	BMI	2B	4	2										N = 1	•	•	•	•	•	•
Branch If Not Equal Zero	BNE	26	4	2										Z = 0	•	•	•	•	•	•
Branch If Overflow Clear	BVC	28	4	2										V = 0	•	•	•	•	•	•
Branch If Overflow Set	BVS	29	4	2										V = 1	•	•	•	•	•	•
Branch If Plus	BPL	2A	4	2										N = 0	•	•	•	•	•	•
Branch To Subroutine	BSR	8D	8	2											•	•	•	•	•	•
Jump	JMP				6E	4	2	7E	3	3				See Special Operations	•	•	•	•	•	•
Jump To Subroutine	JSR				AD	8	2	BD	9	3					•	•	•	•	•	•
No Operation	NOP										01	2	1	Advances Prog. Cntr. Only	•	•	•	•	•	•
Return From Interrupt	RTI										3B	10	1		⑩					
Return From Subroutine	RTS										39	5	1		•	•	•	•	•	•
Software Interrupt	SWI										3F	12	1	See Special Operations	•	•	•	•	•	•
Wait for Interrupt *	WAI										3E	9	1		•	⑪	•	•	•	•

*WAI puts Address Bus, R/W, and Data Bus in the three-state mode while VMA is held low.

SPECIAL OPERATIONS

JSR, JUMP TO SUBROUTINE:

INDXD

PC	Main Program
n	AD = JSR
n + 1	K = Offset*
n + 2	Next Main Instr.

*K = 8-Bit Unsigned Value

	SP	Stack
→	SP−2	
	SP−1	[n + 2] H
	SP	[n + 2] L

[n + 2] H and [n + 2] L Form n + 2

PC	Subroutine
INX + K	1st Subr. Instr.

EXTND

PC	Main Program
n	BD = JSR
n + 1	SH = Subr. Addr.
n + 2	SL = Subr. Addr.
n + 3	Next Main Instr.

	SP	Stack
→	SP−2	
	SP−1	[n + 3] H
	SP	[n + 3] L

→ = Stack Pointer After Execution.

PC	Subroutine
S	1st Subr. Instr.

(S Formed From S_H and S_L)

BSR, BRANCH TO SUBROUTINE:

PC	Main Program
n	8D = BSR
n + 1	± K = Offset*
n + 2	Next Main Instr.

*K = 7-Bit Signed Value;

	SP	Stack
→	SP−2	
	SP−1	[n + 2] H
	SP	[n + 2] L

n + 2 Formed From [n + 2] H and [n + 2] L

PC	Subroutine
n + 2 ± K	1st Subr. Instr.

JMP, JUMP:

INDXD

PC	Main Program
n	6E = JMP
n + 1	K = Offset
⋮	
X + K	Next Instruction

EXTENDED

PC	Main Program
n	7E = JMP
n + 1	K_H = Next Address
n + 2	K_L = Next Address
⋮	
K	Next Instruction

RTS, RETURN FROM SUBROUTINE:

PC	Subroutine
S	39 = RTS

	SP	Stack
	SP	
	SP + 1	N_H
→	SP + 2	N_L

PC	Main Program
n	Next Main Instr.

RTI, RETURN FROM INTERRUPT:

PC	Interrupt Program
S	3B = RTI

	SP	Stack
	SP	
	SP + 1	Condition Code
	SP + 2	Acmltr B
	SP + 3	Acmltr A
	SP + 4	Index Register (X_H)
	SP + 5	Index Register (X_L)
	SP + 6	N_H
→	SP + 7	N_L

PC	Main Program
n	Next Main Instr.

Table A1-5

CONDITION CODE REGISTER MANIPULATION INSTRUCTIONS

		IMPLIED				COND. CODE REG.					
						5	4	3	2	1	0
OPERATIONS	MNEMONIC	OP	~	#	BOOLEAN OPERATION	H	I	N	Z	V	C
Clear Carry	CLC	0C	2	1	0 → C	•	•	•	•	•	R
Clear Interrupt Mask	CLI	0E	2	1	0 → I	•	R	•	•	•	•
Clear Overflow	CLV	0A	2	1	0 → V	•	•	•	•	R	•
Set Carry	SEC	0D	2	1	1 → C	•	•	•	•	•	S
Set Interrupt Mask	SEI	0F	2	1	1 → I	•	S	•	•	•	•
Set Overflow	SEV	0B	2	1	1 → V	•	•	•	•	S	•
Acmltr A → CCR	TAP	06	2	1	A → CCR			(12)			
CCR → Acmltr A	TPA	07	2	1	CCR → A	•	•	•	•	•	•

CONDITION CODE REGISTER NOTES: (Bit set if test is true and cleared otherwise)

1	(Bit V)	Test: Result = 10000000?
2	(Bit C)	Test: Result = 00000000?
3	(Bit C)	Test: Decimal value of most significant BCD Character greater than nine? (Not cleared if previously set.)
4	(Bit V)	Test: Operand = 10000000 prior to execution?
5	(Bit V)	Test: Operand = 01111111 prior to execution?
6	(Bit V)	Test: Set equal to result of N⊕C after shift has occurred.
7	(Bit N)	Test: Sign bit of most significant (MS) byte = 1?
8	(Bit V)	Test: 2's complement overflow from subtraction of MS bytes?
9	(Bit N)	Test: Result less than zero? (Bit 15 = 1)
10	(All)	Load Condition Code Register from Stack. (See Special Operations)
11	(Bit I)	Set when interrupt occurs. If previously set, a Non-Maskable Interrupt is required to exit the wait state.
12	(All)	Set according to the contents of Accumulator A.

Table A1-6

INSTRUCTION ADDRESSING MODES AND ASSOCIATED EXECUTION TIMES
(TIMES IN CLOCK CYCLES)

	(Dual Operand)	ACCX	Immediate	Direct	Extended	Indexed	Implied	Relative
ABA	•	•	•	•	•	•	2	•
ADC	x	•	2	3	4	5	•	•
ADD	x	•	2	3	4	5	•	•
AND	x	•	2	3	4	5	•	•
ASL	•	2	•	•	6	7	•	•
ASR	•	2	•	•	6	7	•	•
BCC	•	•	•	•	•	•	•	4
BCS	•	•	•	•	•	•	•	4
BEA	•	•	•	•	•	•	•	4
BGE	•	•	•	•	•	•	•	4
BGT	•	•	•	•	•	•	•	4
BHI	•	•	•	•	•	•	•	4
BIT	x	•	2	3	4	5	•	•
BLE	•	•	•	•	•	•	•	4
BLS	•	•	•	•	•	•	•	4
BLT	•	•	•	•	•	•	•	4
BMI	•	•	•	•	•	•	•	4
BNE	•	•	•	•	•	•	•	4
BPL	•	•	•	•	•	•	•	4
BRA	•	•	•	•	•	•	•	4
BSR	•	•	•	•	•	•	•	8
BVC	•	•	•	•	•	•	•	4
BVS	•	•	•	•	•	•	•	4
CBA	•	•	•	•	•	•	2	•
CLC	•	•	•	•	•	•	2	•
CLI	•	•	•	•	•	•	2	•
CLR	•	2	•	•	6	7	•	•
CLV	•	•	•	•	•	•	2	•
CMP	x	•	2	3	4	5	•	•
COM	•	2	•	•	6	7	•	•
CPX	•	•	3	4	5	6	•	•
DAA	•	•	•	•	•	•	2	•
DEC	•	2	•	•	6	7	•	•
DES	•	•	•	•	•	•	4	•
DEX	•	•	•	•	•	•	4	•
EOR	x	•	2	3	4	5	•	•

	(Dual Operand)	ACCX	Immediate	Direct	Extended	Indexed	Implied
INC	•	2	•	•	6	7	•
INS	•	•	•	•	•	•	4
INX	•	•	•	•	•	•	4
JMP	•	•	•	•	3	4	•
JSR	•	•	•	•	9	8	•
LDA	x	•	2	3	4	5	•
LDS	•	•	3	4	5	6	•
LDX	•	•	3	4	5	6	•
LSR	•	2	•	•	6	7	•
NEG	•	2	•	•	6	7	•
NOP	•	•	•	•	•	•	2
ORA	x	•	2	3	4	5	•
PSH	•	•	•	•	•	•	4
PUL	•	•	•	•	•	•	4
ROL	•	2	•	•	6	7	•
ROR	•	2	•	•	6	7	•
RTI	•	•	•	•	•	•	10
RTS	•	•	•	•	•	•	5
SBA	•	•	•	•	•	•	2
SBC	x	•	2	3	4	5	•
SEC	•	•	•	•	•	•	2
SEI	•	•	•	•	•	•	2
SEV	•	•	•	•	•	•	2
STA	x	•	•	4	5	6	•
STS	•	•	•	5	6	7	•
STX	•	•	•	5	6	7	•
SUB	x	•	2	3	4	5	•
SWI	•	•	•	•	•	•	12
TAB	•	•	•	•	•	•	2
TAP	•	•	•	•	•	•	2
TBA	•	•	•	•	•	•	2
TPA	•	•	•	•	•	•	2
TST	•	2	•	•	6	7	•
TSX	•	•	•	•	•	•	4
TSX	•	•	•	•	•	•	4
WAI	•	•	•	•	•	•	9

NOTE: Interrupt time is 12 cycles from the end of the instruction being executed, except following a WAI instruction. Then it is 4 cycles.

APPENDIX 2—ASCII CODE TABLE

HEX-ASCII TABLE

Hex	Char		Hex	Char	Hex	Char	Hex	Char	
00	NUL		21	!	42	B	63	c	
01	SOH		22	"	43	C	64	d	
02	STX		23	#	44	D	65	e	
03	ETX		24	$	45	E	66	f	
04	EOT		25	%	46	F	67	g	
05	ENQ		26	&	47	G	68	h	
06	ACK		27	'	48	H	69	i	
07	BEL		28	(	49	I	6A	j	
08	BS		29	)	4A	J	6B	k	
09	HT		2A	*	4B	K	6C	l	
0A	LF		2B	+	4C	L	6D	m	
0B	VT		2C	,	4D	M	6E	n	
0C	FF		2D	–	4E	N	6F	o	
0D	CR		2E	.	4F	O	70	p	
0E	SO		2F	/	50	P	71	q	
0F	SI		30	0	51	Q	72	r	
10	DLE		31	1	52	R	73	s	
11	DC1	(X-ON)	32	2	53	S	74	t	
12	DC2	(TAPE)	33	3	54	T	75	u	
13	DC3	(X-OFF)	34	4	55	U	76	v	
14	DC4	~~(TAPE)~~	35	5	56	V	77	w	
15	NAK		36	6	57	W	78	x	
16	SYN		37	7	58	X	79	y	
17	ETB		38	8	59	Y	7A	z	
18	CAN		39	9	5A	Z	7B	{	
19	EM		3A	:	5B	[	7C	|	
1A	SUB		3B	;	5C	\	7D	}	
1B	ESC		3C	<	5D	]		(ALT MODE)	
1C	FS		3D	=	5E	∧	(↑)	7E	~
1D	GS		3E	>	5F	—	(←)	7F	DEL
1E	RS		3F	?	60	`		(RUB OUT)	
1F	US		40	@	61	a			
20	SP		41	A	62	b			

APPENDIX 3—BRIEF DESCRIPTION OF 6800 FAMILY DEVICES

The following specification sheets are from the *M6800 Microcomputer System Design Data,* Motorola Semiconductor Products Inc., Phoenix, AZ, 1976 and are reprinted here with the permission of Motorola Semiconductor Products Inc., Phoenix, AZ.

MC6800
(1.0 MHz)
MC68A00
(1.5 MHz)
MC68B00
(2.0 MHz)

PIN ASSIGNMENT

1	V$_{SS}$	Reset	40
2	Halt	TSC	39
3	ϕ1	N.C.	38
4	IRQ	ϕ2	37
5	VMA	DBE	36
6	NMI	N.C.	35
7	BA	R/W	34
8	V$_{CC}$	D0	33
9	A0	D1	32
10	A1	D2	31
11	A2	D3	30
12	A3	D4	29
13	A4	D5	28
14	A5	D6	27
15	A6	D7	26
16	A7	A15	25
17	A8	A14	24
18	A9	A13	23
19	A10	A12	22
20	A11	V$_{SS}$	21

8-BIT MICROPROCESSING UNIT (MPU)

The MC6800 is a monolithic 8-bit microprocessor forming the central control function for Motorola's M6800 family. Compatible with TTL, the MC6800, as with all M6800 system parts, requires only one +5.0-volt power supply, and no external TTL devices for bus interface.

The MC6800 is capable of addressing 65K bytes of memory with its 16-bit address lines. The 8-bit data bus is bidirectional as well as 3-state, making direct memory addressing and multiprocessing applications realizable.

- Eight-Bit Parallel Processing
- Bidirectional Data Bus
- Sixteen-Bit Address Bus — 65K Bytes of Addressing
- 72 Instructions — Variable Length
- Seven Addressing Modes — Direct, Relative, Immediate, Indexed, Extended, Implied and Accumulator
- Variable Length Stack
- Vectored Restart
- Maskable Interrupt Vector
- Separate Non-Maskable Interrupt — Internal Registers Saved in Stack
- Six Internal Registers — Two Accumulators, Index Register, Program Counter, Stack Pointer and Condition Code Register
- Direct Memory Addressing (DMA) and Multiple Processor Capability
- Simplified Clocking Characteristics
- Clock Rates as High as 2.0 MHz
- Simple Bus Interface Without TTL
- Halt and Single Instruction Execution Capability

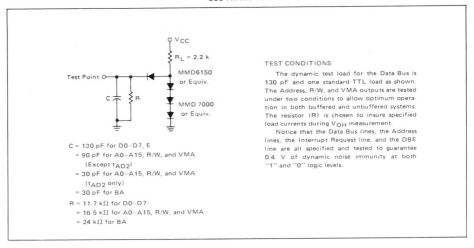

$C = 130\ pF$ for D0–D7, E
= 90 pF for A0–A15, R/W, and VMA
(Except t_{AD2})
= 30 pF for A0–A15, R/W, and VMA
(t_{AD2} only)
= 30 pF for BA
$R = 11.7\ k\Omega$ for D0–D7
= 16.5 kΩ for A0–A15, R/W, and VMA
= 24 kΩ for BA

TEST CONDITIONS

The dynamic test load for the Data Bus is 130 pF and one standard TTL load as shown. The Address, R/W, and VMA outputs are tested under two conditions to allow optimum operation in both buffered and unbuffered systems. The resistor (R) is chosen to insure specified load currents during V_{OH} measurement.

Notice that the Data Bus lines, the Address lines, the Interrupt Request line, and the DBE line are all specified and tested to guarantee 0.4 V of dynamic noise immunity at both "1" and "0" logic levels.

FIGURE 7 – EXPANDED BLOCK DIAGRAM

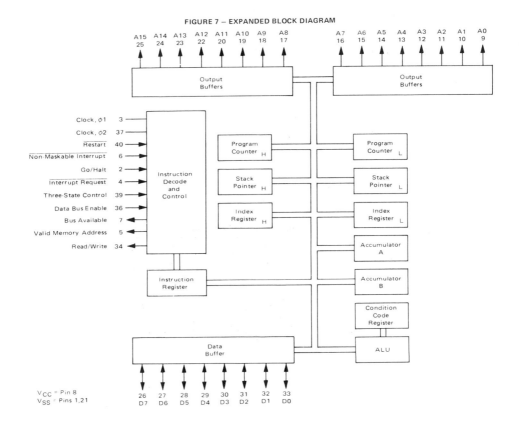

393

MC6821
(1.0 MHz)

MC68A21
(1.5 MHz)

MC68B21
(2.0 MHz)

PIN ASSIGNMENT

```
 1 [ V_SS    CA1 ] 40
 2 [ PA0     CA2 ] 39
 3 [ PA1    IRQA ] 38
 4 [ PA2    IRQB ] 37
 5 [ PA3     RS0 ] 36
 6 [ PA4     RS1 ] 35
 7 [ PA5    Reset] 34
 8 [ PA6      D0 ] 33
 9 [ PA7      D1 ] 32
10 [ PB0      D2 ] 31
11 [ PB1      D3 ] 30
12 [ PB2      D4 ] 29
13 [ PB3      D5 ] 28
14 [ PB4      D6 ] 27
15 [ PB5      D7 ] 26
16 [ PB6       E ] 25
17 [ PB7     CS1 ] 24
18 [ CB1     CS2 ] 23
19 [ CB2     CS0 ] 22
20 [ V_CC    R/W ] 21
```

PERIPHERAL INTERFACE ADAPTER (PIA)

The MC6821 Peripheral Interface Adapter provides the universal means of interfacing peripheral equipment to the MC6800 Micro-processing Unit (MPU). This device is capable of interfacing the MPU to peripherals through two 8-bit bidirectional peripheral data buses and four control lines. No external logic is required for interfacing to most peripheral devices.

The functional configuration of the PIA is programmed by the MPU during system initialization. Each of the peripheral data lines can be programmed to act as an input or output, and each of the four control/interrupt lines may be programmed for one of several control modes. This allows a high degree of flexibility in the over-all operation of the interface.

- 8-Bit Bidirectional Data Bus for Communication with the MPU
- Two Bidirectional 8-Bit Buses for Interface to Peripherals
- Two Programmable Control Registers
- Two Programmable Data Direction Registers
- Four Individually-Controlled Interrupt Input Lines; Two Usable as Peripheral Control Outputs
- Handshake Control Logic for Input and Output Peripheral Operation
- High-Impedance 3-State and Direct Transistor Drive Peripheral Lines
- Program Controlled Interrupt and Interrupt Disable Capability
- CMOS Drive Capability on Side A Peripheral Lines
- Two TTL Drive Capability on All A and B Side Buffers
- TTL-Compatible
- Static Operation

ORDERING INFORMATION

Speed	Device	Temperature Range
1.0 MHz	MC6821P, L	0 to +70°C
	MC6821CP, CL	−40 to +85°C
MIL-STD-883B MIL-STD-883C	MC6821BQCS MC6821CQCS	−55 to +125°C
1.5 MHz	MC68A21P, L	0 to +70°C
	MC68A21CP, CL	−40 to +85°C
2.0 MHz	MC68B21P, L	0 to +70°C

FIGURE 16 – IRQ RELEASE TIME

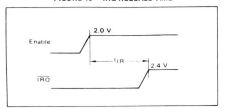

FIGURE 17 – RESET LOW TIME

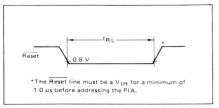

*The Reset line must be a V$_{IH}$ for a minimum of 1.0 μs before addressing the PIA.

EXPANDED BLOCK DIAGRAM

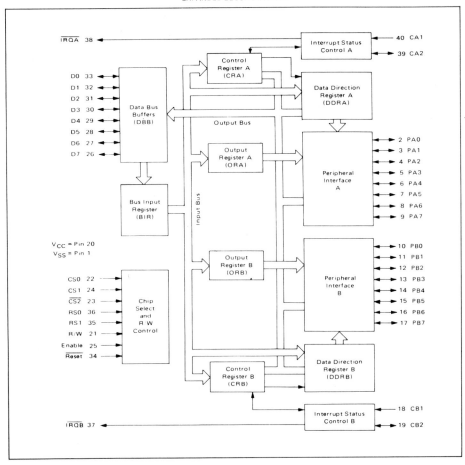

INTERNAL CONTROLS

There are six locations within the PIA accessible to the MPU data bus: two Peripheral Registers, two Data Direction Registers, and two Control Registers. Selection of these locations is controlled by the RS0 and RS1 inputs together with bit 2 in the Control Register, as shown in Table 1.

TABLE 1 – INTERNAL ADDRESSING

RS1	RS0	Control Register Bit CRA-2	Control Register Bit CRB-2	Location Selected
0	0	1	X	Peripheral Register A
0	0	0	X	Data Direction Register A
0	1	X	X	Control Register A
1	0	X	1	Peripheral Register B
1	0	X	0	Data Direction Register B
1	1	X	X	Control Register B

X = Don't Care

INITIALIZATION

A low reset line has the effect of zeroing all PIA registers. This will set PA0-PA7, PB0-PB7, CA2 and CB2 as inputs, and all interrupts disabled. The PIA must be configured during the restart program which follows the reset.

Details of possible configurations of the Data Direction and Control Register are as follows.

DATA DIRECTION REGISTERS (DDRA and DDRB)

The two Data Direction Registers allow the MPU to control the direction of data through each corresponding peripheral data line. A Data Direction Register bit set at "0" configures the corresponding peripheral data line as an input; a "1" results in an output.

CONTROL REGISTERS (CRA and CRB)

The two Control Registers (CRA and CRB) allow the MPU to control the operation of the four peripheral control lines CA1, CA2, CB1 and CB2. In addition they allow the MPU to enable the interrupt lines and monitor the status of the interrupt flags. Bits 0 through 5 of the two registers may be written or read by the MPU when the proper chip select and register select signals are applied. Bits 6 and 7 of the two registers are read only and are modified by external interrupts occurring on control lines CA1, CA2, CB1 or CB2. The format of the control words is shown in Table 2.

TABLE 2 – CONTROL WORD FORMAT

	7	6	5	4	3	2	1	0
CRA	IRQA1	IRQA2	CA2 Control			DDRA Access	CA1 Control	
	7	6	5	4	3	2	1	0
CRB	IRQB1	IRQB2	CB2 Control			DDRB Access	CB1 Control	

Data Direction Access Control Bit (CRA-2 and CRB-2) – Bit 2 in each Control register (CRA and CRB) allows selection of either a Peripheral Interface Register or the Data Direction Register when the proper register select signals are applied to RS0 and RS1.

Interrupt Flags (CRA-6, CRA-7, CRB-6, and CRB-7) – The four interrupt flag bits are set by active transitions of signals on the four Interrupt and Peripheral Control lines when those lines are programmed to be inputs. These bits cannot be set directly from the MPU Data Bus and are reset indirectly by a Read Peripheral Data Operation on the appropriate section.

TABLE 3 – CONTROL OF INTERRUPT INPUTS CA1 AND CB1

CRA-1 (CRB-1)	CRA-0 (CRB-0)	Interrupt Input CA1 (CB1)	Interrupt Flag CRA-7 (CRB-7)	MPU Interrupt Request IRQA (IRQB)
0	0	↓ Active	Set high on ↓ of CA1 (CB1)	Disabled — IRQ remains high
0	1	↓ Active	Set high on ↓ of CA1 (CB1)	Goes low when the interrupt flag bit CRA-7 (CRB-7) goes high
1	0	↑ Active	Set high on ↑ of CA1 (CB1)	Disabled — IRQ remains high
1	1	↑ Active	Set high on ↑ of CA1 (CB1)	Goes low when the interrupt flag bit CRA-7 (CRB-7) goes high

Notes:
1. ↑ indicates positive transition (low to high)
2. ↓ indicates negative transition (high to low)
3. The Interrupt flag bit CRA-7 is cleared by an MPU Read of the A Data Register, and CRB-7 is cleared by an MPU Read of the B Data Register.
4. If CRA-0 (CRB-0) is low when an interrupt occurs (Interrupt disabled) and is later brought high, IRQA (IRQB) occurs after CRA-0 (CRB-0) is written to a "one".

MC6850
1.0 MHz
MC68A50
1.5 MHz
MC68B50
2.0 MHz

ASYNCHRONOUS COMMUNICATIONS INTERFACE ADAPTER (ACIA)

The MC6850 Asynchronous Communications Interface Adapter provides the data formatting and control to interface serial asynchronous data communications information to bus organized systems such as the MC6800 Microprocessing Unit.

The bus interface of the MC6850 includes select, enable, read/write, interrupt and bus interface logic to allow data transfer over an 8-bit bi-directional data bus. The parallel data of the bus system is serially transmitted and received by the asynchronous data interface, with proper formatting and error checking. The functional configuration of the ACIA is programmed via the data bus during system initialization. A programmable Control Register provides variable word lengths, clock division ratios, transmit control, receive control, and interrupt control. For peripheral or modem operation three control lines are provided. These lines allow the ACIA to interface directly with the MC6860L 0-600 bps digital modem.

- Eight and Nine-Bit Transmission
- Optional Even and Odd Parity
- Parity, Overrun and Framing Error Checking
- Programmable Control Register
- Optional ÷1, ÷16, and ÷64 Clock Modes
- Up to 500 kbps Transmission
- False Start Bit Deletion
- Peripheral/Modem Control Functions
- Double Buffered
- One or Two Stop Bit Operation

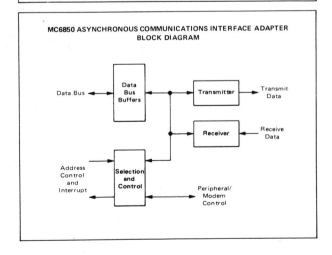

MC6850 ASYNCHRONOUS COMMUNICATIONS INTERFACE ADAPTER
BLOCK DIAGRAM

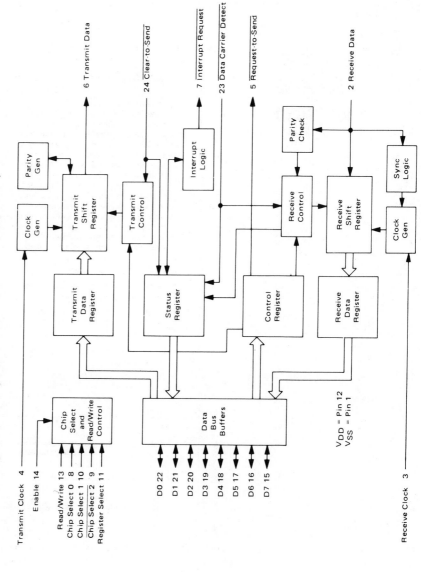

Expanded block diagram of the Motorola MC6850 Asynchronous Communications Interface Adapter. (Courtesy of Motorola Semiconductor Products).

STATUS REGISTER

Information on the status of the ACIA is available to the MPU by reading the ACIA Status Register. This read-only register is selected when RS is low and R/W is high. Information stored in this register indicates the status of the Transmit Data Register, the Receive Data Register and error logic, and the peripheral/modem status inputs of the ACIA.

Receive Data Register Full (RDRF), Bit 0 — Receive Data Register Full indicates that received data has been transferred to the Receive Data Register. RDRF is cleared after an MPU read of the Receive Data Register or by a master reset. The cleared or empty state indicates that the contents of the Receive Data Register are not current. Data Carrier Detect being high also causes RDRF to indicate empty.

Transmit Data Register Empty (TDRE), Bit 1 — The Transmit Data Register Empty bit being set high indicates that the Transmit Data Register contents have been transferred and that new data may be entered. The low state indicates that the register is full and that transmission of a new character has not begun since the last write data command.

Data Carrier Detect (DCD), Bit 2 — The Data Carrier Detect bit will be high when the DCD input from a modem has gone high to indicate that a carrier is not present. This bit going high causes an Interrupt Request to be generated when the Receive Interrupt Enable is set. It remains high after the DCD input is returned low until cleared by first reading the Status Register and then the Data Register or until a master reset occurs. If the DCD input remains high after read status and read data or master reset has occurred, the interrupt is cleared, the DCD status bit remains high and will follow the DCD input.

Clear-to-Send (CTS), Bit 3 — The Clear-to-Send bit indicates the state of the Clear-to-Send input from a modem. A low CTS indicates that there is a Clear-to-Send from the modem. In the high state, the Transmit Data Register Empty bit is inhibited and the Clear-to-Send status bit will be high. Master reset does not affect the Clear-to-Send Status bit.

Framing Error (FE); Bit 4 — Framing error indicates that the received character is improperly framed by a start and a stop bit and is detected by the absence of the 1st stop bit. This error indicates a synchronization error, faulty transmission, or a break condition. The framing error flag is set or reset during the receive data transfer time. Therefore, this error indicator is present throughout the time that the associated character is available.

Receiver Overrun (OVRN), Bit 5 — Overrun is an error flag that indicates that one or more characters in the data stream were lost. That is, a character or a number of characters were received but not read from the Receive Data Register (RDR) prior to subsequent characters being received. The overrun condition begins at the midpoint of the last bit of the second character received in succession without a read of the RDR having occurred. The Overrun does not occur in the Status Register until the valid character prior to Overrun has been read. The RDRF bit remains set until the Overrun is reset. Character synchronization is maintained during the Overrun condition. The Overrun indication is reset after the reading of data from the Receive Data Register or by a Master Reset.

Parity Error (PE), Bit 6 — The parity error flag indicates that the number of highs (ones) in the character does not agree with the preselected odd or even parity. Odd parity is defined to be when the total number of ones is odd. The parity error indication will be present as long as the data character is in the RDR. If no parity is selected, then both the transmitter parity generator output and the receiver parity check results are inhibited.

Interrupt Request (IRQ), Bit 7 — The IRQ bit indicates the state of the IRQ output. Any interrupt condition with its applicable enable will be indicated in this status bit. Anytime the IRQ output is low the IRQ bit will be high to indicate the interrupt or service request status. IRQ is cleared by a read operation to the Receive Data Register or a write operation to the Transmit Data Register.

PIN ASSIGNMENT

1	Vss	CTS 24
2	Rx Data	DCD 23
3	Rx Clk	D0 22
4	Tx Clk	D1 21
5	RTS	D2 20
6	Tx Data	D3 19
7	IRQ	D4 18
8	CS0	D5 17
9	CS2	D6 16
10	CS1	D7 15
11	RS	E 14
12	VDD	R/W 13

PACKAGE DIMENSIONS

CASE 716-02
(CERAMIC)

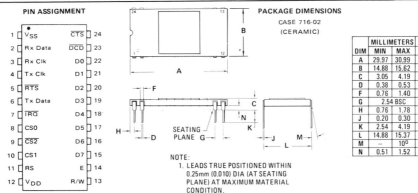

DIM	MILLIMETERS		INCHES	
	MIN	MAX	MIN	MAX
A	29.97	30.99	1.180	1.220
B	14.88	15.62	0.585	0.615
C	3.05	4.19	0.120	0.165
D	0.38	0.53	0.015	0.021
F	0.76	1.40	0.030	0.055
G	2.54 BSC		0.100 BSC	
H	0.76	1.78	0.030	0.070
J	0.20	0.30	0.008	0.012
K	2.54	4.19	0.100	0.165
L	14.88	15.37	0.585	0.605
M	–	10⁰	–	10⁰
N	0.51	1.52	0.020	0.060

NOTE:
1. LEADS TRUE POSITIONED WITHIN 0.25mm (0.010) DIA (AT SEATING PLANE) AT MAXIMUM MATERIAL CONDITION.

128 X 8-BIT STATIC RANDOM ACCESS MEMORY

The MCM6810 is a byte-organized memory designed for use in bus-organized systems. It is fabricated with N-channel silicon-gate technology. For ease of use, the device operates from a single power supply, has compatibility with TTL and DTL, and needs no clocks or refreshing because of static operation.

The memory is compatible with the M6800 Microcomputer Family, providing random storage in byte increments. Memory expansion is provided through multiple Chip Select inputs.

- Organized as 128 Bytes of 8 Bits
- Static Operation
- Bidirectional Three-State Data Input/Output
- Six Chip Select Inputs (Four Active Low, Two Active High)
- Single 5-Volt Power Supply
- TTL Compatible
- Maximum Access Time = 450 ns — MCM6810
  360 ns — MCM68A10
  250 ns — MCM68B10

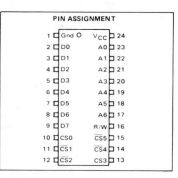

MCM6810
1.0 MHz
MCM68A10
1.5 MHz
MCM68B10
2.0 MHz

PIN ASSIGNMENT

1	Gnd O	V_CC	24
2	D0	A0	23
3	D1	A1	22
4	D2	A2	21
5	D3	A3	20
6	D4	A4	19
7	D5	A5	18
8	D6	A6	17
9	D7	R/W	16
10	CS0	$\overline{CS5}$	15
11	$\overline{CS1}$	$\overline{CS4}$	14
12	$\overline{CS2}$	CS3	13

ORDERING INFORMATION

Speed	Device	Temperature Range
1.0 MHz	MC6810P, L	0 to 70°C
	MC6810CP, CL	−40 to +85°C
MIL-STD-883B	MC6810BJCS	−55 to +125°C
MIL-STD-883C	MC6810CJCS	
1.5 MHz	MC68A10P, L	0 to +70°C
	MC68A10CP, CL	−40 to +85°C
2.0 MHz	MC68B10P, L	0 to +70°C

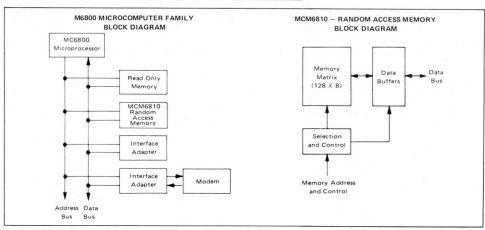

M6800 MICROCOMPUTER FAMILY BLOCK DIAGRAM

MCM6810 — RANDOM ACCESS MEMORY BLOCK DIAGRAM

1024 X 8-BIT READ ONLY MEMORY

The MCM68A30A/MCM68B30A are mask-programmable byte-organized memories designed for use in bus-organized systems. They are fabricated with N-channel silicon-gate technology. For ease of use, the device operates from a single power supply, has compatibility with TTL and DTL, and needs no clocks or refreshing because of static operation.

The memory is compatible with the M6800 Microcomputer Family, providing read only storage in byte increments. Memory expansion is provided through multiple Chip Select inputs. The active level of the Chip Select inputs and the memory content are defined by the customer.

- Organized as 1024 Bytes of 8 Bits
- Static Operation
- Three-State Data Output
- Four Chip Select Inputs (Programmable)
- Single ±10% 5-Volt Power Supply
- TTL Compatible
- Maximum Access Time = 350 ns — MCM68A30A
  250 ns — MCM68B30A

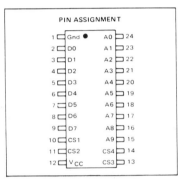

MCM68A30A
MCM68B30A

PIN ASSIGNMENT

1	Gnd	A0	24
2	D0	A1	23
3	D1	A2	22
4	D2	A3	21
5	D3	A4	20
6	D4	A5	19
7	D5	A6	18
8	D6	A7	17
9	D7	A8	16
10	CS1	A9	15
11	CS2	CS4	14
12	V_CC	CS3	13

ABSOLUTE MAXIMUM RATINGS (See Note 1)

Rating	Symbol	Value	Unit
Supply Voltage	V_{CC}	-0.3 to +7.0	Vdc
Input Voltage	V_{in}	-0.3 to +7.0	Vdc
Operating Temperature Range	T_A	0 to +70	°C
Storage Temperature Range	T_{stg}	-65 to +150	°C

NOTE 1: Permanent device damage may occur if ABSOLUTE MAXIMUM RATINGS are exceeded. Functional operation should be restricted to RECOMMENDED OPERATING CONDITIONS. Exposure to higher than recommended voltages for extended periods of time could affect device reliability.

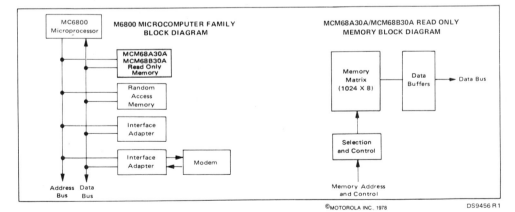

©MOTOROLA INC., 1978

DS9456 R1

APPENDIX 4–LABORATORY INTERFACES AND PARTS LISTS

These are the interfaces required to perform the experiments in this manual. Explanations of the functions and operations of the individual interfaces are contained in the experiments.

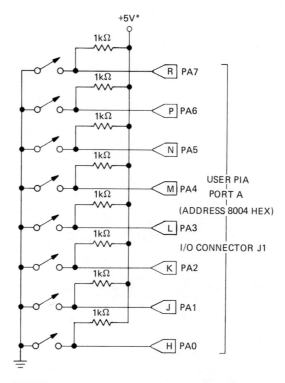

FIGURE A4-1. Attachment of switches to user PIA port A.

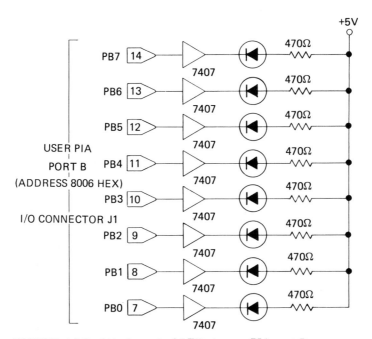

FIGURE A4-2. Attachment of LEDs to user PIA port B.

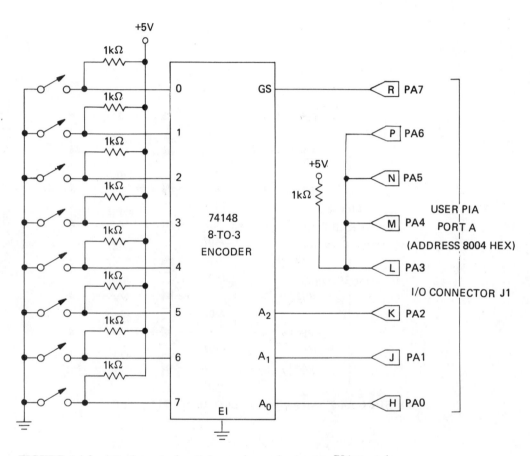

FIGURE A4-3. Attachment of switches and encoder to user PIA port A.

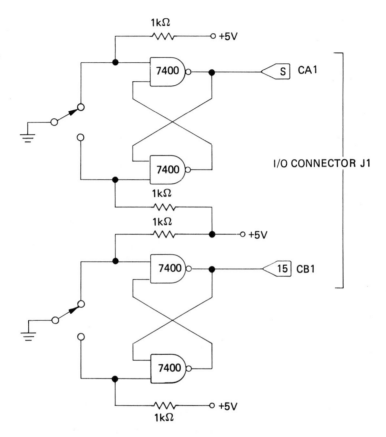

FIGURE A4-4. Attachment of switches to user PIA control lines CA1 and CB1.

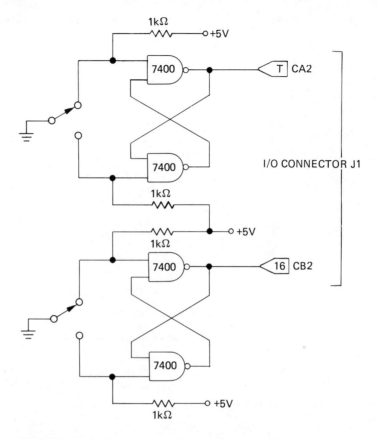

FIGURE A4-5. Attachment of switches to user PIA control lines CA2 and CB2.

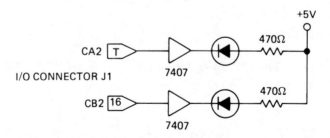

FIGURE A4-6. Attachment of LEDs to user PIA control lines CA2 and CB2. *Note:* Jumper wires are an easy way to select between the configurations of Figures A4-5 and A4-6; otherwise, using CA2 and CB2 as outputs could damage the AND gates in Figure A4-5.

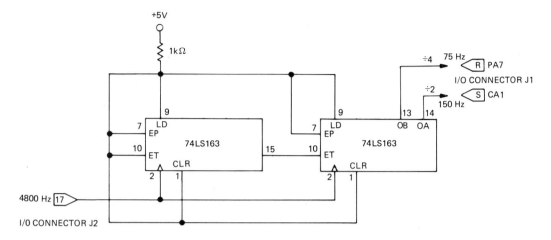

FIGURE A4-7. A simple low-frequency clock generation circuit.

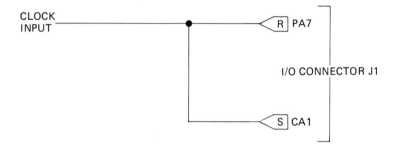

FIGURE A4-8. Connection of clock input to user PIA port A (address 8004 hex). *Note:* Jumper wires can be used to select this configuration as opposed to those used in Laboratories B and C.

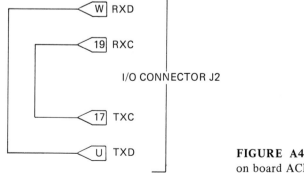

FIGURE A4-9. Connections required to use the on board ACIA in an echoing mode.

PARTS LIST FOR LABORATORY EXERCISES

ITEM	DESCRIPTION	QTY	LABORATORIES	USER PIA PORT
SPDT switch	Alco TT 11DG-WW-2T	8	2, 7, C	A
1K resistor pack	Bourns 898-1-R1K	1	2, 7, C	A
or 1K resistors		8	2, 7, C	A
Decimal switch		1	4	A
74148 IC	Priority Encoder	1	4	A
1K resistor pack	Bourns 898-1-R1K	1	4	A
SPDT switch		2	B, C	A (CA1), B(CB1)
1K resistor pack	Bourns 898-1-R1K	1	B, C	A (CA1), B(CB1)
or 1K resistors		4		
7400 IC	Quad NAND	1	B, C	A (CA1), B(CB1)
LED display	Red	8	3, C, D, E	B
500-ohm resistor pack	Bourns 898-1-500	1	3, C, D, E	B
or 500-ohm resistors		8		
7407 IC	Hex Buffer/Driver	2	3, C, D, E	B
LED display	Red	2	B	A (CA2), B(CB2)
500-ohm resistor		2	B	A (CA2), B(CB2)
7407 IC	Hex Buffer/Driver	1	B	A (CA2), B(CB2)
74LS163	Counter	2	D	A (bit 7)
Miscellaneous:				
Vector prototyping board 377-2		1		
50-pin connector		1		
50-pin termination		1		
50-conductor ribbon cable		30 cm		
14-pin wire-wrap sockets		3		
16-pin wire-wrap sockets		7		

EXAMPLE LABORATORY CONFIGURATION

The example laboratory configuration was constructed on a Vector prototyping board. Figures A4-7 and A4-10 through A4-13 show the arrangement of this board and its connection to the MEK6800D2 Microcomputer Module.

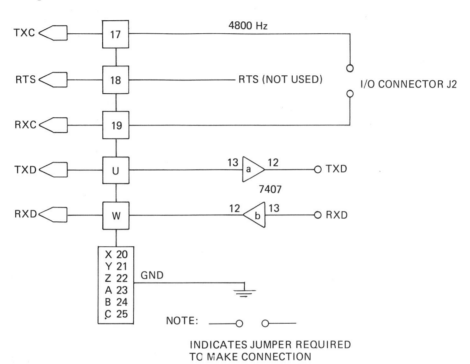

FIGURE A4-10. ACIA connections for echoing or transmission between microcomputers.

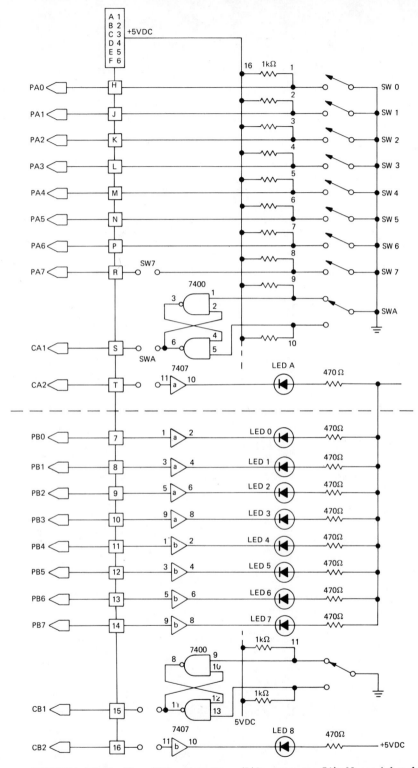

FIGURE A4-11. User PIA connections (I/O connector J1). *Note:* A break indicates the need for a jumper wire to make the connection.

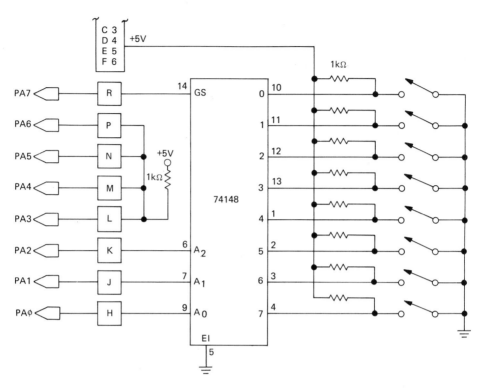

FIGURE A4-12. Encoder connections for Laboratory 4.

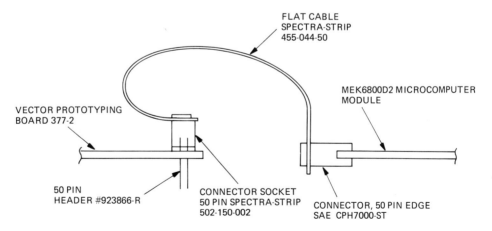

FIGURE A4-13. Connection of prototyping board to Microcomputer Module.

APPENDIX 5–SUMMARY OF MEK6800D2 (JBUG) MONITOR

The following descriptions are taken from the *MEK6800D2 Evaluation Kit II Manual* (1977 edition) and are reprinted here with the permission of Motorola Semiconductor Products Inc., Phoenix, AZ. The table of monitor subroutines also appears in Laboratory A as Table A-1.

The Kit also permits several different memory configurations. The two MCM6810 128 x 8 RAMs provided with the standard Kit will accommodate programs of up to 256 bytes in length (the third MCM6810 is reserved for use by the monitor program). Addition of the two additional optional RAMs expands the capability to 512 bytes. Strapping options for the additional ROM sockets permits any of the following combinations:

1024 bytes in 512 x 8 bit PROMs (MCM7641)

2048 bytes in 1024 x 8 bit EPROMs (MCM68708)

2048 bytes in 1024 x 8 bit Mask-Programmed ROMs (MCM68308 — same pin-out as MCM68708)

4096 bytes in 2048 x 8 bit Mask-Programmed ROMs (MCM68316 — same pin-out as MCM68708 except EPROM programming pin is used as additional addressing pin.)

Adding the optional buffers in the spaces provided upgrades the Kit to EXORciser-compatible status; hence, all the EXORciser I/O and Memory modules (see included data sheets) can also be used with the Kit. For example, addition of MINIbug II, an 8K Memory board, and the EXORciser's Resident Editor/Assembler to the Microcomputer Module creates a complete development/prototyping tool.

START-UP PROCEDURE

Connect the cable attached to the Keyboard/Display Module to connector J2 on the Microcomputer Module. Apply 5-volt dc power. Pushing the reset switch on the Microcomputer Module should now cause the JBUG prompt symbol, "dash", to be displayed in the left-most display indicator on the Keyboard/Display Module. The remaining five displays will be blanked. The JBUG control and monitor program is now in operation and any of the functions described in the next section may be invoked by means of the data and command keys on the Keyboard/Display Module.

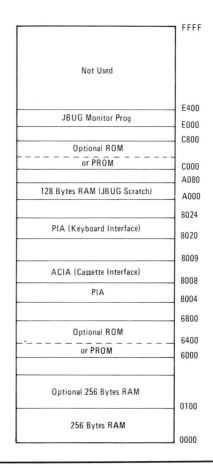

Not Used	FFFF
	E400
JBUG Monitor Prog	E000
	C800
Optional ROM	
or PROM	C000
	A080
128 Bytes RAM (JBUG Scratch)	A000
	8024
PIA (Keyboard Interface)	8020
	8009
ACIA (Cassette Interface)	8008
PIA	8004
	6800
Optional ROM	6400
or PROM	6000
Optional 256 Bytes RAM	0100
256 Bytes RAM	0000

FIGURE A5-1. Memory Map for MEK6800D2.

OPERATING PROCEDURES

The Keyboard/Display Module, in conjunction with JBUG, provides a means of examining operation of the Microcomputer Module and entering and trouble-shooting programs. The Keypad has sixteen keys labeled 0-F for entry of hexadecimal data and eight keys for commanding the following functions:

M — Examine and Change Memory

E — Escape (Abort) from Operation in Progress

R — Examine Contents of MPU Registers P, X, A, B, CC, S

G — Go to Specified Program and Begin Execution of Designated Program

P — Punch Data from Memory to Magnetic Tape

L — Load Memory from Magnetic Tape

N — Trace One Instruction

V — Set (and Remove) Breakpoints

Operating procedures for each of these functions are described in the following paragraphs. The display should be showing the prompt "dash" before any command is invoked.

1-4.1　MEMORY EXAMINE AND CHANGE (M)

This function permits examination and, if necessary, change of memory locations. A map of the MC6800 instructions is included as Table 1-4.1-1 and is useful in translating memory data to instruction mnemonics.

Open the memory location to be examined by entering the address (as 4-digits of hex via the hex keypad) followed by closure of the M key (hhhhM). The display will now show the address that was entered in its group of four displays on the left and the contents in the two on the right. The user at this point has three options: (1) Leave this location unchanged and move to the next location by closing the G key. The new address and its data would then be displayed. (2) Change the data by simply entering the new data via the hex keypad (hh). In this case the display would then be showing the new data that was entered. In the event that an attempt is made to change Read Only Memory (ROM), the display will continue to show the original data. (3) Close the Memory Examine function by means of the E key. Closure of the E key will return operation to the monitor and the prompt will again be displayed.

1-4.2　ESCAPE (ABORT)

This function provides an orderly exit from the other functions and/or user programs. Examples of its use are included in the accompanying descriptions of the other functions.

1-4.3　REGISTER DISPLAY (R)

This function permits examination of the MPU's registers and may be invoked at any time the JBUG prompt is being displayed by closing the R key. Following closure of R, the display will show a 4-digit hex value, the present contents of the Program Counter. The remaining registers may now be examined by sequencing with the G key and will appear in the following order: Index Register, Accumulator A, Accumulator B, Condition Code Register, Stack Pointer.[1]

This display is circular, i.e., a G key closure following display of the Stack Pointer will cause the Program Counter to be displayed again. The E key may be used to escape back to the monitor at any point in the display sequence. If required the contents of any register can be changed by using the Memory Change function. The monitor executed an interrupt sequence when R was invoked. In servicing an interrupt, the MC6800 saves its registers on a stack in memory (it is these memory locations that the R function "examines"). On exit from the R interrupt service routine, the MPU retrieves these values and reloads its registers; hence if the data on the stack is changed with the M function, the new data will go into the MPU. The following locations are used to stack the registers:

> $A008[2] — High order byte of Stack Pointer
> $A009 — Low order byte of Stack Pointer
> S + 1 — Condition Code Register
> S + 2 — Accumulator B
> S + 3 — Accumulator A
> S + 4 — High order byte of Index Register

---

[1]It is a characteristic of the display routine that the value displayed for the Stack Pointer is seven less than the actual value.
[2]In this manual, hexadecimal data is identified by preceeding it with a dollar sign symbol, $.

S + 5 — Low order byte of Index Register

S + 6 — High order byte of Program Counter

S + 7 — Low order byte of Program Counter

where "S" is the current Stack Pointer as saved in $A008 and $A009. Note that it is necessary to exit the R display function and enter the M in order to change register values.

1-4.4   GO TO USER PROGRAM (G)

If the Prompt is being displayed, and assuming that a meaningful program has been previously entered, the MPU can be directed to go execute the program simply by entering the starting address of the program (via the hex keypad) followed by closure of the G key (hhhhG). The resulting blanking of the displays is an indication that the MPU has left the monitor program and is executing the user's program. The MPU will continue executing the user program until either an Escape (E key) is invoked or the program "blows". Control, indicated by the prompt "dash", can normally be obtained with the E key. It is possible that an incorrect program could have caused the monitor's variable data to be modified. In this case, it is necessary to regain control using the reset switch on the Microcomputer Module.

1-4.5   PUNCH FROM MEMORY TO TAPE

The Punch function allows the user to save selected blocks of memory on ordinary audio tape cassettes. Before invoking Punch, the Memory Change function should be used to establish which portion of memory is to be recorded. Using Memory Change, enter the desired starting address into locations $A002 and $A003 (high order byte into $A002, low order byte into $A003). Similarly, enter the high and low order bytes of the desired ending address into $A004 and $A005, respectively. Escape from Memory Change via the E key, thus obtaining the monitor prompt dash. With the audio recorder's microphone input connected to the corresponding point on the Keyboard/Display Module and the prompt present, the Punch function is performed as follows. Position the tape as desired (fully rewound is recommended) and put the recorder in its record mode. Close the P key. The prompt will disappear during the Punch process and then re-appear to indicate that the Punch operation is completed. Typically, the prompt is "off" for over 30 seconds since the recording format specifies that a thirty second header of all ones be recorded ahead of the data. See sections 2-7 and 3-7 for additional details on the recording format.

1-4.6   LOAD FROM TAPE TO MEMORY

The Load function can be used to retrieve from audio magnetic tape data that was recorded using the Punch function described in the preceding section. With the audio recorder's earphone output connected to the corresponding input on the Keyboard/Display Module (and with the monitor prompt present on the display), the Load function is performed as follows. To load the desired record, position the tape at the approximate point from which the Punch was started and then put the recorder into its playback mode. Close the L key. The prompt will disappear, then re-appear when the Load function is completed. After the prompt re-appears, the Memory Examine function can be used to examine locations $A002 and $A003. They will contain the beginning address of the block of data that was just moved into memory. The end address is not recovered by the function, hence the data in locations $A004 and $A005 is not significant during the Load function.

1-4.7 BREAKPOINT INSERTION AND REMOVAL (V)

Because of the difficulty in analyzing operation while a program is executing, it is useful during debug to be able to set breakpoints at selected places in the program. This enables the user to run part of the program, then examine the results before proceeding. The breakpoints are set by entering the hex address of the desired breakpoint followed by a V key closure (hhhh V.). This may be repeated up to five times. The breakpoint entry function can be exited after any entry by using the E key. The monitor program will retain all the breakpoints until they are cleared.

If at any time an hhhh V entry is made and the hhhh (hex data) does not appear on the display, there were already five breakpoints stored and the last one was ignored. At any time the prompt is displayed, entry of a V command not preceeded by hex data will cause the current breakpoints to be removed. If a breakpoint is entered and the program is subsequently executed to that point, the display will show the current value of the Program Counter in the four indicators on the left. (This will be the same as the breakpoint address that was inserted.) The right hand two displays will contain the data stored at that location — that is, the operating code. At this point the G key can be used to sequence through the other MPU registers exactly as in the register display function. If it is desirable to proceed on from the breakpoint simply use E (to get the prompt) and then the G key. At this point, the MPU will reload its registers from the stack and continue with the user's program until another breakpoint is encountered or the E key is used again.

1-4.8 TRACE ONE INSTRUCTION (N)

The Trace function permits stepping through a program one instruction at a time. The Trace function can be invoked any time the user program is at a breakpoint or has been aborted with the E key. However, tracing cannot begin from start-up because the trace routine does not know where the starting address is. Therefore, an hhhh V command must be given at least once before Trace can be used.

Enter the Trace function by first setting a breakpoint at the location from which it is desired to trace and then invoking hhhhG to begin program execution. The breakpoint can be set at the very beginning of the program if desired.[3] Following the hhhhG command, the program will run to the breakpoint and stop, displaying the Program Counter as before. If the N key is now closed, the MPU executes the next program instruction and again halts. The display will then show the address of the next instruction (Program Counter) and the operating code located there. The G key can be used to sequence the other registers on to the display as for a breakpoint if desired. The N key can now be used to trace as many instructions as desired.[4]

The Trace function cannot be used directly to trace through user IRQ interrupts. The NMI is higher priority and will cause the IRQ to be ignored. Repeated attempts to execute the Trace command when user IRQ interrupts are active will result in JBUG continuously returning with the same address. See sections 2-6 and 3-8 of this manual and the *M6800 Microprocessor Applications Manual* for additional information.

---

[3]This procedure assumes the program is in RAM since breakpoints are handled by substituting an SWI for the op-code. If the program to be traced is entirely in ROM, use a convenient RAM location to insert a jump to the desired ROM address. Then set a breakpoint at the address of the jump instruction and proceed as above.

[4]It is a characteristic of the Trace function that all breakpoints in effect at the time Trace is invoked will be removed and must be re-installed following exit from Trace.

Interrupt service routines may be traced by setting a breakpoint at the beginning of the service routine. The Go function may then be used to start program execution, allowing a normal entry into the $\overline{\text{IRQ}}$ service routine. Once in the service routine, Trace can be used as usual. The E key may be used to exit from Trace at any time.

1-4.9   CALCULATION OF THE OFFSET TO A BRANCH DESTINATION

The instruction format for conditional branch instructions calls for the offset to the destination to be entered immediately following the branch instruction op-code as a signed two's complement number. Mental calculation of the offset is awkward due to the required two's complement format. A short program for making this calculation is included in JBUG (lines 62-70 of the assembly listing included as Appendix 1 of this manual). Use the following procedure with this program:

1. Obtain the prompt "dash" by escaping from the current operation.

2. Find the current value of the stack pointer by entering the Register Display.

3. Exit from Register Display and open memory location S + 2, where S is the current value of the stack pointer as obtained in Step 2. S + 2 is the location of the current stacked value of Accumulator B. Enter the high order byte of the destination address in this location. Next, enter the low order byte of the destination into Accumulator A in location S + 3.

4. Put the high and low order bytes of the branch instruction's op-code address into S + 4 and S + 5, respectively. This loads the stacked Index Register with the op-code address.

5. Use the "E" key to exit from the Memory Examine/Change function and then enter $E000G to begin executing the program starting at location $E000 in JBUG.

6. The program runs to location $E013 and hits the SWI breakpoint located there. Examine the contents of Accumulators A and B by invoking Register Display and sequencing through the Registers with the G key. The offset, in the correct form for entry in the program, is now in Acc.A. If Acc.B contains $FF, the offset is valid (within the allowed range) and is in the negative direction. If Acc.B contains $00, the offset is valid and in the positive direction. Any other value indicates that the destination is beyond the allowed range.

1-5   OPERATING EXAMPLE

The following example program is suitable for gaining familiarity with the JBUG monitor features. The program adds the five values in locations $10 through $14 using Acc. A and stores the final result in location $15. The intermediate total is kept in Acc. A; Acc. B is used as a counter to count down the loop. The Index Register contains a "pointer" (i.e., X contains the address) of the next location to be added. The program, as follows, contains an error which will be used later to illustrate some of JBUG's features.

In the following listing, the leftmost column contains the memory address where a byte (8 bits) of the program will be stored. The next column contains the machine language op-code and data for a particular

SIGNALS DECODED																					
DEVICE	ADDRESSES	φ2	R/W	SYMBOL	VMA	A15	A14	A13	A12	A11	A10	A9	A8	A7	A6	A5	A4	A3	A2	A1	A0
ROM	E000-E3FF	1	1	ROM =	1	1	1	1				x	x	x	x	x	x	x	x	x	x
PROM	C000-C3FF			PROM =	1	1	1	0			+	x	x	x	x	x	x	x	x	x	x
RAM (Stack)	A000-A07F	1	x	STACK =	1	1	0	1	0			0	0	0	x	x	x	x	x	x	x
PIA	8020-8023	1	x	I/O =	1	1	0	0								1		0*	0*	x	x
ACIA	8008-8009	1	x	I/O =	1	1	0	0								0*		1	0*		x
PIA	8004-8007	1	x	I/O =	1	1	0	0								0*		0*	1	x	x
PROM	6000-7FFF			6/7 =	1	0	1	1			+	x	x	x	x	x	x	x	x	x	x
USER	4000-5FFF			4/5 =	1	0	1	0													
USER	2000-3FFF			2/3 =	1	0	0	1													
RAM (User)	0000-007F	1	x	RAM =	1	0	0	0				0	0	0	x	x	x	x	x	x	x
RAM (User)	0080-00FF	1	x	RAM =	1	0	0	0				0	0	1	x	x	x	x	x	x	x
RAM (User)	0100-017F	1	x	RAM =	1	0	0	0				0	1	0	x	x	x	x	x	x	x
RAM (User)	0180-01FF	1	x	RAM =	1	0	0	0				0	1	1	x	x	x	x	x	x	x

x = Decoded by the device addressed

* = Required but not decoded by the device addressed

+ = Decoded by 2K x 8 bit optional RAM

TABLE 2-2-1: MEK6800D2 Evaluation Kit II Address Map

device whenever the MPU outputs addresses in the range of $E000 to $EFFF. The particular locations within the ROM are selected by applying MPU address lines A0 thru A9 to the ROM address inputs. The JBUG ROM is located at the highest addresses in the kit's memory field. Note that A12 from the MPU is not applied to this ROM so it will also be selected when the MPU outputs its Restart and Interrupt Vector addresses, $FFF8 — $FFFF. Start-up and interrupt capability is obtained by placing the appropriate interrupt vector addresses in locations $EEE8 — $EFFF of the monitor program.

Additional addresses are decoded for the optional ROMs that can be added for user-generated programs. The Microcomputer Module is layed out to accept either two MCM68708 1024 x 8 bit Electrically Programmable Read Only Memories (EPROM) or two MCM7641 TTL 512 x 8 bit Programmable Read Only Memories. The PROMs are more economical but cannot be erased like the EPROM. Two MCM68316 2048 x 8 bit ROMs can also be used in the PROM locations. In this case, MPU address line A10 is applied to the MCM68316 for decoding the additional 1024 bytes. Jumpers on the PCB are provided for selecting the desired combination of ROM (see note 6 on the schematic diagram of Figure A3-a).

The MC6810 (128 x 8) RAM occupying memory locations $A000 — $A07F is used by the MPU for temporary storage of its internal registers during interrupts and subroutines and is selected by the signal STACK. The MPU also uses this area for storage of flags and temporary data used by the JBUG monitor. This organization allows a clean separation between monitor requirements and user RAM. The system assigns, via the RAM signal, the four user RAMs to the bottom of memory in locations $0000 — $01FF (first 512 bytes). This RAM is useful for small user programs or for scratchpad memory in the MPU's direct addressing range for larger user programs. To prevent contention with these RAMs, expanded systems should avoid these memory

SOFTWARE DESCRIPTION (JBUG MONITOR)

GENERAL DESCRIPTION

The control and diagnostic capability of the MEK6800D2 Kit is provided by the JBUG monitor program resident in the MCM6830 1K x 8 bit ROM supplied with the Kit. The characteristics of this program are described in the following sections. An assembly listing of JBUG is included (Appendix 1) and may also be referred to in studying the flow of the program.

Several RAM locations are used for temporary data storage and as flags by the monitor in communicating between the various routines. Some of the more significant ones are described below and are referred to in the description of JBUG.

SP
($A008)
A RAM location in which the user's Stack Pointer is saved whenever the monitor resumes control. The user's Stack Pointer is required for locating user Registers on the stack and to restore these Register when returning to the user program.

DISBUF
($A00C)
Eight RAM locations used as a buffer to hold the current values being displayed. In the first six locations, the high order 4 bits of each location represent the display digit-count while the low order 4 bits contain the value that is to be displayed on that digit. For example, the high order 4 bits of the sixth location in DISBUF identify the right-most display. The last two locations in DISBUF are used for temporary storage of data that is input from the keypad during a Memory Change function.

DIGIN4
($A014)
A flag that is set to one (LSB) when at least four hex digits have been entered from the keyboard (as in Memory Examine)

DIGIN8
(A015)
A flag that is set to one (LSB) when six hex digits have been entered from the keyboard (as in Memory Change)

MFLAG
($A016)
A flag that is set to one (LSB) when the M key is depressed to invoke the Memory Examine Mode.

RFLAG
($A017)
A flag that is set to one (LSB) when the R key is depressed to invoke the Register Display Mode.

NFLAG
($A018)
A flag that is set to one (LSB) when the N key is depressed to invoke the Trace Mode.

VFLAG
($A01D)
A flag that is set to the number of breakpoints (up to five) that have been set.

XKEYBF
($A01A)
A pointer to the next empty location in DISBUF where the next hex key entry will be stored.

The flow of JBUG is straightforward and is shown in Figure 3-1-1. After release of the RESET button, the monitor goes through an initialization sequence in which the stack pointer is initialized to $A078,

JBUG MONITOR SUBROUTINES*

NAME	CALLING ADDRESS (HEX)	FUNCTION
BLDX (BUILD TWO BYTE ADDRESS)	E0E4	Builds a 2-byte address from the first four locations of DISBUF.
CLFLG	E0B2	Clears display buffer and all flags.
CLRDS	E0C4	Clears display buffer and blanks display.
DISNMI (DISABLE NMI INTERRUPTS)	E084	Disables nonmaskable interrupt from keyboard/display PIA.
DLY1	E0E0	Provides a time delay by counting the index register down to zero.
DLY20	E0DD	Delays 20 ms using index register.
HDR	E0D7	Places prompt (—) in first entry of display buffer.
MDIS (MEMORY DISPLAY)	E269	Displays contents of memory location addressed by first four locations of DISBUF.
MDIS1 (MEMORY CHANGE)	E27E	Changes contents of memory location addressed by first four locations of DISBUF to digits in DISBUF + 6 and DISBUF +7.
MDIS2 (MOVE NIBBLES)	E29A	Moves low nibble (4 bits) of A to B and high nibble of A to low nibble of A.
MINC (INCREMENT MEMORY)	E2A4	Increments memory address display.
OUTDS (OUTPUT DISPLAY BUFFER)	E0FE	Displays six digits in DISBUF. Waits 1 ms between digits. Operates continuously with no return unless a key is pressed.
REGST (DISPLAY REGISTERS)	E2C6	Displays registers on user stack.
REGST5 (MOVE A TO DISPLAY BUFFER)	E31C	Moves two digits in A to first two locations in display buffer.
SETBR (SET BREAKPOINT)	E06A	Makes an entry in the breakpoint table.

*Address DISBUF is A00C, the starting address of the display buffer.

References

BOOKS

Bishop, R., *Basic Microprocessors and the 6800,* Hayden, Rochelle Park, NJ, 1979.

Blakeslee, T. R., *Digital Design with Standard MSI and LSI, 2nd Ed.,* Wiley, New York, 1979.

Hart, J. F., et al., *Computer Approximations,* Wiley, New York, 1968.

Hughes, J. K., and J. I. Michtom, *A Structured Approach to Programming,* Prentice-Hall, Englewood Cliffs, NJ, 1977.

Hwang, K., *Computer Arithmetic,* Wiley, New York, 1979.

Kernighan, B. W., and P. J. Plauger, *The Elements of Programming Style,* McGraw-Hill, New York, 1978.

Leventhal, L. A., *6800 Assembly Language Programming,* Osborne/McGraw-Hill, Berkeley, CA 1978.

Leventhal, L. A., *Introduction to Microprocessors: Software, Hardware, Programming,* Prentice-Hall, Englewood Cliffs, NJ, 1978.

Lipovski, G. J., *Microcomputer Interfacing: Principles and Practices,* Lexington Books, Lexington, MA, 1980.

Luke, Y. L., *Mathematical Functions and Their Approximations,* Academic Press, New York, 1975.

McNamara, J. E., *Technical Aspects of Data Communications*, Educational Services Department, Digital Equipment Corp., Maynard, MA, 1977.

Motorola Semiconductor Products Inc., *Microprocessor Applications Manual*, McGraw-Hill, New York, 1976.

Osborne, A., *An Introduction to Microcomputers, Vol. 1: Basic Concepts*, Osborne/McGraw-Hill, Berkeley, CA, 1976.

Osborne, A., *An Introduction to Microcomputers, Vol. 2: Some Real Microprocessors*, Osborne/McGraw-Hill, Berkeley, CA, 1978.

Osborne, A., *An Introduction to Microcomputers, Vol. 3: Some Real Support Devices*, Osborne/McGraw-Hill, Berkeley, CA, 1978.

Peatman, J. B., *The Design of Digital Systems*, Mc-Graw-Hill, New York, 1972.

Peatman, J. B., *Microcomputer-based Design*, McGraw-Hill, New York, 1977.

Schmid, H., *Decimal Computation*, Wiley, New York, 1974.

Weller, W. J., *Practical Microcomputer Programming: The M6800*, Northern Technology Books, Evanston, IL, 1977.

ARTICLES

Aldridge, D., "Analog to Digital Conversion Techniques with the M6800 Microprocessor System," Motorola Semiconductor Products Application Note AN-757, Phoenix, AZ, 1975.

Allison, D. R., "A Design Philosophy for Microcomputer Architectures," *Computer*, February 1977, pp. 35-41.

Andreiev, N., "Special Report: Troubleshooting Instruments," *EDN*, October 5, 1978, pp. 89-99.

Babb, S. M., et al., "A General Purpose IEEE-488 Interface," IECI 1979 Proceedings, pp. 121-125.

Bainter, J. R., "Dual 555-Timer Circuit Restarts Microprocessor," *Electronics*, March 18, 1976, pp. 106-107.

Barnes, J., and B. Bergquist, "Unite Microprocessor Hardware and Software," *Electronic Design*, March 29, 1976, pp. 74-76.

Barnes, J., and V. Gregory, "Use Microprocessors to Enhance Performance with Noisy Data," *EDN*, August 20, 1976, pp. 71-72.

Baunach, S. C., "An Example of an M6800-based GPIB Interface," *EDN*, September 20, 1977, pp. 125-128. An expanded version of this article with schematics and program listings is available from Tektronix Inc., PO Box 500, Beaverton, OR 97077.

Boney, J., and E. Rupp, "Let Your Next Microcomputer Check Itself," *Electronic Design*, September 1, 1979, pp. 100-105.

Bradshaw, P., "Two-Chip A/D Converter," *Electronic Design*, March 29, 1979, pp. 128-136.

Bram, M., "Adapting the M6800 Processor for Automatic Telephone Dialing," *Electronics*, July 6, 1978, pp. 128-129.

Breikss, I. P., "Nonmaskable Interrupt Saves Processor Register Contents," *Electronics,* July 21, 1977, p. 104.

Buzen, J. P., "I/O Subsystem Architecture," *Proceedings of the IEEE,* June 1975, pp. 871-879.

Cannon, L. E., and P. S. Kreager, "Using a Microprocessor: a Real-Life Application," *Computer Design,* October 1975, pp. 81-89.

Deal, J., and R. Bass, "Program PROMs with a 6800," *EDN,* June 5, 1979, pp. 177-181.

Diehl, W., and W. Reynolds, "Microprocessor Based Engine Dynanometer Data Acquisition System," IECI 1979 Proceedings, pp. 210-213.

Dollhoff, T., "Microprocessor Software: How to Optimize Timing and Memory Usage. Part One. Techniques for the Intel 8080 and Motorola 6800," *Digital Design,* November 1976, pp. 56-69.

Donn, E. S., and M. D. Lippman, "Efficient and Effective Microcomputer Testing Requires Careful Preplanning," *EDN,* February 20, 1979, pp. 97-107.

Edgar, A. D., and S. C. Lee, "FOCUS Microcomputer Number System," *Communications of the ACM,* March 1979, pp. 166-177.

Eidson, M. E., and L. A. Parker, "Synchronous Adapter Reduces Complexity of Floppy Disc Controller," *Computer Design,* April 1977, pp. 102-106.

Eufinger, R. J., "Integrating Peripherals into Processing Systems," *Computer Design,* December 1978, pp. 77-83.

Farrell, J., "Mating Micros to the IEEE-488 Bus," *Electronic Design,* November 22, 1978, pp. 152-157.

Ferguson, M., "MIKBUG with Muscle," *Kilobaud,* July 1978, pp. 64-66.

Fronheiser, K., "Device Operation and System Implementation of the Asynchronous Communications Interface Adapter," Motorola Semiconductor Products Application Note AN-754, Phoenix, AZ, 1975.

Fullagar, D., et al., "Interfacing Data Converters and Microprocessors," *Electronics,* December 9, 1976, pp. 81-89.

Geist, D. J., "MOS Processor Picks Up Speed with Bipolar Multipliers," *Electronics,* July 7, 1977, pp. 113-115.

Gooze, M., "How a 16-Bit Microprocessor Makes It in an 8-Bit World," *Electronics,* September 27, 1979, pp. 122-125.

Grappel, R., "Technique Avoids Interrupt Dangers," *EDN,* May 5, 1979, p. 88.

Hargreaves, J. C., and R. A. Krakowski, "Distributed Process Control: a Micro-Mini Marriage," *Computer,* September 1977, pp. 44-56.

Harrington, W., "MEK6800D2 Microcomputer Kit System Expansion Techniques," Motorola Semiconductor Products Application Note AN-771, Phoenix, AZ, 1977.

Hemenway, J., and E. Teja, "EDN Software Tutorial: File Structures," *EDN,* June 20, 1979, pp. 153-155.

Hemenway, J., and E. Teja, "EDN Software Tutorial: Hash Coding," *EDN,* September 20, 1979, pp. 108-110.

Hill, S. A., "Multiprocess Control Interface Makes Remote Microprocessor Command Possible," *EDN,* February 5, 1976, pp. 87-89.

Holderby, W. S., "Designing a Microprocessor-based Terminal for Factory Data Collection," *Computer Design,* March 1977, pp. 81-88.

Holt, O., and F. Shirley, "Let a Microprocessor Cut Test Time," *Electronic Design,* October 25, 1976, pp. 156-160.

Hootman, J., "See How the IEEE-488 Bus Works by Designing a Compatible A/D — D/A System," *Electronic Design,* September 27, 1978, pp. 88-91.

Jennings, P. D., "Automatic Service Monitor for Telephone Switching Systems," IECI 1978 Proceedings, pp. 10-14.

Kaufmann, J., "Let a Microprocessor Keep Track of Your Process," *Electronic Design,* December 20, 1975, pp. 66-69.

Kelly, S., "Low-Cost Data Acquisition Systems," *Electronic Design,* November 22, 1976, pp. 152-157.

Khanna, V., and T. Daly, "Making the Most of Your Micro," *Digital Design,* July 1975, pp. 36-48.

Landau, J. V., "State Description Techniques Applied to Industrial Machine Control," *Computer,* February 1979, pp. 32-40.

Lange, A., "OPTACON Interface Permits the Blind to 'Read' Digital Instruments," *EDN,* February 5, 1976, pp. 84-86.

Larsen, D. G., et al., "INWAS: Interfacing with Asynchronous Serial Mode," *IEEE Transactions on Industrial Electronics and Control Instrumentation,* February 1977, pp. 2-12.

Le-Huy, H., "Microprocessor-controlled Pulsewidth Modulated Inverter," IECI 1978 Proceedings, pp. 223-226.

Levasseur, D., "Simplify IEEE-488 Implementation with a Multifunction Interface," *EDN,* March 5, 1979, pp. 105-113.

Leventhal, L. A., "Cut Your Processor's Computation Time," *Electronic Design,* August 16, 1977, pp. 82-88.

Leventhal, L. A., "Put Microprocessor Software to Work," *Electronic Design,* August 2, 1976, pp. 58-64.

Leventhal, L. A., "Structured Programming Formulates Microprocessor Program Logic," *Digital Design,* October 1978, pp. 30-40.

Leventhal, L. A., "Take Advantage of 8080 and 6800 Data-Manipulation Capabilities," *Electronic Design,* April 12, 1977, pp. 90-97.

Levine, S. F., "Assembly Language for Microprocessors," *Electronic Design,* December 20, 1975, pp. 58-63.

Logan, J. D., and P. S. Kreager, "Using a Microprocessor: a Real-Life Application. Part 1–Hardware," *Computer Design,* September 1975, pp. 69-77.

Mann, K. L., "Precision Analog Computer Operates in Real or Machine Time," *EDN*, February 5, 1976, pp. 81-84.

Martin, B., "Summary of New Industrial Applications of a Microprocessor to Transmission Systems," IECI 1979 Proceedings, pp. 244-249.

Melear, C., and J. Browne, "Simplify Video-Display Design by Using a Versatile IC Controller," *Electronic Design*, June 21, 1979, pp. 94-102.

Morris, G., "Make Your Next Instrument Design Emphasize User Needs and Wants," *EDN*, October 20, 1978, pp. 100-105.

Morris, G., "Task Analysis Lets You Design without Injecting Personal Quirks," *EDN*, November 5, 1978, pp. 82-88.

Morris, R., "6800 Routine Supervises Service Requests," *EDN*, October 5, 1979, pp. 73-81.

Mrozowski, A., "Analog Output Chips Shrink A-D Conversion Software," *Electronics*, June 23, 1977, pp. 130-133.

Mulder, M. C., and P. P. Fasang, "A Microprocessor Controlled Substation Alarm Logger," IECI 1978 Proceedings, pp. 2-6.

Nash, G., "Microprocessor Software Programs Bit-Rate Generator," *EDN*, August 20, 1977, pp. 134-137.

Newman, S., "Microcomputer System Generates Arbitrary Waveforms," *EDN*, August 20, 1979, pp. 67-68.

Ogdin, C. A., "A Floppy-Disc Interface Is More Than Just a Chip," *EDN*, August 20, 1978, pp. 115-119.

Odgin, C. A., "Interfaces on a Chip," *Mini-Micro Systems*, November 1978, pp. 95-104.

Ogdin, C. A., "Setting up a Microcomputer Design Laboratory," *Mini-Micro Systems*, May 1979, pp. 87-94.

Ogdin, C. A., "Some Simple Hardware Techniques Allow Fail-Safe LSI Interfacing," *EDN*, February 20, 1979, pp. 117-122.

O'Neill, P., "Optically Coupled Triac Driver Chip Interfaces Logic to AC Load," *Electronics*, August 30, 1979, pp. 145-148.

Padmanabhan, J., and M. S. Swaminathan, "Teleprinter Option Unites PROM Programmer to MC6800," *Electronics*, August 30, 1979, pp. 157-159.

Patterson, W., and K. Frisbie, "Reduce Your Microcomputer System's Overhead," *Electronic Design*, June 7, 1978, pp. 122-126.

Peuto, B. L., and L. J. Shustek, "Current Issues in the Architecture of Microprocessors," *Computer*, February 1977, pp. 20-25.

Ringel, C., and J. Tamburri, "Use of Microprocessors to Control and Monitor Operations of Gas Turbine Generators," IECI 1976 Proceedings, pp. 36-46.

Ripps, D. L., "Help a Real-Time Multitasking OS," *Electronic Design*, June 21, 1979, pp. 86-91.

Ripps, D. L., "A Multitasking Operating System Simplifies Real-Time Applications in Many Ways," *Electronic Design,* September 13, 1979, pp. 146-151.

Ripps, D. L., "Simplify Your Real-Time Application," *Electronic Design,* September 27, 1979, pp. 82-86.

Rooy, G., and A. Oumamar, "Direct Digital Control by Microprocessor of a Dual AC/DC Thyristor Converter," IECI 1979 Proceedings, pp. 8-13.

Schindler, M. J., "Fit Your Microprocessor with the Right Software Package," *Electronic Design,* July 5, 1978, pp. 64-72.

Seim, T. A., "Numerical Interpolation for Microprocessor-based Systems," *Computer Design,* February 1978, pp. 111-116.

Sohrabji, N., "Microprocessors Extend Scope of Automated Manufacturing," *EDN,* March 5, 1978, pp. 101-106.

Staab, R. I., and D. M. Shiroma, "Microprocessor Energy Controllers for Navy Buildings," IECI 1979 Proceedings, pp. 110-114.

Stec, H. J., "Low-Cost Interface Automates EPROM Loading," *Electronics,* November 8, 1979, pp. 151-153 (describes a low-cost 2708 PROM programmer for the MEK6800D2 microcomputer).

Steiner, K., "Verify 6800 Data During Recovery," *EDN,* April 20, 1979, pp. 101-102.

Tavora, C. J., "A Hierarchically Distributed Energy Management System," IECI 1979 Proceedings, pp. 156-160.

Tuthill, M., and D. P. Burton, "Low-Cost A/D Converter Links Easily with Microprocessors," *Electronics,* August 30, 1979, pp. 149-155.

Volp, J., "Software Switches Baud Rate," *EDN,* November 5, 1979, p. 83.

Wagner W. S., "Digital Voltmeter Has Audible Output," *Electronics,* March 29, 1979, pp. 120-122.

Wagner, W. S., "12-Hour Clock Tells Time Out Loud," *Electronics,* August 16, 1979, pp. 132-133.

Wakerly, J. F., "Microprocessor Input/Output Architecture," *Computer,* February 1977, pp. 26-33.

Weisberg, M. J., "Designer's Guide to Testing and Troubleshooting Microprocessor-Based Products," *EDN,* March 20, 1980, pp. 177-214.

Weissberger, A. J., "Data-Link Control Chips: Bringing Order to Data Protocols," *Electronics,* June 8, 1978, pp. 104-112.

Wiles, M., et al., "Compatibility Cures Growing Pains of Microcomputer Family," *Electronics,* February 2, 1978, pp. 95-103.

Wong, J., et al., "Software Error Checking Procedures for Data Communications Protocols," *Computer Design,* February 1979, pp. 122-125.

Woods, D. E., "A Microprocessor Based Supervisory Control and Data Acquisition System Communications Controller," IECI 1979 Proceedings, pp. 58-61.

Yalof, S., and D. Gregg, "Collect Data via Pulse-Code Modulation," *Electronic Design,* March 15, 1978, pp. 94-99.

Zsombar-Murray, P. J., et al., "Microprocessor Based Frequency Response Analyzer," IECI 1978 Proceedings, pp. 36-43.

Note: IECI Proceedings refers to the Proceedings of the IEEE Industrial Electronics and Control Instrumentation's Annual Conference on Industrial Applications of Microprocessors, held in March of each year (since 1975) in Philadelphia, PA. The Proceedings are available from the IEEE Service Center, 445 Hoes Lane, Piscataway, NJ 08854, or from the IEEE Computer Society, 10662 Los Vaqueros Circle, Los Alamitos, CA 90720.

Index